MANITOU

MANITOU

The Sacred Landscape of New England's Native Civilization

JAMES W. MAVOR, JR. & BYRON E. DIX

Inner Traditions International
Rochester, Vermont

Inner Traditions International, Ltd.
One Park Street
Rochester, Vermont 05767

Library of Congress Cataloging-in-Publication Data

Mavor, James W., Jr. (James Watt), 1923-
    Manitou : the sacred landscape of New England's native civilization.

    Includes bibliographical references.
    1. Indians of North America—New England—Religion and mythology. 2. Sacred space—New England. 3. Indians of North America—New England—Antiquities. 4. New England—Antiquities. I. Dix, Byron E. II. Title.
E78.N5M38 1989   974'.01   89-17106
ISBN 0-89281-078-5

Printed and bound in the United States

10 9 8 7 6 5 4 3

Distributed to the book trade in the United States by American International Distribution Corporation (AIDC)

Distributed to the book trade in Canada by Book Center, Inc., Montreal, Quebec

Contents

Dedicated to the memory of
Alexander Thom

Acknowledgements

The late Alexander Thom, of Ayreshire, Scotland, was the inspiration for our work in New England. Known as a leading pioneer of archaeoastronomy in Great Britain and Brittany, Thom's careful and voluminous surveys of megalithic sites have caused most archaeologists and historians to pay attention to astronomy as a major ancient cultural feature. But when we visited Thom in 1978, he demonstrated to us a breadth of knowledge and sensitivity to the natural world that was far greater than that of the meticulous engineer implied by his writings and acknowledged by his critics. Thom appreciated the importance of the meeting of land and sky as both a physical and spiritual event, an approach that we have come to accept as the key to understanding the sacred landscape of ancient peoples. We resolved to follow in Thom's footsteps across the water in North America and he encouraged us. He saw our efforts to bring to light the sacred landscape of New England as a parallel to his long struggle in Great Britain.

Since we make theories and observations outside of the mainstreams of history and archaeology, we are particularly thankful to those who, whether or not they agree with us, have respected our work by seriously attempting to understand it and participating in it. Some have contributed skills and ideas while others have provided the moral support and friendship necessary in an endeavor of this kind. In this spirit we acknowledge particularly the following individuals: Christopher Bamford, Jack Cable, George Calhoun, Warren Cook, the late Grant Corwin, Warren Dexter, William M. Dunkle, Jr., John Eddy, William W. Fitzhugh, Kate Foos, Melody Gale, William N. Goetzmann, Robert Goldsborough, Curtis Hoffman, Joseph Jasniewski, Alice D. Kehoe, Thomas F. Kehoe, George Krusen II, Chief Little Horse, Sigfrid Lonegren, William Lovering, Dan Lynch, Nancy Lynch, Euan MacKie, William P. Marsh, James W. Mavor III, James R. McCullough, June P. Miller, Martin Miller, Eleanor Ott, John Place, Peter Reynolds, Susan Robinson, Anne Ross, James W. Rymcszewicz, Barbara Sager, Betty Sincerbeaux, Robert Sincerbeaux, Steven Sharon, Gale Smith, Melody Smith, Ted Timreck, John Todd, Nancy J. Todd, Barbara Waters, James P. Whittall II, and Ray Williamson. We also thank the members of Early Sites Research Society, The New England Antiquities Research Association, and numerous historical and archaeological societies throughout New England with whom we have enjoyed exchanging ideas and observations over the years. In particular, James Whittall has generously made available Early Sites' excellent archive of observations and excavation reports of stone structures in New England and Europe.

During the course of our research, we have received grants for equipment and expenses for which we thank The Cecil Howard Charitable Trust, Mrs. Elizabeth

Young, Mrs. Margaret Morely, the late Mrs. Joseph C. Hartwell, and Mr. and Mrs. Robert Sincerbeaux. Most of these grants were made to and administered by Associated Scientists at Woods Hole, of which the authors are members.

We thank Harold McCarthy, owner of the Calendar One bowl, for permission to study this most important place. Also in Vermont, we thank Jesse C. Curtis for permission to excavate her stone chamber, Irene Crowe for permission to study the Calendar Two site, Hubert Benoit for permission to excavate and study standing stones and other structures on his land, and Audrey and William Gall for permission to study the Indian fort and environs. We are grateful to the several elders in residence over the past ten years at the Joseph Smith Birthplace Memorial in South Royalton, Vermont, located at Calendar One. We thank them for their hospitality in making the campground available and value their interest in our research. In Massachusetts, we are indebted to the owner, who chooses to be anonymous, of the Freetown stone mound which we excavated with his permission, and to Walter Cyr for allowing us to survey the Upton chamber.

In our research, we have learned to appreciate the important and sometimes unique historical collections to be found in the hundreds of small town libraries throughout New England. The cordiality of the staffs and accessibility of collections make working in them a delight. Those libraries that we have used the most are The New Bedford Free Library Genealogical Room, Tozer Library of Harvard University, Sterling Library of Yale University, Harvard Public Library, Littleton Public Library, Natick Public Library, Sudbury Public Library, Concord Public Library, Newport Public Library, Falmouth Public Library, Library of the U. S. Air Force Geophysical Laboratory, and the Marine Biological Laboratory Library.

The following photographs are used with the kind permission of the photographers: Figure 1–1b, Sigfrid Lonegren; 1–23, Martin Miller; 5–6, Warren Dexter; 7–2, 7–4, Rod Bull; 9–41, Ted Timreck; 11–6, 11–12, 12–16, 13–4, Martin Miller.

We thank especially Lindisfarne Press, which did much of the development and production work for this book, and our editor, William P. Marsh, for his thoughtful and meticulous labors which have much improved the presentation of our subject.

Our children, Anne H. Mavor, Salley H. Mavor, James W. Mavor III, Maia D. Porter, William C. Dix, and Lauren M. Dix have all been part of our explorations, tramping through the woods, ideas, and enthusiasms during much of their lives. They have been curious, encouraging and we hope enriched by these experiences.

Finally and most important of all, we acknowledge the loving help and forbearance of our wives, Mary H. Mavor and Diane Dix. We thank them for numerous important contributions to all aspects of our research and in the writing and production of this book which could not have happened without their support.

Prologue

The early seventeenth-century English settlers of America called the land New England because, among other reasons, it reminded them of home; they saw stone walls, standing stones and stone heaps like those of the English countryside. This remarkable collection of man-made works, now largely hidden and ignored in the modern forests, is awesome in quantity, size, and complexity, but its origins and functions have remained unknown. We might expect that New England's many academic scholars would have addressed the problems posed by these ruins, but they have seen greener pastures in the elegant antiquities of far places. Also, the accepted theories of cultural sequence in New England have no place for the stone structures. William Goodwin, one of the first investigators of these remains, wrote in 1946, "No one apparently has hitherto been cognizant, at least from an archaeological point of view, of these curious monolithic stone remains right in the heart of our own New England."[1] Malcolm D. Pearson, who introduced Goodwin to the stone structures in the 1920s, has through his persistence and photographic skills recorded examples of most types of structure. During the past thirty years, gradually increasing numbers of avocational investigators have observed and speculated about the stone remains.

From our experience, stone structures, including not only walls, standing stones and mounds, but also more enigmatic underground chambers, perched boulders and special enclosures, are found throughout New England's six states, but we make no attempt to catalog them here. Rather, we have chosen to describe representative structures and places where we believe we have been able to gather sufficient information, both by direct observation and the study of historical records, to justify our conclusions about their origins and use. We have, however, obtained observational data from many other sites, some with similar stonework, some with greater quantities and more spectacular, all of which fit the landscape architectural patterns which we present here. For comprehensive catalogs of New England's lithic sites, we suggest consulting the files of the Early Sites

Research Society and the New England Antiquities Research Association, which have documented such descriptive material over the past twenty-five years.

The builders and users of New England's stone structures may have been travelers from far places on this or other continents at periods during many thousands of years, as well as indigenous people. However, there is such a tremendous amount of stonework on the New England landscape that nothing less than a massive migration into the land by a foreign people who stayed and multiplied for at least hundreds of years could displace the natives as the dominant responsible culture. We believe that ancient traditions of Native Americans, some of which are still practiced today, were the driving forces in the creation of the stone structures, and that these structures have been built from the time of the last glacial retreat up to the present. But these traditions were probably modified by foreign influences over thousands of years.

We suspected from the beginning that the stone structures, like similar material the world over, might be part of ancient peoples' preoccupation with the rising and setting of the sun, moon and stars. Father Paul Le Jeune, one of the early Jesuit missionaries to the Indians of Canada, observed in 1636 that,

> They address themselves to the Earth, to Rivers, to Lakes, to dangerous Rocks, but above all, to the Sky; and believe that all these things are animate, and that some powerful Demon resides there. . . . They have recourse to the Sky in almost all their necessities and respect the great bodies in it above all creatures. . . . Indeed, it is, after man, the most vivid image we have of Divinity; . . . . When they make some promise of importance, . . . The Sky knows what we are doing today.[2]

By observing the natural landscape and the sky together, we were struck by the abundance and placement of earthen and stone man-made constructions, and they have communicated to us a way of life that was in harmony with nature. Eventually, we realized that the subject encompassed all of the human perception of the natural world and have come to feel that the Algonquian word *manitou* best describes this perception. *Manitou* is not a familiar word in modern New England, but in the spirit-centered world of the Algonquian-speaking Native American, it was fundamental. Roger Williams, one of the earliest English colonists to take a sympathetic interest in the Indians, noticed this and wrote in 1643,

> Besides there is a generall Custome amongst them, at the apprehension of any Excellency in Men, Women, Birds, Beasts, Fish, etc., to cry out Manittoo, that is, it is a God, as thus if they see one man excell other in Wisdom, Valour, Strength, Activity etc., they cry out Manittoo, A God.[3]

More recent observers define manitou as any one of the spirits which control the forces of nature, but we believe that the meaning defies a concise English definition. Attempts to explain Native American beliefs in written modern languages have had limited success. The best attempts are the legends and stories which are interpreted by skilled and sensitive poets. Most Indian languages were not written and modern languages have built-in beliefs which are quite different.

Our approach to understanding and communicating native beliefs within Western society is to describe physical objects that we and others have seen on the landscape and in the sky. In this context, we consider two related aspects of the stonework, its role in shamanistic belief and practice and as ritual landscape architecture complementing the natural environment. We show not only that these two aspects were dominant characteristics in the Native American way of life, but also, perhaps surprisingly, that they were also in the heritage of both the prehistoric and historic European immigrants.

Oral traditions of Indians throughout North America tell us that they view the natural world as a complete whole of which they are a part. Rather than attempting to dominate and change it, they try as individuals and as groups to live harmoniously within it. In this view, all activities are part of both the natural and spiritual world, and reality is not absolute. Indians see white people as compartmentalizing everything and not understanding the whole. They see the white man's concept of progress as narrow and valueless, while what to the white is primitive ritual is to the Indian an expression of a unified philosophy.

However, we must be careful not to overidealize the aboriginal way of life or to think that it did not alter the natural environment, for humans have always managed the landscape to varying degrees in their own interests. Reflecting the diversity of Native American cultures, there are obvious differences between the structures built by Indian groups in various parts of North America. Large urban centers were built by the Anasazi and Pueblo peoples of the American Southwest. Also, the Adena and Hopewellian peoples built great structures of earth and stone along the rivers of the American Midwest and Southeast. In these places and epochs, Native Americans were not averse to making major alterations to their surroundings. Nonetheless, these works have basic similarities to the more subtle stoneworks of New England and the North American Arctic, and seem to express a similar cosmology. And even in the Northeast, native culture caused alteration of the environment. We consider the probability that Native American beliefs and customs in other parts of North America may apply to New England in ways that have been forgotten, even by many of the remaining Indians themselves.

The history of the interaction between the Indians and European colonists of New England indicates that some colonists knew of the stone structures and that a few had sufficient knowledge of Indian ways to know their origins and functions. Our knowledge of the seventeenth-century English settlers and their relationships with Indians comes largely from the writings of clergymen and land conveyance records. It is not generally appreciated that we know nothing about the intellectual and religious lives of at least eighty percent of the European inhabitants of the New England colonies in the seventeenth century, many of whom, like the Indians, could not write in a manner intelligible to later readers. Also, in most localities, their lack of membership in the established church prevented their voting or participating in the government or the mainstream of society that was described in contemporary writings.

During the seventeenth, eighteenth and nineteenth centuries, numerous religious cults appeared in New England, many of which seem to have had special relationships with Indians though their exact nature remains obscure. Those cases that are known, such as the Quakers, Mormons and Shakers, lead us to believe that relations between the Indians and many of the settlers were less confrontational and that there was less difference in religious beliefs than the Puritan clergymen led us to expect.

Most archaeology in New England has attempted to reconstruct the lives of the early Native Americans through excavation of settlements where tools and implements of everyday life reveal something about their material existence. But most of their thoughts, attitudes and actions beyond subsistence have eluded modern investigators.

We are not preoccupied with whether or not the native remains we find are classified as Woodland, Archaic or PaleoIndian, or with catalogues of projectile points and other implements. These are matters that were invented by the white man and, while they provide orderly process, create, in our opinion, artificial boundaries which are distracting in an attempt to comprehend Native American behavior. Without considering these classifications, we can sense a continuity through time and a geographical commonality in ritual. And traditions and legends recorded or maintained through oral transfer by the remaining few descendants ring true to the spirituality which is known from other parts of America.

Scholarship has until recently done little to change European attitudes towards Native Americans. In the early part of and extending through most of the nineteenth century, it was common among both scholars and laymen alike to believe that the great earthworks of the American Midwest were built by a race of materially advanced people from across the Atlantic and that Indians were not capable of such works. In 1881, anthropologist L. H. Morgan wrote, even though he became an adopted Iroquois, that the Indians were incapable of quarrying stone and did not possess the lintel, and therefore could not use stone for building structures. Morgan's attitude is still widely held in New England, where the hallmark of the study of indigenous cultures remains the familiar projectile points, hand implements, pottery and skeletons. The possibility that Native Americans here left substantial stone and earthen structures that remain around us unrecognized and can shed new light on their ways comes as a shock to those who hold tightly to the prejudices of the past.

However, we do have to consider the fact that the evidence of artifacts indicates that immigrants from Europe probably crossed the Atlantic intermittently over several thousand years past and had lasting effects upon the natives, a notion that some may dismiss as a reversion to the excesses of the nineteenth century. But some of the stone material seen in New England is undeniably very like that in Europe and at the same time architecturally a demonstrated part of Native American heritage. We attempt to resolve this apparent contradiction.

Scientific discoveries seldom come about in orderly fashion so that the most lucid way of presenting results is not usually as a narrative of discovery. However, we have chosen to use inductive logic in weaving our story of personal adventure through the explanation of our theories and observations in order to encourage readers who are unfamiliar with our approach to follow in our footsteps, the better to judge our meaning.

Along with the stone ruins solidly anchored to the land, we are investigating the spirit world and its relationships to more tangible realities, a subject to which scientific research is not readily suited. In reporting human behavior and natural circumstances, we are mostly within a familiar reality, but we cannot prove the existence of manitou by scientific methods, nor can we describe or understand completely the religious nature of stone objects. For the most part, we discuss circumstances such as human artifacts, historical accounts, and relationships between the natural environment and human activity. But within these topics there is always the element of personal intuitive perception, as contrasted with reasoning and systematic analysis. It is useful to be aware of this difference in attitude toward natural philosophy, but scholars often tend to sharpen the distinction and to denigrate the importance of speculation and intuition. We attempt to achieve a balanced approach to this sensitive subject.

Our first three chapters present our personal stories of discovery of three major sites in the fields and forests of New England, one in Vermont and two in Massachusetts. They describe, with little attempt at synthesis, the basic elements of a ritual place: stone rows, standing stones, chambers, mounds, marked stones, and natural features of the landscape and sky. These discoveries have a strong thread of celestial observation, for this was our emphasis until we realized that astronomy to us was important primarily as the framework of an anthropological method.

In Chapters 4 through 9 we have built a background of field observation and interpretation of recorded history that enables us to see in new ways the interactions and connections between the natural environment, stonework and people. We have found numerous specific architectural parallels between the New England structures, and the works of the Midwestern Mound Builders and Indians of the west coast of North America. In searching for the meaning of manitou, we have presented the observations of Jesuit priests, Pilgrims and Puritans, and interpreted the attempts at converting the Indians to the white man's Christianity. We have considered human interaction with the natural world in shamanistic societies, as well as Native American ritual life in various parts of North America. We have compared stone structures in Europe and America and suggest the foreign contacts that might have influenced New England's native ways.

In Chapters 10 through 12 we have described three major ritual sites in different parts of New England, having different kinds of natural settings, which have all been in use in historic times but have ancient origins. We have interpreted the historical record and the land and sky in each case to reveal a revised history in which Indians kept alive their shamanistic ways in spite of the overlay of Christianity placed upon them by Puritan clergymen. All three sites express a common cosmology and role in society. Each was part of an ancient network of people and places which came to be used to resist the invasion of the white man and his ways.

In the last chapter, we have brought together our thoughts on the meaning of manitou and drawn our general conclusions.

1

First Discovery in Vermont

In the summer of 1974 Byron Dix discovered, in the steep, green hills of central Vermont, the first of many places in New England that we believe were ancient ritual sites. Discovery, the most exciting part of science, is also the least understood and cannot be explained by its rules. It is invariably the unrepeatable experiment. Byron can describe some of the circumstances surrounding his discovery but not why it came about. He was looking for one of the three stone chambers said to be in the area, but he was not sure of its location and his path was a wandering one.

After climbing up a gully from the First Branch of the White River, Byron came out of the woods on a bare hilltop plateau, a former pastureland that had not yet reforested itself. A mostly straight stone row, looking somewhat like a ruinous stone fence, ran along the east edge of the plateau, oriented north and south. To the south the row ended abruptly a few feet short of an oval mound of stones. Many stones in this row had surfaces marked by U-shaped, finger-sized grooves, some parallel, some crossing one another. Byron had seen marks of this type before, in other stone rows on a hilltop twenty-one miles to the south.

East of the row, the land dropped off steeply into a natural amphitheater. From his elevation, Byron could see other stone rows that enclosed the base of the bowl-shaped valley, which looked to be some twenty acres in extent. On the east, the land bounding the bowl climbed more steeply to a higher, heavily wooded ridge. A saddle to the north connected the east and west ridges and provided a northern boundary for the bowl. To the south, the bowl was open, and the land descended through a swamp which fed a stream. Further to the south was a hill whose summit was on the north-south axis of symmetry of the bowl.

Still looking for the chamber, Byron walked north, turned east onto the saddle, and walked a clockwise spiral route down into the bowl. There was a fine view of distant mountains to the south including Vermont's Killington, Pico and Ascutney peaks, a view that was framed by the steep east and west ridges on either side. After completing a circuit of the bowl, he realized that none of the features which he saw around him matched those that had been described as being near the chamber. He thought that either he was lost or his informants had not seen the landmarks that caught his attention. Nevertheless, he explored the stone rows within the bowl. When he came to the north-south row at the east side of the bowl, he saw that it contained three adjacent vertical slabs of quartzite rock, each about three feet high, five feet long and one foot thick. They were standing beneath two of the three large and singularly impressive sugar maple trees in the area. Two of the slabs had grooved markings in rectangular grid patterns, and another stone about twenty-five yards north in the same row was also marked by a grid. Byron saw that the grooves were quite similar to ancient petroglyphs found throughout the world, often related to the sun. The four by five grid is found among historical Sioux and Ojibway pictographs and means "goods."[1] Byron already felt intuitively that he was at a very special place and that the decorated slabs fitted their surroundings, but, lacking a camera, he returned home without recording his discovery.

In February, 1975, Byron returned to the bowl to photograph the grooved markings on the slabs. This time he snowshoed up an old stagecoach road from the north into the bowl, where he found the waist-high slabs buried in snow. After brushing the snow from the markings, he sketched and photographed them, but photography was difficult because the marks were all on the eastern faces of the slabs and the afternoon sun over the west ridge shone directly into the camera lens. This led him to wonder if the sunset over the west ridge were intended to be observed from these stones. He was immediately intrigued by the astronomical possibilities of the bowl, partly because he is an avid skywatcher and designer of telescopes, but also because the place invites, by its shape and orientation, looking to the sky. Byron wondered if the rising and setting sun over specific peaks and depressions of the high eastern and western horizons could be observed at important times of the year, thereby forming a basic solar calendar. Might there be evidence that people before him did this as they had in many other parts of the world?

After photographing the markings (Figure 1–1), Byron wandered about the bowl, which by now seemed most unusual and awesome. In the center was a mound about six feet high and sixty feet in diameter, later proven to be a bedrock formation. Quite by accident, he saw, built into the mound and hidden by a growth of shrubbery, a stone chamber which fit the landscape so well that he had not at first noticed it. This was one of the chambers photographed by Pearson and published by Goodwin (Figure 1–2).[2] Not equipped to make measurements at this time, he had to wait for an opportunity to return with instruments.

1–1 Grid markings on stone slabs in Calendar One bowl

Byron came back on the equinox, 21 March 1975, accompanied by Betty Sincerbeaux of Woodstock, Vermont, who had guided him to special places before and whose sensitivity to nature and ability to locate forgotten standing stones and underground stone chambers is a legend. They witnessed the changing colors of the sunset from the inscribed slabs, noting that the sunset took place just north of the peak of the west ridge which was outlined clearly by the stone row tracing the horizon. But this observing station, on the eastern side of the bowl, seemed an unlikely position from which to observe all the other events that make up a practical solar calendar. For one thing, the eastern ridge rose very steeply, making viewing in that direction awkward, so Byron thought that there may have been a place in the center of the bowl, unmarked today, from which all of these events could be observed.

That Byron went to the bowl three times without making measurements or recording more than photos of the grooved slabs may seem strange to readers who feel that prompt recording of field data is essential to proper science. But he was in the habit of observing first without artificial aids, sometimes many times over a period of months or years, with time for reflection between. Only then

1–2 Stone chamber, Calendar One bowl

1-3 Equatorially mounted field telescope for discovering astronomical alignments

would he record, because recording can be a distraction from holistic observing and participating. Too often, measurements are trivial or too narrowly focused, yet are mistakenly perceived to represent the whole. Byron probably owes his discovery to this field method, and it became our established practice.

Later that spring, Byron looked for the observation point with instruments. He used an equatorially mounted telescope he had designed and built (Figure 1-3) that can be swung about an axis parallel to the earth's north-south axis of rotation, simulating the path of any celestial body across the sky at past, present and future epochs. It is an ancient instrument, rather like a portable planetarium, appearing first in China before A.D. 400, although an earlier instrument which embodied the same principles, the armilary sphere, was used in Mediterranean countries as early as 500 B.C. The equatorially mounted telescope is the ideal optical device for finding the place where an astronomical observation might have been made from in the past, using known or suspected horizon markers. Byron set the instrument at several trial positions in the approximate center of the bowl, in each case swinging the telescope from horizon to horizon to simulate the sun's path at the solstices and equinoxes. He noted how near the rising and setting points were to the peaks and notches on the horizon. After each successive trial, the telescope was moved by an amount calculated from observations during the previous trial. Eventually, he reached the true single observing station, where all the events were marked by natural horizon features. This place was unmarked by surface indications.

In the summer of 1975, Byron and Betty Sincerbeaux went to the bowl again. As they walked up the trail to the site, Byron told Betty his ideas about the unique astronomical character of the bowl and how it seemed to him to cradle time. He meant by this that the daily passage of the sun, moon and stars overhead was emphasized by the bowl-like shape of the land, which kept a record in its peaks and valleys of the passing of seasons, centuries, and millennia. Betty caught Byron's excitement about the place and asked him not to show her the observing station he had located. Upon entering the bowl, using some sixth sense, she walked directly to the precise place, which Byron had marked by a small stake hidden within a juniper bush.

During the next two years, all eight major solar events, sunrise and sunset at the winter and summer solstices and the equinoxes, were witnessed from this single place, confirming the predictions of the equatorial telescope and Betty's intuition. At the summer solstice, the sun rose over the northern peak of the east ridge and set at a dip in the northern part of the west ridge. At the vernal and autumnal equinoxes, the sun rose at a notch in the east ridge between the northern and southern peaks, and set at the peak of the western horizon, marked by a stone row. At the winter solstice, the sun rose at the southern peak of the east ridge and set at a notch at the southern end of the west ridge. Because of his findings Byron named the site Calendar One.[3]

At this stage of research, the theory was not only entirely circumstantial but also the only man-made features involved were the inscribed grids and the stone row on the west ridge, whose origins were completely unknown. The central observation point was not even marked. Byron could not point to any convincing evidence that the astronomical alignments were not accidental or that ancient people actually used them. However, working alone for the most part, he gradually found bits of supporting evidence. Two standing rock slabs on the east ridge were located approximately at the horizon locations of the winter and summer solstice sunrise sightlines. Also the major axis of the stone chamber in the bowl's central mound was proved to be oriented to the equinox sunrise in the natural notch on the east ridge horizon (Figure 1–4).

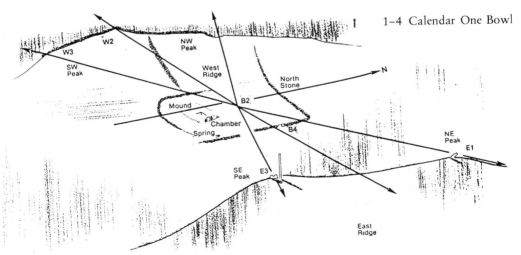

1–4 Calendar One Bowl

Byron also investigated a hilltop site to the south of Calendar One at South Woodstock, Vermont, which he named Calendar Two because he felt it had a similarity to Calendar One. There, the natural symmetry directing one's attention to the sky is missing, but several man-made features signal possible similar calendrical astronomy. A large rectangular mounded stone chamber is oriented so that an observer within can see the winter solstice sunrise in a horizon notch in line with the chamber axis. Byron was that observer on a day when the temperature was thirty-five degrees below zero.

In the early spring of 1978, just after the melting of the snow but before the frozen ground had turned to mud, the best time of year to observe celestial sites in New England, Mavor and Dix met for the first time at a conference and field trip in Norwich, Vermont. Although Mavor had been only casually interested in ancient New England up to this point, he had read of Byron Dix and had wanted to meet him. Like many others, he had been attracted to the glamour of ancient Europe and had excavated in Greece while seeking an Aegean Atlantis. Since 1969, inspired by Alexander Thom of Scotland, he had been surveying ancient sites in Europe and North Africa for possible astronomical functions and had published, in 1976, a megalithic stone ring in Morocco.[4]

The meeting between Dix and Mavor had such a magical character that they left the meeting and dashed south to Calendar One and Two, where Mavor had an unforgettable whirlwind tour. Immediately, the two formed an inseparable research team and set to work to study Calendar One thoroughly, with emphasis at first on the astronomical thesis. We had no favorite theory about who might have built or used the astronomical observatories that seemed to lie on the landscape, or when that might have happened. The only assumptions necessary for pursuing our work were those connected with astronomy, which was just as well, because archaeological and historical background data for Vermont turned out to be very scanty. Archaeologists have tended to concentrate, in New England at any rate, on subsistence sites, places where people lived and dealt with the material needs of daily life. But Calendar One was clearly not such a site, so we could not expect to find tools, pottery sherds, or other subsistence artifacts. What was the significance of this special place? That was the task we set for ourselves. Part of this task was to seek out the historical records, during which we started many intertwined lines of inquiry. Though we did not know where they would lead, they ultimately created a fabric of knowledge relevant to the origins and meaning of the stone and earthen structures.

History of Calendar One

Central Vermont's few early records date from 1761, much later than southern New England, and the records that do exist are scattered. Both New York and New Hampshire claimed the territory that is now Vermont until 1764, when the King of England declared the west bank of the Connecticut River to be the boundary between these two colonies. Then in early 1777, a new colony, named New Connecticut and located where Vermont now lies, was formed. On 4 June 1777, its name was changed to Vermont. Finally, in 1791, Vermont became a state of the Union. As a result of all this pulling and pushing of the territory about the northern Connecticut River, colonial records are disbursed among the archives of three states and Canada.

No archaeological excavations had ever been performed in the region in which we worked, and writings of the white man have very little to say about the prehistoric and historic Indians of Vermont.[5] Vermont was thought by most writers to have been uninhabited before the English arrived and only thinly populated by Indians since then. But recent excavations in northern Vermont have proved an Indian presence several thousand years ago.

The first recorded English settlers came to Royalton in 1771 and to the Calendar One area about 1780. For some unknown reason, Royalton, the most desirable land of its region, was not granted by New Hampshire in 1761 as were the surrounding towns but granted in 1769 by New York.[6] The land was sub-divided into so-called Dutch allotments, from the Dutch traditions of New York, and bought by farming families, primarily named Dewey, Bingham and Woodard. June Miller has matched existing houses and ruined foundations to the historical records and found that a few records and oral traditions may refer to the early presence of some of the eight stone chambers at Calendar One.[7]

There are three recorded traditions about the Calendar One region. Two are accounts of Indian forts. Nash mentions an Indian fort on the hill across the road from the site of the 1782 Ebenezer Dewey house. The hill is Dairy Hill and the road, Dairy Hill Road, as shown on modern maps. Ebenezer Dewey, the first recorded owner of the land, purchased 260 acres, including Dairy Hill, in 1782.[8] Dairy Hill, elevation 1261 feet, lies true south of the Calendar One bowl and has many rock outcrops on its summit and rock ledges to the south. There is an earthen ditch and bank about 120 yards long that partially rings the summit on the east, which is probably the origin of the fort tradition. Along the bank are several structures which include stone mounds, standing stones, stone rows, stone and earth pits and old trees whose limbs appear to have been forced into strange shapes when the trees were young. Several stone features appear to be parts of astronomical alignments from other structures in the Calendar One region. For example, on May Day, an important solar calendar date, the sun sets behind one of the Dairy Hill standing stones as viewed from a chamber to the southeast in the valley below.

The other Indian fort tradition can be traced to the burning of Royalton in the early morning of Monday, 16 October 1780 by a band of 300 Mohawk Indians of the Caughnawaga Indian Christian mission village near Montreal. They were led by an English officer, Lieutenant Horton, whose second was a Frenchman named LeMotte, and were guided by a man named Hamilton. They had apparently intended to burn Newbury, Vermont, about twenty miles to the northeast, but upon hearing that it was well defended, changed their plans.

They travelled down the First Branch of the White River through Tunbridge to Royalton. As the story goes, they intended to attack on Sunday when people were expected to be at church. There happened to be no service that day so they camped on a hill west of the First Branch at Tunbridge, where they remained through the Sabbath, before moving on Royalton on Monday morning. Tradition has it that they camped in a stone enclosure, still existing and known locally as the Indian fort, which overlooks the First Branch and can be seen from the west ridge of the Calendar One bowl. There are astronomical alignments connecting features of the bowl with the fort.[9]

Both structures that tradition calls Indian forts are enclosed spaces on hilltops commanding panoramic views for miles about, and are within our expanded concept of Calendar One. As we show later, although such places in New England were typically labelled forts by the European colonists, a hillfort was a concept alien to Indian ways, and the places were most likely primarily places of cosmological ritual.

Another part of the story of the burning of Royalton relates that a "stone cell" was used for refuge from the raiding Indians. According to the account, Hannah Hunter Hendee and nine children, whom she had persuaded the Indians to release, went to a stone cell three miles from the meadow outside Royalton. Within the memory of persons living at the time the account was written, the stone cell was found and in it were bottles and other ancient objects.[10] It is likely that the stone cell was one of the several stone chambers in the Calendar One area, possibly in or near the bowl, which is three miles from Royalton.

The third tradition relates to Indian Rock, which is a natural sheltering rock overhang on the southern slope of Dairy Hill where Indian artifacts have been found, some from the Archaic period.

Historical records document the subdivision and transfer of lands and show that almost all of the uplands of Calendar One were clear and used as pastures by 1880. But as to origins of stone chambers, stone fences, cairns and standing stones, history is silent except for the traditions just cited. By 1804, the westward migration of farmers had started, and in the early 1900s the farmers that were left began to move down from the hills, leaving the hill farms abandoned. After 1910, the hilltops returned to woodland.[11]

Excavations at Calendar One

Another research thread was archaeological excavation, which we undertook cautiously. Since no previous work had been reported for this part of Vermont, we felt obliged to tailor our methods to the place and our objectives. This was the start of a method of excavation attuned to the environmental and holistic nature of our research. Places are chosen because of subtle clues in our perception of the natural environment and circumstances which may be man-made but unusual or not in the mainstream concepts of history. We had no expectations of what we would find or preconceived notions of the meaning of artifacts except the conviction that celestial observation was a preoccupation of ancient man. We have described in this chapter only the earlier excavations at Calendar One, in order to illustrate how our method evolved. The results of later excavations, performed with the benefit of experience at Calendar One and other places in New England, and reflection on the broader role of Calendar One appear in Chapter 12.

Our first excavation at Calendar One was on 9 September 1978, at a field of about seventy stone piles high up on a spur of the east ridge at about 1500 feet altitude. Dix, Mavor, James W. Mavor III and William Lovering excavated the eastern half of a small stone pile, about six feet in diameter. The piles of this group were built of broken pieces of mica-schist and weathered quartzite which had clearly been quarried from the numerous outcrops of this metamorphic rock that abound on the ridge. We picked this site because the origins of the piles were unknown and we felt that, of the structures available, we could do least damage by destroying one-half of one small pile of seventy apparently similar examples. We emphasize this point because as we have learned more, we have become more humble about the ability of twentieth-century investigators to understand the remains left by ancient people and are doubtful that the knowledge acquired from most archaeological excavation justifies the destruction of evidence that is overlooked.

We found that the stone pile had been built on bedrock, which was one foot below the surface, and that there the stones were smaller in size than above ground. We discovered one small ceramic sherd within the pile, three inches below the ground surface. It was about one-half inch square and, from a 60-power microscopic examination, we found it to be a low-fired earthenware rich in quartz, mica and iron, as is the natural rock and soil of the area. We speculated that it was from Woodland Indian pottery, possibly as much as 2,000 years old. We mention this apparently trivial artifact because it remains the only ceramic artifact likely to have been traditional Indian ware, other than colonial-period ceramics found within and near the Calendar One chamber, found since 1978. It represented our first evidence pointing, albeit sketchily, to Indian influence in the Calendar One structures. We were to find later that a dearth of conventional artifacts characterizes the sites in New England which we consider places of Native American ritual.

In September 1979, we again excavated at Calendar One, at a location on Dairy Hill, about a mile south of the bowl, that we called Genesis. We selected the place in part intuitively but also because it is on a hillside plateau with a fine view, adjacent to a stone slab with grooved markings having the same appearance as those seen in the bowl. We excavated to bedrock over an area of fifteen square meters about the stone and found a small cairn or stone mound on bedrock three feet beneath the surface. We did not know at this time the significance of this result nor that of the sherd found in the stone pile on the east ridge, but we became familiar with the nature of the soil and the rock. We backfilled the excavations and left further disturbance until our experience justified reopening them.

On one of his many walks through the wooded hills and valleys of Calendar One, Byron had found a particularly impressive standing stone near the summit of Dairy Hill which he renamed the Dairy Hill monolith. Above ground, it appears as a thin, flat triangular slab three feet high (Figure 1–5). We excavated the monolith in September 1979 as the third of our many excavations at Calendar One. We dug only around the north end of the slab at first, for we did not want to disturb its position. Three feet below grade, we found mica-schist bedrock and exposed the monolith as a six-foot-high slab balanced somewhat precariously on its bottom edge which was just wide and flat enough for it to be stable. On the eastern and downhill side, a smaller oblique slab was set in the bedrock which prevented the monolith from sliding (Figure 1–6). We then firmly back-filled the north end of the monolith and excavated one side of the south end, where we found a small pile of stones possibly intended to retain the monolith from sliding south. Wedged between these chocking stones, three feet under-ground, we found a knapped chopper stone of green metamorphic rock (Figure 1–7a and b and Figure 1–12d) and nearby a small deposit of red ochre, a material traditionally used by Native Americans for ceremonial purposes. The stratigraphy of the soil section followed the three-layer pattern typical at Calendar One, about eight inches of humus on top, then red and yellow sandy subsoil, and below that about six inches of a dark, grey-green, finely packed material of

1–5 Dairy Hill monolith from southwest

1–6 Dairy Hill monolith after excavation

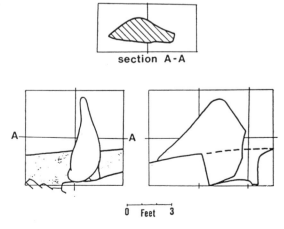

section A-A

A   A

0   Feet   3

1-7 Green chopper found at base of Dairy Hill monolith

clay-like consistency in contact with the crumbling bedrock. The two lower layers appeared not to have been disturbed by the placement of the monolith or the chopper stone, implying that the monolith had been erected in great antiquity, perhaps when bedrock was exposed.

Our interest focused on the curious green layer, whose characteristics we were careful to record wherever we found it. It was encountered not only at the standing stone excavation on Dairy Hill, but at the excavation of the astronomical center in the bowl, in the bowl stone chamber, at the "Indian Fort" in Tunbridge, and at the underground mound at Genesis. In all cases, bedrock had been modified by human hands beneath the green layer, even where the layer appeared undisturbed.

We took soil-core samples from Calendar One and submitted them to geologists, but because of the lack of baseline data in Vermont, pollen analysis of the samples provided no dates for the age of soil layers. However, these geologists analyzed the green soil and were of the opinion that it was either the first soil laid down after recession of the last glacial ice or the soil remaining from an interglacial period before the last glaciation.[12] This astounding result implies antiquity of at least 10,000 years for material in the undisturbed green layer.

We started to excavate the stone chamber in the bowl in 1980. Since the interior was nearly full of earth, our first task was to remove and record some sixteen tons of dirt, wood, stones, and historical artifacts. After that, we excavated outside the walls and discovered that the chamber had been built snugly within a cavity excavated into the bedrock that is about three feet deep as shown in Figure 1-8. The chamber walls were built directly on the bedrock, displacing the green soil layer. The chamber is surrounded, for the most part, by a secondary oval wall which was also built on bedrock, and the space between the two enclosing walls is filled with earth and quarry rubble. We do not know when the chamber walls or the quarried recess were built and there may have been a long interval of time between the two phases of construction. The stone piers forming the passage walls appear not to have been built into a quarried recess and have but tenuous rock interlocks with the chamber walls, implying a later phase of building.

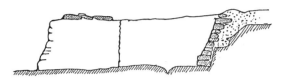

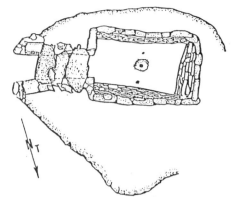

1-8 Stone chamber, Calendar One bowl

Furthermore, the horizontal courses of stone forming the chamber walls change character about halfway up from their bases, also implying a phased construction that could have taken place over a long time (Figure 1–9). The plan view of the chamber (Figure 1–8a) is not a rectangle, but a quite complex shape with the four walls composed of six plane surfaces curiously arranged in parallel pairs. The west or back wall is inclined.

Within the chamber and extending into the entrance passage, the stone floor was covered with a firmly packed layer of the fine green soil, about five inches thick in the passage and thinning to about one inch at the western or upper end of the chamber. It appears that, since the walls displaced the green layer and

1-9 North wall
of chamber

the stone floor has been worked by man — three holes carved in the floor, one
on the equinox sightline axis — the green soil in the chamber was either placed
by man to form a thin compacted floor or laid down by natural causes, after
construction of at least part of the chamber.

We developed the habit of treating as artifacts all of the many stones found
during an excavation and have classified them by shape, material and color,
including many which can be described as quarrying tools, hammerstones and
gravers (Figure 1-10). Other stones which we classify as artifacts are those

1-10 Selection of tools from
Calendar One bowl

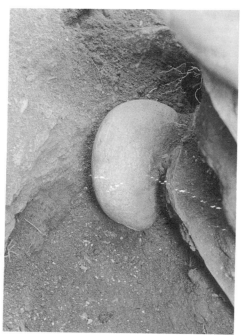

1–11 Greenstone from northwest corner of chamber

located out of a geological context, such as large smooth pebbles of metamorphic greenstone far from present-day streams. One, shown in Figure 1–11 and 1–12a, was found wedged between the northwest outside corner of the chamber and the bedrock cavity, three feet below the top of the walls. Another, with a finely

1–12 *clockwise from bottom right:*
a. Greenstone from northwest outside corner of chamber
b. Greenstone anvil from southeast inside corner of chamber
c. Disk from chamber green layer
d. Dairy Hill chopper
e. Hammer stone from chamber across valley from Dairy Hill

polished concave surface indicating use as a grindstone, was found within the chamber, partly in the green layer in the southeast corner (Figure 1–12b). These may be Indian magic stones.[13] The Diegueno Indians of California have a ceremony for women about to give birth, in which Atulka, a large crescent-shaped stone about thirteen by fifteen inches in size and weighing thirty-five pounds, similar to those found in the Calendar One chamber, was used for healing. Also, when it was heated and placed between the woman's legs, it would soften the abdominal tissues and render motherhood easy and safe. The stones are considered sacred.[14]

Most of the stones which we consider to be tools or implements were found within the yellow-red sandy layer, but some were in the green layer. Many are identical in shape to Archaic tools used in the ancient soapstone quarries of Massachusetts. A well-shaped disc five inches in diameter, shown in Figure 1–12c, was found just above the green layer within the chamber in the northeast corner. Such stones have been widely published as of Native American manufacture and are usually found at Archaic quarrying sites, but with unknown origin and function.[15]

In 1979, in an effort to leave no doors unopened, we helped to initiate an approach separate from but parallel to our own work. We founded, together with Eleanor Ott, Professor of Anthropology at Goddard College, and Sigfrid Lonegren, a specialist in earth divination, the Goddard Archaeological Research Group, known as GARG. One of its functions was to encourage professional archaeologists to study the Vermont stonework, in the belief that this might be a worthwhile complement to our efforts. Anthropologists Dena Dincauze of the University of Massachusetts, Bernard Wailes of the University of Pennsylvania, James P. Whittall II of Early Sites Research Society, Anne Ross of the University of Southampton, astronomer Kenneth Brecher, and Peter Reynolds, director of the Butser Ancient Farm Project in Hampshire, England, were gathered in order to try to make the plan work. The political climate surrounding stone chambers was such that for these scholars to meet together on the subject was most unusual. Eleanor Ott, acting as spokesperson for the group, sought the financial sponsorship of the National Geographic Society.

Peter Reynolds was picked to direct a two-week excavation of a stone chamber. In planning meetings, we (Mavor and Dix) urged that a broad approach be adopted in the research method so as to include the possibility that the chamber might have had astronomical and ritual functions. Our suggestion was rejected, and it became evident to us that the excavation would be conducted under the assumption that the chamber was part of a colonial farm settlement, with possible Celtic overtones. We withdrew from GARG and from participation in the project, convinced that the approach that was taking shape was too narrow. We describe the project here because it shows how very different results can be obtained from two different approaches to studying the same place.

1–13 Entrance of Eagle stone chamber at Calendar One

The project went ahead. After a number of chambers had been examined, one was selected, code named Eagle, and excavated. It was a chamber within Calendar One in South Royalton with which we were quite familiar (Figure 1–13). In fact it is only one-quarter mile from the Calendar One bowl chamber, and, in the absence of trees, each chamber could be seen from the other. The excavation took place in the summer of 1980, at the same time that we were excavating the chamber in the bowl.

The National Geographic Society decided that the results of the dig did not justify an article in their magazine. Seven years after the excavation, Peter Reynolds has not yet issued a report, but June Miller, who participated with him and has worked with us, produced a summary report as part of an M. A. thesis at Goddard College. No clear evidence of origin or original use of the chamber was found. Reynolds' reported opinion of colonial origin is based on finding on the chamber floor a bottle manufactured before 1860, and on stratigraphy of the soil over the roof slabs.[16] However, the floor had been quarried out of bedrock — all chambers that have been excavated have either quarried bedrock or flagstone floors — so artifacts found within the chamber could only be indicators of construction context if they were integral with construction, which was not proven in this case (Figure 1–14). Chambers in general have been used for many purposes in historical times, from burial vaults to root cellars. To confuse the issue even more, Narragansett Indians in historical times used colonial artifacts such as cutlery, jewelry, tools, bottles, etc., as votive objects, and these are found in burials. For instance, a complete set of stone cutter's tools was found in an Indian burial of the seventeenth century. So the bottle could

1-14 Interior of Eagle chamber showing
bedrock floor and bedrock right-hand wall

1-15 Standing stone on axis of Eagle chamber

have been placed by historical Indians, and the roof soil cover altered since
construction. More recently, one of the participants has reported at some length
that the chamber was probably used to store apples from a nearby orchard.

Although June Miller did a sound and important job of historical research on
the area in which the Eagle chamber lies, the excavation showed that the secret
of Vermont's stonework needs more than a conventional approach to archaeology. When we walked through the Eagle's excavation, we saw markings on
stones, as well as shaped stones which we believe to have been used for ritual
and quarrying. We brought these to the attention of the excavators, who ignored
them or threw them away. After the excavation, we pointed out a standing stone
on the chamber axis that appears on the horizon as seen from within the chamber
(Figure 1-15). Near the chamber, there is a great ancient pin oak tree marked
by distortion of its branches when it was young, known locally as the Indian
Council Tree (Figure 1-16a). This tree, now rotting, would have looked like
the Indian council tree in Dighton, Massachusetts, shown in Figure 1-16b.
Evidence of the Indian practice of ritually shaping trees by trimming and tieing
up branches to control their direction of growth is widespread but only occasionally reported.[17] Also nearby, two large boulders of quartzite have been
placed one above the other to form a stack on bedrock. They have been cut

a. Calendar One

1–16 Indian council trees:

b. Dighton, Mass.

away, as shown in Figure 1–17, so that a person can sit within the rock and view the distant northwest horizon across the First Branch of the White River. The name Eaton, presumably after a local settler, Amos Eaton, is inscribed on the boulder in large letters. Later, we came to believe the site of this rock to be a place of Indian vision quest.

The Eagle project presented a direct comparison between our methods and those of the mainstream archaeological community. It convinced us that new techniques better suited to the remains that we were studying were called for, and we set about developing these on our own or with the help of kindred spirits among artists, architects, engineers, environmental scientists, and the diverse membership of the Early Sites Research Society and the New England Antiques Research Association. Members of these two organizations have been patiently recording New England stone structures over the past twenty years. Their work, however, and the structures themselves are largely ignored by professional archaeologists.

1–17 Rock Stack
near Eagle chamber

Structures and Astronomy

The more we investigated the Calendar One bowl and its surroundings, the more circumstantial evidence we found of astronomical sightline alignments using both natural horizon and man-made stone markers, especially the many stone mounds, standing stones and underground stone chambers.[18]

The shape of the hills east and west of the bowl enabled observers in the bowl to see the four basic divisions of the year, winter, spring, summer and fall (Figure 1–18). More precisely, horizon features mark the times of the winter solstice, the shortest day of the year, the summer solstice, the longest day of the year, and the equinoxes, when the length of day and night are equal. The word solstice is a combination of two words, *sol* (sun) and *sistere* (to cause to stand still). However, the sun appears to the unaided eye to rise and set from the same place for about five days before and after the solstice, so in order to determine the day of the actual event, ancient people probably recorded the sun's horizon position for weeks about the solstice. They then could have interpolated halfway between days on which the sun was equidistant on the horizon from its extreme position. Having found the solstices, the equinoxes could be found by counting the days between the solstices and dividing this number in half. Further

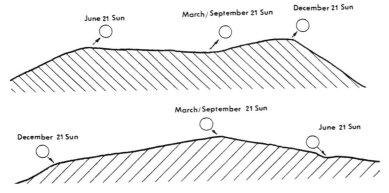

June 21 Sun   March/September 21 Sun   December 21 Sun

December 21 Sun   March/September 21 Sun   June 21 Sun

1–18 Eastern *(top)*
and western horizons,
Calendar One bowl

1-19 Equinox sunrise from
Calendar One bowl chamber

subdivisions could then be found by dividing the number of days between solstices and equinoxes by two. Thus the observers would arrive at May 6, halfway in a day count between the spring equinox and the summer solstice. August 7, November 7, and February 4 were found in a similar way. These eight subdivisions of the year made up the traditional eight-part calendar. They have long been observed by festivals throughout the world and among all the major religions.

Visiting the Calendar One bowl today, one sees the remains of a tunnel-like passageway leading to a small underground chamber built of dry-stone walling. It is empty of the sixteen tons of earth and artifacts which we removed by excavation. The chamber is built into the side of a large natural bedrock and earthen mound, within an egg-shaped perimeter wall (Figure 1–8a). It occupies the southern part of the enclosed space and a man-made stone pile fills out the northern or pointed end of the egg-shaped perimeter. The long axis of the passageway to the chamber is aimed fifteen degrees south of true east toward a notch between two hills. The back wall of the chamber is inclined to the vertical by fifteen degrees and is perpendicular to the equinox sunrise sightline. On the equinox, the sun rises from the notch precisely in line with the passageway as seen from within the chamber (Figure 1–19). The chamber's special position within the bowl, built into the natural central mound, its alignment to the equinox, and its exterior shape all suggest ceremonial significance uniting the experience of the land, sky and the passage of time. The interrelationship of land and sky, seen from the chamber, provides a map of time, a calendar.[19]

This kind of structure is similar to the kiva, an underground ceremonial structure which is also aligned to solar events and occurs in a variety of shapes, used by the American Indians of the Southwestern United States from the dim past up to the present (Figure 1–20). In the Midwest, the Hopewell people of the Mississippian culture of 300 B.C. to A.D. 900 built many stone chambers with rectangular interiors and walled entranceways. These earth-covered structures were used as burial vaults and were aligned to sunrise at the equinoxes or solstices.

Generally they were located on elevated places enclosed by earthwork embankments. The Hopewellian chamber (Figure 1–21a and b) is very similar to the stone chamber in the Calendar One bowl, and Hopewellian artifacts have been found in New England excavations. To the north, the Archaic Maritime peoples of Labrador also built stone chambers and cairns.[20]

Two years after discovery of the Dairy Hill monolith, we noticed that it could be seen from one of the eight Calendar One stone chambers, one-half mile to the east across a stream valley. We surveyed the position of the monolith from a transit station on top of the mounded chamber and found that the stone projected above the horizon and aligned with sunset on May 6 and August 7, two of the division dates of the eight-part solar calendar.[21] Furthermore, the triangular shape provides a left hand edge perpendicular to the path of the setting sun. The chamber is a free-standing structure covered by a mound of earth. A 130-year-old tree is growing on the mound over the calendar, which is of irregular shape with one sharp corner in the north. A single capstone weighing seven tons roofs the chamber proper with smaller capstones covering the entrance passage which opens gradually into the chamber proper after a narrow constriction. The walls are slightly corbelled, each course of stones overhanging that below

1–20 Top of Edge of Cedars kiva, Utah. Distant hills form solar horizon calendar.

1–21a, *top r* Hopewellian burial chamber, Waldron, Mo. (from Wedel, see note 20)

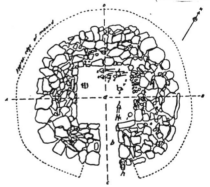

1–21b Hopewellian chamber, north of Kansas City, Mo. (from Fowke, note 20)

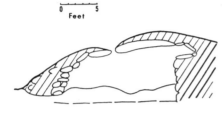

1–22 Stone chamber
across valley from
Dairy Hill monolith

it, to reduce the size of roof slab required. The entrance is oriented 210 degrees true toward a distant view of hills and notches. A large port is centrally located in the top of the rear wall, said to have been modified by historical owners for use as a vegetable chute (Figure 1–22).[22]

We, assisted by June Miller, excavated the interior floor of this chamber in the fall of 1979. Beneath the present dirt floor, we found a neatly placed flagstone floor set on a gravel base. We lifted two flags and beneath one found a hammer-

1–23 Scribed markings
on hammer stone

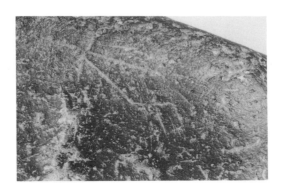

stone of metamorphic rock of the same composition as the chopper found at the monolith, but black instead of green in color. It is covered with orderly scratched linear markings (Figures 1–23 and 1–12e). Similar marks were found on an Indian pendant in Wayland, Massachusetts, which, under microscopic examination, were unlike sharpening cuts and therefore considered to be decorative.[23] We also found patent medicine bottles from the mid-nineteenth century above the flagstone floor.

The stone marker located at E3 in Figure 1–4, on the southern peak of the east ridge of the bowl, marking the winter solstice sunrise from the astronomical center, is a stone slab about five feet long, two and one-half feet high and ten inches thick. A notch one and one-half feet wide has been cut from the center of the top edge, this enabling it to serve as a sighting instrument. We excavated this stone and found that it was set up on a bedrock foundation three feet below ground. Underground, there was a curious arrow-shaped stone set up beside it, shown in Figure 1–24, pointing in the direction of the path of the rising sun, moon or a star, as if to signal the event.

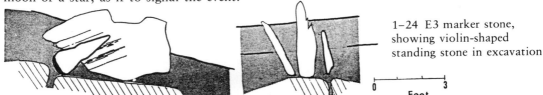

1–24 E3 marker stone, showing violin-shaped standing stone in excavation

Most of our quantitative observations and speculations at Calendar One are of the sun's regular path at different seasons, which nearly repeats year in and year out, with very little annual change. Surely, the ancient people who watched the Vermont sky observed and recorded the paths of the stars, the moon and the planets as well, but it is difficult to argue today that they did in specific cases. There are so many stars that we do not know which ones were recorded. The moon's motion is complex and its cycles are out of phase with the solar year. The planets also have complex motion and even Venus, the morning and evening star, known from many historical records as an important celestial body in ancient times, is very difficult to verify as the particular object of observation on a particular date without historical reference.

Nevertheless, at Calendar One, we have recorded circumstances under which the moon could have been observed. It is particularly interesting, even if speculative, because it implies the possibility of a date many thousands of years ago, in the Archaic Indian period. We speculate that early man observed all of the three lunar cycles, monthly or 29.53 days, semiannual or 173.3 days, and 18.6 years, by noticing the changes in the point on the horizon where the moon rose and set. This is plausible because we can do the same today without instruments. There is a vivid sense of the passage of time if we watch the moon rise and set night after night on a hilly horizon. It changes position rapidly; when near true east or west, its rising and setting points change at the rate of six degrees per day.

Less obvious than the monthly cycle but clearly noticeable by a regular and careful observer is the wobble or minor perturbation over a 173.3-day period in which the moon changes its rising and setting points by 0.20 degrees. If distant, high resolution foresights such as mountain peaks and notches were used, the six-month wobble would be difficult to miss. In addition, over a period of 18.6 years, the moon moves slowly away from extreme north and south positions, called the major and minor standstills, and back again. It would have taken decades of observation to discover this, but it is a motion of very large amplitude, about fourteen degrees between extremes on the horizon. Eventually, if regular observations are made, lunar eclipses will be seen to occur at the equinoxes when the full moon is at the standstills. Also, eclipses of the sun and moon can only occur when the moon is at the extreme positions of the six-month wobble as well. All this adds up to the importance of lunar observations as a means for predicting lunar eclipses, which can be seen at a frequency of about one a year from any point on earth.

Now as to observing the moon. The setting of the moon differs from the sunset largely because of the difference in contrast between the land horizon and the sky during day and night. Because of this, it is unlikely that tangency of the lower edge of the moon's disk would be a clear reference event at moonset. The only observable evidence of the event would be a flattening of the lower edge without warning. Similarly, the rising moon appears suddenly, without twilight, and the twinkle of the top edge in a notch may easily be missed. The only lunar horizon event that is clearly defined for an observer is the last gleam of moonset, when the horizon is silhouetted against the moon, preferably when it is full.

About 100 yards southwest of the chamber in the Calendar One bowl, a stone seat has been carved out of the bedrock on the eastern hillside, facing southwest. An observer sitting in the seat has a spectacular view of the peak of Mount Killington, twenty-three miles away and 4,234 feet high, framed in the notch

1-25 Moonset at Mount Killington at maximum southerly standstill from Calendar One

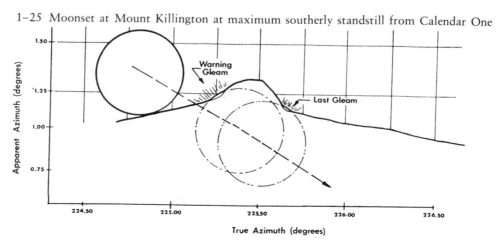

Apparent Azimuth (degrees)

Warning Gleam

Last Gleam

1.50   1.25   1.00   0.75

224.50   225.00   225.50   226.00   226.50

True Azimuth (degrees)

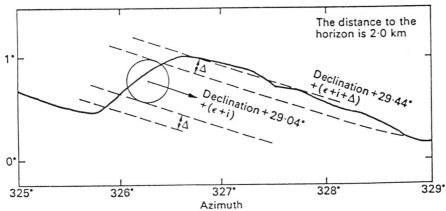

1-26 Moonset at maximum northerly standstill at Ballinaby, Scotland.
From J.E. Wood, *Sun, Moon, and Standing Stones* (Oxford: Clarendon Press, 1978).

between the nearby west ridge and Dairy Hill of Calendar One. We considered the observing scenario that would give the most precise horizon position of moonset at Killington and determined that it would be one in which the upper edge of the full moon is nearly tangent to the north slope such that the last gleam of the disk would move down the slope (Figure 1–25). Before this, the gradual slicing into the moon's disk by the peak of Killington would give warning of the critical period of last gleam to come. Alexander and Archibald Thom have discovered this same scenario at Ballinaby in Scotland, shown in Figure 1–26.[24]

By comparing the suggested event with calculated lunar events, we found that in the above scenario the full moon is in the most southerly position it reaches in its 18.6-year cycle, the southern major standstill. It is also at the southern extreme of its six-month wobble, when the event could have been used to predict eclipses. In addition, there is a small change in the horizon positions of the standstills with changing centuries which enables us to date the event, provided atmospheric conditions are sufficiently predictable. In this case, we can date the event between 1500 and 700 B.C.

The Calendar One Bowl: A Special Place

Calendar One was unlikely to have been a place where people lived, even though oral tradition records two hermits there in the nineteenth century. It must have been first of all a place to contemplate the sky. An observer standing in the center of the bowl immediately becomes aware of the surrounding horizons looming above.

These hilltops shelter the site from the wind. Even though it is calm down in the center of the bowl, the wind can be heard whistling through the trees on the surrounding hilltops. When camping in the bowl, after the evening coolness has set in, a striking difference in air temperature can be felt between the northern or upper parts and the southern or lower parts. Even in a distance of 100 feet, it is noticeably colder to the south. We discovered early in our research that sound was amplified by the bowl. One of us standing upon the east ridge could hear the other speaking in a normal voice on the west ridge, one-half mile away. The southern approach to the bowl is by a mile-long woodland trail from the nearest road. When working in the bowl, we can always hear the conversations of people approaching up this path even when over a half mile away. The bowl is then a natural amphitheater which heightens the aural, spatial and temporal senses of a person standing within it. It has naturally the attributes of Greek sacred architecture which Vincent Scully describes, based on a religious tradition in which land is a physical embodiment of the powers that rule the world and temples must be situated in a particular relation to the natural landscape.[25]

To the observer located at a point along the north-south axis of symmetry of the bowl, the southern horizon has a shape which accentuates the paths of the stars. The southern ends of the east and west ridges bound a convex skyline formed by a hill to the south. The sun and moon are never seen on this horizon, while the stars pass clockwise nearly parallel to it. If the observer turns around and looks to the north, the horizon is concave and bounded similarly by the east and west ridges; again only the stars can be seen moving clockwise around the north star at an elevation of forty-five degrees. The circumpolar stars, those which never rise or set, are seen between the pole and the horizon. The east and west ridges are the domain of the sun, moon and planets, whereas the north and south horizons blend with the paths of the stars.

Early people would have witnessed the interactions of the heavens and the land at this place where they are accentuated by the characteristics of the bowl. They would have recognized how the surrounding natural peaks and valleys mark the passage of time and would have ultimately noticed that the special horizons served as a natural calendar. No alterations of the land were needed in this setting for them to observe the passing of time.

After spending some nights camping within the Calendar One bowl, we were able to formulate an idea that we had known subconsciously for years. The events which we were watching high in the sky and at the horizon could not exist without us. We were part of the events. Sunrise only exists when it is seen by someone. This experience impressed firmly upon us that we are participants, and that the perceptions of all our senses are part of everything around us and every event of which we are aware. It was in this spirit that we continued our research.

2

A Pleiades and Sun Sanctuary
at the Source of Waters

Another major discovery, after Calendar One, was also an accident. In the fall of 1979, James P. Whittall II, archaeological director of the Early Sites Research Society in Rowley, Massachusetts, asked Mavor to help map a group of curious stone and earthen mounds and stone rows within and adjacent to a swamp in Southborough, Massachusetts. Some of the mounds, of which there were at least 100, were quite large, twenty feet in diameter and eight feet high, while others built with vertical walled sides and closely spaced in an irregular pattern may be effigies. Barry Fell and others would have this site built by ancient Egyptians for solar ritual; although we have not studied it sufficiently to comment on this exotic view, we have seen many of the same characteristics as other sites which we do consider to be places of Native American ritual. As of this writing, highway construction threatens to destroy the site.

After a day of surveying, we decided to visit the stone chamber in Upton, Massachusetts. Mavor had not seen it, and with us was Malcolm Pearson, the man who once owned this spectacular chamber and who brought it to public attention by encouraging William Goodwin to publish it in 1946.[1] The chamber lies between Pratt and Christian Hills on the eastern shore of Pratt Pond which feeds a tributary of the Blackstone River of central Massachusetts and Rhode Island. It is on a slope that rises gently to the east, near the outside corner of two intersecting stone walls. Five large adjacent boulders, each weighing thirty to forty tons, form a portion of one of the walls. The chamber itself is a large stone "beehive," unquestionably architecturally similar to some in Ireland and Scotland. A circular underground inner chamber ten feet in diameter with a domed roof

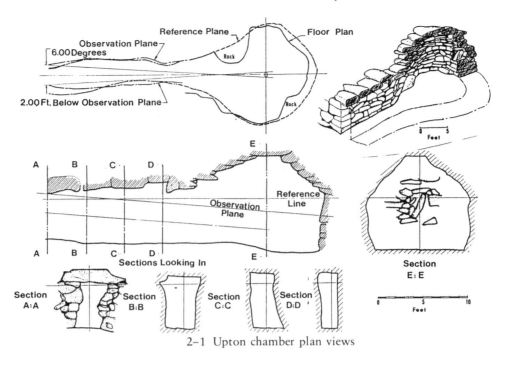

2–1 Upton chamber plan views

over ten feet high is connected to the outside by a long narrow sinuous passage-way between fifteen and twenty feet long with an average width of 2.7 feet (Figure 2–1). It is of dry-wall construction using local granite split from bedrock and glacial boulders, built into the hillside with only the entrance lintel stone and facing stones exposed (Figure 2–2).

2–2 Upton chamber entrance

2–3 Upton chamber interior, showing passage-dome structural transition

The transition from the entrance passage to the domed chamber is effected by a soaring corbelled roof as shown in Figures 2–1 and 2–3, a design that entailed overlapping the passage slabs as the chamber was approached. Such a design can be found in some European chamber tombs 5,000 years old, as well as in Christian cells from 110 to 1,400 years old. However, the most common beehive chamber design world-wide through the ages uses a massive lintel stone of large section to support the weight of the chamber dome; this design is found even in the elegantly finished, tholos tombs of Greece which are later by 2,000 years than similar chambers in northern Europe. At Upton, a gradual rather than an abrupt change in height as well as in cross section is created, evidence of greater structural sophistication than found in the more common rectangular slab-roofed chamber. Each of the two types of chambers presents quite a different aspect to a person entering it, a feature that may be related to an astronomical or cosmological function in some as-yet undetermined way. The region from Upton south to northeastern Connecticut contains several beehive chambers, at least one of which is similar in size and design to the Upton chamber, though with a shorter passage. Near it, there is a circular beehive eighteen feet in diameter, the largest known in New England, which has a lintelled entrance and a shallow dome corbelled with great skill, a design quite different from Upton (Figure 2–4).

While the Upton chamber had been known by the colonists since the early 1700s, apparently no one had looked for indications of possible astronomical use. That was Mavor's first thought upon entering it because we had noticed, on many occasions, stone chambers that are aligned quite precisely to the solstice or equinox sunrise or sunset. We arrived at dusk, and there was just time before dark to take an approximate magnetic compass direction and horizon altitude

2–4 Interior of corbelled beehive chamber in northeastern Connecticut

measurement from within the chamber along the line of the chamber passage toward the distant, elevated horizon, which was obscured by trees. The measurements showed that the line was very near to a summer solstice sunset alignment. We determined to return for more investigation.

Two weeks later, Dix, Mavor, June Potts, Pearson, William M. Dunkle, Jr., of the Falmouth Historical Commission, and Mr. King, a friend of Pearson's and Upton resident, began to seek out in earnest the secrets of this chamber, with the permission of the owner, Walter Cyr. Our plan was to set up our transit outside of the chamber on the line of the entrance passage axis, take a sun sight to determine true north, and determine the orientation of the passage. This was easier said than done, for we had not yet defined the axis of the sinuous passage. For our first attempt, we placed three vertical rods, one at the passage entrance, one at the inside end of the passage, and another at the center of the back wall of the chamber, and aligned them by eye in a straight line so that they approximated a mean chamber axis. This line was measured at 296.57 degrees true, about three degrees south of the summer solstice sunset. As it turned out, this first cut was within 0.20 degrees of the mean axis later determined by measuring successive midpoints of the passage on a fine three-dimensional grid.

Next, our plan called for a climb to the summit of Pratt Hill to the west across a valley, to see if there were a stone mound or other marker on the horizon in line with the chamber passage. This was the moment archaeoastronomers dream of, a chance to check out a theory. From our experience at other New England sites, we were confident there would be one. While four of us inspected the chamber and set up for our sunsight, Pearson and Mr. King drove to the top of Pratt Hill along a dirt road which gives access to the Upton water tower. They returned within a half-hour with the news that they had seen three large stone mounds close to one another on the summit. We received the news with mixed feelings. What were we going to do with three mounds? We only wanted one.

We all went to the top of Pratt Hill to inspect the three stone mounds, which were indeed spectacular. Two, apparently reasonably intact, are long irregular mounds at the eastern edge of the flat summit, oriented approximately north and south and aligned with each other, strung out along the edge of the hill (Figure 2–5). Each is about forty-five feet long with a gap of twenty-eight feet between. Together, they were later found to subtend an angle of one degree from the chamber. The third mound, ruined, is clearly not on the horizon from the chamber.

The mounds posed a challenge in surveying because we had to locate their positions accurately relative to the stone chamber, without being able to see one from the other. They are one mile from the chamber and separated by a valley, a pond, and many trees. Our first step was to use the water tower on Pratt Hill as a reference point from which to run a traverse overland to the mounds. But we needed more than one reference point on the hill, because we did not have the use of a laser transit that could measure distances directly with the necessary precision. We were constrained to the old-fashioned way, measuring angles with the transit and distance with a tape measure, and calculating unknowns by plane trigonometry.

2–5 Looking north along line of mounds A and B

We did not have time on this day to do a complete traverse from the water tower to the mounds because the distance between them is approximately 1,000 feet through dense woods, and the tower could not be seen from the mounds. We did, however, get enough information for a first approximation using a compass and pacing. From this, the previously determined axis of the chamber passage, and the approximate distance between the chamber and the tower from a topographic map, we calculated the position of the mounds. The result was disappointing, several degrees south of the sun's position on the horizon at the summer solstice. Nevertheless, we determined to make more precise measurements at another time.

Before we did this, Mavor went alone to Pratt Hill on 21 December 1979 to check a theory that we had perhaps not yet found the summer solstice mound and that those we had discovered were for some other purpose. (The fact that his visit was on the winter solstice was purely coincidental.) We had made a measurement at the chamber that was interesting in the context of this theory. An observer standing in the center of the domed chamber looking out the passage has a field of view that is six degrees wide, and calculations showed that, at least approximately, the mounds could be seen at the southern limit of this field of view and the summer solstice sunset at the northern limit. From rough calculations, the summer solstice mound, if there were one, should be about 500 feet north of the long mounds, so Mavor walked north from these mounds along the well-defined edge of the hilltop, approximately at the horizon level as seen from the chamber. At 500 feet, measured by pacing, he found his goal, another mound, this one a conical construction of boulders about six feet high at the north end of a large flat outcropping ledge (Figure 2–6). There was also a second

2–6 June solstice sunset mound C

mound, partially ruined, about three feet high and set back from the slope some fifty feet, so that it was questionable whether or not it was on the chamber horizon.

Mavor then ran a traverse with compass and tape from these mounds south to the water tower, some 1400 feet, a process that took two hours. He figured his cumulative distance error was not more than fifteen feet, or one-third of the sun's diameter on the horizon. At home, he calculated positions for the original long mounds and for the newly discovered smaller mounds and found that the position of the top of the six-foot-high north mound, the one on the horizon from the chamber, came out within a fraction of a degree of the sun's position for setting on the summer solstice. We now knew that the extremes of the field of view from the chamber were marked by stone mounds, with a summer solstice sunset at the northern extremity.

This work was the beginning of two years of surveying and mapping of the site, adding new features and repeating measurements to increase their accuracy. Malcolm Pearson, a professional photographer, solved our surveying problem with an ingenious shortcut using a bright strobe light mounted on a pole and triggered from the ground. We set this up at specific locations on the hilltop and at night sighted from the chamber through the transit telescope, synchronizing our activity by using Malcolm's CB radio. The image of the strobe light as seen through the telescope was, to our delight, a bright star, perfect for precise surveying. Using this technique, to our knowledge a first in archaeoastronomical work, we eventually established a surveyed link between the chamber and features on Pratt Hill, accurate to better than one foot in one mile, which we decided would be appropriate, given the dimensions of the stone features. Of course at first, not knowing what astronomical alignments were to be discovered, we did not know how much accuracy was required, but later we found that the level of accuracy

2-7 Sightlines from Upton chamber to Pratt Hill mounds

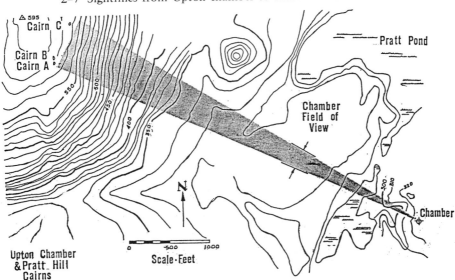

Upton Chamber
& Pratt Hill
Cairns

Scale·Feet

of measurement upon which we had insisted from the start enabled us to date the astronomical events. Throughout our work in New England, we have found that measurements that have been criticized as unnecessarily precise and observations that have been criticized as irrelevant have made the difference between important discoveries and ignorance.

Through the winter of 1979–80, Pearson and Mavor's son, James III, helped us with the surveying, and we established precisely the basic alignments to the three horizon mounds, A, B and C (Figure 2–7). We also mapped the chamber accurately, defined the probable observation position within, and imagined a number of scenarios involving the setting sun. It seemed quite clear that summer solstice sunset at mound C was plausible, but with only one alignment the case for intentional astronomy was weak, especially since there were other mounds. We next considered possible star alignments, but without an archaeologically determined date for the site, we made only slow progress. However, after mapping all of the man-made features on the top of Pratt Hill visible from the chamber, we were eventually able to piece together the components of a complex astronomical observatory of the sun and stars.[2] Before we go into further detail about this astronomy, we want to investigate the archaeological and historical background.

Archaeology and History of the Upton Region

The only previous major archaeological work at the Upton chamber was done in 1955, when the floor of the chamber passage and interior, and an area west of the entrance were excavated by Kelley and Glass.[3] In addition to other historical artifacts, a wooden floor was discovered. However, "no clear evidence of use was found," and it seemed "unlikely that further excavation would answer this problem." Apparently, the excavations did not show whether or not the wooden floor was contemporary with the stone structure or whether or not the chamber was built on bedrock, as so many are. The excavators seem to have given up on getting archaeological results and no one had followed up on their work until we applied our astronomical approach.

Explicit historical references to the Upton chamber and to most other stone structures are rare, and usually vague, particularly regarding origin and function. The region around Pratt Hill was the home of the Nipmuck Indians, a milder and less warlike people than the neighboring tribes, who subjected the Nipmucks and charged them tribute.[4] The first colonial reference to the Pratt Hill region is by John Winthrop, who made an excursion up the Charles River in January 1632 and looked over the area from a distant high hill, but he made no mention of stoneworks.[5] Pratt Hill and Pratt Pond, according to local records, commemorate an absentee English landlord who bought the land from an Indian sachem named John Wampus, alias White, in 1686. The earliest mention of the Upton chamber is dated 1743, when observers were as puzzled as we are today about its origin.[6]

While this material is scanty indeed, there is one important clue in the historical record. Sometime in the 1630s, John Eliot, a young Puritan minister from Roxbury, Massachusetts, set out to learn the native language in order to Christianize the Indians of New England. This became his life work. In 1650, he and Daniel Gookin persuaded the Massachusetts Colony General Court, which claimed all of Massachusetts in the name of the King of England, to allot land for a village called Natick, where the Indians were to be encouraged to become Christians and to live as the Puritans lived. This "praying" village was followed by at least thirteen others, most of them located between Worcester and Boston. The third praying village, Hassanamessitt, set aside in 1654, was a four-mile-square plot of Nipmuck land lying just west of Pratt Hill and the Upton chamber. In 1674, Hassanamessitt was the home of the Nipmuck chief, Wattascompanum, and the center of Nipmuck government.

Eliot's praying villages are important to our story because, as Gookin reported, they were located not by Eliot and Gookin, but by the Indian powwows or shamans, at or near their sacred places of ritual. These sites became magnets for our research because there stone structures still exist in a ritualized landscape that is intact enough to be studied and interpreted. We also began to suspect that the religion of the Indians and their interaction with colonial missionaries could provide clues to the origins and functions of the landscape architecture.

The map of Figure 2–8 shows the Upton chamber, Pratt Hill, Hassanamessitt, and the towns about the region which had been established by the General Court by 1684. A strip of land running east and west was still held and occupied by Indians, and not settled by European colonists, though claimed by the General Court. This included Hassanamessitt, Pratt Hill and the Upton chamber and was bounded on the north by the town of Marlborough, incorporated 1656, and on the south by Mendon, incorporated 1667. Another strip of Indian land ran north from Hassanamessitt.

We became curious about the reason for this spotty arrangement of townships on the colonial frontier and thought to look at the natural setting as an approach to the question. It did not take long to discover that the sources for all of the major rivers of Rhode Island and the eastern half of Massachusetts, except one, lie near Hassanamessitt in land retained by the Indians (Figure 2–8). The Blackstone River flows south to Narragansett Bay from Pratt Pond, where the chamber is located. Whitehall Reservoir, formerly a cedar swamp, drains into the same Pratt Pond and also into the Sudbury River which leads to the Concord River and thence to

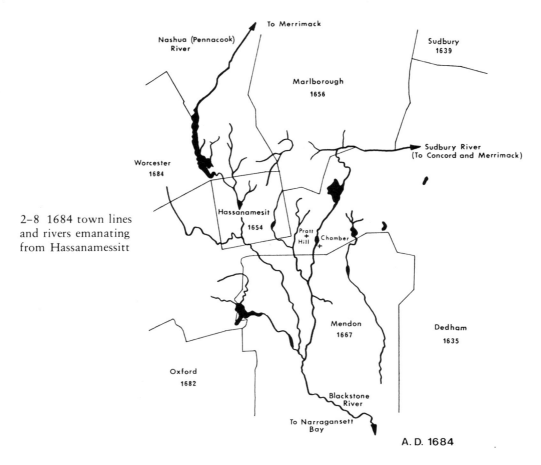

2–8 1684 town lines
and rivers emanating
from Hassanamessitt

the Merrimack and the sea at Newburyport. The Assabet River originates at Hassanamessitt and also flows into the Concord River. The Wachuset Reservoir, just north of Hassanamessitt, drains into the Nashua River, which also flows into the Merrimack. To the east, the source of the Charles River, which empties into Boston Harbor, is North Pond in Upton, just east of Pratt Pond. It is likely that Hassanamessitt, the seat and sacred center of the Nipmuck Nation, was, with the adjoining strips of land, retained by the Indians because of its special location at the source of the waters of Massachusetts, making this area a place of powerful manitou. Only the Taunton River of southeastern Massachusetts does not originate here.

Just north of the Upton chamber and connected to it by a chain of swamps and streams is the Whitehall Reservoir. When the first white settlers came, it was a bog with great white cedar trees hundreds of years old and three small ponds. As late as 1708, salmon, shad and alewives, which made their way up the Merrimack, Concord and Sudbury Rivers to spawn, were abundant. The salmon had disappeared by 1775 and the alewives by 1815.[7]

There is a complex group of stone mounds and earthen banks on the southwestern shore of Whitehall Reservoir, shown in Figure 2–9. Hopkinton Springs, as the place was known in the nineteenth century, is the site of three adjacent mineral springs, one with a large concentration of sulphur, one magnesia, and the other iron. The place thrived as a spa from 1816 to 1837, and some stone structures remain from this period as well as before.[8]

Near the springs and a stream which feeds the reservoir is a large pentagonal enclosure of low earthen banks. Just outside the pentagon on the northwest, there is an oval-shaped stone mound about thirty feet in diameter containing an interior chamber with the entrance facing northwest. To the north and again entirely outside of the pentagon is an elongated group of forty-seven stone mounds extending toward the north. There is evidence of hydraulic management of the watercourses within the site using large boulders, earthworks and stone rows. Other earthen banks, stone rows and stone mounds complete the arrangement. The significance of this array appears to be its location on the shores of a great cedar swamp, at a group of mineral springs, places which are connected by a waterway to the Upton chamber site three miles to the south, and also at the source of waters.

2–9 Hopkinton Springs stone and earthern works: a) Stone mounds, count 69. b) Earthwork. c) Large stone mound with central pit. d) Large boulder. e) Standing stone. f) Sulfur spring. g) Magnesia spring. h) Iron spring. i) Dam. j) Square stone-lined pit. k) Small stream. l) Sluiceway. m) Large stream. n) Pond. o) Whitehall Reservoir, formerly Whitehall Cedar Swamp.

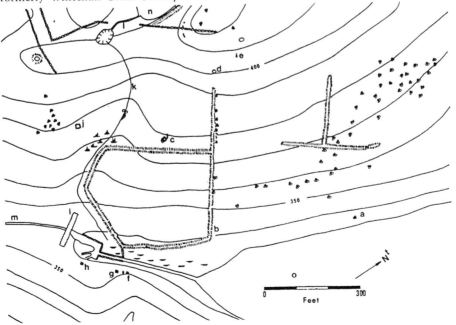

The eastern half of Pratt Hill, containing the stone mounds, and the Upton chamber site were included in lands bought for investment by Harvard College and the Cambridge Grammar School in 1715 from Waban and others representing the Natick Indians. Waban was prominent in the beaver trade and instrumental in setting up the first praying village at Natick. The lands, called Hopkinton after Edward Hopkins who bequeathed the money for the purchase, included within its bounds another of Eliot's praying villages, Magunkaquog, located halfway between Natick and Hassanamessitt.[9]

With the creation in 1715 of Hopkinton and Sutton to its west, all of the Indian land to the east, south and west of Hassanamessitt passed to the colonists' hands. By 1727, more towns had been created and the Indian land to the north was absorbed. And finally, in 1735, the same year that Upton was created out of parts of Hopkinton, Sutton and Mendon, Hassanamessitt became the colonial town of Grafton, although some praying Indians continued to live there.[10]

Historical records are useful not only for the direct information that they provide, be it fact or fancy, but also for the questions they raise about the gaps. These questions are often answered in turn by the records themselves, provided the questions are asked. In this spirit, we raise a number of questions about the lands in the vicinity of what is today called Upton. How were the town boundaries determined, from the earliest times? How were the bounds of the praying towns established? What was the role of the native sachems and shamans, and of the Indian sacred places? Was the strip of land which includes Pratt Hill retained by the Indians until 1715 because of its sacred role? Was Pratt Hill left out of Hassanamessitt purposefully because of some sacred consideration? Why was Hassanamessitt the seat of government for the Nipmuck Nation?

One recent addition to the historical record of the Upton area seems especially tantalizing. In 1948, Sarah M. C. Sullivan, a Nipmuck Indian, wrote from the Indian reservation at Grafton: "Our people were great stone builders. Sometimes those caves came in very handy. You could get in them away from cold and snow. They also helped to hide a lot of the Indians during King Philip's War in 1676. The Indians also helped the slaves by hiding them in caves when they escaped from the slave owners. . . . Upton was once included in Hassanamesitt."[11] This certainly suggests that the chambers and other stoneworks were built by precolonial Native Americans and were still in use during colonial times. The case for precolonial origin was borne out by our discoveries concerning the astronomy of the Upton chamber.

Astronomy of the Upton Site

Viewed from the chamber interior, Pratt Hill is the dominant feature on the horizon, about one mile to the northwest. Astronomical observations on this horizon in the past would have required only that the land be clear in the vicinity of the mounds and the chamber and along sight lines. The hill is now heavily forested with young trees, but we know from an 1851 map that the land was clear during the nineteenth century, and we also know that at the time of the first European settlements in the seventeenth century, the natives were in the habit of clearing large tracts of land by burning.[12]

To investigate the astronomy, we selected as a logical choice the center of the inner chamber as the position where an observer could have stood (Figure 2–1). From here, he could see the elevated horizon on Pratt Hill and a band of sky above it, between the horizon and the passage entrance lintel stone.[13]

We initially focused on the summer solstice sunset at mound C as viewed from within the chamber because all of the ten stone chambers which we have surveyed in central Massachusetts are oriented to a solstice rise or set of the sun. At Upton, there were two probable scenarios, one to make the sunset observation when the lower edge of the sun's disk is tangent to the horizon and one when the upper edge is tangent. Could we decide between the two? By calculation it turned out that it was impossible for the last gleam of the sun to be marked by the mound, because the solstice sunset does not now occur this way, nor would it ever have in the past, at least to the extent that our projections of past sun behavior are correct. On the other hand, the lower-edge scenario was quite plausible. We show it in Figure 2–10 with the lower limb of the sun grazing the top of the pointed mound C.

The question of whether the tangency of the upper or lower limb of the sun to the horizon was the reference point for sunrise and sunset observations in earlier times has been discussed by several writers on archaeoastronomy. It is generally agreed that any intermediate position such as the center of the sun is too

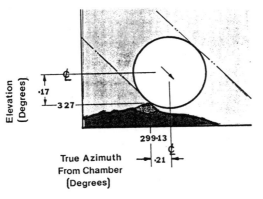

2–10 June solstice sunset over mound C

imprecise and was seldom used. Gerald Hawkins, in describing the convincing alignment of the great temple of Amon-Ra at Karnak, Egypt, where ancient people saw the same celestial events as those in America, presents a midwinter sunrise alignment on a horizon twenty-five kilometers away in which the lower edge is tangent.[14] For our part, sunrise is equally precisely marked by a lower edge or upper edge tangency, but surely the first gleam is more striking and also provides the opportunity to see the green flash, though this is not related to marking with precision. At sunset, however, it seems clear that lower-edge tangency offers the most precise reference for observation of azimuth because the last gleam is partially diffuse and uncertain in time.

We next attempted to establish a date for the chamber's use as a solstice observatory by determining the date when the lower limb of the sun at summer solstice sunset would have been precisely tangent to mound C. Using the 1980 solstice sunset position, as viewed from the chamber, and the known rate of change of the solstice sunset position (1½ feet south per century), we computed a date of A.D. 670 ± 300 years. The range of values is necessary because of uncertainties in the intended position of the sun relative to the mound, possible variations in the height of the observer and his position in the chamber, and the index of refraction of the light path. In other words, it is a fact that during the period A.D. 370 to 970, an observer standing in the center of the chamber dome would have seen the sun set over mound C as shown in Figure 2–10 on the summer solstice. Whether or not someone actually did so is another issue, which will be argued by probability after we have explained the other astronomical events that were marked by features of the site and could have been observed during the same epoch.

Then came the astronomical breakthrough. With a tentative date in hand, we looked at possible events during the same time period that could have been marked by the long mounds A and B. Stars change their positions of rise and set due to precession of the equinoxes and proper motion by about one-half degree per century.[15] This can provide a very precise dating technique. We discovered that in A.D. 710, Alcyone, the brightest of the Pleiades cluster of stars, grazed the top of mound A and set in the notch between mounds A and B. Also, the match between the combined widths of mounds A and B and the width on the horizon of the Pleiades visible to the unaided eye, the eight brightest stars, is precise. Alcyone, Electra, and Pleione set in the notch between mounds, whereas Merope set on the southern end of mound A, Atlas on the northern end of A, and Maia, Taygeta and Asterope on mound B (Figure 2–11).

We now had two celestial events at about the same time in history, the setting of the summer solstice sun and the Pleiades, which occurred at the northern and southern limits of the field of view from a single observation point within the chamber. The field of view is six degrees, which corresponds to a strip of land 560 feet wide on the summit of Pratt Hill. We next concentrated on an accurate survey of all man-made features on the summit, particularly those within the field of view from the chamber, considering seriously the possibility that we

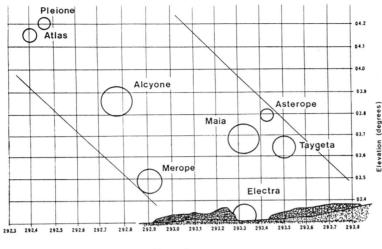

2-11 Pleiades setting over mounds A and B

might be able to correlate specific stars and dates with horizon markers. If a substantial number of such correlations could be found, we could make a case based on probability.

We have identified a total of seven large stone mounds near the summit of Pratt Hill and two about 300 yards to the north. Mounds A, B, E, F and J are elongated piles of irregular shape, each about forty-five feet in length, located as shown in Figure 2–12. Mounds C, D, G and H are of about the same height, five

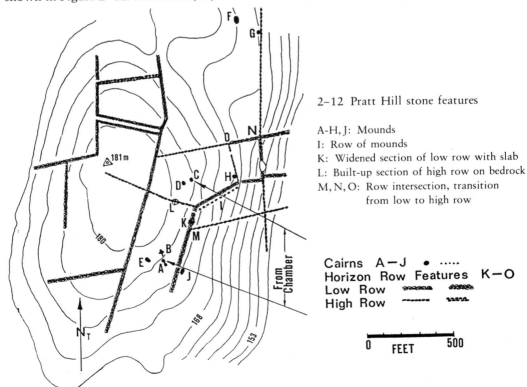

2-12 Pratt Hill stone features

A-H, J: Mounds
I: Row of mounds
K: Widened section of low row with slab
L: Built-up section of high row on bedrock
M, N, O: Row intersection, transition
        from low to high row

Cairns A—J • ......
Horizon Row Features K—O
Low Row
High Row

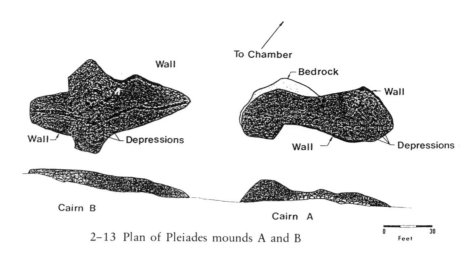

2-13 Plan of Pleiades mounds A and B

to six feet, as the others but of smaller, approximately circular, plan, about four-teen feet in diameter. All of the large mounds are stone piles built upon natural outcroppings of bedrock. All except mound J project above the natural horizon without trees as viewed from the chamber position, but mounds F and G are not visible from within the chamber. They lie well to the north of Pratt Hill and may have been intended to be seen from another place. Mounds A and B are of complex, oblong shape as shown in two views in Figure 2–13, from the chamber and from overhead. In the absence of trees, they would appear as long humps on the natural horizon, two solar diameters in combined length, with a notch in the center of one-quarter of the solar diameter. Mound E lies behind mound A as seen from the chamber and may have been intended as a horizon feature from a point southwest of Pratt Hill. About 150 feet from mound C is a quarry for white quartz and a prominent quartz outcrop not visible from the chamber. Stone mound J is positioned alongside a stone row that has a one-yard-wide gap opposite the central portion of the mound (Figure 2–12). Access to this gap from the east is only possible through the one-yard-wide space between the mound and row, and a person approaching from the west could not see the gap until very close to it. The design limits access through the gap to one person at a time. This specific design feature, which we call a "blocking mound," is character-istic of the Hopewell tradition of the Midwestern Mound Builders, which lasted until about A.D. 800. We have observed this feature at several sacred sites in New England described in later chapters.

There are several unmortared stone rows on Pratt Hill (shown in plan view in Figure 2–12) which fall into two general categories, according to their width and height. Those which are typically about three feet high and a single hand-carried boulder in width are called "high rows" and are generally similar to docu-mented dry-wall stone fences of the eighteenth century used for field boundaries and sheep containment.[16] Those of the other type are about one and one-half feet high and from five to ten feet wide and are called "low rows." A low row typically has more stones in it than a high row of the same length and therefore does not appear to be a collapsed high row. Some low rows have occasional special features which include locally widened sections, local depressions in the row, unusually large stones, raised or built-up sections, curbstones and openings or gaps. Frequently, low and high rows are found in the same locality and may meet or intersect one another, sometimes at astronomically sensitive locations.

Five special features, K, L, M, N and O, are identified in Figure 2–12 because they occur on rows and project above the horizon as seen from the chamber interior, although N and O can be seen from within the chamber only by moving off-axis to the south. K is a slab placed on a widened section of a low row; L is a built-up section of a high row on a bedrock outcrop; M is the intersection of a low and a high row; N is an intersection of three rows from which a high row starts to the north; O is the intersection of two high rows and a low row. M, N and O are the only row intersections on Pratt Hill which lie on the horizon. All of the fourteen man-made structures that could be seen as horizon markers from the position of the chamber are listed in Table 2–1.

Table 2–1   Upton Survey Data

Data is referred to an observer within the chamber, two feet below and twenty-three feet east of the bottom outside edge of the chamber entrance lintel. Unless otherwise noted, reference point on mounds is at their peak.

Marker	*True Azimuth (deg.)*	*Apparent Altitude (deg.)*	*Distance (ft.)*
Mound A	293.25	3.37	4940
South end mound A	292.94	3.32	4917
North end mound B	293.87	3.38	4979
Mound C	299.13	3.27	4999
Mound D	298.76	3.37	5038
Mound E	292.83	3.39	5032
Mound F*	309.84	3.01	5205
Mound G*	310.06	2.90	5061
Mound H	300.88	3.04	4779
Marker K	296.63	3.33	4884
Marker L	297.37	3.39	5022
Marker M	295.98	3.33	4884
Marker N	304.21	2.70	4776
Marker O	302.60	2.64	5009
Passage axis	296.6	3.40	4884

*Mounds F and G lie on the horizon from outside the chamber entrance but cannot be seen from within. Mound J is not on the horizon.

Small stone mounds, typically one and one-half feet high and three to six feet in diameter, spaced thirty to fifty feet apart, are found in groups in certain limited areas. A group of forty is within the enclosure surrounding mounds A, B and E. In addition, there are twenty small mounds in a straight line spaced more or less uniformly alongside a low stone row, I in Figure 2–12. Such a row of mounds could be an evolutionary stage in the building of a low row, but in this case there is already one right beside it. This row of mounds lies parallel to the horizon and just below it and is precisely bisected by the setting summer solstice sun. Mound groups of these types number in the hundreds in New England and are documented elsewhere in Nipmuck country in a Native American context.[17]

Because the Pleiades set at mounds A and B appears to have been a major feature of the site, we investigated the heliacal behavior of the Pleiades, which has been used as a calendrical reference point for millennia all over the world.[18] Heliacal set of the Pleiades, the last setting before a period of invisibility, occurred just after sunset about mid-April during A.D. 700 to 750, and would have been visible from the chamber interior. The first rising after over a month of invisibility, or heliacal rise, occurred just before sunrise at the end of May.[19] The midnight culmination, when the Pleiades were overhead at midnight, occurred on October 30, but these two latter events would not have been visible from the chamber interior.

Our discovery of the Pleiades set alignment was startling enough, but it was not the complete story. The seven stars listed in Table 2–2 are, in addition to the Pleiades and the sun, all of magnitude 2.8 or brighter, the brightest being Arcturus at magnitude 0.24. During the period A.D. 700 to 750, they would have been the nine brightest stars in the field of view from the interior of the chamber, *and all set precisely at horizon markers* (Figure 2–14). No such spectacular combination of events occurred during any other epoch within the past 12,000 years.

The observation post within the Upton chamber is at the end of a long, narrow subterranean passageway. In the twilight hours and in darkness, an observer here can see faint objects and subtle contrasts in his field of view outside of the chamber considerably better than he could if he were outside the chamber. This occurs

2–14 Pratt Hill horizon features as seen from chamber

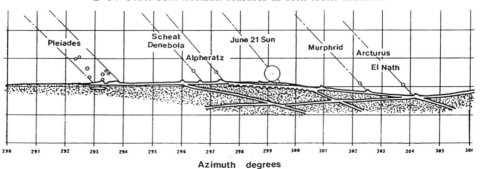

Table 2-2   Star Sets Associated with Markers

Setting Star	Marker	Date A. D.	Declination*
Scheat	K	738	+21.51
Denebola	K	738	+21.51
Alpheratz	L	738	+22.16
El Nath	N	700	+26.37
Arcturus	N	700	+26.37
Algeiba	O	750	+25.54
Murphrid	O	655	+25.54
Alcyone	A	710	+19.21
Other Pleiades	A, B	710	+18.95–+19.66
Sun	C**	370–970	+23.60
Sun	M***	370–970	+20.7
Scheat	Passage	720	+21.60
Denebola	Passage	720	+21.60

*Astronomical declination is the angular distance of a celestial body north or south of the celestial equator and corresponds to latitude on earth. The celestial equator is the projection of the earth's equator on the celestial sphere. At the equinox, declination zero, the sun follows the celestial equator from rising true east to setting true west on a level horizon.
**June solstice
***May 24, heliacal rise of Pleiades A.D. 675–775

because ambient light from outside entering through the undulating passage is limited to a six-degree-wide sector. It is therefore much darker inside than out, and when the observer enters the chamber, the pupils of his eyes dilate, enabling them to gather up to four times as much light as they would outside. Except for Arcturus, the stars whose past settings are marked on Pratt Hill are of relatively low brightness, even when high in the sky. At setting, they would be less bright and barely visible because brightness diminishes near a low-lying horizon. Alcyone, magnitude 2.86, and Denebola, magnitude 2.23, set at apparent altitudes of 3.37 and 3.33 degrees respectively. On the basis of the rule of thumb that extinction angle equals magnitude, both stars are marginally visible on the horizon in clear weather to an observer outside the chamber. Because of enhanced seeing ability due to the chamber design, an observer within the chamber might have a good chance of witnessing the set of these and other stars over markers on Pratt Hill.

The statistical probability that the results of Tables 2–1 and 2–2 could have been obtained if the matching of events and markers at the site were the result of random location and orientation was calculated in four parts. First, considering all possible markers in an area of seventy acres about Pratt Hill summit, the probability that eight of the nine mounds and three of the seventeen row intersections on the summit would have been in positions to be observed as visual horizon markers from within the chamber was calculated. Second, the probability that the chamber field of view would have been oriented in the particular direction that includes the mounds was calculated. Next, the probability that the markers would have proper locations for significant astronomical events to be observed from within the chamber at some period within the past 12,000 years was calculated. Finally, the compound probability of all the above factors was calculated. The net result is that if the observed markers were randomly placed, the probability of the observed astronomical results is less than one part in several million. Even considering the possibility of, say, ten additional unknown markers on Pratt Hill which had been missed and showed no astronomical association, the probability would still be large in favor of astronomy, showing that if we missed some markers or if some had been destroyed, the result is not necessarily invalidated. It can be inferred then that there is a high probability that the structures were intended for astronomical use.

There is an alternative to astronomy that may explain the structures on Pratt Hill and therefore cannot be overlooked. The building of mounds as a result of field-clearing for agriculture is frequently suggested as a logical, albeit undocumented, origin of stone mounds, and it is reasonable that field-clearing piles would be made on bedrock outcrops, even possible that they could have been constructed with laid-up walls like mounds A and B and located on the brow of a hill. It is also possible that they would typically be found in closely spaced groups of forty to one hundred and would be carefully built. But in the case of the Upton chamber, we feel that the evidence is overwhelming that the stone mounds fit an astronomical model.

The Pleiades

The Pleiades have been admired and critically observed in all ages of world history, second among the heavenly bodies only to the sun and moon. According to the historical astronomical literature, their heliacal rise and set and their midnight culmination have marked festivals, seasons, and calendars throughout the world. The Greeks saw this group of tightly interconnected quivering stars as a flight of doves, carriers of ambrosia to the infant Zeus, and used it for orienting their temples. The date of the midnight culmination was observed in the ancient Druids' rites of November first, and it became the traditional date of the Witches' Sabbath or Black Sabbath in medieval Europe. This tradition has come down to the modern world as Halloween, though the midnight culmination has now slipped to November 21.

In Central and South America, archaeological and historical records provide an encyclopaedic resource in archaeoastronomy which may be valuable to the researcher working in other geographical areas. Here and everywhere else that the cosmology of ancient peoples has become known, astronomy has played a vital role, and we do not expect that the northeastern United States would have been fundamentally different. We reason that knowledge of the detailed cultural role of the sun and the Pleiades in the American tropics can be extrapolated to temperate North America, whether or not there was contact between peoples. Much the same events were seen in the sky and they could have evoked similar responses. In the valley of Cuzco, Peru, the heliacal rising and setting and midnight culmination of the Pleiades occurred at approximately the same times of year as they did at Upton, Massachusetts, for any given epoch. The Incaic calendar of A.D. 1500 records the heliacal setting of the Pleiades about a week later than the date we calculated at Upton because of differences in epoch, horizon elevation and latitude. Therefore, we could expect cultural parallels.

The role of the Pleiades in the life of the Inca is known through historical records and surviving structures. The Inca saw this cluster of stars as a universal mother who gave birth to the other stars, as well as to the new sun of the June solstice and the new year. The earth mother, the sun and the Pleiades were also related in Inca myth by association with crystal, or quartz: a crystal fell into the water before the sun god emerged, and the rising of the sun from a spring was considered to be a birth not only from the water but also from the Pleiades. Further, these stars were related to water in the forms of springs and rain. All of these elements were brought together at the Coriancha Sun Temple, the most magnificent structure in Cuzco, originally sheathed in gold. There the rise of the Pleiades over a basin of water, also used for libations to the sun god, and the June solstice sunrise are marked by structural alignments as seen from a single observation point at the great gate.[20] We have already pointed out that all of these elements are likewise present at Upton, where there is a single observation point for the summer solstice sunset and the Pleiades set, and the Pleiades set sightline passes over a lake. And quartz from the nearby quarry is frequently used in the stone rows. Thus hydrography and topography at the Upton site indicate a cosmology in which the Pleiades and water are parts, with the Pleiades representing an earth mother, observed from a stone chamber buried in the earth.

Researchers see a correspondence between the patterns of increase and decrease of the sun, the Pleiades, and Inca agriculture. June, the beginning of the Inca year, was marked by the heliacal rising of the Pleiades and dedicated to the harvest. Also, the Chimu, A.D. 1000–1700, and the Moche, 200 B.C.–A.D. 700, of coastal Peru, regulated their agricultural calendars by the heliacal behavior of the Pleiades.[21] In Aztec Mexico of about A.D. 1500, and in Paraguay, the heliacal rising of the Pleiades at the end of May marked the planting season, while the midnight culmination on November 17 was marked by the Fire ceremony, beginning the dry season. In the Amazon valley, however, the heliacal rising of the

Pleiades marked the beginning of the rainy season. The association of the Pleiades with the planting of corn among agricultural peoples and with the rains among hunter-gatherers is general all over Mesoamerica.

The importance of the Pleiades in the agricultural calendar of the Indians of southern New England was written of by Giovanni da Verrazzano in a letter to the King of France after his voyage to America in 1524. A translation of the *Cellere Codex*, generally considered to be the most complete and reliable version of this letter, states that "when sowing, they observe the influence of the moon, the rising of the Pleiades and many other customs derived from the ancients."[22] However, this translation may miss two key astronomical possibilities. The phrase *"Li'fluxio Lunare, il nascimendo de Le plyade"* from the *Codex* can be translated as "the flux of the lunar course, the birth [first rising] of the Pleiades," an interpretation which implies a more sophisticated astronomy since it suggests concern with the moon's path, not only its influence, and with a heliacal rising of the Pleiades, the first day of visibility. In 1524 the heliacal rising would have occurred about the end of May, perhaps marking the end of the sowing season.

Roger Williams noticed the importance of astronomy not only in the Indian cosmology, but also as a universal religious theme. He wrote, "The Sunne and Moone, and Starres and seasons of the yeere doe preach a God to all sonnes of Men, that they which know no letters, doe yet read an eternall Power and God-head in these." North American Indian lore has many specific references to the Pleiades. The Shasta and Onondaga placed them prominently in their legends, as did the Iroquois, who considered the Pleiades their favorite constellation, representing seven persons who guarded the holy seed during the night.[24] The Blackfeet observed the Pleiades at the planting of seed. The Kiowa and Cheyenne associated them with the *Mateo Tepe* or Devil's Tower, which was raised by the Great Spirit to protect seven Indian maidens pursued by giant bears; the maidens were afterwards placed in the sky as the Pleiades. In the traditions of the Yurok Indians of northwestern California, who have eastern Algonquin roots, there is a saying that the Pleiades are invisible for one month only: they disappear at the end of the fifth month after the winter solstice, are gone to lie in the water in the sixth, and in the seventh reappear just before daybreak.[25]

Comparisons between the ways in which people responded to their observations of the sky in different geographical locations should be valid, provided due consideration is given to astronomical differences. In view of the documented roles of the Pleiades among people of all the Americas and the connection between the June solstice and Pleiades heliacal behavior, we suggest that these events were related at Upton to signal the beginning of the calendar year, and also that the heliacal set of the Pleiades in mid-April was recorded to note corn planting time. A.D. 1000 is usually given as the earliest date for the growing of cultivated plants in New England,[26] but the alignment of the Upton chamber to the Pleiades may indicate that corn and other crops were grown as early as A.D. 700.

At Upton, we became persuaded that there is strong circumstantial evidence to support the theory of prehistoric Indian origins and use of stone structures throughout New England which heretofore have been either ignored or considered part of the colonial farm scene. Although we propose a construction date of A.D. 710, the design of such a complex site must have required many generations of continued tradition. Also, the proximity of the site to Hassanamessitt, seat of government of the Nipmuck nation, a location selected by the Indian powwows in 1654 for a praying village, and centered in a strip of land held by the Indians and not settled by the colonists until after 1715, implies a long tradition of sacred places and a shamanistic practice of astronomy that persisted for at least 900 years.

3

Stone Mounds
in Massasoit's Domain

New England stone mounds are, for the most part, assumed to have been the work of historical farmers clearing their fields of boulders for cultivation, a view that persists in spite of the fact that similar mounds are found all over America and attributed to aboriginal people. Although New England farm lore includes the use of so-called "manure stones,"[1] scattered heaps in a cultivated field built to enrich the soil beneath them, a great number of groups of stone heaps are located on land with no historical record of cultivation and clearly unsuitable for it. Many groups of up to 200 mounds are located on rocky hilltops where cultivation is out of the question. And while we know that isolated stone mounds were used as markers in laying out seventeenth-century town boundaries and were similarly used as property bounds through the nineteenth century,[2] at least some of these were preexisting, and in any case this accounts for only a few. Many mounds were constructed with curbs, walls, pits, cavities, or in curiously regular or irregular shapes suggesting effigies, while others mark astronomical sightlines from stone structures to the horizon.

We first studied groups of stone mounds on Cape Cod because patterns were revealed by the unique geological environment. Elsewhere in New England, the composition of the landscape is more complex, masking the clues to their origins. Cape Cod was created by glacial lobes which retreated northward about 15,000 years ago. It is composed entirely of glacial debris overlying bedrock located from 300 to 700 feet below today's land surfaces. The strip of land about two to three miles wide on the western and northern coasts is a terminal moraine where great piles of gravel and boulders accumulated at the end of the glacier's southerly advance. Elsewhere, the Cape is a glacial outwash plain, mostly sand with occasional rocks.

The town of Mashpee, an Indian town until recent decades, is located entirely on the outwash plain where few boulders are found, and as a result is devoid of stone rows and the other stone structures which we have come to associate with places of Indian ritual. On the other hand, Falmouth, adjacent to Mashpee in the southwest corner of Cape Cod, is largely moraine and contains a great many stone structures. In common with most New England towns it has 100 to 200 miles of stone rows, probably more than the average number of mounds, and standing stones and perched boulders. It has no known stone chambers, perhaps because it has no bedrock for them to rest upon.

Over the period 1979 to 1984, together with William M. Dunkle, Jr., Chairman of the Falmouth Historical Commission, and James McCullough, a local resident, we mapped the groups of stone mounds of Falmouth, placing them on the town's large scale topographic maps, probably the first time that large numbers of mounds had been accurately mapped in a New England town.[3] The mapping was first done because of the threat of destruction, but the Falmouth Planning Board, led by Victoria Lowell, had the foresight in 1981 to insist that the planning for an industrial park and a sewage treatment plant be done in such a way as to avoid the stone mounds. This board is to be particularly commended because they acted in spite of the fact that archaeologists of the Massachusetts Historical Commission dismissed the mounds as of no consequence without even looking at them.[4]

Eventually we mapped about 1,000 stone mounds in Falmouth. The mounds are found in several configurations, pictured in Figure 3–1. In most cases heaps of boulders, each small enough for a person to carry, are piled on top of larger

3–1 Types of stone mounds in Falmouth

 A Pile of small boulders, about 25 pounds each, on top of large boulder; most frequently found, most easily noticed and most easily destroyed type

 B Pile of small boulders with no visible foundation boulder

 C Small stones piled between large boulders

 D Ring of small boulders surrounding a large boulder; rare, usually only one is found in a group of other types

 E Standing stone beside a stone pile

 F Single course of closely spaced small stones of oval or irregular plan, a pavement

3–2 Stone mound
on boulder

boulders, as shown in Figure 3–2; since there is no near-surface bedrock, the
mounds are not connected with it as they often are elsewhere. They are commonly found in groups numbering 10 to 100 on the south or east flanks of kettle holes
of the moraine. These depressions, often ponds, were formed, according to present geological theory, by great blocks of ice left by the glacier as it receded. As
the blocks gradually melted, their weight caused the earth to sink relative to
adjacent land, forming hilly knobs and kettles on the landscape with only a little
level land between.

As in most other places in New England, the origin of these mounds is obscure, but some do have Native American connections. In the midst of several
groups of stone mounds in Falmouth is a large boulder known as Great Rock,
which was rediscovered in recent years by Charles White, former Town Engineer.
According to Jehu Norton, an eighteenth-century Indian, it was an Indian do-

3–3 Astronomical alignments
from Great Rock (a) over stone
mounds (b) and kettle holes (c)
d Summer solstice sunrise
e Equinox sunrise
f Winter solstice sunrise
g Summer solstice sunset
h Equinox sunset
i Winter solstice sunset

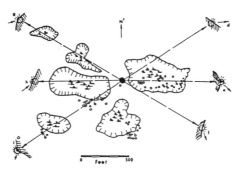

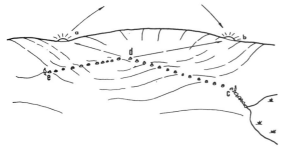

3-4 Shanks Pond aligned rock stacks
a Winter solstice sunrise
b Equinox sunset
c Observer at end of rock stack row near Shanks Pond
d Corner of rock stack row
e Observer sighting equinox sunset along rock stack row

nation boulder, upon which passing natives would place branches as a token of respect. It is also thought to have been a marker for the northern boundary of Suckanesset, land purchased from Indians in 1660 by the early English settlers of Falmouth.[5] The rock lies on a hilltop overlooking several large kettle holes, as shown in Figure 3–3. Points on the horizon for the six solar calendrical events, winter and summer solstice sunrise and set and equinox sunrise and set are marked by standing stones or natural peaks and notches, as shown in the figure. Groups of stone mounds are also located along these sight lines.

A unique row of stone piles adjacent to Shanks Pond in Falmouth is seen in Figure 3–4. A rambling stone row climbs from the kettle hole on the southwest corner of the pond and then changes to a row of stone piles spaced about ten feet apart. These in turn climb a gentle hillside in a straight line, turning at the summit to form another straight line along a natural ridge. The ascending line from the end of the stone row is a winter solstice sunrise alignment, and the line along the ridge from its east end is an equinox sunset alignment, an event that can be witnessed there today because trees on the horizon have fortuitously been cut away for a road. In Figure 3–5, a cat sitting on one of the stone piles faces the equinox sunset along this row of piles. The equinox sunrise can also be observed

3–5 Equinox sunset over Shanks Pond rock stack

from the west end of the ridge along this line since the ridge and the horizon in both directions are level. The piles, or more precisely stacks of boulders, used here are small and do not sit on large boulders. They could easily be destroyed, a fact which suggests that they are fairly recent in origin. It is known that about 1800 an Indian family named Shanks or Shawnks lived in a wigwam on the shore of Shanks Pond.[6]

Isolated stone mounds in Falmouth have been connected with Wampanoag Indians who lived there. In adjacent Bourne and Sandwich, donation piles of stone mark locations where passing Indians left selected rocks out of respect for the spirit or manitou of each place. In Mashpee, which has relatively little stone, brush piles served the same purpose up to recent times. Sometimes, these locations are called wishing or praying sites in folklore, which implies that they were places that visions were sought.

A Tract in Falmouth

We selected for detailed study and mapping a 180-acre wooded tract in Falmouth where several groups of stone mounds occur in conjunction with other stonework. One reason for choosing this site is that its history of usage since the seventeenth-century European settlement of the area is well-established and records little disturbance of the natural landscape. During the past 300 years there were few buildings of record and the land has been used only as woodland and pasture. We mapped not only the stone mounds but also the locations of all the man-made features that we could find, because we believe that the total environment must be considered in any study of stone structures. The tract, which we call Boulder Ridge, is adjacent to seventeenth-century European settlement and within the Wampanoag domain but it had attracted no recorded interest among archaeologists.[7] A part of a glacier stopped for a time and released its load of rocks, forming a ridge of boulders in the middle of the tract.

Figure 3–6 is an illustrated catalogue of the details of stone structures seen at Boulder Ridge and also commonly encountered in walking many of the woodlands of Cape Cod moraines in the wintertime when leaves do not obstruct the view. Among the details shown, in addition to the mounds, are embrasures, vertical slabs in stone rows, different lengths of stone row, and shaped slabs which we call spirit of the creator after Hopi practice for similar stones. Of special interest to our story, these spirits-of-the-creator slabs often resemble a human head and shoulders effigy (Figure 3–7) and are usually found built into stone rows at the locations of other special structural details or discontinuities in the natural landscape. Certain low enclosures of boulders found here and throughout New England resemble Indian "prayer seats." Here, one shown in Figure 3–8, was built of small boulders placed on a horizontal slab between large boulders, with a vertical slab forming one side of the enclosure. These "seats" are usually just large enough to accommodate one sitting person.

Stone row: one or more linear courses of closely spaced stones. Long, over 200 feet; intermediate, from 50 to 200 feet; short, from 5 to 50 feet

Embrasure: U or V shaped recess in a row, usually about 6 feet long, sometimes with adjacent standing stone

Enclosure with adjacent standing slab

Enclosure without slab

Serpentine stone row

Boulder stone mound: a group of head-sized or smaller stones on top of large boulder

Stone mound: a pile of boulders on the ground

Rock group: one course of quarried stone and boulders, larger than in rows or mounds, in a closely knit group up to 30 feet in extent, usually shaped

Standing stone: tall, narrow obelisk

Excavation: Excavated, shaped depression in soil of unexplained origin

Linear earthwork: not built for carriage roads

Stone bound: quarried rectangular granite marker

Other special man-made features: spirit-of-the-creator stones; corner-notched stones; stone basins; perched boulders in stone rows

Knob: natural glacial isolated peak

Exceptionally large boulder

Kettle hole: natural depression created by the weight of an ice block left by receding glacier, often a swamp or pond today

3–6 Catalog of stone structures and natural features at Boulder Ridge

3–7 Spirit-of-the-creator stone in Falmouth

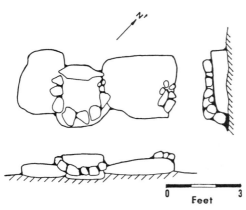

3–8 Stone enclosure resembling
Indian prayer seat

The plan of the Boulder Ridge site is shown in Figure 3–9. It shows some 170
separate man-made features consisting of 76 stone mounds in three major groups,
18 short stone rows, and several lengths of longer stone rows. At first the stoneworks appear as unconnected parts, but repeated features and patterns become

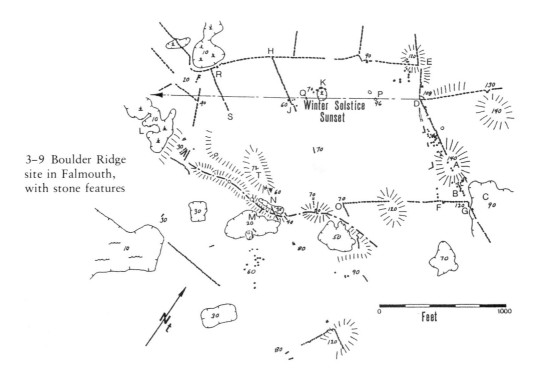

3–9 Boulder Ridge
site in Falmouth,
with stone features

evident as the place is seen as a whole. Because of trees in the way today, astronomical alignments appear only after the stone features have been mapped and visualized in the context of their local horizons. All of the stone features catalogued in this area seem connected to kettle holes, knobs, ravines, swamps, rocky ridges or major hilltops. There are two major concentrations of features, one about the rocky ridge and the other about the highest hill in the area.

To the southeast of the highest hilltop, A, is a group of eleven stone mounds, B, along the edge of a gully which falls away into a kettle hole, C, to the north. In the gully is a curious two-lobe man-made excavation with a stone mound at its base separating the two lobes. From A, a stone row descends the hillside toward D, the joining of three long stone rows, where there is a triangular stone enclosure. We find many stone mounds, all southwest of the row AD, on the flank of this dominant hill where the land slopes steeply from an elevation of 147 feet to 10 feet above sea level.

At corner E, on top of a knob, there is a large split boulder, probably broken naturally, but curious because of its commanding view and the way in which the two pieces enclose a natural place where a group might meet or observe (Figure 3–10). The split is in line with the sightline to the winter solstice sunset over Buzzards Bay. South of this boulder, on the opposite side of the nearby stone row, there are several stone mounds on a steep slope. Three of these are unusually large and one was formed of small boulders piled between and on two large boulders (Figure 3–11).

In this tract there are twelve embrasures in stone rows, eight of which have orthostats nearby, usually stone slabs one and one-half to three feet high. In addition to one embrasure at F and two at the northwestern swamp, there is an embrasure with an orthostat, open to the northeast toward a kettle hole, adjacent to corner G. Stone row AD has two embrasures, and row DE, one, all

3–10 Large split boulder at Boulder Ridge

3–11 Stone pile between boulders

opening to the southwest. Proceeding northwest from A to D, the first embrasure is directly opposite an exceptionally large boulder and the second at the top of a local hill. The third is at a marked change of slope. An embrasure with orthostat in row EH is next to a larger triangular embrasure, and the embrasure with an orthostat at J near the end of the row southeast of H signals nearby mounds.

Proceeding to the small kettle east of J, we find a deep swampy hole, the northwest flank of which is paved with a group of boulders K over an area thirty by twenty feet in extent. On the northwest flank is a large boulder mound and on the west flank a stone mound which may be a continuation of the pavement.

South of the northwest swamp a kettle hole L, which is a pond in the spring, marks the west end of a prominent rocky ridge of large glacial boulders, for which the tract is named, that winds from east to west across the site for 500 yards. On the plateau between the pond and the end of the ridge is an arrangement of serpentine intermediate-length and short stone rows. At the ends of two of the intermediate rows, James W. Mavor III noticed that the tops of boulders had been worked to form basins, like those commonly described as Indian mortars or libation bowls (Figure 3–12). There is also a stone mound and a rock group nearby.

Proceeding east along the rocky ridge for about 600 feet, we come to a wide stone row M of large boulders, thirty-six feet long and six feet wide, which extends from the summit of the ridge down the steep slope into the large kettle hole to the south. One hundred feet farther to the east along the ridge, an intermediate-length stone row N passes over the ridge from the northeast edge of the large southern kettle through a small kettle to the north.

The long stone rows of the tract describe what one might call a solar parallelogram CEHO, 400 yards on a side, that dominates the overall layout of stone features. Observers on the knob at E and at the row corner G can see the winter solstice sunset by looking along the two legs of the parallelogram, in the direc-

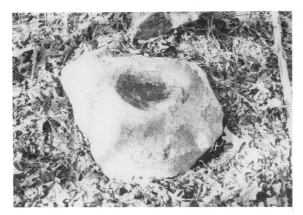

3–12 Boulder worked to form a basin

tions of the row EH and GO respectively and toward the north shore of Cutty-hunk Island. But, the focus of astronomical activity appears to have been at D, the triangular stone enclosure where an observer could see the winter solstice sunset precisely at the north coast of Cuttyhunk eighteen miles away (Figure 3–13a) over a nine-foot-high triangular boulder located at P in Figure 3–9 and shown in Figure 3–13b, and an oblong stone mound at Q. This sight line has been dated astronomically between A.D. 1500 and 1800. An observer at .the triangular enclosure would have also seen the winter solstice sunrise over the summit A. As if to complement these alignments to the southwest horizon, the largest group of stone mounds is located on the southwest slope of the high hill.

Leg HJO consists of a long stone row extending from H to an embrasure with an orthostat and stone mounds adjacent, then across a gap to a short stone row, slightly skewed from line HJO, that is isolated from other mapped features but adjacent to some large boulders. The line continues across another gap to corner O, where an intermediate-length stone row extends it beyond the parallelogram.

3–13 a) Winter solstice sunset alignment to Cuttyhunk north shore from triangular enclosure at three-row intersection, Boulder Ridge. b) Visual features along sightline. The nearby nine-foot-high pyramidal boulder signals the approximate location of winter solstice sunset, more precisely marked by the last gleam of sun at north coast of Cuttyhunk. Small islands are the Wee Weepeckets.

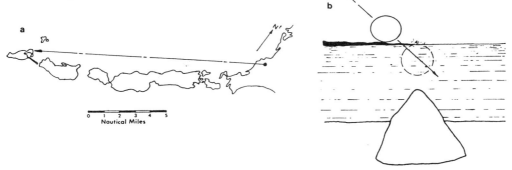

This line marks the winter solstice sunrise on a nearby level horizon as seen from H. The nearly parallel and slightly curved stone row RS from the northwestern swamp, runs southeast toward the knob T, which is the horizon for a winter solstice sunrise alignment from R, the juncture of this stone row and another at the swamp edge.

These arrangements suggest that the site is a vast and complex architectural work. It is diffuse and its elements are simple and not easily recognized, but the architectural plan is sophisticated in that it reflects a sensitivity to the natural environment in space and time. The subtle positioning of the stonework in relation to the natural features reflects a respect for and understanding of the natural world. All these signs point to a Native American origin.

While industrialized man tends to see time as an endless stream flowing from the past through present into the future, the Indian sees it and all events as cyclical. The seasonal festivals, signalled by the solar alignments, are keyed to astronomical cycles and seen as connecting life on earth with the celestial bodies in an ever repeating way. The solar, lunar and combined solar and lunar calendars of all peoples are a reflection of this concept and the dates of the beginning of the year reflections of different traditions. The English settlers of New England began their year on March 25, following a tradition originating with the vernal equinox, until 1752 when the Gregorian calendar was adopted. The Jews begin the year at the new moon following the autumnal equinox. The Wampanoag "divided the year into spring, autumn and winter, and counted the year by the lunar months. The first of the annual religious festivals began at the first appearance of the first new moon after the vernal equinox and the sun was the adored god of great divinity and power."[8]

An Excavation Reveals Origins of Stone Mounds

Freetown, lying east of the Taunton River in southeastern Massachusetts, is a land of Atlantic white cedar swamps, separated by ridges. It has many morainic accumulations of sand, gravel and boulders which were deposited about 12,000 years ago by the Wisconsin Glacier as it melted away from the terminal moraines a few miles southeast at Cape Cod. Freetown became important to our research when we discovered that it is the location of numerous groups of impressive stone mounds which we suspected were built by Native Americans. The mounds might shed light on a native way of life now forgotten since the traditional ways of the Wampanoag Indians who lived here died with them, and previous archaeology in the region had provided only the subsistence relics that survived the acidic soil.

Our introduction to the stone mounds of Freetown was a telephone call from James P. Whittall II announcing that a large group of stone mounds in Freetown was being destroyed by logging operations prior to the building of a hazardous waste treatment plant. He had his information from Fred Rhines, reporter for the Fall River *Herald-News*, who had written that a New Bedford resident had discovered an Indian burial site.[9] This sequence of events started a political controversy that reverberated through the newsrooms of Fall River, New Bedford and Providence for the next six weeks because local people opposed to the plant as a neighbor were quick to seize on the possibility of an important archaeological site to hold up development of the plant. Another consideration was that the site for the plant was right on top of the water mains supplying New Bedford. Whittall and Mavor were invited to inspect the site and mapped some sixty mounds in a group of well over one hundred, unaware of the unfolding political drama.

Later, Dix and Mavor visited the same site with Freetown officials and gave the opinion that the mounds were probably not burials, but were likely to be part of an important Indian ritual site. We also observed that the mounds extended beyond the property under consideration for the plant, to the south and to the east into Bolton Cedar Swamp, and noted extensive earthworks that looked worthy of investigation as possible Indian constructions similar to others documented in northern Massachusetts. Of particular interest was an embankment over 1,000 feet long, about twenty feet high and sixty feet wide, built of broken rock and earth, which runs along the northwest side of the water conduit that supplies New Bedford from the Middleborough ponds. While this bank might be spoil from the trench dug for the water conduit some eighty years ago, it seems too massive for this purpose and is separated from the conduit by a wide ditch. Our attention was also drawn to an unroofed, dry-walled stone subterranean enclosure about eight feet square built on top of the embankment, with an entrance facing southeast. We made note of this structure because we had seen many others like it and it fit a pattern which we shall develop later.

On 21 June 1983, Mavor sent a letter report urging conservation of the mounds due to their possible archaeological importance to the Commissioner of Indian Affairs for Massachusetts, with a copy to the State Archaeologist, who represented the Massachusetts Historical Commission. We received no response from either office, which should perhaps have been expected, since Mavor had experienced a similar lack of interest in his 1979 report of the discovery and mapping of the several hundred stone mounds in Falmouth. Nevertheless, the Indian Commissioner was interviewed by the *Providence Journal* and was quoted as saying, "Some farmer just started building a stone wall and never finished."[10] A staff archaeologist of the Massachusetts Historical Commission was quoted by the *Standard-Times* of New Bedford as saying, "They are just piles of fieldstone — it is common in all pasture areas where farmers just dropped them in piles."[11]

Realizing that the Freetown plant site was a political hot potato, we concluded that a nearby site out of the public eye might answer the scientific questions and serve as well to help to preserve others. John Place of Freetown offered to

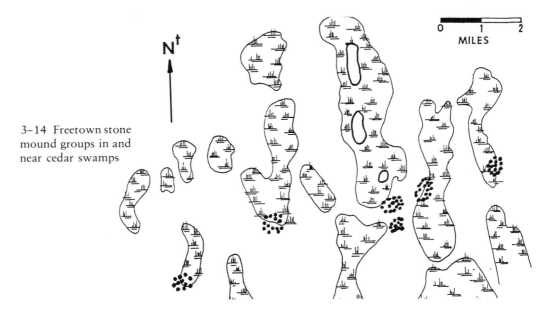

3-14 Freetown stone mound groups in and near cedar swamps

show us additional locations where he had seen groups of stone mounds. Chief Little Horse of Westport and the Wollomonopaug Indian Tribal Council, unlike the Indian Commissioner (also of Indian descent), was anxious to see these mounds preserved because he felt that they were of Indian origin. We undertook a survey of a wide geographical area surrounding the threatened site and found many stone mound groups of a similar character, all on easterly facing slopes of the rising land between cedar swamps. We found that there are at least 1,000 mounds in East Freetown and more in adjacent towns, characteristically associated with stone rows. Figure 3-14 shows six groups, all at swamp edges over a distance of ten miles. Freetown also contained an abundance of hematite, which was once extensively dug and worked. As bog iron, hematite was an important ore in the eighteenth and nineteenth centuries. As red ochre, it played an important ceremonial role in Native American life.

We selected for detailed study a group of 110 stone mounds that is a half mile from the threatened site and has the same density of the same sized and shaped mounds. The site is 150 feet above sea level on land sloping gently downward to the northeast. The arrangement of stone mounds within the group (Figure 3-15) appears to have some elusive kind of order to it. Stone mounds follow along a curved stone row, just visible above the ground surface, and lengths of stone row connect stone mounds to the west. We infer that stone mounds and stone rows at Freetown were designed to relate to one another and also that many of the groups of mounds have similar origins and functions.

We reluctantly decided to excavate a mound only because we thought that this would produce quickly the kind of information that might persuade governmental archaeological authorities to conserve the mounds. Of course we were

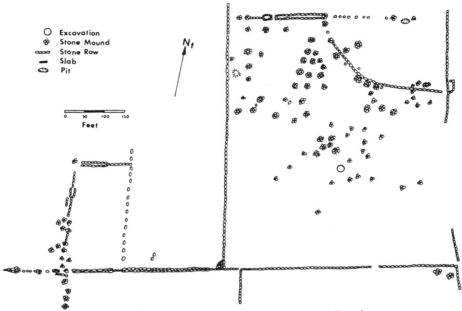

3–15 Plan of stone mound group at excavation site

wrong in this hope, but our intuitive reluctance to excavate has been confirmed time and time again since. The mound selected for excavation appeared typical of those in the group, twelve feet in diameter and thirty inches high above ground level (Figure 3–16).

3–16 Mound before excavation, with Chief Little Horse, *right*, and John Place

After some preliminary excavation of the selected stone mound, a Freetown conservation group arranged for us to meet with the selectmen, to whom we submitted a report. As a result of this meeting, the *Standard-Times* of New Bedford reported that the "Boston Historical Commission" had "vehemently disagreed with contentions of two Cape Cod researchers that mounds on the site were left by early Indians. . . . Boston says that most likely they were glacial deposits. . . . Neither Byron Dix nor James Haver [sic] of Associated Scientists of Woods Hole, a non-profit research organization, is an archaeologist." The article went on to say that "the local Historical Commission would not support having the site regarded as a historic landmark."[12]

Dix and Mavor, along with Diane Dix, John Place, James Rymciewicz, James P. Whittall II, and Chief Little Horse, participated in the excavation, which started in June and continued on into November of 1983. Prior to excavation, Chief Little Horse performed a traditional Indian ritual of respect. We undertook this phase of research with a heavy sense of responsibility, knowing that excavation is a nonrepeatable experiment and should be the culmination of a study, undertaken only to answer questions that cannot be addressed in other ways. We justified it at this stage as the only way to find sufficient evidence to stop destruction of this important and numerous type of antiquity. There are many apparently similar examples in the Freetown groups, so we sacrificed one to save many. This was the first attempt to excavate a New England stone mound with a sense that it was a sacred monument and that every part of it and its surroundings were important to this role. For this reason, we go into some detail.

The plan view (Figure 3–17) shows the mound to be triangular, of arrowed form, and directed true south. The excavation proceeded in two phases, the first to achieve a quick result that might prevent further destruction of the threatened group. A trench, including squares P2, Q2, R2 and S2, through the northern part of the mound revealed a stone and earthen row, made of boulders about one foot in diameter, oriented east-west, with its base at least 2½ feet below present ground level, so that it was either underneath or integral with the mound. Because of this circumstance, we conclude that the row was built either before or contemporary with the mound.

This row, shown as feature E in Figure 3–18, is slightly curved and built on the transition to grey-green gravel soil. The row is different in structure and clearly distinct from the soil profile away from the row, verified by excavating a control square 25 feet northeast of the center of the mound. In the control square, the soil profile was similar to that within the mound in color and chemistry but no stones were found, until at a depth of 16 inches a layer of large boulders was discovered. As to precedents for ancient underground stone rows in New England, Huntington reports a dry-laid stone wall 24 inches high constructed during the late Archaic Period by occupants of a rock shelter in Marlborough, Massachusetts.[13] The destruction of the site of this wall was permitted by federal and state authorities for the construction of the highway interchange connecting Routes 495 and 295.

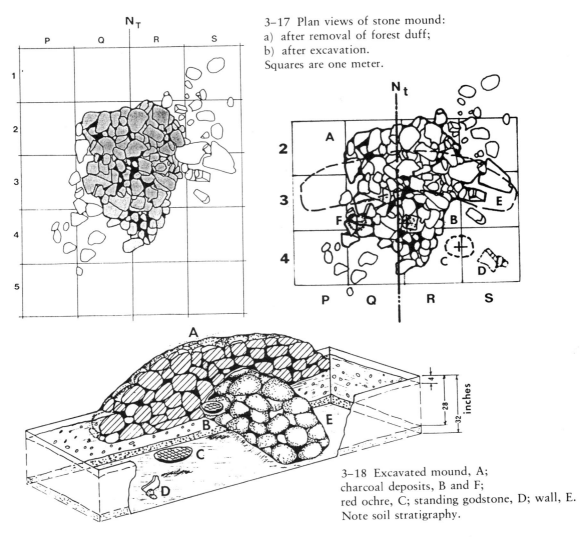

3-17 Plan views of stone mound:
a) after removal of forest duff;
b) after excavation.
Squares are one meter.

3-18 Excavated mound, A; charcoal deposits, B and F; red ochre, C; standing godstone, D; wall, E. Note soil stratigraphy.

The second phase of our excavation consisted of removing the remainder of the stones in the mound, recording size, shape and location, and trowelling down the interstitial soil. In the southern squares, P3 and 4, Q3 and 4, R3 and 4, and S3 and 4, we removed 972 stones altogether that were greater than 2 inches diameter, of which 12 percent exceeded 8 inches and 5 percent were larger than 12 inches. The mound, shown as feature A cut by a north-south cross section in Figure 3-18, was built entirely of larger stones, 8-14 inches diameter, from the top down to 4 inches below present ground level. From 4 to 8 inches depth, there was an interior layer of smaller stones, 4-6 inches diameter, surrounded by larger boulders, shown in Figure 3-19. From 8 to 12 inches depth, there were large boulders in squares P3, Q3, R3 and P4 and smaller stones in squares Q4 and R4.

Two separate, isolated charcoal deposits 12 inches in diameter and 4 inches

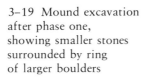
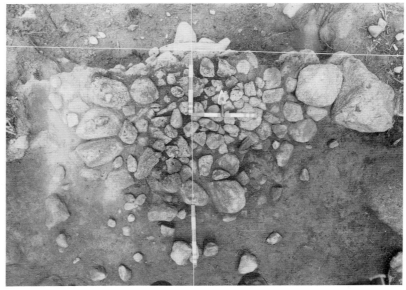

3–19 Mound excavation after phase one, showing smaller stones surrounded by ring of larger boulders

deep were found between 8 and 12 inches depth below the layer of smaller stones and above the layer of larger boulders at the joining of square Q3 and Q4, shown as features B and F in Figure 3–18a and b. Carbon 14 dates of 875 ± 160 years ago and 790 ± 150 years ago were determined from these charcoal deposits.[14] Below 12 inches depth, the excavated regions of squares Q4 and R4 consisted of densely packed smaller stones, 2–6 inches diameter, with larger boulders around the periphery of the mound.

We found a large deposit of chunks of red ochre or soft hematite, consisting of 120 pieces weighing ten pounds within a three-foot diameter lens from 14–18 inches depth in squares R4 and S4, shown in Figures 3–17b and 3–18 as feature C and

3–20 Typical red ochre chunks found in excavation

in Figure 3–20. Occasional pieces of red ochre were removed from depths of 10 to 30 inches. The red ochre was located beneath the larger boulders of the mound and among densely packed smaller stones uncharacteristic of the typical soil profile away from the mound. Whether or not the red ochre is prehistoric, it is strong evidence that this was a Native American ritual site, since red ochre is typically associated with their ritual from the Archaic Period up to the present day. It appears in burials as a symbolic blood offering to the spirit, as a hunting charm in medicine bags, and as the pigment for ritual body paint.[15] This stone mound in Freetown produced more red ochre chunks than were collected at Wapanucket, a nearby extensively excavated Archaic Indian site, in twenty years of excavation. This may point to a previously unrecognized role for red ochre at ceremonial lithic sites detached from habitations and burials.

The most interesting single stone artifact was a worked standing slab of diamond shape with point up, 20 inches high, found in square S4, propped up and inclined 30 degrees to the vertical, with its base at a depth of 2½ feet (Figure 3–18a and b, feature D, and Figure 3–21. It is similar to underground standing slabs of unnatural appearance found in our excavations of lithic sites in Vermont[16] and may be akin to Algonquin image stones or Hopi spirits of the creator.[17]

The profile of soil properties within the mound, in the excavation border at the mound edge and in the control excavation 25 feet away were exactly the same.[18] This suggests that the mound may have been built a long time ago when the ground level was 2½ feet below what it is today, and the processes of wind-blowing, leaching and eroding produced a soil profile that is the same inside and outside the mound. It is less likely that the mound was built in a dug pit on a gravel bed, followed by backfilling through the ages by natural processes. Further excavation along a profile radiating outward from the mound might clarify this question, but either possibility may imply greater age than the carbon 14 analyses indicate, which is quite possible since these give only the most recent possible date for the mound.

3–21 Standing godstone in excavation

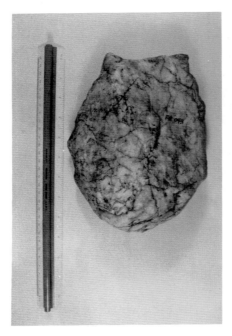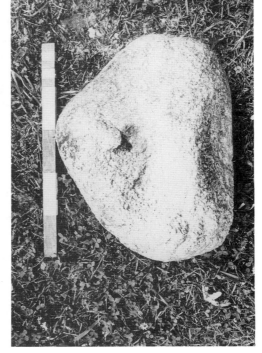

3-22 "Horned" quartz stone and anvil stone found in excavation

Many stones throughout all levels of the mound showed markings indicating possible use as tools or implements, but they were limited to hammerstones, scrapers, choppers and anvils (Figure 3-22). Noticeably absent were the stone projectile points, axes, chisels, atlatl weights, knives, gouges, bowls and pottery that define a subsistence site. Since history reports that some stone mounds consist of material ritually donated by Indians as they passed by and the implements in the mound consisted of large numbers of limited types, the stones in this mound could have been individually selected for their roles in ritual and not just random boulders or rejected tools.

The most extensive burial and habitation site of prehistoric provenance in southern New England that has been excavated is the Wapanucket site,[19] located four miles north of the Freetown stone mounds, at Lake Assawompsett, in a similar environmental setting and with a similar soil profile down to 2½ feet. Charcoal and diagnostic artifacts in the 7 to 25 inch levels are dated from 3,435 to 9,000 years ago. The Wapanucket and Freetown sites appear to be of quite different character. Wapanucket was a place where people settled, worked, subsisted and buried their dead. Freetown has only stone implements of very limited types, charcoal, a large quantity of red ochre and a standing slab. Freetown, therefore, could have been solely a ceremonial site with a quite different set of artifacts from a subsistence site. This separation of everyday living places from heliolithic ritual sites is, we believe, characteristic of New England because the kinds of artifacts found in the two types of places are universally different. We were led to these places initially by circumstantial evidence of astronomy and later by typical patterns of the natural environment, by stone structures and by hand-held artifacts showing little work by man compared with most tools and implements found at places of settlement and subsistence. These sites seem to have more to do with the way people celebrated the uniqueness of their local landscapes than with the daily business of survival.

We conclude from the excavation that the mound, and by implication many others, was built by prehistoric Native Americans for ceremonial use, and was certainly not the result of English colonial field clearing. Stone mounds are extremely stable, can survive earthquakes and, if undisturbed by animals or plants, can last a very long time. Therefore, we believe that many of the stone mounds are monuments to a way of living in a continuous harmony with nature.

History of Freetown Area

In these first three chapters, we are attempting to convey a feeling for the process of discovery. The discoveries took place first on the New England landscape and only later in historical archives. There, the evidence of Indian origin of stonework is subtle and obscure but does gain weight by sheer quantity. We can sense from the record, and from the absence of records of Indian life except as it supports English righteousness, that relations between Indians and colonists were not as confrontational as appears on the surface.

The white man's written history treats the New England Indians as an obstacle to colonial expansion, so it only incidentally sheds light on the Indian ways. Nevertheless, here, as in other chapters, we present the historical record as a backdrop to our observations to highlight inconsistencies in and to raise questions about historical portrayals of both Indians and the European colonists, as well as to present evidence of Indian stonework. Incidents in the lives of prominent characters during the period of growth of the Plymouth Colony have become legend and, as legends do, have grown in the telling.

At Freetown, we are more interested in the physical location and the people than in the governmental jurisdiction. However, tracing Freetown's evolution lends insight into the natural environment and both its native and immigrant inhabitants. Since Freetown is on the old Indian trail from Plymouth to Sowams, where Massasoit lived, it was crossed as early as 1621 by Pilgrims Edward Winslow and John Hopkins. In 1623, when Edward Winslow and John Hamden visited the dying Massasoit and saved his life, they were accompanied by Corbitant, sachem of the Pocasset tribe, who occupied the Freetown region and were the largest tribute tribe of the Wampanoags under Massasoit.

Two principal Indian gods or spirits were recognized by the colonists, Kichtan and Hobomock. The story goes that once there was no sachem, only Kichtan, a self-existent creator of the heavens. Men never saw Kichtan nor prayed to him but they held him to be good. Hobomock resembled the Devil of scripture. The Indians prayed to him, often musically, to heal wounds or diseases and to remove evils. When diseases were curable, Hobomock was considered responsible for the complaints and the prayers answered. If diseases were not cured, they were ascribed to Kichtan. The name Hobomock was given to many ponds and swamps in New England including one in Freetown containing a large group of stone mounds.[20]

The colonists also perceived two classes of Indian officials in addition to the hereditary sachems or chiefs. Powahs or powwows were seen as priests who had certain powers. They could make "rocks move" and "trees dance." In a community of warriors, paneses were seen as an aristocracy, who inflicted severe penances upon themselves in order that the spirit Hobomock might appear to them. Both powwows and paneses sought Hobomock, and so had overlapping shamanistic roles.

The Indian who acted as a liaison between Massasoit and the Pilgrims had the name Hobomock, a paradox, because he was reported to have been converted to Christianity. After Massasoit's death in 1661/1662 of plague, Alexander or Wamsutta, his eldest son, became the great sachem of the Wampanoag Federation, which included all the tribes of southeastern Massachusetts. Since his wife was Weetamoe, daughter of Corbitant and his successor as sachem of the Pocassets, the Pocassets and Pokanokets, Massasoit's tribe, became more closely joined. When Wamsutta died within a year of his father and was succeeded by Metacom, called King Philip by the colonists, the tribes came even closer together because Metacom was married to Corbitant's other daughter, Wootonekanushe.

The largest single body of warriors available to Metacom during the Second Puritan War were Pocassets, who were crucial to his early successes. After the war of 1675 and 1676, almost all of the Pocassets had been either killed or sold into slavery. The few who remained were those who had been friendly to the English, including direct descendants of Massasoit.

The English history of Freetown began in 1659 when a group of enterprising colonists consisting of Josiah Winslow, son of Edward, governor of the Plymouth Colony, James Cudworth, Constant Southworth, father-in-law of Benjamin Church, later famous as a hero of the Second Puritan War, and twenty-two others bought what is known as the Freemen's purchase from Ossamequin (Massasoit), Wamsutta and Tattapanum (Weetamoe).[21]

The name, Freetown, adopted in 1683 at incorporation, came from "Freemen's Purchase," as all the purchasers were "old freemen" who had lived in the Plymouth Colony since 1640 and had preference over more recent comers. They each paid eleven pounds for one-half square mile of land. This region, which came to be called "old Freetown" to distinguish it from the later "new Freetown," was a rectangular plot of land four by seven miles in extent along the east side of the Taunton River, all lots having prime river frontage (Figure 3–23). It was the

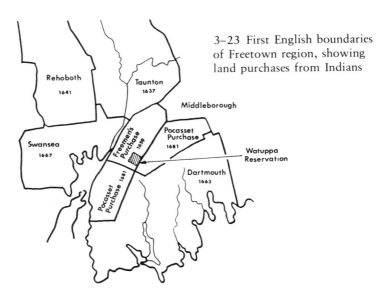

3-23 First English boundaries of Freetown region, showing land purchases from Indians

last major land purchase from the Indians before the Second Puritan War.

In 1671, Awashonks, sister of Tokamona, of the Sogkonate tribe of Little Compton, Rhode Island, broke away from the Wampanoag Federation and claimed that the Freemen's Purchase land was Sogkonate territory and the purchase therefore invalid. The Plymouth Colony government, under Governor Prence, argued that the land had been bought in good faith when the Sogkonates were part of the Wampanoag Federation. Awashonks disagreed, so the Plymouth Colony appointed Major Josiah Winslow, one of the purchasers and later governor, to lead one hundred troops and proceed to Assonet Four Corners to hold the land at all costs. This threat brought about agreement before violence erupted; Awashonks recognized the Freemen's Purchase and Plymouth Colony recognized the Sogkonates as an independent tribe.[22]

Also in 1674, Benjamin Church from Duxbury bought land in Sogkonate and erected two buildings. He was the first white settler there, and he won the friendship and respect of the Sogkonates to such an extent that he was able to persuade Awashonks to support the English in the war. Church led a number of delicate and hazardous diplomatic missions on behalf of the Plymouth Colony before the war. Once the war had started, he became a captain in the Plymouth Company, and his troops eventually cornered and executed Metacom. He pursued Metacom for 15 months with a dedication and a vengeance which contrasts sharply with his friendships and intimacy with other Indians both before and after the war, behavior which caused us to probe deeper into the character of Benjamin Church.[23] He considered some of the Plymouth Colony officers incompetent and felt that had he been in charge at the start, the war would have ended very quickly. Church saw Metacom not only as the instigator of the war and therefore an enemy, but as a personal adversary. Church appears to have had a genuine interest in the welfare of some Indians, and at the same time was an exterminator of others.[24]

After the killing of Metacom and the decimation of the Indians between Narragansett Bay and Cape Cod, Benjamin Church, like most colonial leaders, organized a major land purchase. The land records of the Plymouth and Massachusetts Colonies show that, whatever other adventures colored his life, Church was deeply committed to real estate and other businesses. He and his brother Caleb owned three mills and were the chief owners of water power along the Fall River, which flowed from South Watuppa Pond to Mount Hope Bay. On March 5, 1679/80, Benjamin Church and seven others paid the Plymouth Colony 1,100 pounds for land called the "Pocasset Purchase." The grand deed states that the land belonged to the Plymouth Colony and was conveyed by it. But in spite of this, the sale was negotiated with a few remaining Pocasset Indians, by name John Briggs, Thomas Prudence, Ephraim Allen and Samuel Briggs, in negotiations that dragged on to March 1681, when the sale was recorded. It remains unclear how much of the purchase price went to the Plymouth Colony and how much to the Indians.[25]

We decided to learn more details about the history of the Pocasset Purchase because the Freetown mound which we excavated was located within it, and we hoped that the history would tell us something about the origins of the mounds. The Purchase contained two separate parcels of land, one along Narragansett Bay in present-day Tiverton, Rhode Island, and the other east of the Freemen's Purchase, called Pocasset Outlet (Figure 3–24).

It was not until 1713 that the Pocasset Outlet, the lands of the stone mounds, were subdivided. The greater part was divided into twenty-five Great Lots and

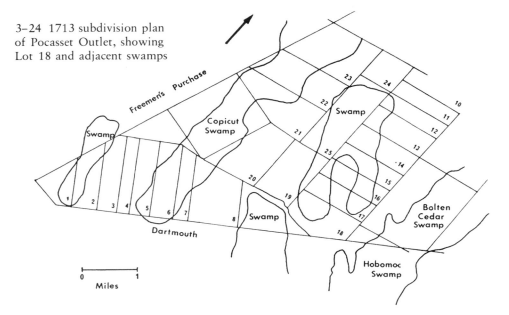

3–24 1713 subdivision plan of Pocasset Outlet, showing Lot 18 and adjacent swamps

eleven Copicut Swamp lots and was considered to have little historical importance by historian Philips. The tract shown in Figure 3–15, where the excavated
mound was located, was part of Great Lot Number 18, of the Pocasset Outlet
division of 1713 (Figure 3–23), of the Pocasset Purchase of 1679. In order to
follow the owner's wishes and to preserve the mound group we do not divulge
the location in further detail. Lot 18 is shown on the subdivision plan to have
been owned by Josiah Winslow, Jr., son of the then governor, and Constant
Church, son of Benjamin Church. The relationship of these families with the
Indians is perhaps the best documented of any in the Plymouth Colony. They
were also owners of several other lots of the Pocasset Purchase.[26]

The original deed to the Great Lots of Pocasset Outlet, dated 1715, including
lot number 18, shows the bounds of the various lots as stations in a narrative
as the surveyor of this, the first survey, walked the bounds. Numerous reference
points are described as "a read oke tree with some stones about it," and the like.
On casual reading, one might assume that the stones were set about the trees by
the surveyor. However, we interpret the document to mean that the stone heaps
and trees used as bounds were in place before the surveyor came upon them and
were used because they were convenient in a survey that did not require much
precision. A description of lot 18 includes "a stake — with a considerable heap
of stones about it," and "a black oke chopt in many places with a heap of stones
to pine." Other bounds are indicated by "a small sassafras with stones about it
with stones on a rock close to it," "white oke sapling with a heap of stones on
a rock close to it," "white oke tree with some small stones about it," "a pitch
pine tree with a big stone against it, and a stake and stones about it."[27] We
observed that the surveyor did not mention groups of mounds, only individual examples.

Bounds were indicated by a total of forty marked trees and twenty-one stone
heaps. The surveyor notes the distinction between a considerable heap of stones,
a heap of stones and a small heap of stones. He also, in a few instances, notes a
heap of stones on a rock close to a marked tree. He refers to a tree with a big
stone against it and a stake with stones about. Lots 1 through 7 are not marked
by heaps of stone, whereas all the others are. While we can offer no certain
explanation for this, the surveyor, who apparently conducted the lot surveys in
sequential order, implies that he had not been in the habit of using stone heaps
as markers, until he came to some in lot 8 that were already there and convenient
for his use. To corroborate this theory, we examined later original deeds of the
Pocasset Purchase and found explicit statements that the surveyor had made
certain stone heaps for markers, but in the same deeds he referred to trees with
heaps of stones about them, using the same phrasing as the Pocasset Outlet
deed. This indicates a mixture of contemporary and older stone heaps.

In an attempt to correlate this historical data with our observations, we
plotted the locations of the 1713 boundaries on our map of the six stone mound
groups of Figure 3–15, not shown in order to preserve the mounds. No groups

were within 300 yards of any boundaries of the lots which were typically over 300 acres in area and contained large areas of swamp, making the survey difficult. We concluded that there were individual stone mounds present before the survey of 1715 but no evidence that stone mound groups were or were not. The surveyors could have missed the groups or ignored them because numerous mounds would have been confusing as markers. Thus history is vague or silent about stone mounds, as it is about most stone structures in New England. If the groups of mounds were there, European settlers from the seventeenth-century to the present seem to have been unaware of any important cultural significance to them.

After 1659, the Plymouth Colony laws were strict as regards the purchase of lands from the Indians. Express authority from the court was required and a colonial deed alone confirmed the purchase. The effect of this apparently salutary procedure was somewhat diminished by the fact that the members of the court were the largest and most aggressive purchasers of land from the Indians. Daniel Wilcox, one of the Pocasset Purchasers, was a cousin by marriage of Benjamin Church, lived in Sogkonate near him, had a great proficiency in speaking the Indian language, and broke the law by buying land directly from an Indian. He was convicted of "high misdemeanors" in 1681 and was fined 150 pounds by the General Court at Plymouth. Twenty years later, he paid the fine to the Province of Massachusetts by deeding land abutting North Watuppa Pond, just south of the present Fall River–Westport boundary.

In 1704, a group of Indians of the Pocasset tribe, petitioned the governor of Massachusetts to grant them a plot of land, and the land given by Wilcox in 1701 was granted to them. A committee of the Massachusetts General Court (for Plymouth Colony had been absorbed by Massachusetts in 1692) was appointed to receive the property from Wilcox and hold title in trust for the Indians. On the committee was Benjamin Church, and he was appointed the Indian guardian or trustee and received for their benefit the funds from later Pocasset Purchase distributions. The Indians, it turned out, were the members of Church's company who had turned against Metacom and most of the Pocassets and supported the English.[28]

The Indians settled on their new reservation but were dissatisfied with it partly because it was divided into two separate parcels on opposite sides of the Watuppa Ponds. In 1707, they petitioned the General Court for their holdings to be consolidated into one property so they might have a common place for public worship and a school. In 1709, Benjamin Church accommodated them by exchanging lands which he owned in the Freemen's Purchase for the former Wilcox property, and the reservation was moved in 1709 to a 160-acre lot "in Easterly part of Freetown, 1¼ miles long by 64 rods wide bounded westerly on Great Watuppa Pond." It was part of the Freemen's Purchase Great Lots Numbers 2 and 3 and is centered about 1½ miles north of the present Fall River–Westport boundary (Figure 3–24). Church's deed to the Province of Massachusetts describes the land as, "lyeing more Commodius for the Indians settlemt and more Remote from the English." It was conveyed, "allways to be continued and used for a plantation and settlement for the Indian natives . . . Divers of whom have been very serviceable in the present and former wars and some of them brought up in English families."[29] It was further specified that the Indians would pay one quarter of good venison to the governor each year on December 10 (Old Style), which was the winter solstice and implies that the Indians continued to celebrate the feast of dreams.

The Indians who settled on this small reservation in Freetown were a privileged group, distinct from most of the Pocassets who lived in Freetown. They probably needed protection from the other Pocassets. But Benjamin Church had a practical motive in settling his Indian warriors, which is revealed by the conditions of his grant of land at Sogkonate to Indians who had served under him on military adventures of the Plymouth Colony. They promised to remain ready to serve him at any time in the future.[30] However, it is possible that Church had a personal interest in both the Pocassets and the Sogkonates and their ways beyond the bond of military service. The Church family continued its interest in the reservation by making improvements from time to time. In 1763, there were twenty-five families living on the Watuppa reservation, four of which had Church as their surname and two others with the first name of Benjamin.

Organized religion in Freetown had a curious history. Until 1793, or 110 years after incorporation, Freetown had only one settled minister, Silas Brett, of English ancestry, who served from 1747 to 1776. His only salary, aside from trifling freewill offerings, came from the Honorable Board of London Commissioners for propagating ye Christian knowledge among the natives, for preaching to the Indians at the Watuppa Pond reservation. This was the organization that sponsored John Eliot's mission and his praying villages, but there is no record of a praying village in this region. During most of this period of the Europeans' concern for Christian knowledge among the Indians, the European settlers of Freetown themselves were without Christian religious leadership. The Reverend Fowler attributed this lack of piety to his view that they were children of the *Mayflower* Pilgrims who were "not distinguished for that superior intelligence and devoted piety, which were conspicuous in their fathers." They in fact resisted the settling of a preacher or teacher in the town. The first meetinghouse in Freetown was probably the Indian church at the Watuppa Pond praying village, followed in 1714 by a combined meetinghouse and townhouse built by the town. Until 1821, when Quakers built a house of worship, there were no other meetinghouses built. We can probably conclude that the Freetown English in this period were indifferent, if not antagonistic, toward the Puritan Church.[31]

The reservation today has two old, neglected cemeteries. When we inspected the one on a bluff overlooking North Watuppa Pond, we found stone mounds within its boundaries. Across Blossom Road, also within the reservation, James Rymciewicz took us to an exceptionally large oval stone mound, sixty-five feet long and seven feet high, on the summit of the most prominent hill overlooking the southern part of North Watuppa Pond. We might ask how a spectacular monument of this type came to be within the reservation and not mentioned in historical records, and it also seems strange that Benjamin Church saw merit in having the plantation remote from the English, whom the Indians on the reservation had fought for. We do not know Church's views on Indian religion, but perhaps the location of the reservation was selected to permit the continuation of the ancient ways, using stone monuments already there, in peace. The Puritan frenzy was at its peak, but apparently not in Freetown, so the Indians may have held to the traditional religious practices without disturbance from the English.

The stonework and location of the land on Watuppa Pond sold to the Massachusetts Colony by Church for an Indian reservation have the earmarks of a place sacred to the Indians, but we do not know whether the stone mounds in the cemetery or on a nearby hilltop are prehistoric, historic or both. Archaeological evidence implies that some of the Freetown stone mounds are 800 to 900 years or more old. Our interpretation of land records implies that individual stone mounds were in place before the first English surveys, yet the many large groups are not mentioned in historical records. As we read about the English settlers, more and more unanswered questions arise about their thoughts and actions with respect to the natives, for which, in later chapters, answers gradually emerge, answers that depend for their meaning on a sense of much detail that comes to light while following our route of discovery.

4

Native American Traditions of Stone and Earthworks

The first clue to native origin of the works of stone and earth was our realization of their sheer quantity and wide dispersion. True, there seemed to be concentrations near rivers and ponds, which were the focus of both Indian and European colonial settlements, but there are also concentrations on rocky hilltops and in the wilderness of inland New England. That all this would have been built by European colonists between 1700 and 1850, the period of most documented stone fence-building, seemed to us most unlikely.

In the previous three chapters we told of the process of our discovery of places where stone structures were integrated with the landscape. Here, we attempt to convey the awesomeness of and respect due these structures by focusing on several different types, describing each one and the scope of our thoughts as we view it, with little regard for place.

Stone Rows

New England's most obvious, lasting man-made works are the thousands of miles of piled stone usually called stone walls or fences. These are the most common and widely recognized of all lithic structures, and they are evident in nearly every picture or other visualization of the New England countryside (as shown in Figure 4–1), but they are treated as such an integral part of the natural landscape that their origins as man-made structures are ignored and have been little studied. Historians, anthropologists and archae-

4–1 Stone rows, Sutton, Mass., 1876 engraving

ologists have extrapolated from a few anecdotal accounts of the European settlers that people of their culture constructed most of the stone walls and fences of New England. The remainder are assumed to have been built by Indians under the colonists' employment or influence. It is implied that all were built to mark boundaries or as fences or revetments.

We came to question, initially on astronomical grounds, whether or not all New England linear stone structures are of colonial origin. We observed that many of them are aligned to solar horizon events and that many do not appear to mark land boundaries or to be functional as fences. Also, they are found at a great variety of locations, including narrow river valleys, streambeds, hilltops, and the seacoast. We realized that there are other possible uses for such structures and that we should not be limited by historical records in considering their origins. They could have served as barriers, boundaries, conduits, horizon modifiers, ceremonial markers, artistic creations or signs of respect. The case for such a diversity of uses is supported by the great variety in design of the structures. Some structures use boulders as they come from the fields; others are made of naturally broken or quarried rock from nearby ledges. Some contain intermittent boulders (Figure 4–2), standing stones or rock piles. Others are unusually wide or high and inexplicably their geometry is often seen to change abruptly. Lengths of massive rows or boulders are to be seen in the woods isolated from any other stonework or habitation, as shown in Figure 4–3. We have seen rows of piled stones that link natural rock outcroppings, boulders, standing stones, hilltops, streams and landscape discontinuities. In addition, rows are often connected to or near modified natural structures such as balanced rocks, rocking stones, rock overhangs and perched boulders.

Rather than use the functionally limiting terms *fence* and *wall,* we prefer to call the linear stone structures by the name of *stone row*. We are

4–2 Unusual boulder structure in Vermont stone row

then not confined to a utilitarian image but can visualize them as landscape architecture following land contours, connecting tops of hills with valleys and ponds, connecting large boulders and rock outcrops, defining the shapes of the wetlands and highlighting distant horizons. This landscape architecture of precolonial America was not destroyed by the European invaders because they found uses for it, and perhaps because they did not recognize its significance and saw no threat in it. It may even be that these familiar structures and the fascination of such a landscape helped create an alluring impression of home and kin among the early European settlers. Perhaps this contributed to their inclination to assimilate the landscape architecture into their own history. Between 1622 and 1627, Thomas Morton may have sensed a landscape subtly planned by the Native Americans because he saw in New England a land that reminded him of home, where "the trees grow here and there as in our parks."[1]

The examples of barriers and boundary markers that can be identified most easily as historical are stone structures utilized for land division, animal containment and revetment. Quite specific details are available

4–3 Row of large boulders perched on smaller ones, Franklin, Mass.

about the wall-building methods used by English colonists, which may help to distinguish between their constructions and others of Indian or unknown origin. Gathering the stones and transporting them by stone boat to the fence site often took more labor than building the fence. The average competent European fence-builder could build twenty-four to sixty-four feet of fence per day if the stones were piled at the site ready for use, and a stone fence requires about 180 common-sized stones per rod. Based on these numbers, a fence-builder working a nine-hour day and placing one stone a minute could build three rods of fence per day.[2]

These average figures come from historical records such as the unusually complete information on some of the stone fences of Naushon Island, which has a number of fences that run entirely across the island and were built between 1760 and 1820. In 1767, Isaac Peterson was paid two shillings a rod to dig and transport the stones for and build a stone fence four feet high. He was also instructed to plow a ditch alongside both sides of the walls for the planting of locust, oak and beech trees as windbreaks.[3] But these European-style boundary fences do not account for the many other stone structures on Naushon island or for stone rows having the special design features such as embrasures (Figure 4–4) which fit architecturally with the places that we consider Native American ritual sites.

The colonial scenario applies to structures that were high and sturdy enough to serve as practical fences or to retain earth. In these, the stones were stable, fit closely and had large areas of contact. But many stone rows do not fit this pattern. They are loosely built with large gaps

4–4 Embrasure in stone row, Falmouth, Mass.

4-5 Loosely built stone row
with wind holes,
Martha's Vineyard

between stones and with boulders precariously perched or easily moveable, suggesting quite different functions and probably different construction procedures. Our suspicion is supported on Martha's Vineyard where most stone fences have large gaps between stones and are held by tradition to have been built by Indians who made provision for the wind to blow through (Figure 4-5).

Research into historic records of New England with this broadened view reveals that the Europeans' history may have recorded more stone rows built independently by Native Americans than by the European settlers. The white man's history acknowledges the building of stone rows by the Abenaki, Nipmuck, Narragansett, Mahican, Sakonnet and Wampanoag groups, to name a few. In the early 1700s, Thomas Church, son of Benjamin Church, the conqueror of Metacom, reported to the Massachusetts Colony General Court, of which he was a member, that his town of Little Compton, Rhode Island, had over 120 miles of stone walls, largely built by Indians, who were noted for the excellence of their stone walls. Since he also reported that there were but 100 Indian men in Little Compton in 1700, most walls probably remained from an earlier time. The many stone rows that wander through the dense woods of Monhegan Island off the Maine coast, are said to have been there in the 1600s, before most New England colonists started building stone fences.[4]

Jonathan Bourne, after whom the town of Bourne was named when it was set aside from Sandwich in 1884, was presented with all the land that he could blaze between sunup and sundown. He hired an Indian to build a stone wall around a portion of this land, promising him a barrel of rum after it was finished. The Indian worked hard for years until, when he was but a few hundred yards from completion, he fell dead and so never received the rum. The stone wall that he built can be seen today in the woods, in a fair state of preservation, but it no longer bounds anything and so appears to wander aimlessly.[5] This typical anecdote, for there are others in the historical record, may be the English interpretation of the many Indian-built stone rows to be seen on Cape Cod and elsewhere in New England.

A few stone rows in New England have been shown by excavation results to be prehistoric. We showed in Chapter 3 that a stone row beneath a stone mound in Freetown can be dated to A.D. 1100. The oldest documented stone row of which we know is that excavated at the Flagg Swamp rockshelter in Marlborough, Massachusetts. Here a wall built upon the terrace at the drip line in front of a natural rock overhang was dated by stratified small-stemmed projectile points to the Late Archaic period, or at least 3,000 years ago.[6]

Stone Mounds

Our surveys indicate that in New England there are at least several hundred thousand laid-up stone heaps or piles, which we call mounds, and that many towns contain over 1,000.[7] We have found large groups of stone mounds both on rocky hilltops and in swampy lowlands. At sites containing chambers, stone rows, standing stones and other signs which we consider characteristic of ritual places, there are always groups of stone mounds. Very large mounds, up to sixty feet in diameter and fifteen feet high, while numerous in total, are generally few in number at any single site.

Early historical references to the origins of the New England stone structures are few and obscure, which is not surprising if they are Indian, because few Indian oral traditions survived the almost complete elimination of the native population by disease, war and forced emigration before A.D. 1700.[8] In addition, conventional archaeological studies of Native American works in New England today are largely confined to settlement and the means of subsistence, almost totally ignoring religion and stone structures that might reflect this important part of life. Speck writes that there are anthropological references to stone mounds in eastern North America but that "archaeologists, however, have so far apparently paid them scant attention," and "ethnologists have described them but casually."[9] For these reasons, stone architecture has been placed by default in the colonial farm setting. However, there is some historical documentation, oral tradition, and primary data to support alternative views.[10]

A few stone mounds in New England have been linked to Indians in published reports. Speck and Squier observed that some memorial mounds of brush or stone were constructed by historical Indians to mark scenes of tragedy and that stone mounds were used to mark the places where warriors were killed and sometimes buried. A donation mound in Greenville, Connecticut, built in 1643 marks the place where the Narragansett sachem Miantonomo was captured by the Mohegan sachem Uncas, but there is some doubt that he was ever buried there. Other mounds were erected from materials donated to a spirit or manitou, and later passersby would add votive stones or branches to them. Speck reports a Mohegan oral tradition in which dwarfs, carrying lights about the swamps, stopped at rock piles where the lights would flare up. Algonquian dialects, which are rich in environmental description, contain numerous words for stone mounds, implying that they played a cultural role.[11]

There is a heap of stones in Great Barrington and another in Bourne, Massachusetts, to which each passing Indian added a stone, according to oral tradition. The mound in Great Barrington, located on a promontory, could be seen for miles around in the absence of trees and is the termination of a stone row fifty yards long. A stone mound on Martha's Vineyard was erected in 1657 by Indians as a memorial to the Puritan missionary Thomas Mayhew, Jr., and passing Indians have since placed stones on it. Stone mounds can be seen today in Indian tribal cemeteries in Fall River, Massachusetts, and Charlestown, Rhode Island. Some mounds have shapes, either columnar or low and wide, similar to those of the Plains hunting tradition, while others, up to 500 square yards in area and fifteen feet high, may be effigy mounds.[12]

Most of the few brief reports of archaeological excavations of New England stone mounds are limited to noting the absence of artifacts usually found at habitation or burial sites and to describing the mound size, shape, and method of construction. However, Frank Glynn, from 1952 to 1954, opened two "stone heaps" at Pilot's Point in coastal Connecticut just west of the Connecticut River, and reported important findings. The foundations of the two heaps were beneath the junction of topsoil and subsoil, and artifacts suggested an Archaic-Woodland overlapping period with some Adena-like tools. Glynn concluded that the mounds were prehistoric and Indian, a conclusion contrary to the prevailing view that there were no prehistoric stone heaps in New England. That view has not changed since, in spite of his work. While Glynn recognized that there were many stone mounds in New England and that some occurred in groups, he attached no significance to the fact of the groupings.[13]

Outside of New England, Noble found groups of stone mounds in Ontario that were part of the vision quest ritual tradition among Algonquin Indians, marking successful communion with spirits. In the southeastern part of the United States, Swanton cites innumerable heaps of stones made by the Creek Indians, who had a tradition of donation similar to that known in the Northeast. Bushnell reports many groups of 100 to 150 small mounds in Missouri which have no implements, gravegoods or signs of habitation connected with them, characteristics that fit New England mound groups as well. Stone mounds and stone rows in association make up the medicine wheels of western Canada and the United States, used for ritual astronomy and commemorative monuments by prehistoric Indians of the Plains. Hopi stone mound shrines, some built by donation, are part of sun ceremonies. The Yurok and Wiyot peoples of northern

California even today use stone mounds, stone rows and stone enclosures called "prayer seats" in their vision quest ritual. The origins of these peoples are traced to lands east of the Great Lakes more than 500 years ago and they speak Algonquian languages.[14]

Even though the historical lines of research are as yet inconclusive about the nature of groups of stone mounds, a case for their antiquity and Indian origin can be made from the results of excavation and from geographical association between groups of stone mounds, and other stone structures, as well as from astronomy. In the first three chapters, we described these connections at Calendar One, Upton and surroundings, Cape Cod and Freetown, and they appear in all later chapters. Gradually, because of their concentration in certain areas of New England, stone mounds are becoming the major challenge of New England stonework.

Standing Stones

Besides the familiar gravestones of the past 300 years, there are in New England many thousands of standing stones or upright slabs set in the ground or supported by other stones, of a variety of sizes and shapes. Most are of unknown origin. Some are tall obelisks, others slabs in stone rows that are wider than high called orthostats, anthropomorphized stones called god or manitou stones, and memorial stones of all shapes.

Their purposes are varied as well, whether monuments to spirits, astronomical or other place markers, or memorials to individuals. Their origins and functions can seldom be detected without considering their surroundings and other associations in depth, so they are best thought of as a very general type whose examples only have meaning in particular places. Because of this we have chosen to say no more about them here, leaving them to the descriptions of specific stones in places having integrated stonework.

Stone Chambers

Stone chambers were the first structures that we studied. They have received more attention than other enigmatic lithic structures in New England, probably because they are more structurally complex than other stonework and invite architectural comparison with similar structures all over the world. We were drawn to them, like many others, because of this. The strongly held views that have fueled debate about the origins and functions of these chambers are, in our opinion, largely a reflection of twentieth-century social and religious attitudes, rather than knowledge of the chambers themselves and their surroundings. As we became aware of the vast amount and diversity of stone structures, we came to believe that stone chambers are but one of many components of a larger cultural scene. The number of catalogued stone chambers in New England, 300 to 400 and increasing steadily, seems large to those who consider them in isolation from their surroundings, but the number is miniscule when they are considered part of the total assemblage of enigmatic stone structures. We became immersed in the controversy and were therefore led to investigate and learn more about the chambers than might otherwise have been the case.

One general theory of the origin of the chambers, put forward by William Goodwin, holds that Irish Culdee monks fleeing from Norse raiders went to New England about A.D. 1000.[15] There they are thought to have built the stone chambers for the same purposes which they served in Ireland, both as living quarters and as chapels. Goodwin sees the numerous chambers as parts of missions built to aid the conversion of the Indians to Christianity. His principal argument holds that there are design and construction similarities between the New England chambers and Irish beehives and cloghans. There are indeed such similarities and a few chambers could plausibly have had such an origin, or have been used in such a way. However, as we show later, the effect of this possible imported culture would have been small when seen in the context of a comprehensive view of America's landscape and native cultures.

Few New England archaeologists have written on the subject, but most who have claim that the Vermont stone chambers were built by historical farmers of European origin as root cellars and other practical buildings of rural life in the eighteenth and nineteenth centuries. This theory is neither plausible nor imaginative. The Vermont State Archaeologist, in presenting the case for "root cellars," wrote: "Absolutely no archaeological or ethnological evidence exists at present which suggests that prehistoric or historically known Indian groups undertook the level of stone construction represented by the stone chambers."[16]

This denial of American Indian stone construction at the chamber level is, quite simply, wrong. As we show later, many Indian groups throughout North America built stone structures similar to or even more sophisticated than the New England stone chambers. Influential scholars hold to the "root cellar" theory and the research method that leads to it without having studied the chambers seriously themselves. Some even echo anthropologist L. H. Morgan's nineteenth-century view that Native Americans could not build permanent structures of stone and that the lintel was beyond their capability.[17]

Such magnificent stone structures, with lintels, as Pueblo Bonito in Chaco Canyon, New Mexico, have convinced scholars of the Western Indians that Morgan's view was a myth, but it is a myth that still persists in New England. Here, scholars have in general concerned themselves with what they unfeelingly label the "subsistence strategies" of the Native Americans as represented by their tools, implements, weapons and funereal customs at sites largely selected because of accidental finds.

The "root cellar" theory draws on supposed similarities between root cellars and stone chambers. But stone chambers typically make poor root cellars. Only ten percent of those in Vermont and less in other parts of New England have vents, and these are not suitable for the control of temperature and respiration so critical to their use as root cellars. Furthermore, the orientations of chambers do not reflect a concern for maintaining a constant temperature inside. Most chambers are built on near-surface bedrock, not soil as recommended for root cellars. Oral traditions of use typically refer to later functional adaptations of existing structures and therefore are probably secondary. Today, the chambers stand empty and disused, relics ignored by most farmers and scholars alike.[18]

Stone chambers differ in design as much throughout New England as similar structures around the world differ among themselves. Different structural features of the native stone call for differences in design. Therefore, the chambers cannot be considered a particular class of monument except in a very general sense, and they have a variety of possible uses and origins. The quality of construction in many cases is comparable to chambers in Europe that have stood for 5,000 years, yet some may have been built 100 years ago.

The historical record accounts for only a few stone chambers in New England and these are clearly exceptional, for example hollow chimney foundations built into house foundations. The oral tradition of chambers, when examined carefully is found to be conflicting in many cases.

In our view, the root of the difficulty in researching New England's stone chambers and other enigmatic stone structures lies in research method. One archaeologist wrote that "the chambers, on their own merits, are demonstrably ancient or they are not," and are "independently verifiable and should not ride coattail to inscription or other purportedly ancient evidence."[19] We disagree emphatically with this view, common in archaeological circles, that research can be carved into convenient pieces and that one context precludes another. We hold that chambers and other cultural aspects must be perceived within the broadest possible framework, considering all possible influences nonexclusively. More specifically, some stone chambers are both ancient and modern and have served many roles, and nothing is independently verifiable. All of the theories described above are worthy of careful consideration, and each probably contains some truth.

Also, the myth that equates European colonists with civilization and Indians with savagery still dominates American society, and there is a tendency to reject field observations rather than theory when the two conflict. This myth, that the present American culture is a transplant of European culture to American soil and that the Indians are a mere foil, has led to the separation of historic and prehistoric archaeology. Another point of view is presented by Francis Jennings, who writes, "Our society, like all others, is the product of its entire antecedent history," a history that is particularly difficult to identify in the eastern United States where the living native heritage has all but disappeared.[20]

Indian Forts

New England history abounds with descriptions of palisaded Indian villages, the walls constructed of closely set poles placed in the ground, some with ditch and bank earthworks. Champlain saw them on his coastal travels and, later, the Great Swamp fight in Kingston, Rhode Island, was fought over a palisaded stronghold enclosing several hundred houses. These were not generally called forts for they were not primarily military outposts, but ordinary villages.

When the English discovered stone enclosures, usually on hilltops, they called them Indian forts, by analogy to the many hilltop enclosures of Great Britain and Ireland, also called forts. There are at least twenty "Indian stone forts" in New England, built of earthworks, stone rows and mounds. They represent perhaps the only large stone construction that is acknowledged, reluctantly, by scholars to be of Indian origin, most believed to have been built in the early seventeenth century. Even at that, they are largely assumed to follow designs brought from medieval Europe by the colonists. These structures are not well known nor are they considered historically important, probably because no battles took place there. It seems to us that they are important as evidence of Indian stone construction, some of prehistoric origin, and that they may have been primarily places of ceremony. One of these, Ninigret's fort in Charlestown, Rhode Island, overlooking an oceanic bay from a promontory, has been excavated and shown to be at least 1,500 years old. It is a large rectangular enclosure having a ditch adjacent to a bank built of stone and earth. It was modified a number of times and actually used as a fort in historic times after European-style bastions had been added at the corners. We describe here three additional Indian stone forts which taken together imply a thread leading back into prehistory and possibly to the Midwestern Mound Builders.

Tunbridge, Vermont

We investigated the Indian fort in Tunbridge, Vermont, mentioned in Chapter 1, because it is near the Calendar One bowl. Reportedly a stopping place of Caughnawaga Mohawk Indians from Canada before they burned Royalton in 1780, it is located on a promontory of a northwest-southeast ridge overlooking the First Branch of the White River and the hills surrounding the Calendar One bowl.

There are several parts to the hilltop site. A rectangular enclosure of stone rows with three intact sides with the northwest or uphill side open is located at the narrowest part of the ridge, about one-third mile south of its summit. The southwestern row is six feet high, the others lower. Northwest of the enclosure and nearer the summit of the ridge, a row of stones runs along a few feet from the edge of a steep dropoff to the east. It has several features not ordinarily seen in colonial stone fences. A slab is set vertically in the row, propped up by an inclined slab. Nearby is another vertical slab in the row where two parallel short rows extend six feet eastward ending just short of the steep dropoff and forming an opening facing east across a deep valley to a steep conical hill a mile away. The third component of the Indian fort site is a group of rectangular pillar-like stone mounds located about fifty yards west of the stone row (Figure 4–6). Finally, there is a spring on the western part of the ridge summit.

As is our practice, we looked for solar horizon events from the various features of this fort to the natural horizon of near and distant hills. We set up Byron's equatorially mounted telescope at the propped slab to follow the path of the sun at the equinoxes. Sunrise appeared to be in the direction of the conical hill to the east, but at a more distant horizon above it. Nevertheless, out of curiosity, we swung the telescope along the sun's path so that it was aimed at the summit of this hill. Byron looked through the scope and saw a standing stone precisely in the center of his field of view, as shown in Figure 4–7. We were off down the hill in short order and made the strenuous climb up the 400-foot conical hill, which was very steep on all sides. At the summit, we found the standing stone wedged in a crevice of bedrock outcrop. After setting up the telescope and sighting back to the propped stone at the Indian fort site, we realized that it was the horizon marker or foresight for an observation of the equinox sunset from our position at the standing stone.

In succeeding visits we discovered that both the Indian fort enclosure and the propped stone were connected by solar and lunar horizon sightlines in the eastern quadrant to the ridges surrounding the Calendar One bowl two miles away.

4–6 Stone mound near Indian fort, Tunbridge, Vermont

4-7 Sightlines from propped stone near Indian fort, Tunbridge, Vermont

Since we had explored all of those hilltops previously, we immediately suspected that prominent stones which we had seen on their summits were markers for these alignments (Figure 4-7). On one summit, the winter solstice sunrise as seen from the propped slab was marked by a large spherical perched boulder, a rarity in this area. The major lunar extreme position was marked by a standing stone on another peak. Observing from the enclosure, we identified both of the lunar extreme standstills, and the winter solstice sunrise at hilltops.

The visual and astronomical connections between the Indian fort and Calendar One turned out to be two-way, for an observer on the ridges at Calendar One can see the Indian fort. Today, with much tree growth, only the west ridge is clear enough to permit this sighting.

What started out as an historical Indian fort turned out on closer examination to have many features bearing no known relation to defensive or any other military functions. Instead, the dominant characteristics are those which we find associated with ritual. If the enclosure served as a campsite for invading Indians, this is likely to have been a strictly secondary function. More interesting is the implication that the Indians knew about the site and camped there before their attack. Nourse writes that Indians who had been driven from their heritage in New England to the north and west "did not forget the beautiful valley residence of their fathers nor cease to desire revenge. . . . Marauders from Canada never lacked guides familiar with all approaches to and weak points of defense of each frontier town."[21] The historical record that the attackers, after finding that Royalton was defended on Sunday, returned three miles up the First Branch to camp at an exposed and indefensible location could mean that the "Indian fort" had a particular attraction and perhaps a sacred role in Indian life.

The Queen's Fort

The "Queen's Fort" in Exeter, Rhode Island, is traditionally believed to have been built by Native Americans, and we studied it for this reason. It is an arrangement of rows of laid-up boulders connecting larger boulders on the summit of a most spectacular feature attributable to glacial action, a great pile of large boulders some fifty feet high. The site is considered historically significant because folklore gives it a role in the Second Puritan War of 1675. Like many Indian sites in New England, it would be completely ignored if it had no association with battles with the whites.

Contemporary accounts have this to say about events that may refer to the Queen's Fort. In December 1675, just before the Great Swamp Fight at Kingston, Rhode Island, a large force of Massachusetts and Connecticut troops under General Josiah Winslow, estimated at 1,000 men, was assembled at Richard Smith's castle in Wickford, Rhode Island. On December 14, five days before the Kingston fight, many of the force attacked and burned the village of the Old Queen Quaiapen, destroying 150 wigwams, killing seven and capturing nine Indians. Quaiapen, also known as Magnus, Matantuck and Sunke Squaw, was the leader of the Niantics, and as the sister of Ninigret and widow of Makanno, son of Canonicus the first, she was one of the most influential sachems of the Narragansetts. Her domain included the present towns of North and South Kingston and Exeter.

On December 15, the army headquarters at Wickford was visited by Stonewall John, an Indian who came as an emissary from the Narragansetts to negotiate peace. In a separate contemporary account, of a similar if not the same episode, Roger Williams was asked to parley with three Indian leaders, one of whom, named Nawwhan, he knew as John the wall-maker, a servant of Richard Smith. Shortly after the parley with Stonewall John, several companies of English troops were attacked by Indians who lay in ambush behind a stone wall. The final episode in Quaiapen's story occurred in June 1676, when Major Talbot "killed the Old Queen of Narragansett, and an arch villain of their party, that had been with them at the sacking of Providence, famously known by the name of Stone-wall, or Stone-Layer John, for that being an ingenious fellow he had learnt the Mason's Trade, and was of great Use to the Indians in building their Forts, etc. Likewise Potucke, the Great Indian Counsellour, (a Man considering his Education of a wonderfull Subtlety) was brought Prisoner into Rhode Island."[22]

These sketchy contemporary accounts of events in 1675–6 have been embellished over time to create a "history of the Queen's Fort," some of which is plausible. Since the hilltop structure was within Quaiapen's domain, near Wickford, and probably near the village destroyed on December 14, it may well have been connected with Quaiapen. Stonewall John was established as a stonemason, builder of forts, and a Narragansett leader under Quaiapen, and from this it has been inferred that he designed and built both the Queen's Fort and the palisaded fortifications in the Great Swamp. But here, another character enters the story, Joshua Tefft, a renegade Englishman who left his people to live among the Wampanoags. Along with others of Metacom's people he sought and was given refuge by the Narragansetts and was with them at the Great Swamp Fight. When he was captured a few weeks later, he admitted to Roger Williams that he had worked on the fortifications in the Great Swamp. Tefft was hanged, drawn and quartered four days later. Since the fortifications were well planned and built, the colonists assumed that Tefft was primarily responsible, a view that has persisted. However, Calloway, writing in 1984, accepts the notion that the fortress was built by Stonewall John, possible with Tefft's help.[23]

The first historical account that specifically mentions the structure called the Queen's Fort was E. Potter, Jr.'s *The Early History of Narragansett*, published in 1835. Since then, a folklore has grown in which the structure was a fortified stronghold of Queen Quaiapen and the base for several attacks on colonial troops prior to the Great Swamp Fight. A broadened story was given by James N. Arnold, when he wrote that the territories along the Queen's River, one mile west of the Queen's Fort, from its source to its union with the Usquepaug were set aside for the use and support of the squaw sachem and a guard of twenty-four warriors.[24] Another source presents an entirely different perspective. It tells that the Queen's Fort was a stopping place for the Nipmuck Indians of central Massachusetts and also mentions a rock cave known as the Queen's Chamber which was used by the Indian princess, Queen Bess.[25] While we do not know the authority of this last item of folklore, it opens up the possibility that nineteenth-century antiquarians had reason to suspect that the site was not principally a fort but rather a place where Indians from other parts of New England gathered.

Now, to the structure itself and what it can tell the observer today. Sketch maps were made in 1865, 1910, 1931 and 1932.[26] They differ in the number of "bastions" shown. We have made a drawing of the structure as it exists today (Figure 4–8). On the north and east sides, the hill drops off precipitously, while on the south and southeast, the slope is gradual but strewn with large boulders which a person approaching from or leaving these sides must climb over and around. The only easy approach is from the west, where there is a path today. There are two stone rows at the summit, the longer one on the west and a shorter one on the northeast. The space between the rows, on the north and at the most precipitous place is partially occupied by a row of intermittent large boulders, leaving a gap of about 100 feet with a single standing stone in the center.

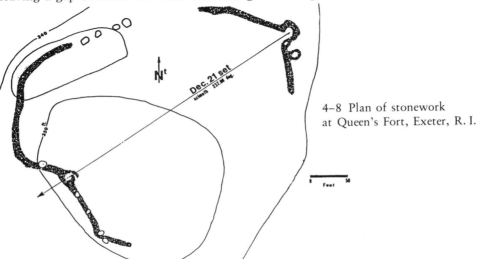

4–8 Plan of stonework at Queen's Fort, Exeter, R.I.

4-9 Spiral enclosure
at highest point
of Queen's Fort,
Exeter, R. I.

An impressive spiral enclosure, with room enough inside for ten people to sit comfortably (Figure 4-9), is built into the highest part of the main stone row, at the hill's summit, an elevation of 350 feet above sea level. The wall of the enclosure may have been partially rebuilt in recent years. In the northeast row is a partial enclosure, which could be described as a bastion if the structure were a fort. Next to it, but outside the main row and set several feet lower, is a circular enclosure of stone, smaller in diameter than either of the other two. Looking south from the summit, one sees a lone stone row extending from the base of the hill south for several hundred feet. There is a boulder cave on the western flank of the hill known as Queen Quaiapen's bedroom. When we explored it, we found a curious pile of straw but were not impressed by its size, another feature that has grown in the telling.

We observed that by standing in the enclosure in the northeast row we could see the spiral enclosure in the southwest row on the horizon. Naturally we took measurements of direction and elevation and found that there was a winter solstice sunset alignment between the enclosures. Winter solstice alignments are the most frequent in our experience with New England stonework, not surprising because the winter solstice was the most important Algonquin Indian festival, the Feast of Dreams.

The summit enclosed by the rows is literally a pile of boulders. There is no room to set a wigwam, and it is most uninviting as a campsite, but as a spectacular geologic feature it is awesome. As a fort, it is indefensible. The stone rows are presently only about two feet high, but even if they were higher in the past, they would not stop an attack from the south over the boulders. Attackers and defenders alike would be chasing each other over and around boulders. And most important of all, there is apparently nothing to defend but a great pile of rocks on the summit. We know that many rocks were sacred to Native Americans so that from this perspective, the Queen's Fort could perhaps be a sacred place, signalled by stone rows and a solar alignment. If this were the case, it would be expected to be a place of much spiritual power or manitou.

Lochmere, New Hampshire

We describe a third Indian fort because it is particularly large and introduces a different perspective, similarity to the Midwestern Mound Builders. E. G. Squier published in 1849 a drawing of an "Indian Stone Fort" at Lochmere, New Hampshire, on the Winnepisogee River where it widens into Little Bay (Figure 4–10). The site is relatively large compared with other New England "stone forts," and consists of wide stone rows forming a pattern of enclosures and avenues on the bank of the river. At three locations there are gaps in the rows with stone mounds blocking the line of sight in or out but providing a narrow access passage. A ditch runs across the site and is labeled a millrace by Squier. There is also an island in the river with mounds upon it.[27]

Squier published this structure because he noted architectural similarities between it and the great earthen and stone works of the Mound Builders of the river valleys of the American Midwest. We noticed the similarities, too, and have called attention to Squier's observation in our lectures and papers over the past several years.[28] For example, we noted that the Lochmere fort is similar to the Hopewellian structures at Marietta, Ohio (Figure 4–11), where there are also mounds which visually block gaps in the enclosure rows and an avenue formed by parallel embankments from an enclosure entrance down to the river bank. Both works are adjacent to a major river bend; in addition, the Lochmere structure signals an island while Marietta is a joining of the Ohio and Muskingum rivers.

4–10 Indian fort, Lochmere, N. H.   4–11 Earthworks, Marietta, Ohio (from Squier, n. 28)

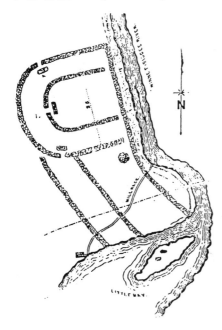 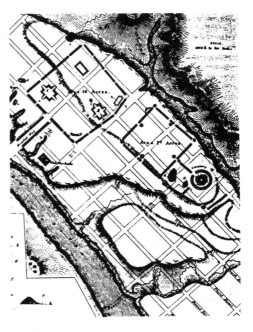

4–12 Mound with manitou
stones, Marietta, Ohio
(from Squier, note 28)

At Marietta, there are two additional features which invite comparison with
New England. On the top of the steep bluff overlooking the earth works from
the southwest is a group of several stone mounds, also a common feature in New
England. At the southeast end, there is a great conical mound surrounded by a
ditch and bank, still well preserved, probably because it is surrounded by a
cemetery founded in 1788 with the birth of the city. Nearby once stood several
straight walls, now destroyed. A painting of the cemetery and mound made
in the early nineteenth century (Figure 4–12) shows eleven tombstones of a
curious shape. On a visit to this mound in 1986, Mavor observed that these
stones were no longer in the cemetery, which today is well filled with stone
markers all around the mound, none like those in the painting. We are struck
by the resemblance of these missing stones to the stone spirit of the creator,
the manitou stones which we have observed in New England and which are
recorded historically as part of Indian ritual in both the eastern and western
parts of America.

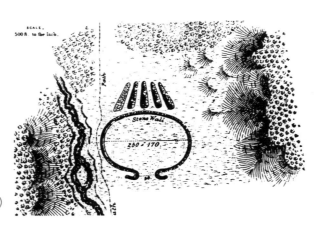

4–13 Stone work
with five fingers,
Ross Co., Ohio
(from Squier, note 28)

Stone rows of great variety are to be seen in New England and also in the works of the Midwestern Mound Builders. In Figure 4–13, a curious geometrical arrangement of massive stone rows is shown in which each of the five fingers is a pile of rock 200 feet long and 65 feet wide. Destruction of sites in the Midwestern river valleys has been extensive wherever the land has been suitable for agriculture.

We have prepared a list of New England Indian forts which we prefer to call sacred enclosures. In Table 4–1, opposite each site is an indication of which features are present, including construction material, standing stones, mounds, springs, astronomy, embrasures, historical references, and marked stones.

Table 4–1 Sacred Enclosures (Indian Forts)

Location	Earth-stone	Stone-earth	Earth	Stone rows	Mounds	Embrasures	Perched Boulders	Standing Stones	Water	Marks	Astronomy	Hist. Ref.
Sanbornton, NH	x			x	x	x			river	?		x
Ninigret, RI	x		x			x			sea	?		x
Uncas, Conn				x	x				spring	?		x
Tunbridge, Vt	x			x	x	x		x	river	many	x	x
Queen's Fort, RI				x		x		x	swamp	?	x	x
Montauk, NY	x		x			x			sea	?		x
Franklin, Mass	x	x	x	x	x		x	x	river	many		x
Shantok, Conn	x								river	?		x
Gungywamp, Conn	x	x		x	x	x	x	x	sea	many	x	x
Peperell, Vt	x	x	x	x	x	x		x	spring	many	x	x
S. Woodstock, Vt				x	x	x	x	x	spring	many	x	
Putney, Vt	x	x	x	x	x	x		x	spring	many	x	
Heath, Mass	x	x	x	x	x		x	x		few	x	
Upton, Mass			x	x	x	x	x	x	spring	few	x	x
Harvard, Mass	x	x	x	x	x	x	x	x	spring	few	x	x
Boxborough, Mass	x	x	x	x	x	x	x	x	spring	many	x	x
N. Salem, NH				x		x		x	spring	few	x	x
Freetown, Mass	x		x	x	x		x	x	spring	few		x
E. Thompson, Conn	x		x	x	x	x		x	spring	?	x	x
Falmouth, Mass			x	x	x	x		x	spring	few	x	

Earthworks

Ditches were dug by the European colonists for various agricultural purposes, including sheep pens, and this must be kept in mind when assessing the ages and functions of earthworks, but numerous earthworks cannot be explained by any agricultural tradition or record. They are usually ditches with adjacent banks and seem to connect topographic features, usually near water. One in Pocasset on Cape Cod connects a hilltop with a spring in a valley. Some are near the sea in the outwash plain. Cape deeds of 1727 specify "digged ditch" and "divil's ditch" as boundary markers and landmarks.[29]

Champlain reported that he had seen ditches three to six feet deep on the slopes of hills in New England and that they were built by Indians, who used them for planting corn. DeForest reported that trenches dug by the Nipmucks of central Massachusetts and the Narragansetts of Rhode Island were visible in 1850, but their functions seem to have been lost to history. More recently, in the first part of this century extensive earthworks were observed in New England by Warren Moorehead and Charles Willoughby, who mapped long and complex ditch and bank systems in several towns of eastern Massachusetts, inspected the surface features and concluded that they were most likely of Indian origin. Moorehead's conclusions were concise: "First; Forts Graham, Goldsmith, Baker, Shawsheen, Benner, Hagget's and Foster's Pond were not constructed by white people to control forest fires. Second; they are not boundaries of land. Third; they were not for purposes of drainage. Fourth; they were not built by the Whites during the Colonial or French and Indian Wars. Fifth; they are supposedly of Indian origin." When Willoughby published his second report in 1935, he reiterated his opinion that these works were of Indian origin, all except those at Millis, Massachusetts, about which he had become uncertain.[30]

Willoughby wrote of a circular embankment fifty feet in diameter, enclosing a small hill at Marblehead, Massachusetts, now mostly destroyed by quarrying. It was first mentioned in a 1658 deed as "the Indian fort." The most elaborate and extensive earthworks reported by Willoughby, in his first article, and by Moorehead are those in Millis, Massachusetts, which run for miles over hilly terrain and include enclosures. The trenches are always on the inner side of the embankments except in the few cases where they are on both sides.

Moorehead also published some detail about the earthworks in Andover, Massachusetts, which are mostly adjacent to wetlands and perhaps have some functional connection to them. They are earthen banks and ditches from three to six feet high sometimes connected to stone rows and sometimes with stone rows as part of the bank, shown in Figure 4–14. In 1942, archaeologist R. P. Bullen reported his excavations at two Andover earthworks that had been mapped by Moorehead, and disagreed with Moorehead's view that the works were Indian.

One of Bullen's excavations was of an earthwork known as "Fort Graham." He found an area where there were a few angular rock fragments and one projec-

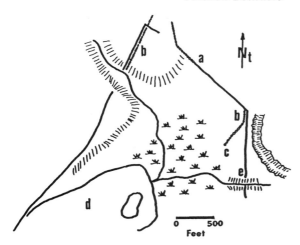

4-14 Earth and stoneworks, Andover, Mass.
a Junction, earth bank and stone row
b Stone row
c Stone row ending in swamp
d Earthwork
e Stream intersecting earthwork

tile point overlying an ash deposit on both sides of a ditch and bank. He defined this as an Indian site and dug a trench through the earthwork and the ash deposit. The stratigraphy of the soil indicated to him that the ditch had been dug through a preexisting Indian site. He argued that because the ditches were dug later than nearby Indian sites, they therefore were "post-Indian." Observing possible sod-clods in the thrown-out dirt, he concluded that since no Indian tools were found, the ditches must have been dug with metal shovels. He also considered the possibility of an Indian stockade and looked for post holes but found none. Noting that the earthwork is some 5,000 feet long and finding no evidence of a heavy Indian population, he argued against Indian origins. On the colonial side of the ledger, Bullen found no colonial artifacts and cited no historical record in eastern Massachusetts of the origins of these or similar earthworks. His final conclusion was that all the earthworks of this type in Massachusetts were the work of the early settlers and that they were built for various reasons but chiefly as ha-has, ditches retained by stone walling on one side found in England. Bullen's conclusion that the works were colonial English seems to bear no relationship to the evidence presented in his report, but nevertheless the earthworks have not been excavated since because his paper has convinced archaeologists that New England earthworks are colonial and that's that.[31]

Throughout this book, we report the discovery of numerous earthworks in conjunction with stoneworks which we believe identify Indian sacred places where shamans practiced their art, visions were sought, and much manitou exists.

Perched Boulders

Natural boulders and bedrock formations have played a major role in folklore, superstition, ritual and cosmology of peoples throughout the world from the distant past to the present. In North America, this is well established in historic Indian folklore. Large isolated boulders, perched upon bedrock, are characteristically found at sacred places, and in New England they are typically associated with nearby stone mounds, stone rows, standing stones and natural landscape features that identify a place of ritual. Some are entirely the result of natural processes while others have been modified in recognition of the connection between the Indian and his natural surroundings.

There are a number of perched or balanced rocks which have connections with Indian traditions. In the town of Bourne, Cape Cod's rockiest town, many great boulders are known as Giant's Graves and at least one was the object of ritual journeys. A true balanced rock or rocking stone is located in Bourne on a hilltop. Two others, shown in Figure 4–15, can be seen in Falmouth. As elsewhere in New England, unusual rocky places were called places of the devil in colonial records, a likely indication of Indian ritual. In Bourne, the Devil's Dumping Ground has two acres of boulders set in a curious depression. At another location, a heap of large boulders is called the place where "the devil broke his apron string." Even kettle holes are identified with the devil. Squaw Hollow was said to have been pressed into its present shape by the devil's heel. Praying rocks are common on Cape Cod, unusually large boulders where shamans are thought to have sought communion with spirits. It is probably no accident that early Christian missionaries chose these sacred rocks as places from which to preach to the Indians.

Sacrifice Rock is the site of an anecdote involving Richard Bourne, the Cape's leading seventeenth-century Christian missionary to the Indians. When he witnessed dancing and riotous ceremony on this rock, he said, "If you do not stop your horrible work I will call upon my God to visit his wrath upon you." The Indians disregarded the warning and a flash of lightning split the rock into strangely shaped pieces, killing some of them. This great rock, flat on top, can be seen today split into two main divisions with a four-foot gap between.[32]

4–15 Perched boulders, Falmouth, Mass.

4–16 Hokum split rock, Dennis, Mass.

Similarly, on a hilltop in Dennis is a gigantic boulder called Hokum Rock, which has also been split in two (Figure 4–16) and also has a place in Indian tradition. Each of the two pieces weighs 600 tons, and one is perched on three points. Numerous pebbles have been placed in the space between the great pieces of rock, as if donated.

The emerging science of geology late in the nineteenth century placed perched boulders entirely outside human material culture. The new geologists considered that the existence of perched boulders on both sides of the Atlantic Ocean proved that they were placed naturally on both continents by receding glacial ice or local rock disintegration. In Europe, antiquarians speculated that the megalithic cultures were responsible for perching boulders in the spectacular settings on hilltops, and lively debate ensued between the geologists and antiquarians. When the geologists learned that no megalithic culture was to be found in North America, they enthusiastically embraced the idea in support of their theory. Also, they observed that often such boulders are of rock that is different from the bedrock on which they are set, from which they inferred that glaciers transported the boulders from places in the north, sometimes hundreds of miles away.

Those concerned only with the natural origins of these boulders to the exclusion of possible human roles in modifying or moving them, and others who have focused exclusively on man-made or supernatural origins, have missed the most likely answer, that both agencies have been at work.

With some trepidation, we now depart temporarily from our attempt at a holistic view in order to categorize several types of perched boulder configurations which are quite distinct in appearance and structure and therefore perhaps in their roles in human society. Boulders of the first type are balanced on one or two points of support on bedrock or on a second boulder, and appear frequently in American Indian folklore as either rocking stones or drum rocks. Algonquins call them *tataesset* or *tattahassun*. They are balanced in stable equilibrium and can be rocked back and forth with very little energy.

A particularly impressive example is Rolling Rock in Fall River, Massachusetts, preserved by the city as an historic and scientific curiosity; there are nearly iden-

4-17 Rolling Rock,
Fall River, Mass.

tical rocks in Taunton and Swansea. Rolling Rock was called the Goose Nesting
Rock in old boundary descriptions and is a 140-ton, egg-shaped, conglomerate
boulder, containing many smoothly fractured quartzite pebbles. It is supported
by two small bearing surfaces on a natural granite outcrop (Figure 4–17). Now
nearly surrounded by houses in a dense residential area of the city, it was shown
in its present location on an 1812 map of Fall River, just nine years after the
town was formed, and was still described as free to rock in 1841. Until about
1900, it could be moved easily with one hand and could be made to oscillate
two or three inches at the top.[33] It is strategically located for visibility on the
horizon from some distance to the east and west because it crowns the brow of
the southerly spur of the highest hill in Fall River, overlooking North Watuppa
Pond. It is also on the old Indian trail from the falls of the Fall or Quechechan
River to the narrows between North and South Watuppa Ponds. In the nineteenth
century, the stone could have been seen from the falls, an important Indian fishing
spot. The site of the North Watuppa praying village described in Chapter 3 lies
just across the pond to the east.

Most large rocking boulders have been stabilized by either natural weathering
or human activity depositing sediment and small stones under them to prevent
the rocking motion. The Fall River stone, stabilized in the 1930's, has only a
few small pebbles under it, but they have put a stop to its rocking ability. We
imagine that the boulder could have been used as a signalling device as rocking it
in sunlight about its axis, which is oriented ten degrees true, would cause changes
in reflective patterns when seen from the east and west.

Several of the rocking boulders that we have encountered in New England
have depressions carved into them than can be used as seats. Such a depression
can be found on a rocking boulder in the Shaker domain at the northeast corner
of Harvard, Massachusetts. This stone, weighing about a ton, can be rocked
back and forth easily with but slight pressure from one finger.

During the process by which a boulder is set upon a flat platform, the local
contact surface, usually curved, and the platform both crush until the contact

area has increased to the point that the compressive stress in the boulder and shear stress in the platform have decreased to less than the strength of the rock's material. Then, if the rock is stable, that is it returns of its own accord to its initial position if rolled a small amount, and the required force can be exerted by a person, it is a rocking or roll stone.

Rocking stones range in weight from tens of pounds to hundreds of tons and are found in a variety of forms from egg shapes to long planks, as shown in Figure 4–18. Some, when rocked, strike their platforms creating deep booming sounds that can be heard or felt in the earth some distance away. While all operate on

4–18 Rocking stones *(clockwise from top 1):* Foxboro, Mass.; Boxborough, Mass,; Boothbay, Maine; Lunenburg, Mass.; Harvard, Mass.; Boxborough, Mass.

4–18*(cont.)* Rocking stones:
Shrewsbury, Mass. *(above)*; Charlestown, R. I.

the same physical principles, the smaller sizes and some shapes are more common than others. Small stones shaped either like planks or almost like spheres are easily balanced by accident of nature or the work of man, but the very large stones require shapes and weight distribution that are relatively rarely achieved in nature and would be very difficult for man to accomplish.

While the rocking feature is the reason for our interest in them, rocking stones must roll in order to rock. The stone resists being rolled because of its stability and its resistance to elastic deformation of the contact surface, and the larger the rock the greater this resistance is, while the starting force available from a person's push remains constant. For this reason, a large rocking stone, as compared with a small one, requires a weight distribution and curvature of the contact surface within narrow limits in order to function. In addition, there is an absolute limit to the size of rocking stones because the strength of stone is the same for large rocks as for small. Consequently, the area of contact with its platform increases with size in order to support the stone. This increases the force necessary to roll the stone quite independently of its weight distribution or elastic properties. We estimate by extrapolating from idealized conditions that this absolute maximum is about 300 tons.[34]

Natural weathering of a boulder over a long time could create a rocking stone. Freezing and thawing could create spalls on the underside and eventually slight rocking excited by wind would weather the contact surface to a curve. Few, however, would achieve the precise conditions required by the large rocking stones that we see today. It is very unlikely that ancient people could have created large rocking stones from ordinary boulders, but they could have tuned the behavior of existing rocking stones. For example, the underside of the Fall River Rolling Rock, between supports, has a rough-surfaced concavity in the otherwise convex surface that could have been made by hammering. If rock had been removed at this location, a feasible human modification, it would have decreased the force necessary to rock the stone. It is also possible that rocking stones were moved from one place to another or changed in orientation to meet the demands of signalling or ritual.

Rocking stones have a well-documented history world-wide, from as early as the days of Pliny the Elder, A.D. 23–79, who wrote about them in his *Natural History*. In Great Britain, there is a wealth of antiquarian literature about rocking or balanced stones. Many have rock basins carved into their surfaces or have rock chairs associated with them. The European settlers of America were familiar with balanced rocks, having seen them in their native countries. Many of the perched and rocking boulders sites of New England were given names that usually incorporated Satan or the devil, a holdover from English ecclesiastical authority which labeled these monuments as diabolic devices and the idols of blasphemers.[35] There was much speculation in the seventeenth and eighteenth centuries about the origins and use of these stones by Druids and others for religious ritual. With the rise of Cromwell and the Puritans, many rocking stones in Europe were toppled because of the belief that they were pagan idols. In New England, many have survived destruction by nature and man.

The second type of perched boulder is naturally stabilized and restrained from movement by three or more points of support. Some were set directly on bedrock and others are supported by stone rows, earthen banks, or piles of smaller boulders; several examples are shown in Figure 4–19.

4–19 Perched boulders of the second type: Acton, Mass. *(top l)*; Hokum Rock, Dennis, Mass. *(top r)*; Row of perched boulders, Franklin, Mass. *(bottom l and r)*

4–20 The Rollstone,
Fitchburg, Mass.

One boulder of this type in Fitchburg, Massachusetts, well known in Indian lore, once rested on the summit of Rollstone Hill, 300 feet above the streambed below. This egg-shaped boulder, approximately eight feet in diameter and twelve feet long, weighs over fifty tons. When photographed in the nineteenth century, the base was surrounded, but not necessarily supported, by a circular enclosure constructed of quarried stone. The enclosure was about three feet high and appeared to cradle the boulder like a giant egg in a small stone nest. This is the only perched boulder we have encountered with a supporting structure of this specific design. The hill was quarried for its granite by the English settlers and the Rollstone, as the boulder was named, was threatened with destruction. In order to preserve it, citizens of Fitchburg in 1929 split the rock into manageable pieces, transported them down the hill and reassembled the rock as a monument supported by granite pedestals at a major city intersection (Figure 4–20).[36] Those who preserved this rock, which had always overlooked the city, did so because of its place on the landscape, its role in folklore, and their emotional attachment to it, but its home had been destroyed. We suspect that the Rollstone and many others of this type were formerly rocking stones which have been stabilized by additional supporting rocks. People could have done this for safety, to make a signalling stone inoperative or as a ritual killing of a sacred artifact.

In many New England locations, very large perched boulders of this type rest on top of stone rows unquestionably built by man. While they may have been delivered to their locality by glaciers, they were certainly not placed on the stone rows by this agency. In Franklin, Massachusetts, at a site known locally as the Indian Fort, hundreds of twenty-to-forty-ton boulders resting on long stone and earthen banks are seen to march down the meadows into a swamp (Figure 4–19). Similar stone-row supported boulders, clearly erected by man, are to be seen in Littleton, Massachusetts.

The third type of perched boulder consists of a large boulder partially or entirely supported by one or more, and frequently three, small boulders or quarried pieces of rock set as pedestals on bedrock (Figure 4–21). We have coined the

4-21 Pedestaled boulders
a) North Salem, N.Y.

b) Sullivan, N.H.

c) Montville, Conn.

name pedestaled boulder for these structures, which are often quite spectacular, especially when set upon a hilltop and entirely supported by three pedestals. They are structurally similar to megalithic constructions in other parts of the world usually called dolmens, which are often considered to have been prehistoric tombs. The New England structures are always found on bedrock, and structures identical to them can be seen in Great Britain and in Korea.

4–21 *(cont)*

d) Dunkeld, Scotland

e) Agassiz Rock, Manchester, Mass. This 600-ton cubical boulder is supported at three corners; one support is a curious triangular boulder (*r*). It was cited by Louis Agassiz, the nineteenth-century naturalist, as illustrative of the work of glaciers.

Pedestaled boulders supported by quarried pedestals, clearly erected by man, have been identified in New England. It is most likely that they were erected by historic or prehistoric Native Americans for ritual use, but we cannot eliminate an intercontinental influence of several thousand years antiquity. Even if some pedestaled boulders are glacial creations, which could be the case if they are supported entirely by natural boulders, they could have figured in ancient ritual among prehistoric people. In fact, if they are entirely natural, they were present when the first post-glacial people arrived in New England and could have been part of ritual from that time.

A particularly spectacular specimen of pedestaled boulder is a massive boulder of ninety tons supported by five standing stones, located by the roadside in North Salem, New York (Figure 4–21a). It is not on a hilltop but beside a stream in a valley. In Figure 4–21b, we show a pedestaled boulder in Sullivan, New Hampshire, which is supported by quarried pedestals of mica schist quite different in character from the granite of the boulder. By comparison, a similar pedestaled boulder from the summit of a hill overlooking Burnham Wood of Macbeth fame at Dunkeld, Scotland, is shown (Figure 4–21d). It is called a rocking stone, which it is not, in historical literature, and local folklore tells of Druid ritual performed about it.

A fourth type of perched-boulder structure is the table rock or quarried flat slab set on three or four supporting rock pedestals. It is unquestionably man-made and therefore a form of rock sculpture. We have seen these on hilltops and in swamps, always associated with other man-made lithic material, and we have found four roughly quarried ones set on boulders or on roughly quarried or broken pieces of ledge. Early colonial records associate these vaguely with Indians, but we also know that the colonists used this type of monument for tombstones in certain limited cases. Many colonial cemeteries contain a few monuments of this type, with the horizontal slab well cut, dressed and inscribed and we know of no reason why this design was selected. For example, in Little Compton, Rhode Island, the graves of Benjamin Church and his descendants for two generations are interred in a few such tombs, the only tombs of this design in the cemetery, which contains hundreds of graves. It is a curious coincidence that a few miles away is the site of Queen Awashonks' village, located by a meandering stream through a swamp, marked by standing stones and a group of table rocks made of dressed slabs. Only one stands, while others have been knocked over. Queen Awashonks was close to Benjamin Church during the Second Puritan War when he persuaded her to join the English forces against Metacom. Similarly, in Lunenburg, Massachusetts, the first cemetery contains three table-rock tombs.

Also in Lunenburg is the most interesting table rock of the undressed type that we have seen in New England. In order to demonstrate how the holistic perspective invariably causes us to find more than we are looking for, we relate the story of Mavor's first visit to this rock, which he had learned of in his reading. It was described as a large boulder balanced on top of a fifty-foot-high rock broken to form a crevice that a person could crawl through.[37]

On Sunday, 19 January 1986, Mavor, along with his son-in-law Robert Goldsborough, sought out the table rock. Our directions placed it just north of the east end of a pond a half mile from the nearest road. We had also heard that Luther Burbank, the famous horticulturist, who had discovered the Burbank potato while living in Lunenburg from 1870 to 1875, had planted a row of pine trees aimed at the rock. We tramped through the woods and over fields and eventually came to the pond, which had been formed by damming up a stream at its west end where there was a natural falls. To avoid a swamp at the east end of the pond, we crossed the dam and faced a steep rocky hill running the length of the pond.

Rather than climb the hill immediately to reach the east end of the pond where the rock was supposed to lie, we walked over to some large boulders which were about 100 yards from the dam and which we could see from it. We examined a large boulder of quite irregular shape, rather like a Y, flat on top, perched on a

4–22 Prayer seat
adjacent to stone row,
Lunenburg, Mass.

granite ledge that dropped off precipitously about fifty feet to the stream gully below. We decided that this boulder met the criteria for the table rock except that we saw no crevice in the ledge. This rock was a perched boulder of the second type and, as far as we could tell, it could have been placed by a glacier. At a point 100 feet along the edge of the precipice we saw a smaller, nearly spherical perched boulder of about fifteen tons. This one, shown in Figure 4–18, was perched precariously and was probably balanced at one time before debris had collected under it. Mavor surveyed these boulders with respect to a stone row about 150 feet to the east which climbed from the dam up to the summit of the steep hill and part of the way down the other side. It was evident from the topography and flora that the pond had been a swamp and that the present mortared stone dam had probably been preceded by a simpler one and before that a natural sill.

We climbed to the stone row and walked along it, as is our practice in exploring sites. At about thirty feet from the summit, Mavor came upon a stone structure attached to the row but not integrally fastened to it, so that it must have been built at a different time. It consisted of two projecting stone rows one yard apart and one yard long forming an enclosure large enough for one person to sit facing east toward its opening (Figure 4–22). It fit the description of a Yurok prayer seat in structure, orientation and location.

Looking along the axis of the enclosure to the west, Mavor found himself looking directly at the smaller balanced boulder. When this summit location was viewed from each of the two perched boulders below, it appeared as the horizon for alignments to the extreme positions of the moonrise in the northeast quadrant.

Though we felt that the large Y-shaped boulder could be the table rock, there was the nagging lack of a crevice, and it was at the west end of the pond not the east. So we walked east along the summit ridge of the hill where we saw a few large boulders but none of exceptional interest, until Mavor came to a cliff dropping off some fifty feet with a great rocky ledge across the gorge facing him. On top of the cliff was a classic table rock, a flat-sided quarried slab about three feet thick perched on three points, two of them small boulders and the third the parent ledge (Figure 4–23). We climbed down into the gully and up the other side for a closer look. There was ice and snow about, making footing somewhat hazardous, but we eventually felt sure enough of our footing to climb all the way around the rock, which was perched precariously on the edge of the cliff, similar to the boulders at the west end of the pond. The rock was set next to a deep crevice about one-and-one-half feet wide. A large piece of the great ledge had split off and was displaced one and one-half feet horizontally from its original position.

Robert first noticed the evidence of the table rock's origin. The four sides are not at right angles, and he observed that the line of two adjacent sides of the table were precisely parallel to two sides of a cavity in the ledge next to and below the table rock. This not only showed exactly where the rock had come from, but that it had been lifted and placed so that it was oriented in exactly the same direction as it had been before it had been quarried, raised about six feet and moved over about six feet. Could this be to preserve its natural magnetic orientation? While moving a twelve-ton boulder would not be considered particularly difficult as a general proposition, doing so at this particular place would be something of a feat without modern equipment. There are no drill marks on the table rock or the ledge, but there are subtle splitting marks. This rock is perched at a place of particularly rugged beauty and probably great manitou, overlooking a swampy pond. It marks the eastern end of the rocky hill, and the other two perched boulders and the enclosure mark the west end.

Later Mavor sought out the early records of the Lunenburg proprietors, when the first lots were laid out in 1719. The first white owners of the land where the table rock lies are on record and their property corners were marked by "pillars of stone," but no table rock is mentioned. Similarly the biography and letters of Luther Burbank reveal nothing about the origins of this table rock. He was,

4–23 Lunenburg, Mass., table rock, showing wedge shape and supports

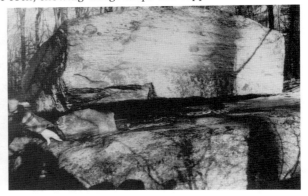

4–24a Rock stack with rocking stone on top, Mount Wachuset, Mass.

however, a man of diverse talents and interests, including a curiosity about spiritualism. If he knew of the rock, he would probably have been interested, but the pine trees he allegedly planted would be at least 110 years old, and those that exist today certainly are not, so the story may have no basis in fact.

A fifth type of perched boulder, the rock stack, two or three large boulders placed one upon the other, is really a combination of the other types. In our experience the top boulder is usually a rocking stone; examples of such stacks are shown in Figure 4–24a, b and c.

During the winter of 1985, Joe Lada, of Keene State College in New Hampshire, videotaped an interview with us at one of the sacred places which we have come to know in the Nashoba Indian lands at Boxborough, Massachusetts. One of the more striking examples of what we believe to be ritual remains was a giant rock stack positioned on the summit of a ridge overlooking Highway 495 near the Route 111 exit (Figure 4–24b). The rock stack consisted of two similarly shaped boulders placed one on top of the other. Each boulder had been worked

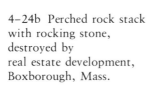

4–24b Perched rock stack with rocking stone, destroyed by real estate development, Boxborough, Mass.

so that it created a shelf or overhang large enough to shelter a person. The lower boulder was twice the size of the upper and both together exceeded ten feet in height. The upper one probably rocked before stones had been placed to wedge it in a fixed position. Sadly, the ridge and the rock stack with it were recently destroyed in order that an industrial park could be built. Probably the theory that perched boulders are entirely the work of a nature that has no connection with people is responsible. This view is not only in conflict with the ethnohistory that surrounds these magnificent landscape monuments of balance and harmony, but it has also contributed to their destruction. Ironically, the construction company that cleared the land for the industrial park and destroyed the rock stack is named "Algonkian."

4-24c Rock stack with rocking stone, Holliston, Mass.

We describe perched, balanced, pedestaled and table rocks in other chapters, but they are presented as elements of ritual sites or even in broader contexts. We show how they form markers for astronomical alignments and call attention to geological phenomena which Indians perceived as sacred. Whatever the origins of the rocks, they figure prominently in the folklore of both the Indians and the English colonists. We have seen them in every town in New England that we have investigated.

5
Land and Sky

People dwell where the land and sky meet. The natural form of the land affects their day-to-day existence in practical ways, since they use it and the fruits of the land to protect themselves from the sky's harsh cold, snow, rain, winds and darkness. However, in choosing their dwelling places, people are influenced both by practical factors and by a subjective feel for place, which grows as they attempt to live in harmony with the natural forms upon the land beneath the sky. Not only do these forms affect the way in which the sky behaves, by changing weather patterns for instance, but they also affect the way people feel. From a mountain summit, the land stretches away and a person seems much smaller compared with his place than he does when he is enclosed in a valley where his visual limits are more confined. The rising and setting of the celestial bodies on the horizon provide further evidence of the interrelation between the sky and the land, and of the uniqueness of each particular place. It is therefore only natural that people have developed rituals and codes of behavior for the placing and design of their dwelling places.

Through all the ages of humanity, people have felt that they could improve upon the natural architecture of the land and the sky for motives of religious belief, political power, aesthetic choice or practical necessity. The great pyramids of Egypt, built 5,000 to 4,000 years ago, remain as monuments to the attempts of man to change permanently the face of the place where land meets sky. Our modern tall buildings, bridges and highways are similar but more transient efforts.

From time to time, there have been those who preferred to participate in the natural relationships between land and sky in perhaps a more respectful manner, by subtly working with the landscape rather than by changing it in spectacular or monumental ways. Through the ages, the practices of cultures on diverse parts of the earth have demonstrated this point of view. We believe that the people who inhabited the eastern part of North America from 10,000 years ago up to the sixteenth century were inclined in this way and their descendants continue practices such as ritual shaping of trees (Figure 5–1). But, whatever the intentions, all people, as all life, alter the natural world about them according to their nature and numbers. It is a matter of degree and whether it is enhancement or destruction depends upon point of view.

It is perhaps remarkable that subtle remains of ancient peoples could survive in the modern industrialized world. But the rugged topography of much of New England has tended to be avoided by industrial and residential development, and it has had only 400 years of destruction by Europeans, compared with thousands of years in Europe. The places in the world that are considered the seats of early advanced civilization are probably the places where subtle prehistoric remains are least likely to be found. There each succeeding culture has destroyed and buried the remains of the previous one.

The survival of the European settlers who came to America from Europe depended at first upon good relations with the native inhabitants and upon learning aspects of their way of life peculiar to the environment. After these settlers had displaced the natives, they introduced the European way of life into the new land. The surviving writings of the sixteenth- and seventeenth-century settlers tell little about the native inhabitants or the ways in which the settlers adapted to Indian ways. A traditional picture of New England history was built largely upon conjecture that was logical from an English perspective, one that continues to be

5–1 Modern Indian marked tree, Charlestown, R. I., Indian Church

accepted with little question. The motive for this tradition was and continues to be a desire among the immigrants, with local exceptions, to eliminate the native inhabitants, their customs and way of life from the national consciousness. The early English settlers considered this way of life primitive, depraved and indolent, and their descendants continue to hold this view.

While we cannot bring back all the customs of the native inhabitants, and probably would not if we could, it may be possible to recall a respect for the meeting place of the land and sky which once existed. Reminders can be seen today all about us if we but observe appropriately. In order to see these reminders, however, we must set aside, for the moment, our baggage of much historical writing and folklore. Even the conclusions of modern archaeological excavations depend heavily upon circumstance and conjecture. Many of the rude stone structures about the New England countryside which have been attributed to European settlers may have much different origins and functions than supposed. There are stone rows, stone mounds by the hundreds of thousands, standing stones, perched boulders, areas of stone paving, and structures of many designs having laid-up stone walling, some with great stone-slab roofs, some enclosing space and some which are solid masses. This tremendous wealth of stone structures, which we have barely touched on here, pervades our landscape, yet few people have thought it worthy of serious investigation. Thousands of miles of New England stone "walls" are casually attributed to eighteenth- and nineteenth-century farmers of European origin on the basis that a very small sample can be verified by historical records.

We offer a new perspective, recognizing the importance of seeing the place where we live as the meeting place of land and sky, and asking how people might respond to this perspective. What might they leave for posterity as reminders of this response and why? We find that there are certain places, with common types and patterns of features, which we believe record the perceptions of ancient people. Probably each community of people had one or a few of these places, separate from their places of daily living, which explains the general absence of habitation debris at such sites.

Our method is one of primary observation and participation. It depends upon the experience and perceptions of the observer and realizes that we sense things differently from those of different backgrounds. What can be sensed today is the first step of the method and independent of past observations or interpretations.

The Native Americans treated every aspect of the natural landscape as sacred, and we believe that they signalled this fact in subtle ways, some of which can be detected today. Also, in maintaining an ecological balance, there were practical considerations such as planting or hunting at the appropriate times in the appropriate places, which were likewise treated as sacred. As a result, some places, such as swamps, were ritualized in ways that reflected both cosmic and everyday subsistence concerns. Therefore, although the common anthropological designations of upland and lowland to describe the major regimes of the landscape may be appropriate for some studies, we prefer to use different, more specific designations that relate to our observations. For example, a swamp can be in an upland or a lowland, as can a horizon, or a stream.

Astronomy

The invasion of America which started during the sixteenth century and continues to the present day is one of the most overwhelming cultural discontinuities on record. By A.D. 1700, most of the residents of New England were European immigrants with only remnants of the native population remaining after a century of invasion. Today, we know very little about the nature and ways of the native people before this date, and the historical records and artifacts of the European colonists are open to diverse interpretations. In our research we found that much possible evidence of native culture prior to this great discontinuity still lies abundantly about us unrecognized today, and that a consideration of the possible astronomical significance of this evidence provides an entirely new image of native life in colonial times and earlier. We use astronomy not as an esoteric science with elaborate jargon and complex techniques, but as a fundamental and creative way of looking at everyday things. We have found that most of the elements on which our knowledge of the past is based can be interpreted in new ways by means of the astronomical approach, resulting in equally or more plausible reconstructions of our heritage. Astronomy takes the structure of familiar things and opens them to the infinite scale of the universe.

When the land and sky are considered together, our experience of the world is changed and perhaps given profound new meaning. Horizon phenomena such as the rising and setting of the sun and moon and the resulting patterns of light and shadow on the land become humbling and awesome manifestations of our connection with the cosmos.

A Coastal Astronomical Site

A single rock stack marks the observation point for an astronomical alignment that can be clearly witnessed today because it is on the shore of the Elizabeth Islands off Cape Cod, which have been mostly denuded of trees by sheep farming. In 1982, Mavor noticed a rock stack consisting of a two-ton granite boulder placed upon a larger one with a dished-out top. In addition, a vertical face of the smaller boulder was decorated by a pecked serpentine figure and a group of at least four small circular depressions (Figure 5–2).

The stack is situated on a bluff some twenty-five feet above sea level and fifty yards from the shore of a semicircular cove. An observer standing at the stack and looking to the west across the waters of the cove sees a promontory which forms the far side of the cove. A pair of boulders, one triangular and one rectan-

5-2 Perched boulder
with serpentine marks *(l)*
and four dots *(r)*,
Elizabeth Islands

gular, on the promontory at the center of a concavity in the land contour, form a
horizon marker. These boulders, probably placed by the last glacier, are in fact
100 feet apart but from the position of the stack appear to overlap as shown in
Figure 5–3. Mavor surveyed the sightline, one-half mile long, with a transit
and found that when the sun's declination[1] is zero degrees, at the equinox, the
setting sun's disk frames the pair of boulders symmetrically, and the last gleam
is seen in the notch formed by the triangular boulder and the level ground (Figure 5–3).

The equinox, the time when the center of the sun crosses the celestial equator
at zero declination, occurs twice a year on March 20, 21 or 22, and on September
21, 22 or 23, when day and night are equal in length. It does not, in general,
occur at sunset. At sunset on the day of the equinox, the sun's declination may
vary from +12 to –12 minutes of arc, which is the angular width of the pair of
horizon boulders. Once every four years, the sun's declination at equinox sunset
comes within a few minutes of arc of zero and the sun fits neatly on the foresight
as described and witnessed by Figure 5–4, taken in September, 1984. Ancient
people could have determined the days of the equinoxes by recording the solstices
and counting to the days equidistant between them, or by observing equal length
of day and night on a gnomon.

The vertical face of the perched observation boulder is oriented 312 degrees
true, and an observer facing the marks on this face would face 48 degrees true.
Star charts are common among western American Indian works, so we speculated that the four depressions on the rock might have represented a star arrangement. However, the possibilities cover the period from thousands of years ago
to the present.

Most of the Elizabeth Islands have been preserved from exploitation by
human development since 1842. The locations of all of the limited number of
buildings built since the 1600s are well known, as are the stone walls built during

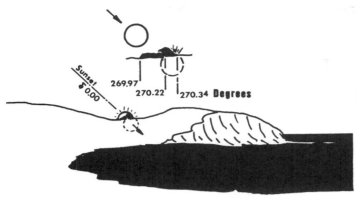

5-3 Equinox sunset geometry, Elizabeth Islands

the time of James Bowdoin, a previous owner. The natural landscape of the islands has been changed primarily by sheep farming and by the gradual ravages of wind, waves and salt spray. With this background, there is reason to expect that the perched and marked boulder signalling solar and, perhaps, stellar alignments has been in place for at least hundreds of years.

The celestial bodies were and continue to be a pervading passion among indigenous peoples. The practice of observing all celestial behavior for its practical significance while simultaneously admiring it as vast and wonderful has continued from the distant past into the present. Religions, which are based in part on the need to sense our place in the natural world around us, are molded by the cycles of the sun, moon, stars and planets. It was observed long ago that biological cycles on earth are related to these cosmic events. These observations were not explained by physical laws in the modern fashion, but by a sense of the overwhelming power of natural events over the comings and goings of people and other species on earth.

5-4 Equinox sunset on promontory horizon, Elizabeth Islands

Hilltop sites are characteristically important astronomically in many parts of the world, but with notable differences among them. In several places in New England, it appears that the observer stations himself at markers placed around the periphery of a hilltop and observes looking toward a peak common to all stations. In Great Britain, where ancient astronomical sites have been studied extensively, alignments generally radiate from a central observation point outward to distant horizon features. This difference may imply a different social structure or different cosmological view. In New England, for example, the design may mean that many observers in a community focused their attention on a single sacred place, perhaps implying a democratic society with a monotheistic religion. In Britain, on the other hand, an elite priesthood may be implied.[2]

In Chapter 4, we mentioned briefly that early Algonquian speakers from northeastern North America migrated west to California about 500 years ago. They naturally took with them the tradition of the interrelation of land and sky which they had known in the east. Ethnologist T. T. Waterman, in describing the cosmology of these Yurok Indians, states that, to the Yurok, overhead is as real and concrete as is the earth on which he treads. The Yurok word *Ki-we'sona* meaning "that which exists," is their word for the sky dome and the expanse of landscape and water it encloses.[3]

The idea that natural processes proceed by fixed natural laws originated at least as early as Aristotle. By the seventeenth century, many people in Western Europe believed that human beings could, by applying these laws, control the earth's events. Accordingly, modern science was born, dedicated to this premise, and God took human form. Among indigenous peoples, or most of the world's population, including the natives of America, none of this happened. They continued in their way to see man as a humble part of nature, and respected the natural balances.

Ecology

The astronomical nature of the landscape architecture led us to consider the ecology of the Indian way of life because stone markers on the horizon can be seen only if the land is clear of obstructing trees and shrubs. There are many references in the historic record to an Indian tradition of burning the trees and other vegetation off large areas of the land annually and semiannually.[4] Pollen studies show that the tradition may go back 12,000 years in northeastern North America and 40,000 years in Australia.[5] The trees would first be killed by cutting away a band of bark; then, after the tree had died and fallen, it was burned in place. This process, though long in elapsed time, required very little human effort. With large areas of land cleared, the ecological balance was undoubtedly somewhat different from what we see today. A lively scientific debate centers on the amount of land burned over in eastern North America, with estimates varying from ten to ninety percent. In the seventeenth century, this tradition was prohibited by the white man's laws, and the new forest which resulted obstructed the sight lines to the meeting of the land and sky. The tradition of observing ritually the rising and setting of celestial bodies at horizon markers became increasingly difficult to practice soon after contact between the Native Americans and the European settlers.

Abrupt foresting of the land coupled with the absence of cyclical burnings may have directed the climate in ways that are misunderstood today. The early peoples of the northeastern United States may have knowingly controlled the burning cycles to soften the harshness of the coming winter. The release of smoke, heat and ash into the atmosphere during these burning periods may have caused a greenhouse effect over large areas of land in the Northeast, leading to brief periods of warming. Also, the diffusing ash particles may have "seeded" the water molecules in the atmosphere, increasing the normal rainfall. This cycle following a November burn could have been a passive form of climate modification designed to lengthen the growing season. The size of this effect would depend upon the population density of the land, a matter about which there is also a scientific debate. Recent estimates claim a much larger precolonial Native American population than previous assessments.[6]

This scenario and others of aboriginal climatic modification are confirmed by recent research. Pollen studies in Australia have suggested a correlation between aboriginal burning of the land and climatic change over the past 40,000 years. This span of time covers two glacial and interglacial cycles. It was observed that the increasingly dry period between 40,000 and 9,000 years ago brought an almost total replacement of the rain forest by hard-surfaced desert-like plants. The natural climatic change, evaluated from global sea-level changes and sea surface temperatures, seemed unlikely to account for this drastic floral change, a suspicion that was confirmed by the discovery of increased charcoal particles in the soils, indicating a sharp and frequent increase in burning of the land about 38,000 years ago, the date assigned to the first human habitation.[7] At 9,000 years ago, a sudden vegetation change to lush rain forest accompanied the wet Holocene period during which the Pleistocene ice melted to its present-day condition.

Pollen profiles from Guatemala and Venezuela provide convincing evidence of the unstable and short-lived nature of tropical rain forests in the Americas. Eleven thousand years ago, the lands subsequently occupied by the Maya were marshy savannahs with juniper scrub, in contrast to today's tropical forest. In addition, between 3,000 years and 400 years ago, much of the forest was levelled by the Maya. The diversity of the tropical forest is now seen by ecologists as caused by instability and dynamic turnover rather than environmental stability as was previously thought. Since these forests are now seen in this way, the role of man in substantial environmental manipulation over many thousands of years becomes a more logical possibility.[8]

In North America, we can now visualize the retreat of the Wisconsin IV glacier beginning 11,000 years ago as a time of unstable vegetation, accompanied by regular burnings of the land by the Indians. The soil was artificially darkened by charcoal from the burning, increasing its absorption of the sun's energy and warming the land. This in turn accelerated the melting of the ice. Thus, the mechanism is in place to suggest that aboriginal ritual burning of the land not only caused a measurable change in global climate over the past 40,000 years, but also played a significant and perhaps large role in accelerating the warming during the last glacial retreat, an event that has not yet been satisfactorily explained by natural science.

We can visualize the cyclical burning of the land as a carefully controlled ritual process which purified the environment. The ditch and bank earthworks, which often surround wetlands as discussed in Chapter 4, may have been built as a fire barrier to preserve these sacred wetlands from burning. Enriching large areas with charcoal and ash balances the soil and purifies the water that drains over the land. Sacred, here, is meant in the Indian sense that all nature is sacred, or spiritual, and there are degrees or different kinds of spirituality or manitou. The water is purified both physically and spiritually.

Lessons applicable to New England can be learned from experience in Australia, where it is now acknowledged that the "natural landscape" has been managed by aboriginal peoples to a much greater degree than modern observers have previously realized. The productivity of the land for the hunters and gatherers of Australia was enhanced greatly in ancient times by controlled burning of vegetation which increased the yield of certain plants and thereby attracted grazing animals to the new shoots. By maintaining a controlled diversity of vegetation, destructive brush fires, which are common in farming communities, are avoided, the land is cleaned and certain predators such as snakes can be controlled.[9]

Of particular relevance to aboriginal use of New England wetlands is the discovery in Australia's Kakadu National Park that as recently as 1845, and for at least 1,000 years before, there were dense aboriginal settlements on dry patches within and on the edges of wetlands. The resources used by the aborigines included many swamp plants and animals. Over a million stone artifacts have been found in swamps and marshes; these must have been carried in from a distance because there is no natural surface rock in these wetlands. It is estimated that 50,000 stones were dropped each year over a period of 1,000 years at the sites studied.[10]

The elements of the New England landscape appear to be connected into a network of sacred spaces in a way that enables each element to share in the experiences of all of the others. The connectors which we see are the arteries of stone rows, the astronomical and sightline alignments which connect surface features to the celestial bodies, and the mounds and perched boulders and other stone structures which connect the bedrock to the biosphere. The seeker of visions who, as we shall show in later chapters, makes use of these elements, both draws energy from them and contributes it to them.

We in the modern world have become used to our attempts to dominate and control even the unknown, as if it were a human frailty to be overcome. It is entirely possible that knowledge is sensitivity to surroundings and the balance of the world's ecosystems, not the catalogued and codified information that characterizes Western civilization. To understand the vision quest and its important role in past cultures, we must consider the possibility that it was a process that opened the individual to learning experiences far more holistic and profound than those with which we are familiar.

Language

The very words we speak often direct our perception of the world. A large part of the world's population speaks with greater emphasis upon action and being and with a concept of time that is different from that of the modern Western-language speaker. This emphasis encourages mystical thought, which is now considered to be caused by using the right or creative hemisphere of the brain.

When a Westerner attempts to observe "objectively" and define the structure of American Indian language using his perception of logic and reality, he overlooks the Indian eloquence in abstract and metaphysical matters. He also fails to comprehend the Indian's ability to view nature at its most fundamental levels, a participating, interpenetrating universe in which the dichotomy of observer and observed does not exist.

LaVan Martineau, in learning to understand American Indian rock writing, has perceived that its structure is identical to sign language and to the spoken languages of the people.[11] This perception gives us some idea of the holistic nature of this language group and its relationship to the natural environment. We believe that both the works of stone and earth in New England and the rock writing participate in the natural order in the same manner.

Most of the known rock writing in the United States is located in the arid lands of the Southwest where many canyons and caves with sheer walls of smooth sedimentary rock are suitable for petroglyphs and paintings. In New England there are relatively few known petroglyphs. We do not know the reason for this scarcity but can surmise that the dominance of rough granite with few protected caves and overhangs, along with the abundance of wood, makes writing on bark a more convenient though less permanent alternative.

On the other hand, there are thousands of marked stones in New England, often associated with sacred places (Figure 5–5). Although these stone markings,

5–5 Groove-marked stone, Calendar One bowl, Vt.

5-6 Marked stone near shore of Lake Memphramagog, Quebec

usually ordered sets of grooves or abraded short lines, suggest numerical notation, they may have a greater content, as do known petroglyphs. We have seen examples of both linear markings and pictographic petroglyphs together on the shore of Lake Memphramagog in Quebec, Canada (Figure 5–6). An excavation in Woodstock, Vermont, organized by Warren Cook of Castleton State College, in which we participated, revealed an unusual and complex array of orderly grooves on the bedrock surface which had been covered by a few inches of soil (Figure 5–7).

5-7 Grooved marks on bedrock, Woodstock, Vt.

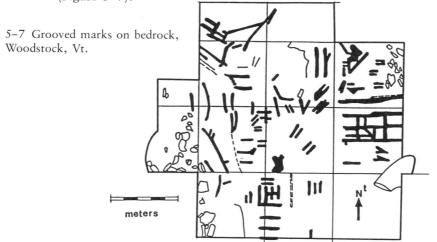

Throughout North America the Indian languages have certain basic similarities. Even though the spoken languages may not have been universally understood, the written forms were. Indian petroglyphs required the reader to exercise logic, common sense and creativity, as well as awareness of the surroundings and geography, in order to understand them. The petroglyphs cannot be read using the marks alone. This aspect contrasts sharply with modern languages, particularly Western European, in which characters contain the entire message and are learned and used by rote. Also, as Martineau shows by examples, Indian petroglyphs often have a meaning that is an extension of the concept conveyed by the writing itself.[12] This requires viewing the writing through the eyes of the Indian and allows for the use of fewer symbols than would be the case otherwise.

An example of a pictograph having this quality is shown in Figure 5–8. It is a rare combination of symbols each meaning "darkened eye," which describes the confluence of two particular rivers having an unusual geometry. The reader of this petroglyph must decipher it by visualizing the symbols as canyons and the general pattern as the complex flow of water at this specific place. One river makes an almost complete circle which is portrayed by the interlocked symbols, one cut off at the end signifying an incomplete circle. Reading the petroglyph requires imagination and a clear concept of natural phenomena such as the one described, and the reader must exercise both logic and intuition.[13]

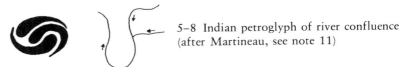

5–8 Indian petroglyph of river confluence (after Martineau, see note 11)

American Indian languages can also express a complex of ideas in a single word. This agglutinative or incorporating characteristic, which emphasizes word and form, is dominant and fundamental, whereas in isolating languages such as the Indo-Chinese family emphasis is on sentences and word order. In Native American languages several ideas retain their separate identity even though fused in one word, just as the simple symbols which make up a petroglyph are fused to form an ideogram of great complexity. In this context, sentences and word order limit clarity; only the word and its form or the design of the petroglyph are important. In the conjugation and declension of Native American languages, the prefixes and suffixes are distinct from the root and therefore easily shifted from one root to another without losing their significance, while Indo-European languages use internal modification of the root which, losing its identity, becomes arbitrary and difficult to analyze.[14]

Because Indian words, when translated into English, usually express entire sentences, the subject-verb-object structure of English is absent and the net effect is that most Indian words contain verbs or otherwise express action or being. This observation expresses a fundamental cultural difference. To the European, subject, object and verb are separate entities and are perceived as independent.

When he says, for example, "he sits on the rock," he visualizes the subject, the action of sitting, and the rock as having no relationship other than that which is directly expressed. The Indian can express the same concept with one word and conveys with that word that the person, the rock, and the sitting are equal parts of the natural world. They are relatives. The action of sitting is not only felt by the person but also by the rock. The Indian, however, would consider such a vague and impersonal statement meaningless and not worthy of expression. He would include the name of the person and the identity of the rock and its location. His word would mean, for example, "Metacom sat gently on the smooth, black rock at the mouth of the stream below the great falls."

We see the stone and earthen works of New England as not only a form of sacred landscape architecture, but also as writing. They convey ideographic images which are built in a manner identical to that of the language and pictographic writing of other American Indians, but on a larger physical scale. A complex site consisting of stone mounds, chambers, earthworks and the natural land and sky conveys a complex image, one word made of many components, which fuses, just as do the spoken language, the rock writing and the sign language.

It is clear that the use of Indian words in a discussion which takes place in the English language is bound to be obscure in meaning. For this reason, we use Indian words primarily in quotations from or paraphrases of historical records, and then in the realization that the writer is struggling with the problem of language.

Swamps

The wetlands or swamps of southern New England, once thought of as wastelands by the European settlers, were mostly the domain of the Atlantic white cedar and the Indians, although the colonists did log them. Our knowledge from historical sources of the Indian use of swamps is confined to records of events in which the colonists participated, mostly the battles and massacres of the seventeenth century, commonly called the Pequot and King Philip Wars, which we call the First and Second Puritan Wars.

The Pequots or Grey Fox Indians, originally members of the Mahican Federation of the lower Hudson River valley, broke away and formed a separate tribe about 1590, after which they settled in Connecticut and established themselves as a local power. In 1637, the Massachusetts Bay Colony under Governor Winthrop went to war against the Pequots. Both the Plymouth and Connecticut Colonies were opposed to the war, and Governor Edward Winslow of the Plymouth Colony accused Winthrop of consciously provoking it. The Pequots were pursued relentlessly from eastern to western Connecticut by Winthrop's troops backed by the Mohegan sachem Uncas. A Pequot village in a swamp between the Thames and Connecticut Rivers was attacked and many of the villagers were executed. On 13 July 1637, most of the survivors were killed in Pequot Swamp in Southport. Sassacus, the last Pequot Great Sachem, and some of his warriors escaped and fled to New York to attempt to buy protection from the Mohawks, who instead killed them.[15]

The most widely known "Great Swamp Fight" took place in Kingston, Rhode Island, in 1676 during the Second Puritan War, when a large fortified Narragansett village on a low island in the Great Swamp was attacked by the English led by the Massachusetts Bay Colony, with great losses on both sides.[16] It is likely that this low island of four acres, where artifacts 3,000 years old have been found, was built by the Indians for a settlement. It lies in the vee between two convergent streams in a large and otherwise level wetland (Figure 5–9).

Earlier, on 26 June 1675, in the first week of the war, a Boston cavalry troop and two Plymouth companies were posted to Swansea after the Indian raid on that town which commenced hostilities. The troops proceeded into the swamps of Swansea and nearby Mount Hope searching for Metacom. They were ambushed, led astray, became lost and finally gave up the search. The inexperienced Major James Cudworth, who with Josiah Winslow owned miles of swamps but knew nothing of them, conducted useless sorties into the Pocasset swamp in Tiverton. But Captain Benjamin Church of Cudworth's Company, whom we have already met, was friendly with Queen Awashonks, who lived in a swamp in nearby Sogkonate, and persuaded her not to join Metacom.[17]

On 18 July 1675, there was a battle in Great Pocasset Swamp in Tiverton. A village of 100 wigwams where Metacom and Weetamoe had hidden their people was raided with 16 whites killed and 100 Indians captured. In the accounts of the war, written by Church, Increase Mather and John Easton, repeated references are made to Indians hiding in swamps and colonial troops searching swamps. Metacom himself was finally ambushed and killed in 1676 in a swamp on Mount

5–9 Great Swamp Fight site, Kingston, R. I.

Hope Neck by troops led by Church. On 28 August 1676, after the death of Metacom, one of his captains, Annawon, and his principal lieutenants were captured by Church in the great swamp of Rehoboth, called Squannacook, at a sacred rock to which they had retreated to await capture. They were executed by the government at Boston.[18]

Every decisive engagement between the colonists and the Indians took place when the Indians were attacked in strongholds on islands within the swamps. Because of this, we can infer that the Indians were very familiar with these swamps, which undoubtedly traditionally played a great role in their lives. When the Indians burned over the land twice a year, they apparently preserved the swamps for settlement and refuge, probably by using stone- and earthworks. It seems likely that the Native Americans recognized the resources available in the swamps and managed them over a long period of time to provide a congenial habitat, an energy and nutrient source, and a water purification system, as well as to control insects and to produce wildlife and food and fiber crops.[19] We also raise the possibility that some islands within wetlands were created by water-level regulation, because earth- and stoneworks which Moorehead and Willoughby attribute to Indians are frequently found within and near New England cedar swamps.[20]

A cedar swamp in East Freetown, Massachusetts, an extension of Bolton Cedar Swamp, is named Hobomock. Salisbury, citing Edward Winslow, writes that the major spirit, Hobomock, "protected and empowered those who obtained visions of him."[21] Several groups of stone mounds, several hundred mounds altogether, are located on the rising land just west of Hobomock Swamp, and one group extends into the swamp itself. It may be that the swamp was named by the colonists after Hobomock, whom they equated to the devil, because of extensive Indian religious activity in the area, of which the stone mounds are the relics. If the mounds were associated with seeking visions of Hobomock, this would be reflected in tradition.

Our research into the origins of groups of stone mounds, stone rows and associated astronomical alignment markers to solar horizon events has shown that they are frequently within swamps or related architecturally to them. We have found through excavation that certain stone mounds related to swamps are of prehistoric Indian origin and were built for ceremonial purposes. Algonquin groups are known to have used stone mounds and rows in their vision quest ritual. Several swamps in New England retain the name Hobomock, the spirit to which most vison quests by Algonquin powwows were directed. Passaconnoway, sachem and powwow of the Pawtucket Indians, worked his spells in the swamps near his settlement for three days and nights in an effort to rid the region of the white man.[22]

The earthworks at Andover, Massachusetts, described in Chapter 4, are located near swamps, and Bullen, though skeptical of Indian origin, found Indian artifacts and no evidence to support colonial origin. These ditch and bank works could have been used to control water level to build up the soil.[23]

Anthropologist Frank Speck reports oral traditions among the Mohegan Indians of Connecticut, of dwarfs who carried lights about the swamps, stopping at rock piles where the light would flare up. These will-o'-the-wisps are said to be spirits or disembodied souls travelling about with lights. Other New England Indian accounts describe glowing light in the night sky, envisioned as liberated souls. Josselyn, writing in 1833, states, "They have a remarkable observation of a flame that appears before the death of an Indian or English upon their wigwams at night: the first time that I did see it, I was call'd out by some of them about twelve of the clock, it being a very dark night."[24]

The Algonquian dialects contain numerous words meaning cedar swamp, with variants depending upon the environment. Similarly, there are many words for the confluence of streams and for stone mounds, implying cultural importance.[22] Curious boulders located at the edges of swamps are part of Indian legend. In the region about Bristol, Connecticut, there was a white cedar swamp which was flooded in the 1870s to make present Fall Mountain Lake, a reservoir for the factories of Waterbury, Connecticut. Norton observed that a large boulder, perched on three smaller boulders was located at the edge of the swamp and known locally as Indian Rock. Also on the edge of the same swamp there is a large rock known as Witch Rock and near it another, balanced precariously on a small area of support, that figures in Indian legends.[26]

Indian Cedar Swamp in Rhode Island is near the Great Swamp that figured in the battle of 19 December 1675. Today, it is in the heart of the lands occupied by the remaining Narragansett Indians, and they have built their stone church on a bluff overlooking this swamp far from main roads. Along the dirt roadway to this church there is a large boulder, balanced upon a bedrock outcrop overlooking the swamp. Its base is smoothly undercut all around giving it a mushroom-like aspect (Figure 4–18h).

The wetlands were apparently left forested by the Indians when they burned off the surrounding areas, and ritual management of the wetlands may have entailed subtle changes in hydrology, including lowering the water level in winter to increase germination, and controlling flora and fauna to make a more congenial habitat. The wetlands' excess production could have been harvested for use elsewhere or left for peat accumulation by hydrological management.[27] We suggest that the earth and stone structures found in freshwater wetlands today may be the remains of this wetland management system. Burning over uplands, draining their products to the wetlands, charcoal filtering of the run-off water, and possibly encouraging or controlling the cedars may have been important aboriginal land-management practices of depth and subtlety.

Ecologists Turner and Harrison and their colleagues have observed hydraulic agriculture in the Yucatan peninsula swamps engineered by the Maya. In a seasonal tropical forest, the Maya constructed canals and raised fields about 100 feet on a side, between 300 B.C. and A.D. 1000. Water remained in the canals year-round, and the top of an adjoining farmed field was about two feet above it.

The fields were built by scraping off the topsoil to the limestone bedrock that underlies the swamp. Then canals were dug into the limestone, and the excavated materials plus some additional upland material were used to build a three-foot-high plat between canals. On top of that a planting surface of topsoil was spread. The net result was that the swamp water was restricted to the canals while a raised dry planting platform was created. Plant forms that do not normally grow in the swamps have been found in the fields. Corn and cotton were grown, with three crops in a year-round rotation. The high productivity of the managed swampland caused food to be produced in excess of local need so it was exported. It appears that such a system took considerable organization and much labor; perhaps as many as 2,000 people may have been required to build in one swamp.[28]

We can only conjecture about whether or not such a system was constructed in New England. It is generally thought that Northeastern Indians did not produce works requiring the organization of large groups of people. This may not, however, have been so, in the light of the discovery of large-scale earthworks of possible Indian origin. On the other hand, the geology of New England is very different from that of the Yucatan, where a flat sedimentary rock base lies a short distance below the soil surface. Cedar swamps in New England are bogs having tens of feet of peat, which would presumably have required a much different technique of hydraulic engineering. If, as suggested, water-level regulation was used to build islands in a swamp, this method could have required a relatively small amount of labor and have been at the same time more subtle and sophisticated than its possible Mayan counterpart. In any case, an additional link between the ancient people of Mexico and those of northern parts of North America would not be a surprising development.

An Example of an Integrated Swamp Site

We feel that the major places of Indian ritual contained works of man which signalled all the elements of land and sky participating together. Among the several groups of stone mounds in Freetown, Massachusetts, that we explored, one in a swamp just over the southern boundary of East Freetown in the town of Acushnet gives a particularly vivid demonstration of these connections. Stone mounds are architecturally connected to a system of stone rows, streams and natural topography, and a tall, pointed standing stone marks an astronomical alignment. The intimate connections between streams, horizon topography, swamps and stonework were recognized only after we observed and became intimately familiar with the place without knowing in advance what measurements or relationships would turn out to be crucial to its understanding. Here our study was confined entirely to nondestructive observation and measurement, unlike the Freetown excavation. Where "land development" does not threaten a site, we apply conversant research methods which, without excavation, entail a highly active involvement with the place and its artifacts. In this case, the

5-10 Standing stone, Acushnet, Mass.

complex geometrical layout, its relationship to the natural land and water ecosystem and to the sky are important and challenging considerations.

A standing stone 6 feet 2 inches high (Figure 5-10) is located so that the winter solstice sunrise can be seen at the stone on the horizon from an observation station at the intersection of two streams or at points along the interconnecting line. The stone appears on the horizon when viewed from the general direction of the stream intersection, and when viewed from that direction it appears at the center of a natural depression formed by rising land on either side (Figure 5-11). All of these circumstances reinforce the notion that the stone was intentionally placed.

5-11 Sightline to standing stone from stream intersection, Acushnet

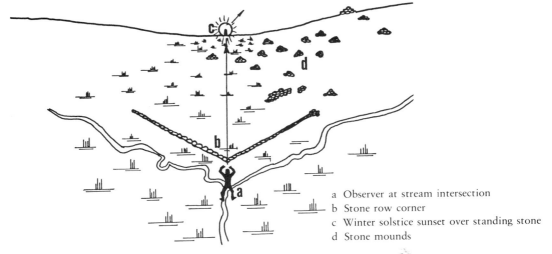

a Observer at stream intersection
b Stone row corner
c Winter solstice sunset over standing stone
d Stone mounds

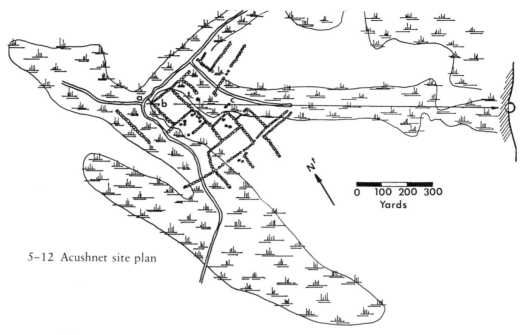

5–12 Acushnet site plan

The two meandering streams, shown in the regional map of Figure 5–12, drain swamps from the north and south, and meet to form a single stream which runs eastward to the New Bedford reservoir.

The prominent standing stone, which is securely anchored in the ground, appears to have been located carefully both to mark a solar event and to signal features of the streams, particularly the intersection and a possible spring which may be the origin of the seasonal tributary on the east. The northwestern face of the stone, which is quite flat and is aligned to 52 degrees true, is directed toward the spring. Near the standing stone and on the sight line from the stream intersection is a table rock, a flat four-sided slab 5 x 6 x 4 x 4 feet, supported on three points, two of which are visible round boulders. South of the table, toward the standing stone, there is a stone mound and just to the north a low standing slab aligned to 60 degrees true.

Our detailed map of the central part of the region of Figure 5–12 is shown in Figure 5–13. It is bounded by the main stream on the north and west and records the locations of stone rows, stone mounds, standing stones and any other obviously man-made features, as well as some large natural boulders which appear to be connected to the man-made architecture. Nestled into the corner formed by the streams is a trapezoidal area formed by stone rows, 346 by 408 feet. The northwest corner, A, includes an angle of 82 degrees and lies on the sight line from the stream intersection, B, to the standing stone, C. This sight line also bisects the 82 degree angle between rows.

Near the northeast corner of the trapezoid is a prominent tetrahedral boulder 5 feet high, shown as feature D in Figure 5–13 and in the photograph of Figure

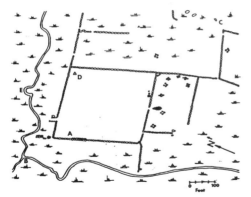

5-13 Central features
of Acushnet site
A Northwest corner of trapezoid
B Stream intersection
C Standing stone
D Tetrahedral boulder
E Embrasure in stream

5-14. This is a type of stone which E. G. Squier reports was venerated by Indians of the Northeast.[29] A sight line from the standing stone to this boulder passes through the center of an embrasure, E, formed by the meanders of the stream, as shown in Figure 5-13. These meanders, which are usually thought to be entirely the consequence of natural hydrodynamic processes, seem both in size and shape to duplicate the earth and stone embrasures commonly found in works along the Midwestern rivers built by the Adena and Hopewell peoples in prehistoric times and also seen in Indian stone forts in New England. The Queen's Fort, or "Quaiapen's Domain" as we prefer to call it, discussed in Chapter 4, has two such embrasures which establish a summer solstice sunset sight line. We suggest that the Acushnet embrasure may be an architectural feature constructed by placing boulders to guide the stream. Embrasures may have originated as representations of natural phenomena such as meanders of rivers and streams in flat country, like those found in the low-lying coastal plain of eastern New England and the Midwestern river basins.

5-14 Tetrahedral boulder,
Acushnet

At the northwest corner of the trapezoid, shown in Figure 5–13, the line of the west row is extended to the stream on the north by a stone mound and a low row of boulders, which begins with a small standing stone. Ninety feet to the east of the corner is a port in the row, with a short avenue of boulders, directed toward the stream at 340 degrees true. The avenue is a low linear arrangement of rocks that makes use of some large boulders already in place. Again, there is a stone mound in line with an arm of the avenue. An observer standing at the small standing stone or at the large boulder in the east branch of the avenue will see the equinox sunrise at the horizon marked by the tetrahedral boulder, D. South of the avenue there is another group of boulders. A stone mound is built into the southwest corner of the trapezoid, where a short, three-foot-long connecting row to a large boulder is followed by a section of row which extends to the stream and meets another large boulder. The north row of the trapezoid is aimed at a large boulder on the bank of the stream to the west.

The smaller trapezoidal arrangement of stone rows south of the larger one contains several stone mounds, and the west and south legs of the trapezoid stop sharply short of the intersection of their lines of direction. A white quartz boulder is seen at the south end of the west row and another in the center of the larger stone mound in the southeast corner. A stone mound is built into the row corner at the northeast corner of the smaller trapezoid. A teardrop-shaped stone mound, a single course of 500 pound boulders, points toward an opening in the row.

The diagonal of the larger trapezoidal row arrangement, if extended south-easterly, passes precisely through the row corner near the prominent standing stone C. Other stone mounds and rows and orthostats are seen in Figures 5–12 and 5–13.

We naturally wonder if all the stone features are contemporary and if they are part of a common architectural plan or concept. In particular, the bulk of the stone rows are constructed of boulders with considerable gaps between them, like those ordinarily labeled stone fences and which may have served as stone fences. In the architectural scheme we envision, the stone rows connect places with one another rather than serve as boundaries or containments. Therefore, they need not be as high as fences. Perhaps the rows we see today were originally lower like the rays of a medicine wheel or like those seen in the Freetown mound sites connecting stone mounds. They may have been built up to make pasture fences within the past 200 years. The permanence of the stream meanders is also a question, but to the extent that they are caused by boulders deflecting the stream, which is certainly the case in many places, they could be quite permanent and of great antiquity.

It seems likely that the Acushnet site is connected to the other stone mound groups to the west in Freetown. It is two miles from the excavated stone mound that we have shown to be prehistoric, Native American, and ceremonial. It is also near other mound groups in Freetown that actually extend into cedar swamps.

6

Indians Meet the Jesuits, Pilgrims, Puritans and Quakers

The coast of New England and Canada as far north as Labrador was visited by European fishermen at least as early as the mid-fifteenth century, according to recent comparisons of Breton and Canadian toponyms. Later, ships from Portugal, Spain, Brittany, Normandy, The Netherlands, England, Ireland and Scandinavia swelled the fishing fleets to considerable numbers. In 1517, 150 French fishing vessels were observed in Newfoundland waters. By 1578, it is recorded that 330 ships fished in American waters annually, with the catch totalling "16,000 tonnes burthen."[1]

Through the 1500s, voyagers sailed up and down the New England coast, and it was during this period that Maine's Monhegan Island became probably the most important settlement in New England. As a safe offshore port, it was always passed and frequently visited by the European explorers. Samoset, who learned English and later met the Pilgrims at Plymouth, knew many of these earlier explorers because of his position as an Abenaki sagamore living on Monhegan Island. Through Samoset and other strategically placed individuals, the New England Indians became informed of the white man's activities. Between 1501 and 1614, no less than seventy New England Indians, on at least ten occasions, were captured and taken to Europe, more or less equally distributed between England, France, Portugal and The Netherlands. Many of them died of infectious diseases, but several returned to America.

Through these encounters the Europeans had their first exposure to Native American spirituality. They became familiar with Indians' reverence for the sun, moon and stars by 1524, as pointed out in Chapter 2, a practice many considered idolatrous, and learned that Abenaki meant Aurora Borealis. At Secotan in South Virginia (present-day North Carolina), they saw the Indians revere anthropomorphic posts, also considered idolatrous. At least one of the captive Indians taken to Europe in 1605, named Maneddo, was a shaman. In Maine, in 1608, an English leader who got on well with one Indian community was killed by "magic" by the shaman of a neighboring hostile tribe.[2] But European understanding of Indian religious beliefs and practices remained slim even when, in the seventeenth century, religious conversion became an element of the official policy of colonial expansion.

The Europeans found a native people who saw themselves as part of the whole of nature, without special privilege, and who treated the animate and inanimate objects about them as equals, all having supernatural aspects, called *manitou*. Life and death were part of a continuum, and the only religious hierarchy was shamanism, a tradition whose origins were lost in the dim recesses of the past. Moral codes were based on practical experiences and codified in unwritten tradition. Many individuals took on a vocation in which they ritually died and were reborn to serve as healers and visionaries.

The religious faith of the Christian European immigrants in America contrasted with that of the Native Americans with whom they came in contact. Organized Christianity compelled its adherents to attempt to convert and to subdue, which led to usurpation of the land and suppression of native religion. On the other side, the Indian animistic religion was capable of absorbing all others into its broad concept, so the idea of persuading others to accept a particular doctrine or belief played no part. Therefore, the Indians reacted to Christianity by absorbing parts of it into their old ways rather than by rejecting those ways and converting. Occasionally, individual Europeans, either because the process of conversion of the Indians required it, or through curiosity, observed and recorded those Indian ways.

What are the remains of ancient Americans that tell us of their spiritual life? Europeans have written of their observations of rock paintings, carved images, stone mounds and other curious structures of earth and stone, charm stones and other shamans' paraphernalia. Historical Indians have reported the ceremonies and described the vision quests and the spirits which inhabit all things in nature. We will look now at some of those sources.

The Jesuit Missions of Eastern Canada

In New France, eastern Canada, the message of Christianity was brought to several thousand Indians between 1608 and 1760 by a few Jesuit missionaries who respected the Indian ways far more than any other missionaries. They were "perhaps the best friends the Native Americans ever had among the Europeans," and wrote copiously of their work in America, describing the religious life of the Indians with an authenticity unequalled by any other European settlers.

Father Francois DuCreux, S. J. (1581–1646), was the official historian of the Canadian mission. He never visited America, and was censored by the Jesuit hierarchy, but at times he wrote with considerable perception.[3] The Algonquian word *manitou*, and the Huron word *okki*, according to DuCreux, were used for both good and evil spirits. When the Indians encountered any unusual object, such as a pebble of unusual shape or a piece of pottery in an unusual setting, they recognized it as an *okki* or *manitou*, a thing with supernatural power. Certain objects, called *aasconandi*, were charms that could change their shapes. All diseases were attributed to a spirit called the wife of manitou; shamans were called *aoutmoins*. DuCreux also recognized the use of many Indian words for what seemed to him to be the same thing, but which to the Indians were not. Unlike Puritan missionaries, he appears to have grasped the breadth of the animism manifested by these perceptions and beliefs. He concluded that the Indian belief in spirits which go toward the sunset was equivalent to his belief in immortality of the soul.

Father Joseph Lafitau, S. J. (1681–1746), lived in a Mohawk village of his mission at Sault St. Louis outside Montreal from 1712 to 1717. The village was named Caughnawaga, meaning "at the rapids," and was recognized by the colonists of New York and New England, as well as by the native people, as the main settlement of "French Praying Indians." But there was a difference between these Mohawks and the inhabitants of the praying Indian villages of Massachusetts. The Caughnawaga Indians were neither forced nor encouraged to live entirely like Europeans. Lafitau sought only to save souls, not to take the Indian lands and force them into an alien mode of living. His writings probably represent the most objective contemporary account of the Indians of northeastern North America at this period.

Lafitau compared what he observed among the Indians of North America with what he had read of the customs of European classical antiquity, a comparison that gave a structure and a frame of reference to his work. In making his investigations of Indian life, Lafitau walked a fine line, exercising caution not to antagonize his Jesuit brothers by seeming to condone native beliefs, while being careful not to arouse suspicion among the Indians by taking too much interest in their culture. By respecting the native ways, he learned much about them.

Lafitau believed that "God had inscribed the elementary truths of natural religion on the hearts of all men," but that ignorance had enveloped these truths in idolatry and magic.[4] The religion of the Indians was then, to him, one of decay. However, he was also open to rational argument when his observations did not fit the orthodox theory and agreed with an astute observation of Lahontan, whom he considered an atheist: "The Indian listens to the Jesuits without contradiction or dispute but is not, therefore, converted."[5]

Lafitau recognized the sun as a universal symbol of the divinity in all European mythologies, and therefore found it not surprising that the sun was also the divinity of all American peoples. He observed that, in addition to the primal being which they identified with the sun, they had "all kinds of spirits" of an inferior order, called *okki* or *manitou*, that were more inclined to do evil than good, and were never confused with the primal being. For example, the Hurons believed that an eclipse of the moon was caused by a demon or dragon eating it.[6]

In Florida, Father DeRochfort observed that among the Apalachee a mountain was consecrated to the sun and had a spiral path cut in solid rock winding from base to summit. On the east side near the top was a natural cave serving as a temple, where four times a year, at the seasons of two sowings and two harvests, the tribe celebrated festivals in honor of the sun. Lafitau commented on the similarity of this anecdote to tales of solar ceremonies all over the world, an elementary practice based on universal need, independent of direct communication among peoples.

The eastern orientation of sacred monuments and temples in America was compared by Lafitau with the practice of placing the altar of ancient churches toward the east. He also observed that fire had always had a religious aspect and that the Indians' burning of the land was no exception. In the question of sacrifices as an act of religion, Lafitau considered it a universal custom for people to sacrifice their most valuable possessions. The small sacrifice to the sun of tobacco and such were consistent given the material poverty of the people. He even felt that the punishment, torture and death endured by captives and prisoners were probably a form of sacrifice.

Lafitau saw that idolatry among the Indians used the same sorts of symbols that are universal among people all over the world, including: heaped up stones, cubic, pyramidal or conic cut and uncut stones, the hermes or divinities of wood and stone (godstones), sacred trees and woods, mountains and high places, anointed stones and idols, anointed stone seats, and sacred posts. That Lafitau observed all of these symbols in northeastern North America and recognized them as part of Indian religion conforms to our observations today and identifies him as the first recorder of these indicators of a way of life whose implications have been largely ignored for nearly 300 years.

Shamanism

Some valuable insight into the Indian shamanic tradition can be found in the earlier observations of Jesuit missionaries dating from 1625 to 1640. According to Father Le Jeune, the Hurons assigned three causes to disease. There were naturally caused diseases requiring natural remedies, sicknesses in the mind cured by realizing desires, and sicknesses caused by poisons from the wickedness of magicians which required expelling from the body the object to which the magic adhered.[7] Le Jeune believed that the healers were cunning and subtle, endowed with a second sight like soothsayers. He thought that they could penetrate with their minds the innermost recesses of the heart of the sufferer and so discern the secret desire which must be realized to effect a cure. They had revelations from an *okki*, which appeared to them as an eagle or deer. The Canadian Indians complained that mortality had increased greatly among their people since the earliest European contact. They attributed this to unholy charms and poisons, including baptism, brought by the Europeans.

Both Fathers Le Jeune and Brébeuf describe their competitions with shamans, but each came to a different conclusion. Le Jeune and the diviner Mestigoit lived together in a lodge and contested for four months. Mestigoit had a dream in which he said that he saw Le Jeune wasted and worn out in the woods, unable to go on. Le Jeune, suspecting that this was but a trick, produced a more optimistic dream of his own, in which the people escaped famine. Le Jeune explained to Mestigoit that when body and mind are at rest, the objects that appear in dreams are connected with the thoughts or events of the day. By expressing this Western view, he inadvertently mocked the shaman, who reacted by behaving like a madman. Le Jeune was afraid he would be killed, but he nevertheless remained passive. The two competed every day in this fashion for four months, until Mestigoit left the lodge to go hunting. Afterward, Le Jeune became seriously ill, but recovered, while Mestigoit died horribly, and "the Indians recognized that it came from God."

In Brébeuf's experience, he prevented a shaman from removing a cross in order to bring rain. Brébeuf, however, allowed the red cross to be painted white. When the change of color did not bring rain, the cross was painted red again, with an image of Christ on it for good measure. The next day it rained.

Brébeuf's contest with a shaman appears to have been superficial, but Le Jeune's account has the ring of authenticity, except perhaps for the outcome. It is similar to reports of contests between shamans, each exerting his spiritual power to overcome the other, and both drawing their powers from similar sources as the result of similar training. These anecdotes, clearly slanted to portray a Christian victory, were published by DuCreux.[8]

Father Christian LeClerq, who went to Canada in 1675 and became historian of the missions to the Gaspé Peninsula, believed, contrary to DuCreux, that shamans were truly in league with the devil and not mere tricksters. Shamans could make trees appear all on fire without being consumed, and they could supposedly kill men fifty leagues distant by burying a knife in the ground. They also healed by chasing out the devil causing the illness. One devil, *tchongis*, would remain in the body of a sick man after death, so that mourners had to cut up the body and take out the devil.[9] LeClerq observed that the natives had no temples, priests or sacrifices but was impressed by their worship of the sun, which they saluted at every sunrise and sunset. The Indians, furthermore, counted years by winters, months by moons, days by nights, and hours in proportion to the sun's height in the sky. They regulated their calendar by various observations of nature, such as the behavior of animals and plants in response to the seasons.

Lafitau concluded that shamans and sorcerers, though they may have had the same abilities, which came from communication with spirits, differed in the motives of their actions. He saw the shamans as people favored by spirits, more enlightened than most and favoring the public good. They could explain dreams, heal, and foresee the future. The Indians had another class of remarkable persons who were akin to sorcerers and witches. There were many of them, and they did only harm, casting spells or curses. The shamans used charms which were usually in themselves but ordinary things, but which through supernatural power could work miracles. Using charms, the shamans went into states of ecstasy and were no longer themselves. They responded to signals from potions, divining wands, and the sounds of cymbals. In these states, they could do bizarre things, including burning or piercing themselves without permanent effect. Anecdotes of clairvoyant episodes are common. The Algonquins and Abenaki professed Christianity even though they still made fire from piles of pulverized cedar wood and prophesied by the direction the fire ran.[10]

LeClerq recorded a curious story of the Miramicho Indians of the Gaspé Peninsula. Their tradition held that a man appeared to them in a dream holding a cross in his hand and told them to make crosses, which would be the remedy for all their ills. The natives, who believed in dreams, took heed and in their council resolved to always wear the cross and to undertake nothing without it. Crosses can still be found in the vicinity of their burial places, sometimes interred with burials, and have been found also at the banks of rivers. Some of these have double or triple cross pieces. When Father Emanuel Juneau arrived in 1682, only a remnant of the cross custom remained among the Miramichos, but it was easily revived by the Jesuits, who naturally associated the crosses with Christianity. However, a very old man reported that the cross and its use had not been brought by strangers, but rather by tradition that came from his ancestors. LeClerq was convinced that the cross had been held in veneration long before the first arrival of the French, and had nothing to do with Christianity. In fact, he reported that the cross-bearers, as they were called, were particularly resistant to conversion or the acceptance of Christianity. He states that this is perhaps the reason why the Jesuit fathers eventually abandoned the Gaspesian Indians and went to the headwaters of the Saint Lawrence River. This was in spite of "the fact that the Gaspesians were the most docile of all the Indians of New France and most susceptible to the instruction of Christianity." LeClerq went so far as to write, referring to all the missions of New France, that even though the missionaries had labored greatly for the conversion of the Indians, there was no solidly established Christianity among the natives.[11]

Lafitau described initiation into the sacred mysteries as again a universal practice, which he observed among the Iroquois. The Iroquois, like the Huron and Algonquin, began the rites of initiation at puberty:

The initiates retreat into the woods, youths under a shaman's direction, young girls under a matron. During this time, they fast and pay careful attention to their dreams and report them exactly to those in charge of them. The elders examine dreams to determine what they should take for their Oiaron or Manitou on whom their future happiness depends.[12]

This *oiaron* was the initiate's personal medicine or familiar guardian, revealed in a mysterious dream after a period of sleeplessness and long fasting. It was the essence of his personal desires or needs detached from the senses and material things. By means of the *oiaron*, he could transform himself, transport himself and do what he pleased. In addition, the initiate became attached to a spirit, called *otkon* by the Iroquois, *okki* by the Huron, *manitou* by the Algonquins, and symbolized by some material object which brought him good luck or otherwise affected his life. This object was held as dear as life itself. If it was an inanimate, permanent object such as a stone, life would be long, but if it was an animal, the initiate might die when the animal died. He could not choose what the soul would attach to, and in this way the dream could have bizarre effects.

Now and then an individual withdrew alone to a little cabin apart from others and fasted for a week or ten days. However, Brébeuf recognized that by his time (early 1600s) the Indians had already lost many of their religious customs and abandoned much of their retreats and fasts.[13] After such initiations and trials, the soul was admitted to intimate communication with the gods, who manifested themselves in dreams or contemplation or in theurgy and divination.

The Huron feast of dreams or desires occurred at winter solstice, a date recorded frequently, as we have pointed out, by astronomical alignments of stone structures in New England. It was called *onnonhouarori* in Mohawk, meaning madness or turning of the head. All the people went into a sort of frenzy and cried their dreams aloud. He who guessed another's dream had to gratify the dreamer's desire. Lafitau compared this with some of the festivals of classical Greece and Rome which can be traced to the earliest times.[14]

Archaeology and Ritual in Eastern Canada

Archaeologists in Canada have considered the spiritual life of the Indians and associated the stone structures with the vision quest. In 1958, J. N. Emerson found some enigmatic stone structures on the shores of Lake Superior on raised beaches of some antiquity. There were rectangular structures with walls, rectangular floors, stone-lined pits which later came to be called Puckasaw pits, circular pits, circular floors, crescent-shaped structures, cairns and post-holes. From the archaeological context, he concluded that some of the structures were 3,500 years old, but their purpose was baffling. Because of lack of cultural material identifying the sites as settlements, he suggested that they were places for vision seeking, which was general among Woodland Indians such as the Ojibway and Cree. The desolate site was suitable for this purpose because it was an area of stone beaches, wild winds, thrashing waves and fog. It was a place of isolation.

Some years later, William Noble found groups of cairns and stone-lined pits like Emerson's Puckasaw pits on the shores of Rock Lake in Algonquin Provincial Park in Ontario. One group contained forty-two rock cairns on a hilltop overlooking the lake. He studied these structures and concluded that they were part of the vision quest ritual of Algonquian-speaking Indians. The mounds are thought to represent successful visions.[15]

The First Plymouth Settlers

The Pilgrims who founded Plymouth Colony in 1620 could be called Puritans since they were part of the Puritan movement that had swept England, but unlike those Puritans who later settled Massachusetts Bay, they were Separatists who had seceded from the established church and organized their own. Hence they were outcasts and refugees. Except for a few of their leaders, they were from humble stations in life, and William Bradford, who spoke for them, gave the impression that they were, as a group, gentle, tolerant, and merciful. However, other shiploads of settlers soon followed the *Mayflower* to Plymouth, and among these were many picked by the English businessmen who sponsored the early voyages. They were probably more interested in wealth than in the simple faith of the Pilgrims.

There was a diversity of religious views among the early settlers and divisive economic and political forces at work which affected relations with the Indians. An important example is the story of Thomas Morton, an English lawyer and not a Separatist or Puritan, who went to New England in 1622 at the advanced age of 50 as a member of Weston's abortive fur-trading partnership at Wessagusset in present-day Quincy, Massachusetts. In 1625, Morton and Captain Wollaston brought over thirty bonded servants to start a plantation and fur-trading post two miles north of Wessagusset at Passonagessit, the former home of Chickatawbut, sachem of the Massachusetts, whose people had been almost wiped out by the plague of the previous decade. Morton got on well with the Indians, including Chickatawbut, who lived nearby; he probably spoke their language, admired their humanity, wrote extensively about their ways, was a successful fur trader, and drew to his hilltop settlement others who were like-minded. Morton wrote that the Plymouth Separatists defaced a monument over Chickatawbut's mother's grave because they saw the monument as a superstitious idol.[16]

On 1 May 1627, a gigantic Maypole, an eighty-foot cut pine tree with buck's horns nailed to the top, was erected, with the help of Indians, at Morton's plantation, which he called Ma-re Mount, because of its grand view of the sea. May Day was celebrated with revels and merriment "after the Old English Custome," and the Plymouth Separatists reacted promptly. Miles Standish and his troops marched the twenty-eight miles to Ma-re Mount, cut down the pole, arrested Morton and shipped him back to England. Returning in 1629, he again erected the Maypole and was again sent back to England, this time by the Boston Puritans. Back in England, he allied himself with the Royalists and attempted to have the Massachusetts Bay Colony Royal Charter revoked. Bradford countered by accusing Morton of selling guns and alcohol to the Indians, and thereby endangering the English community, but Salisbury thinks that the few guns that passed into Indian hands during this period could not have posed a threat to the English.[17] It is more likely that Morton's success in fur trading raised the competitive ire of the other English settlers and that the Maypole served merely as an excuse to harass him. His writings provide a non-Puritan viewpoint tending to balance the interpretations of Bradford, Winslow and other Pilgrim and Puritan leaders which have become the official history of the Plymouth Colony.

The erection of a Maypole and the accompanying pagan festival in seventeenth-century New England was not confined to Ma-re Mount, nor was the incident there the first. In the spring of 1622, Weston's party reached the Damariscove Islands off Maine, where they saw a Maypole set up by English fishermen. In sixteenth- and seventeenth-century England, May Day was definitely a living pagan festival frequently officiated by English monarchs.

Seamen, who were particularly known for their observance of the May festival, probably erected many Maypoles along the coast of New England which, with the ceremonies, were correctly perceived by the Indians as evidence of religious beliefs similar to their own. The Maypole in England probably represented the world tree which supports the universe like the Norse Yggdrasil. Holy trees or poles figure in the myths of many widely separated peoples, including Native Americans, and were part of their perception of immanent divinity or spiritual quality in all natural phenomena. The fertility rites which were part of the May Day festivities represented a renewal of life that was compatible with the Christianity of the ordinary English folk who went to America.[18] Some of the *Mayflower* colonists were farmers from the English countryside, where ancient pagan customs had been absorbed into the religious life. They were likely to have been familiar with, and tolerant of, such practices as solstice, equinox and May Day festivals.

The Pilgrims may have intentionally chosen, for their own protection, one of these festival days for the first landing at Plymouth. They had been prepared to expect not only hostile natives on American shores but also unspeakable cruelties if they were captured.[19] Accordingly, they expected the worst from the natives upon landing. However, they also knew from previous explorers something of the customs of the natives, which very likely included the dates and practices of the important festivals, such as the Algonquin feast of dreams on the winter solstice. In 1620 the winter solstice occurred on December 11 of the Julian calendar then used by the English, or on December 21 of our Gregorian calendar. This was the date that a group of the Pilgrim leaders first landed in the *Mayflower*'s shallop at Plymouth, and it may have been chosen because the natives were expected to be gathered at their sacred places celebrating the winter solstice feast of dreams festival and therefore less likely to threaten the landing. The pilot of the expedition, Robert Coppin, may have known about the festival because he stated that he had been in Plymouth harbor before and accurately described its location relative to Provincetown.[20]

The Pilgrim journals lend support to this theory. The expedition which resulted in the Plymouth landing was planned to scout along the shore of Cape Cod Bay from Provincetown to Plymouth. The shallop started out from Eastham on the morning of Friday, December 8, and, missing Barnstable Harbor, the only navigable harbor along the route, had to sail the full forty-five miles to Plymouth in one day. Once there, the company seems to have dallied unaccountably at Clarke's Island in Plymouth Bay, perhaps in order to land at Plymouth on Monday, the solstice. They are reported to have scouted the island on Saturday, rested on the Sabbath, and sounded Plymouth Harbor and landed there on Monday. The reference to a Sabbath-day rest is unusual and therefore suspect, as it was the only such journal notation made during the five weeks that the *Mayflower* spent in Provincetown.[21]

Having raised this question, we examined the records more carefully and were led to a suspicion that much historically important information was omitted from or lies hidden within the Pilgrim records. The eye-witness accounts of the stout-hearted English settlers of Plymouth contain but superficial descriptions of the Indian ways and nothing directly about their festival days based on solar, lunar and stellar events, which previous explorers had mentioned on much briefer acquaintance with the Indians. Nor does Bradford mention the pagan practices of English country folk, even in criticizing Thomas Morton's May Day festivities. These omissions may have been made on purpose because of the Pilgrim leaders' strong aversion to ceremony and idolatry.

By being alert to historical observations of the solstices and equinoxes, the dates of events during the first year of the Plymouth Colony became clues to Bradford's and Winslow's hidden message. *Mourt's Relation*, the earliest journal of the Pilgrims (1622), which was not intended for publication and therefore presumably more candid than later revisions, reveals that the Pilgrims not only landed on the winter solstice but also appear to have been consistently and strongly guided by solar events in all of their relations with Indians. Taking *Mourt* as authoritative, we found that eight of the reported nine principal episodes involving contact with Indians can be connected with solar events. Five of these occurred precisely on the days of solstices or equinoxes, and three others occurred shortly after an equinox.[22]

In addition, Squanto, who spoke English and was the sole remaining survivor of the Indian inhabitants of Plymouth before the Pilgrims, and who had been taken to Europe, sold into slavery, and rescued by Spanish monks, participated in all five journeys after his appearance at Plymouth on March 22, 1620 (Old Style). This pattern of connections between the Pilgrims' activities, solar events, and Indian contacts implies that the Pilgrims knew about and respected, probably from fear but perhaps also from understanding, the importance of solar events in the lives of the Indians. Squanto not only guided the Pilgrims over the land and acted as interpreter, but also probably organized the journeys and planned the dates.

The Indians of southeastern Massachusetts had been mistreated by English and probably French ship captains and were therefore distrustful of the Pilgrims. An incident was made known to the Pilgrims a short time after their arrival which brought this home:

> The Indians, before they came to the English to make friendship with them, they got all the powaws in the country, who, for three days together, in a horrid and devilish manner did curse and execrate them with their conjurations, which assembly and service they held in a dark and dismal swamp.

Squanto, nevertheless, was apparently responsible for arranging the peace between the Pilgrims and Indians that was ratified during Massasoit's visit on March 22, 1620 (Old Style).[23]

The Pilgrims reported that they found no Indians living within fourteen miles of the Plymouth settlement because they had all been killed by the plague.[24] But the sacred places remained and would have continued to be used by Indians whether or not they lived in the vicinity. They can still be found today near the settlement. There are at least three known donation boulders, called sacrifice rocks, on which branches were piled as donations, along the Old Sandwich Road south of New Plymouth opposite Telegraph Hill and Morey's Hole (Figure 6–1).[25] In the region of Manomet Hill, there are large marked boulders, traditionally Indian sacred places, that signal alignments to solstice solar horizon events. Two miles east of the Plymouth settlement, along Beaver Dam Brook, but separated from it now by a stand of Atlantic white cedar trees, there is an array of stone rows one boulder high connecting larger boulders on a hillside,

6–1 Sacrifice Rock, Old Sandwich Road, Plymouth, Mass.

some of which have stone mounds on top of them. This linear array stands in the midst of a group of stone mounds.[26] At the edge of the brook are more stone mounds, one of which is made of fist-sized pebbles and contains a collection of intact and broken nineteenth-century patent medicine bottles. Upon inspection, they were found to have contained alcohol, and some narcotics as well. According to Speck, such bottles were traditionally donated by Indians to the earth and placed respectfully in pits.[27] In Chapter 11, we cite additional discoveries of donated alcohol bottles within stone structures, which suggests strongly that the stone mound by Beaver Dam Brook is an Indian donation mound to which both stones and bottles have been donated. We believe that the stonework on the hillside above it is Indian ritual landscape architecture.

The Puritans

The Puritans who founded the colony at Salem in 1628 were religious non-conformists, but, as non-Separatists, they were not exiles. They disapproved of the Separatist Pilgrims and had no scruples about their own connection with the Church of England, despite objecting to certain teachings of the Book of Common Prayer and certain rituals which resembled the Church of Rome. They did found the Congregational Church as distinct from the Church of England in America, the latter becoming the Protestant Episcopal Church.[28] Supporters of Cromwell in the English civil war of 1640 to 1646, the Puritans were vigorous, enterprising and powerful. They were educated and of the upper middle class, and brought their considerable means to found a new England in America. Relative to the privations undergone by the Pilgrims, the Puritans lived in comfortable circumstances.

The Puritans transplanted their culture to the new land, building white wooden village meetinghouses that are related to the natural landscape in ways which contrast with the stone structures. Even in their early, simple form without spires, the meetinghouses, center of each town's civic and religious life, crowned the hilltops, attempting to dominate rather than blend with the landscape. In 1630, John Cotton preached to colonists about to sail for America that they need not buy the land nor ask permission to use it of anyone but God, their landlord. This message guided the Puritans in the new land.

During the first few decades of European settlement in New England, the Native Americans and the new settlers shared the country in a more or less peaceful, if uneasy, coexistence. The natives, secure in their homeland environment and traditions, tolerated the visitors from across the ocean. The immigrants, in turn, depended upon the natives' help for their survival. By 1644, the balance of power favored the colonists. The Puritans had increased in number and had appropriated lands to the extent that there were rumors of native rebellion. To maintain their prominence, the Europeans drew up treaties with several sachems of the Massachusetts and Nipmuck people. These stipulated that the natives would accept English Christianity and practice its rituals. The colonists justified this treaty provision by their view that the Indian religion, if it existed at all, was satanic and that it was God's will that the English colony survive and prosper. These imperatives in turn demanded the conversion and subjugation of the Indians. Some individual Puritans, chief among them Roger Williams, held different views about the natives, but they were outside the mainstream and were either exiled or harassed.

To achieve their ends, the Puritan colonies set out to destroy the power of the Indian religious leaders, who were said to be in league with the Devil. This is evidenced by the numerous places in New England named, by the Puritans, after the Devil, places which invariably turn out to be sites where Indian ritual was practiced. However, the natives continued to respect the powwows after their "conversion" to Christianity. Conversion is hardly the correct word, since the Indians saw the new ideas as another element in their holistic image of the cosmos. In cases where powwows and sachems objected to Christianity, it was because of its threat of collecting tribute, not its religious doctrines.

John Eliot and the Praying Indian Villages

Against this background, the young minister from Roxbury, John Eliot, again enters our story. Sometime in the 1630s, Eliot set out on what was to become his life work, the Christianization of the Indians.[29] His mission was eventually supported by the Society for Propagating the Gospel Among the Natives of New England, a corporation funded from England, first set up in 1649 and reorganized as The New England Company in 1662, to support the instruction of the natives in what was perceived as the "proper worship of God." The Corporation was the brainchild of Edward Winslow, one of the original members of the 1620 Pilgrim company and governor of the Plymouth Colony, who was most likely inspired by John Thorowgood's 1646 book suggesting that the Indians originated from one of the lost tribes of Israel, citing the similarity of Indian and Jewish rites, knowledge of the flood, circumcision, dancing, etc. In the view of Winslow and others, "If they be Jewes, they must not be neglected." The Jesuit Lafitau, writing in 1724, had considered but rejected the Jewish theory of Indian origins. Eliot may have supported this hypothesis, because he organized the praying villages following Moses' management of the Israelites in the wilderness. Also, he wrote in a brief discourse for the second edition (1660) of Thorowgood's *Jewes in America*:

> Truly the Bible says that the Ark landed on the eastward of the land of Eden, and if so, then surely into America, because that is part of the Western World. Hence why ought we not to believe a portion of the ten tribes landed in America.

Governor Winslow went to England in 1647 armed with Thorowgood's lost tribe theory, his personal knowledge of Eliot, and Eliot's manuscript describing his first four meetings with the Indians, which Winslow edited for publication immediately upon reaching London. During the printing and distribution phase, he briefed many of his influential friends, including many in Parliament. By the time Eliot's pamphlet, "The Day-Breaking, if not the Sun Rising of the Gospel with the Indians in New England," was on the shelves of bookstores, Winslow had already set the stage for its enthusiastic reception. A second pamphlet three months later entitled "The Clear Sun-Shine of the Gospel Breaking Fourth Upon the Indians in New England" was endorsed with the signatures of many officers of the clergy and government. It included a letter from Eliot stating that "the Indians have utterly forsaken their powwows," though this was more propaganda than actuality.

Winslow, in his dedicatory letter to Parliament, argued that Eliot's mission should be supported because of the possibility that the Indians were the descendants of one of the lost tribes of Israel. In July of 1649, Cromwell's Parliament passed Winslow's bill, providing for a corporation of sixteen persons with authority to collect money, acquire property, and make investments. Collections were made door-to-door in every parish of England and Wales, and in the first year 12,000 pounds were raised. The money was used for schools, clothes, tools and books for the Indians, and for the salaries of Eliot and his native assistants. It also, after 1654, supported the Mayhew mission on Martha's Vineyard.

The Indians took charge of Eliot's mission from the start. In our view, the event that was crucial was the invitation to Eliot from one of the Indian leaders, Waban of Nonantum, to come to speak to the Indians about Christianity. Nonantum, meaning place of rejoicing, was a highland spot east of the present day Newton, Massachusetts. On the eighteenth of October, 1646, Eliot delivered his first sermon to the natives at Nonantum, and there the idea of the praying villages first appears in the record. The circumstances of this event bear scrutiny because they helped establish the nature of Eliot's later work. Waban, whose name meant wind, was a highly respected member of the Nonantum group and was a beaver trader, a special interest that may have led to his invitation to Eliot. Also, Eliot appears to have been especially respectful to Waban by carefully choosing the text of his first sermon from Ezekiel 37:9: "Prophesy unto the wind, prophesy, son of man, and say to the wind, Thus saith the Lord God; Come from the four winds, O breath, and breathe upon these slain, that they may live." The group that assembled at this first meeting included influential Indians from some distance, among them Waban's wife Tassansquaw, Tahatawan of Nashoba and Tahatawan's daughter Rainbow. Daniel Gookin and Cockenoe, Eliot's interpreter, were probably among the three companions of Eliot.

Inspired by his success, Reverend Eliot next wanted to gather a group of Indians into a well-governed, Christianized town, hoping that if the first one were successful there would be many others. He set out to find a proper location but couldn't find one that suited him. On returning from a search one day, accompanied by a group of Indians, he stepped behind a rock and asked God's advice. Then, the Indians told him of a place at a bend in the Charles River, which pleased Eliot, and it became the location of the first praying village, Natick, founded in 1651.[30]

The Natick praying village was operated solely by Indians for over a century, and its history provides us with a great deal of information about the native peoples of New England. The first structure built there was a bridge across the Charles River, engineered and constructed entirely by the natives, and built in part of stone. The bridge was said to have survived the great flood of 1691, while many English-engineered bridges did not.[31]

Natick was a very sacred place to the Indians. The name means the place of seeking, a place that would have been rich in manitou and suited for the practice of the vision quest ritual and the dances that accompany it. An isolated island adjacent to Martha's Vineyard had the same name as early as 1642. The ritual of seeking is well established all over the world among hunting and gathering peoples, and the places where it is practiced are the domains of shamans, or in New England, the powwows. By his invitation to Eliot, Waban initiated the Christianizing of the Indians on their own terms. Thus, it is likely that the Indians' choice of Natick's location resulted from a policy decision by the Indian leaders and probably set the mold for the praying villages that followed. In other words, the Indian powwows chose the places and conditions and set the rules that guided Eliot in his mission.

The ritualized landscape that is the signature of a vision quest domain is found at all of the praying villages, and we believe it was an established architectural form long before the coming of the Western Europeans. All of these special places contain interacting elements, both man-made stone structures and natural landscape features, which we have described in every chapter of this book. The idea of ritualizing landscape is not new. An ingenious theory holds that the Greek gods Apollo and Zeus were nature spirits connected with special places in the natural landscape. Prehistoric stylized temples were developed at these locations by the erection of standing stones and other stone structures.[32]

The Indians participated in their newly acquired Christian rituals on the Sabbath. Gookin wrote that the Indians were assembled on the Sabbath by the beating of a drum and that "bells they yet have not." He was quite wrong, of course, for the Indians had been accustomed to bells in their ritual dances long before the coming of the white man. The Indians, groomed and dressed in an English manner, assembled to the beating of a drum like most other New England churchgoers, because church bells were scarce in the English New World at this time. In a church at Norwalk, Connecticut, the change from drums to bells took place in 1665; there drums were also used to announce the annual time for fence repair.[33] After the worshippers gathered, the Indian preacher intoned a solemn and affectionate prayer. Next, a chapter would be read from the Old or New

Testament, followed by the singing of a psalm. Then the preacher would catechize, pray and deliver a sermon. The ceremony concluded with a prayer, the reciting of a psalm and a blessing. During all of this, the praying Indians were described as pious and reverent.

From this description, it is very easy to suppose that the Indian practice of the Christian religion was like that of the colonists. The literature records that the Indian churchgoers behaved, from a Christian perspective, in an appropriate manner on the Sabbath. However, it should never be assumed from this that they behaved similarly at other times and places. By analogy, the early Christian history of Britain indicates that the Church of Rome was fooled by practitioners of the old earth religion.

From 1651 to 1658, seven praying villages were established through the apparent guidance of John Eliot and Daniel Gookin. In order of their founding, they were Natick, Punkapoag (Blue Hill), Hassanamessit (Grafton), Ockoocangansett (Marlborough), Wamesit (Lowell), Nashoba (Littleton), and Hakunkokoag (Hopkinton).

Marlborough was one of the earliest towns, and from the start was set up as two villages, one an Indian praying town, called Ockoocangansett, and the other for Europeans, called Whipsuppenkke. The smaller Indian town of 6,000 acres, laid out in 1654, was nearly surrounded by the larger English town of 29,000 acres. The Indians who lived here in 1643 were branches of two tribes from some distance away, the Naticks from the east, and the Wamesits from present-day Lowell on the Merrimack River to the north. Daniel Gookin wrote that the Indians of Ockoocangansett had extensive cornfields and apple orchards and that there was considerable conflict over land ownership between the English and the Indians. An Indian planting field, in their section of town, was located on a hilltop which the English coveted for their meetinghouse. Gookin reports that the Indians fenced in their fields here but, because of "their improvidence and bad fences," the English livestock trampled their fields and their crops did not prosper.[34] But these may have been ritual stone rows, not fences, and Eliot may have sensed it because he wrote that there were hypocrites among the Indians of this village who professed Christianity but yet kept to the old religion.

Eliot's fifth praying village, on the Merrimack River at Wamesit, was surrounded by a semicircular ditch, both ends of which terminated on the riverbank. Gookin tells us that these villagers were more difficult to Christianize than those at Ockoocangansett: "Of these strange Indians divers are vitious and wicked men and women, which Satan makes use of to obstruct the propriety of religion here." The Wamesits are also reported to have asked Eliot, "What is the image of God which it is forbidden in the second commandment to worship?" If Eliot answered, the record is lost, but in other chapters we report the discovery of what we believe to have been the images under question, called godstones by those who knew about them. Even today, they remain abundant but unrecognized in New England, after centuries during which they were at first suppressed and then forgotten.

The apparent success of the first seven praying villages led Eliot to establish a second group of seven which he called the new praying towns. They were mostly in the Nipmuck country of central Massachusetts. The majority of the praying villages had very small populations, usually only forty-five to sixty persons representing nine to twelve families or several extended families. Eventually, six more praying village were set up, bringing the total to twenty. The people were described as able, genteel, ingenious, modest, prudent and useful.

During the Second Puritan War of 1675–76, Eliot continued to receive support from England for his praying villages, even though he was harassed in the colonies for unpatriotic activities. Many of the English settlers considered Eliot's Indian "converts" to be "preying Indians." Two of the newly settled English towns adjacent to praying villages were said to have been burned by the praying Indians of Ockoocangansett and Nashoba.[35] Many English thought that the Indians of the Nipmuck praying villages had sided with Metacom, the great Wampanoag chieftain and warrior.

Metacom, known to the colonists as King Philip, was the second son of Massasoit and had assumed the leadership of the Wampanoags in 1662 at the age of twenty-four. He was of striking appearance and character and is described as an eloquent statesman. His goal was to form an alliance of all the New England tribes, including the Mohawks of New York, in order to oust the white man from the land.

The many burnings of English villages in Massachusetts during the war caused great consternation among the settlers, and on 30 August 1675 all except five of the praying villages were shut down. In these, Natick, Punkapoag, Nashoba, Wamesit and Hassanamessit, Indians were confined to the village limits on penalty of death.[36] Then Puritan vigilante groups formed, who, distrustful of the praying Indians under the protection of the Commonwealth, forcibly gathered the natives and interned them on Deer Island in Boston Harbor. During the course of the war, about 500 people from the praying villages were forced onto Deer Island, where many died from exposure and starvation during the most severe winter on record. After the war, a number of the survivors were sold into slavery and others returned to their old homes, but most went to Natick, the first praying village.

The sacrifice of the praying Indians on Deer Island generated a reaction that was felt in Western Europe among those who had participated in the popular support for Eliot's mission. Part of the role of the New England Company was to announce to the world its Christianizing and organizational achievements among the Indians, so news of the Deer Island tragedy as the climax of the Company's work met with great dismay among its European supporters. This may have provided part of the spiritual stimulus that caused the birth of new religious groups in Europe and New England during the religious revival of the early eighteenth century.

Eliot's mission, which had seemed so successful at first, was ended by the Second Puritan War and probably had no lasting effect on the Indians. Even though he had the advantage of a highly organized religion behind his dedicated and prodigious efforts, and realized to a certain extent the difficulty of the problem, he could not overcome the Indians' ancient communion with their natural environment. While he held that the Indians must be civilized in order that they be Christianized, he realized that one season of hunting would undo all his missionary work.[37]

Most of the writings of seventeenth-century clergymen, including John Eliot, show little interest in the religion of the Indians, but the Connecticut Blue Laws of 1678 betray their knowledge that, among some colonists at least, there was dangerous curiosity:

> Whereas notice is taken of some people that doe frequent the meetings of the Indians at their meetings, and dances, and doe also joyne with them in their plays . . . if not encourage them in their Divill worship, for some, acquainted with their customs, doe say their exercises at such times, is a principal part of the worship they attend: for the prevention whereof this court dow forbid all persons in this colony from contenancing the Indians in such meetings, by being present there, upon the penalty of 40 shillings for every breach of this order.[38]

This underground particpation of "some people" in Indian religious ritual continued into the nineteenth century and influenced the Puritans and other religious groups.

Martha's Vineyard

The people of Martha's Vineyard, Nantucket and the Elizabeth Islands off Cape Cod have always led an insular life which has kept them apart from the nearby mainland. During the first fifty years of their English colonial settlement, 1641–1691, the islands were part of the colony of New York, and they are today separate counties of Massachusetts. They do, however, share a common geology and maritime aspect with the Cape, and a tradition of peace between the Indians and the colonists, even through the later seventeenth century when the rest of New England saw much conflict and violence.

The first Puritan religious mission to the Indians of New England, started by Thomas Mayhew, Jr., offers unique insight into the relationship between the Indians and colonists on Martha's Vineyard. Thomas Mayhew and his son, Thomas Jr., emigrated from England in 1631. Thomas Sr. soon became active in the business and political life of the Massachusetts colony. In financial troubles in 1641, he bought for forty pounds the right "to plant and inhabit upon Nantucket and the two other small Islands adjacent." Shortly, the right was expanded to include Martha's Vineyard and the Elizabeth Islands. The purchase, or patent, obtained from the agents of King Charles I and confirmed by the agent of Sir Ferdinand Gorges, who also had a claim, gave proprietorship to Thomas Mayhew and his son jointly. This gave them the exclusive right to purchase land from the Indians. At that time, the Mayhews saw the purchase as a somewhat risky but potentially rewarding adventure in land acquisition, which they accepted in the hope that they could gradually obtain the land from the Indians who occupied it. They dreamt of an island feudal estate, after the English pattern, a dream which was eventually realized. A Christian mission to the Indians, led by the younger Mayhew, was seen as a necessary step toward fulfillment of their dream. Unlike John Eliot, who was an ordained Puritan minister and spent years preparing himself for his missionary task, Thomas Mayhew, Jr., aged 21, had no training or expressed inclination toward the profession of theology. Equipped with little but a flare for languages, which was also Eliot's forte, he undertook the leadership of a band of five Watertown, Massachusetts, adventurers who became the first recorded white settlers of Martha's Vineyard.[39]

In March 1641/42, when Thomas Jr. settled at Edgartown, there were about 3,000 Indians on the island. At first the small band of English settlers remained separate and aloof from the Indians. After a year, Hiacomes, an Indian who was looked upon by the sachems as of no account and ridiculed by his tribe, showed signs of friendliness and the colonists reciprocated. Young Mayhew became acquainted with Hiacomes, quickly learned the Algonquian tongue, and persuaded him to accept the Christian faith.

Through 1643 and 1644, Hiacomes and Mayhew worked as a team, persuading individual Indians of eastern Martha's Vineyard to accept Christianity. In 1645, there was a plague among the Indians, and those who had listened to Mayhew's Christian counsel fared better than others. This proved a great boon to the mission, so that by 1646, the year Thomas Mayhew, Sr., settled on the island, his son was well established and giving regular weekday lectures to the Indians, while Hiacomes preached on the Sabbath.

The letters of the younger Mayhew reveal a humble and pragmatic man, dedicated to the spiritual and material well-being of the Indians, whatever colonial aspirations he harbored. Like the clergymen who followed in his footsteps on the island, he was a combination of clergyman, physician and lawyer, because for many decades it was difficult to attract people of these professions to the insular life. We suppose that the Indians saw these individuals' roles in society as comparable to those of their powwows, or shamans. One of his earliest extant letters about the Indians, dated 1647, describes his success in faith healing; in fact, except for the usual pro forma pious phrases of seventeenth-century correspondence, it is devoted entirely to the matter of healing. It appears to us that he saw that the way to gain the confidence and respect of the Indians, and so further the settlement by the English, was to compete with the powwows, as they competed with one another, as healers, and he had some success.

In 1649, an Indian who had been sent by one of the greatest powwows to spy at the Christian meetings was persuaded by Mayhew to accept Christianity. In 1650, Hiacomes openly challenged the power of the powwows, who threatened his destruction but were unable to hurt him. Shortly afterward, two powwows asked Mayhew if they might accept Christianity. Their confessions, reported by Mayhew, are remarkable documents, unique in New England historical literature. They seem to have been profoundly convinced of their sins of pow-wowing and to have rejected them and their spirits dramatically. By 1652, a total of ten powwows on Martha's Vineyard had accepted Christianity and some felt their spirits struggling for years afterward.[40] Another powwow who accepted the new faith was Tequanomin, "of great esteem and very notorious." He was the powwow of the isolated island south of Martha's Vineyard named Noman's Land, probably after him. By 1702, Noman's Land Indians were mostly Sabbatarian Baptists.

Nowhere else in colonial history do we find such vivid descriptions of, or indeed acknowledgement of, conversion of such large numbers of shamans. Its uniqueness makes it suspect. This dramatic confession and acceptance of Christianity by the powwows may not have been a simplistic replacement of an old religion by a new one, as Mayhew's writings have been interpreted. More likely, it was an example of the ritual death and rebirth that is part of shamanistic tradition throughout the world in which the shaman's power is increased, not destroyed. In this case, the shamans probably absorbed part of Christianity into their cosmology, thereby strengthening their spiritual power.

The powwows or shamans were keepers of sacred knowledge as well as teachers, doctors, visionaries and, on occasion, diviners. A shaman was trained to change his perception of his own environment and of himself, as well as that of others around him. This was done through tonal, rhythmical and other practices which probably produce electrical and chemical changes in the body. In most shamanistic cultures, the shamans are perceived as doers of good, and witches and sorcerers are different individuals. Mayhew apparently saw all shamans as agents of the devil. When they sought visions of Hobomock, they were perceived as seeking the devil. Shamanism is a cultural hierarchy, not a religion. In spite of the reported dramatic "conversions" of the shamans and a large part of the Indian population, there is no reason to believe that the Indians' religion, which attributed spiritual qualities to all things, was substantially changed by the Mayhews' missionary efforts.

Many Vineyard legends of the dim past filled with animistic allusions survive to this day. The Indian legend of the giant Moshup dominates the mythology of the islands. Before the sea rose to surround the land that is Martha's Vineyard, Moshup dragged one of his feet heavily across the marshy ground between the island and the mainland, and the track which was formed was filled by the ocean. It widened and deepened during the course of time, eventually forming what is now Vineyard Sound. According to legend, Devil's Bridge, the rocky reef off Gay Head, is a remnant of a great bridge of stones built by Moshup from Gay Head to the Elizabeth Island of Cuttyhunk. It is tempting to consider these legends as stemming from a Jungian collective unconscious reflecting a time seven to eight thousand years ago when the rapidly rising sea level caused Martha's Vineyard to become an island.

6–2 The Quitsa Dolmen,
Martha's Vineyard

On Martha's Vineyard, works of stone are attributed by tradition to Indians or to other non-English colonists. There is a well-known structure called the Quitsa Cromlech or Dolmen, the European terms being used because some people think that it is of European origin (Figure 6–2). While this theory is possible, the name can be misleading because the structure is connected architecturally with stone rows having embrasures, spirit-of-the-creator stones and other site features which we ascribe to Indians. The Quitsa structure itself is a stone chamber set into a hillside, which may have been earth-covered as are most New England stone chambers. The walls are made with three boulders about three feet high with a short connecting length of wall built with similar stones. It is capped by a single large stone slab split from a nearby boulder. One or two people can sit comfortably inside, and the entrance faces true south. The construction used mostly large natural boulders rather than built-up smaller boulders or quarried rock, as in most stone chambers, probably because the large boulders were near at hand upon the terminal moraine and there is no near-surface bedrock about. The basic elements of the design are similar to many New England stone chambers.

Tradition states unequivocally that the miles of stone walls which fence the Vineyard farms and estates of today were built for the colonists by Indians who were paid with rum for their labors. We cited similar traditional tales on mainland Cape Cod, which because of their consistently pejorative character may not be the whole truth. The tradition on Martha's Vineyard adds an Indian custom of building stone fences with boulders placed so that there were air spaces between them through which the wind could blow (Figure 6–3). Many of these can be seen during even a casual tour of the island today. This can hardly be a practical colonial specification for stone fences, and it is a construction that would result if boulders were deliberately carried and piled one at a time rather than selected from a handy stone boat full of rocks. It is most likely an Indian tradition with prehistoric roots, related to respect for the spirits of the place, the stones and the wind.

6–3 Stone row with spaces between the boulders, Martha's Vineyard

By the time of Mayhew's death in 1657, the number of Indian conversions had reached several hundred. After he was lost at sea on a trip to England in 1657, the Indians commemorated his place in their lives with a traditional stone mound, upon which each passerby placed donation stones for many decades. They loved Mayhew and accepted his religion, but they didn't necessarily thereby give up their own. Thomas Jr. was succeeded in the Indian mission by his father, who observed about 1660 that the Gay Head Indians had "obstinately refused" to accept Christianity and, alone among the island's regional groups, continued to carry on their "heathen rites." After Thomas Sr. came several unrelated clergymen, and three more generations of Mayhews, Thomas Jr.'s son John (1652–1688), his grandson Experience (1673–1758) and his great-grandson Zachariah (1718–1806).

Religion among the English on the island did not remain dominantly Puritan for very long, even though it was the church of the Mayhews. Thomas Mayhew, Sr., who ruled the island from 1646 to his death in 1682, decreed that religion and government among the Indians were to be separate, a curious notion for a Puritan, but, of course, it applied to the Indians only, as a necessary expediency. The Vineyard settlers were actually diverse in their religious beliefs from the beginning, and there were many landed settlers who did not attend a church. Baptists established an early foothold on the island, and most Christian Indians eventually adopted this faith.

Thomas Mayhew, Jr.'s mission on Martha's Vineyard and John Eliot's praying villages of mainland New England were similar in two particulars. The missionaries thought that they had converted the Indian culture into a Puritan society, whereas they had not. Also, both missions took place on the fringes of the colonies as part of the process of colonial expansion. Eliot's praying villages, while located at places of the Indians' choice, were administered according to rules laid down by Eliot and Gookin, and few Indians were actually converted or even accepted the new religion. The Second Puritan War caused the whole scheme to collapse. On Martha's Vineyard Thomas Mayhew, Jr., was far more successful than Eliot. He was aided by an insular situation, adopted the shaman's power to heal and set up a family dynasty of missionaries which was not interrupted by the war. His success was not in overpowering the shamans or in complete conversion from one religion to another, but in contributing to a peaceful transition in the inevitable process of destruction of the Indian culture by the English.

The praying Indians, who ultimately numbered several hundred on the Vineyard, were gathered in about five congregations over the island. Great Point on Chappaquiddick Island, where there was a praying congregation, was originally an island called Natick, meaning place of seeking, which was also the name of the first of John Eliot's later praying villages. In both cases, sites were probably places of the vision quest, chosen by the powwows. There were no praying towns on the Vineyard comparable to Eliot's where the Indians were governed and encouraged to live like the English. Christiantown, a one-mile-square plot in Tisbury, was set off in 1659 by the sachem Josias, who never accepted Christianity, for the use of the four Christian Indians in his sachemship, one of them his uncle. They were to pay the sachem 20 shillings a year tribute. This enterprise, which may have started as a family squabble, was eventually ratified by the Mayhews, and the place became a refuge for Indians in later years. The Indian name of Christiantown was Manitouwattootan, "God's town" in a loose English translation. More likely the name means that the English God was classified as a manitou, one of many spirits. There was a ceremonial dance place called "dancing field," a level plateau northeast of Indian Hill. Another place of praying Indian congregation was called Nashamoiess, akin to Eliot's Nashoba, meaning "he is of the spirit."

Thomas Mayhew, Jr., while primarily engaged in missionizing the Indians of eastern Martha's Vineyard, managed to buy from the Indians large tracts of land in the western part of the island, uninhabited by English. This apparently unexplained venture came to fruition fourteen years after his death, when, in 1671, his father and older brother Matthew, who had also bought large tracts, approached Francis Lovelace, the royal governor representing Charles II in New York, with a proposition. As a result, the western half of Martha's Vineyard, owned by the Mayhews, became the only English manor in New England. Thomas Sr. and Matthew were designated hereditary Lords of the Manor, with title and lands to go with their heirs in perpetuity. Thomas had his long-held dream of a feudal estate, with tenant Indians paying him tribute. To separate the manor from the ordinary folks, it was partially enclosed by a fence, which on Martha's Vineyard at that time meant a ditch. After his father's death, Matthew, less impressed by titles than his father, sold the manor to the governor of New York. In 1711, the manor was bought by the Society for the Propagation of the Gospel as a means of keeping the Christian Indians on the island from reverting to idolatry.

By the mid-1800s, religion on Martha's Vineyard had come full circle when

Methodist camp meetings gathered thousands of people on the island. Their "love feasts" and "parting" ritual included dancing in processions and nocturnal revels on the shore. A brother announced that he had seen John Wesley in a vision and conversed with him. Numbers of the faithful lost all strength and lay for hours without the power to speak or move. Ecstatic experiences of this nature, found among many other Christian groups as well, are fundamentally shamanistic, the direct communication with spirits, which the Puritans so vehemently fought.

The history of religion on Martha's Vineyard since 1642 is one of gradual Indian adoption of a Christian spirit into their native animism, some modification of the roles of individual shamans, but continued respect for nature and the practice of ritual landscape architecture. The European settlers experienced a mixture of changing and liberalized Christianity, real estate grabs, and peaceful relations with and a measure of respect for the Indians not commonly found in New England.

The Quakers

Religion in New England among the English immigrants began to change soon after the first settlements, partly following changes in Europe but also in response to the challenges of life in a frontier land. The first major change was the arrival of the Quakers or members of the Society of Friends, who were inspired by an inner light which superseded, in their view, the scriptural orthodoxy of the Puritans. They also questioned the divine right of the King of England, represented in America by colonial governors.

The persecution of Quakers by the Puritans of the Massachusetts Bay Colony began in 1656, immediately upon the arrival in Boston from England of Ann Austin and Mary Fisher, the first Quakers in America. The early Quakers were given to speaking out during Puritan services and openly questioning the authority of the ministers, which was seen as a criminal act. As a result of persecution, many Quakers went to the more tolerant Plymouth Colony, but even there laws prevented Quakers from being admitted as freemen. In 1657, two Quakers landed on Martha's Vineyard Island to missionize the Indians and were promptly sent packing to the mainland of Cape Cod by Thomas Mayhew, Jr. The Indians were cordial but assured the Quakers that they already had a missionary whom they liked. Their rejection may not have been on theological grounds, but related more to competition for land. The Quakers, Christopher Holden and John Copeland, were accepted in Sandwich by a group of dissenters from the state church and within one year had eighteen families professing Quakerism.[41]

Quakerism bypassed the governmental spiritual teachers. The Puritans, to whom church and state were one, saw the Quaker disrespect for the magistrate on religious grounds as civil disobedience. That Puritans Richard Bourne and Thomas Mayhew, Jr., the leading Christian missionaries on the Cape and islands, participated in the persecution of the Quakers is not surprising, in view of their lack of tolerance of Anabaptists or any other sect. Conversion of the Indians was seen as the means for their political subjection to the English colonists, and confusing the issue with other Christian sects did not suit this objective.

Official persecution of Quakers was abolished in 1661 by a King's order, but in practice it continued for decades. In spite of the persecution, which was considerably less on the Cape than in the Massachusetts Bay Colony, Quakers settled Cape Cod towns aggressively, buying land from the Indians. The early Quakers posed a real economic threat to the Puritans, for in addition to their settlement of Cape Cod, they proceeded to buy up much of the islands as well. Circumstances show that Quakers got on well with Indians whenever they met. The Quakers spoke plainly and did not defer to men of authority, a rather Indian-like manner which may have contributed to their good relations. Relations between the Indians and Quakers of Cape Cod were so congenial by 1675 that they did not participate in the Second Puritan War.

We have read early accounts of Quakers who went into the wilds and lived with the Indians, only to find that they wrote about their own spiritual revelations and omitted the Indians entirely. However, the preservation of some Cape Cod stone structures may be due to the friendship between Quakers and Indians. In Brewster, there is a brook from which alewives and herring were taken by the Indians from precolonial times and by English colonists as well. It is fed by two ponds which lie in what was once the domain of the seventeenth-century sachem Sachemas, who made a long career of selling property in small lots, much of it to Quakers. His home site is unrecorded but may well have been on the last piece of property he sold, which abuts the ponds and contains a group of curious straight, single-course rows of boulders with intermittent groups of standing stones. Some of these have notably avoided becoming land boundaries in centuries succeeding Sachemas' time. In Figure 6–4, we show the rows on this site which

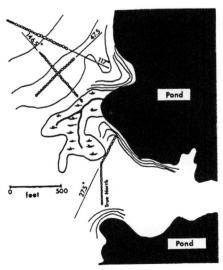

6–4 Stone rows between ponds, Brewster, Mass.

6–5a Row of standing stones
at end of boulder row,
Brewster, Mass.

connect bodies of water. One ends with a particularly spectacular row of standing stones ending with a large Indian grindstone (Figure 6–5) located precariously on the top of the steep bank of the pond, as if this place, though awkward to use, was important, perhaps for ritual.

6–5b Indian corn-grinding
boulder at end
of boulder row,
Brewster, Mass.

Though they did aggravate the Puritans, the Quakers were tolerant of many other faiths, particularly the Indian religion, which also recognized individual revelation. Whether or not they acted purposefully, due to their influence the Americanized versions of Christianity became more tolerant of the Indian religion and subtly took on some of its attributes. We suspect that the first instances of significant influence by Native American spirituality upon the Christianity of the European settlers took place on Cape Cod in the late seventeenth century among the Quakers. Later, other groups throughout New England were slowly affected, an aspect of Indian-European interaction that we follow up in the next two chapters.

Conflict and Confederation on the Western Frontier

Western New England and the Hudson River Valley were the scene of much turmoil throughout most of the seventeenth century, since this was the frontier where the territorial ambitions of the French, the Dutch, the English New York Colony and the Puritan United Colonies of New England (Massachusetts Bay, Plymouth, Hartford and New Haven) came into direct confrontation. In furthering their interests, all of these colonies also routinely armed both sides in Indian conflicts. The New Englanders not only tried to invade Dutch New Netherlands, but also, being Puritans and not friends of either Charles I or Charles II, planned to invade English New York. The French and English alternately fought and made peace with each other and with the Indians of the region, primarily the Mohawks, one of the five nations of the Iroquois Confederacy, and the Mahicans, a confederacy of Algonquian-speaking tribes that included the Mohegans of Connecticut.

Francis Jennings describes a "covenant chain confederation" of Indian tribes and English colonies during this period, with the Iroquois at its heart. The chain, which Jennings sees as a political institution created by treaties, intrigues and other maneuvering, expedited the English colonization of northeastern North America, and reduced the amount of violence. As distinct from creeping conquest by distant imperial powers, it was a series of pragmatic, local arrangements which balanced the interests of the conflicting parties and was quite removed from the myths of kingly divinity, racial superiority, natural law, sovereignty and the like, which other writers have invoked as the driving forces of colonization.[42]

Jennings' perception is important to our story because it shows that conflict between Indians and colonists based on differences in religion, racial prejudice, cultural origins, etc., was not inevitable and in many situations did not occur. It justifies our belief that seventeenth-century colonists, most of whom were not members of the Puritan church, and the Indians treated each other as the practical circumstances of their time and place dictated. It also shows that although the actions of historical figures have frequently been excused on the grounds that they conformed to the supposed norms of their times, those norms may not have existed.

As a result of the pressures from the European colonies, the Native Americans' tribal identities, intertribal relations, social customs and religious practices were greatly disrupted. The Mahicans were the hardest hit in this region, first squeezed to the east by the Mohawks, Dutch and New York English, and then to the west by the Puritans.

By 1660, the New England Puritans, planning for the conquest of the Hudson Valley, supplied the Mahicans and the Mohawks with arms to fight each other. In 1663, praying Indians from eastern Massachusetts were armed by the Christian mission supervisors and unsuccessfully attacked the Mohawks. We presume that John Eliot and Daniel Gookin at least knew of this adventure.

In 1664, while the Hudson Valley was still Dutch, the English further incited New England Indians against the Mohawks and tried to instigate a general uprising of the Indians of New Netherlands to coincide with an English invasion from Massachusetts. This invasion took the form of a show of force at Albany which caused the Dutch and the Mohawks to make peace with the English. New Netherlands became New York, "granted" by Charles II to his brother, James, Duke of York, who later became the unpopular James II. This action effectively squelched the Puritan invasion of the Hudson Valley but did little to change the political situation except to make it more awkward for the Puritans. Their competitor for the territory merely changed from the Dutch to the Duke of York, whom they could not attack with impunity.

In 1666, under orders from Louis XIV of France to exterminate the Iroquois, French troops from Canada burned Mohawk villages. In 1670, French Canada and British New York cooperated, during a temporary treaty between the sovereigns, to suppress the long-standing feud between the Mohawks and Mahicans.[43]

In 1676, New York's Edmund Andros, who as royal governor was more subservient to his king than were the New England Puritans, armed the Mohawks. They attacked Metacom and his allies the Mohegans in southern New England and had considerable influence on the course of the Second Puritan War. Simultaneously, a fugitive band of 200 Narragansetts fled to Stockbridge where they were slaughtered by Puritans guided by a Mohegan. The Puritans wanted to exterminate the defeated Indians but Andros did not. Andros and the Mohawks, as part of the covenant chain, permitted a sanctuary to be set up at Schaghticoke on the northern frontier of New York just north of Troy, on the fringe of the Mahican traditional lands. Indians from all over New England, including Mohegans, Narragansetts and some western Abenakis, lived together here, joined in 1685 by Mahicans from Canada, and remained neutral in the conflicts between the English and French. After the English revolution of 1688 and accession of William and Mary to the throne of England, Andros was arrested by the rebel

Massachusetts Puritans and shipped to England, only to be returned to America as governor of Virginia.[44]

The Schaghticoke Indians sent out little colonies to the Housatonic Valley, one of which, made up of Mahicans and Narragansetts, was located south of Monument Mountain in Great Barrington or Sheffield. It was named Scatekook and was headed by the powwow Umpachene. We shall meet this group again in the next chapter.

7

The Eighteenth Century

Except for the insight of a few individuals, the colonial records show little appreciation for the Indian concept of manitou, the interrelationship of humanity and nature, spirit and matter, individual and cosmos. The religion of the North American Indians is not easily explained in the English language. To start with, the English word "religion" has no counterpart in Indian speech, because the spiritual life of the Indians is inseparable from all other aspects of life. Speech and words are not symbols of ideas to the Indian but are the ideas themselves. The sounds and the act of breathing which produces them are related to the source of breathing in the body and the person's spiritual center. Thus, a word or even an unspoken thought has a potency or power of its own which, when evoked in a ritual context, is enhanced. Similarly, the process by which material things, such as houses, utensils, decorative arts, etc., are created, is imbued with sacred powers.

When Christianity was presented to Indians, they were able to understand the message and the example of those who presented it because their own beliefs were so all-encompassing. They accepted Christianity into their own religion without giving up anything; hence they were not converted, only changed by a new experience. Few, if any, colonists understood this aspect of "conversion." However, the themes of native religion are now and then reflected in New England philosophies and historical records, and the views of some individuals have a quality, usually subtle, that implies understanding. Such an individual was Ezra Stiles.

The Gentle Puritan

Ezra Stiles (1727–1795) was a colonial clergyman and President of Yale College from 1777 to 1795. He left what are probably the most important English records of Native American ritual life in New England, in fragmentary notes of his travels, meetings, and thoughts, in his sermons, in his large international correspondence, and in one book. He lived at a time of religious ferment among the Protestant churches of New England, and he wrote candidly of his religious life. His writings have been of much interest to historians for the broad insight they provide into many aspects of ordinary eighteenth-century life, even though Stiles was an uncommon man.

We were introduced to Stiles by filmmaker Ted Timreck and archaeologist William N. Goetzmann, who told us of Stiles' curious interest in Indians, his religious tolerance and doubts, and his references to a number of Indian stone gods. These gods sparked our interest because we had seen many shaped stones that we thought may have been the New England equivalent of Hopi spirit stones at places we considered sacred to Indians. We decided that we must get to know Ezra Stiles.

Stiles was one of very few people of his time to have recorded stone structures known to be of Indian origin, and his writings are the original source for a number of references to Indian stonework that are not corroborated by other observers. For this reason, he has been accused of gullibility in reporting the stories of informants, but his biography shows him to have been a remarkably precise observer and recorder of a great variety of natural phenomena. He was a respected astronomer and meteorologist who lectured on these subjects at Yale College and who kept throughout his adult life a record of air temperatures that is invaluable today in reconstructing past climate. He recorded the two transits of Venus across the sun's disc that occurred during his lifetime. Benjamin Franklin was a close friend, and Stiles used Franklin's equipment to demonstrate electricity at Yale. We came to the conclusion that Stiles was a reliable and acute observer whose reports of stone structures had been neglected by scholars simply because, as may be the case for our own observations, they conflicted with orthodox theory of these structures.

Stiles was a minister of the Congregational (Puritan) Church for most of his adult life, but his tolerance of other faiths was most unusual for his day.[1] He wrote,

> It has been a principle with me for 35 years past to walk and live in a decent, civil, and respectful communication with all, although in some of our sentiments, in philosophy, religion and politics of diametrically opposite opinion; hence I can freely live and converse in civil friendship with Jews, Romanists, and all the sects of the Protestants, and even with Deists. I am all along blamed by bigots for this liberality. I have my own judgment and do not conceal it.[2]

Shortly after graduating from Yale College in 1746, Ezra, having broadened his perceptions by a deep interest in astronomy, entered what has been called his "period of doubt," from 1747 to 1754. He wrote later about this critical period in his life:

> In the years 1747 and 1748, I had not indeed a disbelief, but I was in a state of skepticism, and ardently sought a clear belief in the being and attributes of God. In conversation with Mr. —— raised scruples and doubts about Revelation which has cost me many a painful hour.[3]

Stiles suffered severe mental difficulties in the fight between his intellectual and spiritual inclinations, and his activities during this period reflect his uncertainty. Nevertheless, in 1749 he took an M. A. at Yale and was licensed to preach. In 1750, he preached a few times to the Stockbridge, Massachusetts, Indians, discussed later in this chapter, and was invited to take charge of the mission there, an offer he declined because he feared that his heretical religious views would be discovered in the examination required for the post. He then gave up the ministry, studied law, and was admitted to the bar in 1753, after which he practiced law for two years in New Haven. Almost all of this critical time from 1749 to 1755 he tutored at Yale.[4] The ministry and law were the only means of livelihood open to an intellectual of his time, and he tried both.

As he settled into his job as a tutor at Yale in 1749, he discovered that he had a tendency to Arminianism, a protest movement growing out of Dutch Calvinism imported to New England, which taught that people could do good works on their own without divine guidance. Stiles decided that by good works he could not only ward off hellfire but ascend to Heaven. This was a rejection of Calvinism, both in the form of his Old Light heritage and the New Light. Old Light preached that sinners were dependent upon Christ and that the first step toward a moral, Christian life was a rational recognition of their sinfulness. The New Light advocated the possibility of sudden and dramatic conversion to Jesus Christ as savior.

In fact, Stiles went beyond Arminianism. He saw that a system of ethics could be arrived at by reason and observation without divine inspiration, and quite independent of the Scriptures. He had arrived at Deism, then a popular underground theology at Yale. Deists accepted God as the creator of the world and the final judge, but regarded him as detached and making no revelation; reason, the light of nature, was humanity's only reliance. Deists, who included George Washington, Thomas Jefferson, Benjamin Franklin and Tom Paine, saw their ideas as a natural, universal religion with roots in mankind's primitive unspoiled simplicity.[5] Stiles was for a time a Deist but eventually accepted revelation while remaining tolerant of the alternatives. Deism was importantly different from Indian religion, and grew from Western science's concept of nature. On a supernatural level the Deist believes that God, being apart from the world, performs no miracles, while the Indian believes that supernatural power exists in everything, thereby combining the rational and the supernatural without the anthropocentricity characteristic of Western religions. Nevertheless, Stiles might have made the jump from Deism to Indian religion, and in so doing would have found himself in a very difficult position, a position he could not communicate or accept and remain within his society. He may have chosen the doctrine of revelation through the Scriptures in order to survive.

Stiles was in the midst of the religious ferment of 1733 to 1760, which was a result of the changing social conditions and environment in America. People saw, many for the first time, that they had a choice, and the differing churches asked them to choose. Also, they reacted to the evil and gloomy picture of the times painted by Puritans with deserted congregations, like Cotton Mather in 1701. What the Indians made of this ferment amid the attempts to convert them to Christianity we cannot tell, but Mather had already pointed out the Puritan failure to convert the Indians. While condemning Muslims, Quakers, Socinians, and papists as pawns of the Devil, he reported that they shamed the Puritans in winning Indians.[6]

By 1755, Ezra Stiles had sufficiently resolved his religious doubts to accept the position of pastor of the Second Congregational Church in Newport, Rhode Island, where he stayed for twenty-two years. It is not clear if he ever acquired positive knowledge that the Scriptures were of divine origin, and he continued to give his doubts away in sermons that presented rational arguments for the authority of Scripture, answering questions which a true believer would never raise.

After Stiles settled in Newport, he began taking the ferry across the bay to visit the Indian villages, where he made a census and drawings of the wigwams and their internal arrangements. He read about the Indians in the books of his time and copied from old letters and manuscripts. He also asked friends, especially missionaries in the western part of the country, to collect information for him. He asked about the numbers of Indians to be found, whether or not the powwows were hereditary, and if they used idols. He was keenly interested in their language and whether or not they recorded events by the use of written characters. In fact, so keen was his interest in the Indians that on the day of his ordination in Newport, that solemn ceremony when his beloved father preached Old Light Christianity with fervor and love for his most prominent child, Ezra found time to discuss Mohegan stone idols with Deacon Avery of Groton.

Stiles was skeptical of the widespread reports of the Indians' acquiescence to English religious views, illustrated by this example:

> New England Indians, upon the accession of the English were soon ashamed of their old religion, or rather finding it ridiculed by us and and considered idolatrous, that they concealed much from us.[7]

But at the same time that Stiles sought understanding of Indian ways, he preached at Newport, 13 June 1773, against divination and necromancy among the Indians.

Powaws of the American Indians are a relict of this antient system of seeking to an evil, invisible power. — Something of it subsists among some
almanach makers and fortune tellers. — When the system was entire, it was a
direct seeking to Satan, and the Indians avow their powaws to be to this day
tho no Powaw now exists in New England.[8]

Stiles observed objects and ways of the Indians which have either been ignored
or treated less comprehensively by later writers, although this may be attributable
to nothing more than his customary thoroughness. Morgan states that if Stiles
had written his proposed book on New England religion, he would have devoted
a large part to the Indians' beliefs and tribal ceremonies. Yet reference to Indian
religion in his extant writings is confined to scattered accounts, some perceptive
enough to leave us wondering if Stiles knew more about the subject than the
record shows and if some of his writings on this subject were destroyed. Yale College
in the eighteenth century was a seat of Deism, a fact that caused Stiles' successor
as president, Timothy Dwight, to claim that Stiles had taken Yale to the depths
of depravity. Dwight held views very much at variance with Stiles, and he felt
compelled to "clean up" Yale. In so doing, he could have destroyed some of
Stiles' more provocative writings, and a number of pages of Stiles' papers, which
from the context concerned Dwight, were obviously removed by someone while
they were in Dwight's custody.[9]

Stiles may have learned much about Indian religion in the course of his studies
and, in view of the breadth of religious views which he tolerated and considered
and his knowledge of astronomy, he could indeed have grasped the essential feature of Native American religion, a holistic view of nature, of which man is but a
part. This essential truth is in part a rational cosmology based on keen observation of nature and realization of man's dependence upon the natural environment.

In Stiles we have a man who was one of the most learned, sensitive, and
liberal of his time and place, and who also was keenly interested in New England
Indians, observing artifacts and ways that his contemporaries and successors did
not notice. Yet there is no direct evidence that he considered incorporating
any part of Indian religion in his religion, even in his Deistic period when he had
rejected Christianity. His interest seems to have been mainly anthropological,
lacking compassion or acceptance of Indians. Nevertheless, Stiles left important
records of specific godstones and places of Indian ritual and, in spite of the
objective evidence, we sense through subtle hints throughout his papers that
there is more to the story than we know.

Stiles saw about twenty Indian worked stones which he called stone gods or
godstones and considered to be idols. In some cases, he described the physical
surroundings or other circumstances of the finding of the stones. One, about
three feet high by one-half to one foot thick and carved to give a human appearance, was found in East Hartford in 1755, standing in the ground, during land
clearing. It was given to Yale College, where presumably it is stored gathering
dust in an obscure cellar to this day; a picture was published by Squier in 1849

7–1 Sketch of godstone found in East Hartford, Conn., given to Yale College by Ezra Stiles (after E. G. Squier, "Aboriginal Monuments of the State of New York," *Smithsonian Contributions to Knowledge* 2, 1849)

(Figure 7–1). Some godstones were found in stone fences, as are many that we have observed. In the Great Awakening of 1741, the Indians, who had previously concealed their godstones from the white men, brought and gave up to the English a number of stone and wooden idols. In 1755, Stiles reported that Pockatunnek, an Indian of Groton, Massachusetts, said that the Mohegan Indians once had idols.[10]

Stiles also wrote about several Indian forts of earthen bank or stone. His description of the palisaded village in the great swamp of Kingston, Rhode Island, is the basic reference for this well-known site.[11] He described stone mounds and large boulders on which Indians cast stones or pieces of wood as donations. He was acquainted with Hobomock swamps which had traditions that the devil came out of them. According to Stiles, Hobomock meant devil in the East Haven Indian language. He further reported an impression that manitou was an evil spirit that needed to be propitiated, as contrasted with a good spirit that was quite inaccessible. This narrow view of manitou was probably a specific observation, not to be taken generally.

Stiles reported an interview of a Mataguissawack Indian, Josephus (1718–1799), by Colonel Thomas Goldthwaite, which reveals wide travels over North America to be customary among the Indians at that time. Josephus lived northwest of Lake Superior, forty days journey from the Penobscots of the Maine coast.

In 1795, Stiles published his only book, *A History of Three of The Judges of King Charles I*, a curious subject considering his career and interests. It is the story, which he researched assiduously for many years, of the lives in America of three of Oliver Cromwell's top military leaders who had participated in the condemnation and execution of Charles I and were known as the regicides. When the monarchy was restored in England in 1660, Major Generals Whalley and William Goffe, Colonel Dixwell and Goffe's wife, who was Whalley's daughter, escaped to America and lived their lives hiding from British spies sent to capture them. Goffe outlived all the others, dying in 1690. Apparently he had been in line to succeed Oliver Cromwell, who died in 1658, which probably explains why the royal avengers hunted him for thirty years.

Many Americans were sympathetic to the Judges' plight, particularly Puritan ministers, who harbored them. Stiles wrote in great detail about the hiding places in Connecticut where the Judges lived, and it is evident from his writings that he believed that these places were, for the most part, Indian sacred places. His curiosity about this matter seems to us to have exceeded that about the Judges themselves, of whom he was ostensibly writing. We believe that he has described stone chambers and their settings and provided rare documentary evidence of seventeenth-century ritual use by Connecticut Indians.

Among those who helped the Judges was Daniel Gookin, a lifelong friend of William Goffe, who was also, as we discussed in Chapter 6, a cofounder with John Eliot of the praying villages. We suspect that Stiles' obsession with the story of the regicides was due to what he learned about Indians from it. The Judges remained in Cambridge, Massachusetts, for a time and then were guided by Indians to New Haven, where they hid in a series of caves and laid-up stone shelters. The story of these hiding places intrigued Stiles. It is perhaps significant that he was the first to write about the Indian aspect of the story a century after the events, at a time when liberal criticism of religion was in vogue.

The first place of hiding was a probably natural boulder cave of great monoliths, fifteen to twenty feet high, at the summit of West Rock in New Haven, Connecticut. Another site was a stone structure built with "stone wall" about eight by seven feet in plan, of which three feet of wall yet stood in 1795. It was partly dug into the side of a hill and dug deeper than the surrounding soil level. The Judges lived here for a time but abandoned it after discovery by Indian dogs.

Another refuge was a cave built up against a rock ledge, ten by seven feet in plan. It was 100 feet from an Indian sacred spring and 800 feet from Deacon Peck's house. Stiles found an Indian godstone at the site. This third place of refuge was called the Lodge, at Spring Fort Rocks. It was a "place of Indian worship and powwowing in ancient and forgotten ages," a place where deer came to eat and drink at the small perennial spring between two trees that first grew at least as early as 1590.

For three and one-half years, the Judges hid in these and similar structures near New Haven. After this they found more permanent quarters in a cellar in Hadley, Massachusetts.

The Stockbridge Indians

Another attempt was made to Christianize the Indians at the colonial frontier, this time in southwestern New England during the New Light revival of the 1730s. The 1700s saw the introduction of liberal criticism of the Scriptures, rationalism, and tolerance into the Christian community.[12] Thinking Puritans experimented with many religious ideas and found themselves actually doubting the divinity of the Scriptures. Most Indians were bystanders to this process, but some were swept up in the fervor of the New Light as part of the continuing change that modified the old Indian ways and dimmed their knowledge of the stones and the landscape.

The Stockbridge experiment of western Massachusetts was politically an aid to colonial expansion in New England and further west. The Indians who participated also served as a friendly buffer against the French in the wars of the mid–eighteenth century. The importance to our work of this attempt at Indian Christianization lies not only in the extensive records of Indian religious life, but also in the evidence of communication between geographically widespread Indian groups. For this purpose, there were four phases of the Stockbridge story: the selection of sites, the establishment of towns, the gathering of Indians from elsewhere, and the dispersion throughout the continent of these Indians after the American Revolution.[13]

The Muh-he-ka-ne-ok, meaning "people of the continually flowing waters," were the focus of this missionary activity, carried out by Puritan clergymen. The name was shortened by the English to Mahican and by the Dutch to Mahikander. Also called the River Indians, these tribes lived east of the Hudson River in New York State and in extreme western Massachusetts and Connecticut. They were probably the root stock of the Mohegans who settled in Connecticut shortly before the Europeans arrived there. If so, the ways of the seventeenth-century Mohegans, discussed at length in Chapter 10, and their kin the Pequots were like those of the Mahicans before they were exposed to Christian missionaries.[14] Some of the Mahicans came to be known as the Stockbridge Indians after a town of that name was granted by the Massachusetts General Court in 1735 where Indians would live and be taught Christianity, the white man's ways and abstinence from strong drink.

In 1604 the Muh-he-ka-ne-ok Nation, before it fell victim to the white man's vice and disease, had, according to a nineteenth-century descendant, Waun-nau-con, alias John W. Quinney, stretched from Manhattan to Lake Champlain and numbered 25,000, including 4,000 warriors. About 1669, the Mahicans were subdued by Mohawk Iroquois and ceased to be an independent nation, becoming subservient to the extent that they sought prior approval for major community decisions from the Mohawk council at present-day Albany. In 1724, the Massachusetts Colony granted land for English settlement along the Housatonic River and paid the Indians 460 pounds, three barrels of cider, and thirty quarts of rum. Twenty-one Indians signed the deed. The once-large Indian population of the area had been decimated by disease and migration, so at the time of the Massachusetts grant, there were only two major Indian villages in the vicinity. One, headed by Umpachene, was Skatekook or Schaghticoke, meaning "where the small stream empties into the larger one and corn lands adjoin." It was located at the junction of the Housatonic and Green Rivers in present-day Great Barrington, and was reserved by the Indians in the deed. The other, headed by Konkapot, was called Wnahktukook and was located at the Great Meadow at the bend of the Housatonic River between present-day Stockbridge village and Monument Mountain. This was outside of the English land grant, and some Dutch settlers were already living in the area.

In 1734, a proposal for a mission to the River Indians was laid before the Board of Commissioners for Indian Affairs in Boston by Reverend Samuel Hopkins of West Springfield. There followed a visit by Hopkins and Reverend Steven Williams, and commissions in the colonial militia for the two Indian leaders, making them Captain Konkapot and Lieutenant Umpachene. The Indians agreed to receive a religious teacher, and John Sergeant, a graduate and tutor at Yale College, was employed in that capacity. Throughout the negotiations and for some time later, Jehoikim Van Valkenburgh, a Dutch settler living in Wnahktukook, served as interpreter between the English and Indians.

Timothy Woodbridge was also employed as teacher because John Sergeant was in residence but one-half of each year, the other half being spent at Yale. Woodbridge stayed on permanently and became increasingly influential. It appears, from his role as the General Court's agent, magistrate and broker in later land takings, that he represented the secular interests of the Massachusetts Colony. Woodbridge was also the great-grandson of John Eliot. His mother, Jemima, who lived with him at Stockbridge for many years, had been ten when Eliot died and presumably was much influenced by him.

Since the two towns to which Sergeant and Woodbridge ministered were eight miles apart, the villagers met at first halfway between and then later about one mile south of Monument Mountain.

A letter written 8 November 1735 from Wnahktukook tells of the ordination of John Sergeant before a large delegation of approving Indians. Afterward, Sergeant and the anonymous writer of the letter went south to Mahaiwe, "place downstream." They crossed a rugged mountain named Mas-wa-se-hi, meaning "nest standing upright," where a trail led by a curious mound on the south side of the peak.

> It is a pile of stones some 6 or 8 feet in diameter, circular at its base and raised in the form of an obtuse cone. It is raised over the grave of the first Sachem who died after they came into the region. Each Indian, as he goes by, adds a stone to the pile. Captain Konkapot tells me it marks the boundary of land agreed upon in a treaty with the Mohawks. . . . The Muheconnucks being entitled to have all the country for their hunting ground, within one day's journey in every direction from said pile. He also says that a chief was buried there, but the stone is added to keep distinct the monument.[15]

The mountain is today called Monument Mountain after the pile, shown in Figure 7–2. The southern peak, called Squaw Peak, is a precipitous pinnacle of pure Lower Cambrian quartzite rock, of toolmaking quality, which towers some 950 feet above the adjoining valley of the Housatonic River and marks the southern limit of the Green Mountains.[16] Near the stone mound are two lengths of

7-2 Stone pile at Monument Mountain,
Great Barrington, Mass.

7-3 Stone row leading to stone
pile on Monument Mountain

stone row which appear to serve no agricultural function, one leading directly to the mound (Figure 7-3). Even though this is a rocky area, there are very few other stone rows or walls. These two rows and earthworks that we have observed at the base of the mountain, combined with the oral tradition of spirituality, indicate to us that it is a sacred place. Near the summit, we have seen wooden sticks placed up against the openings of rock shelters in a way that indicates an Indian ritual presence today, following a practice common among Indians of southern California.[17]

Monument Mountain strikes us as a place with a tremendous amount of manitou, or spiritual power. This impression comes not so much from the historical record as from our observations of the land and sky. Quartz is known to have played an important role in Indian ritual, presumably because of its color, transluscence and piezoelectric properties, as well as its value in toolmaking. The talus slope on the east side of Monument Mountain has gigantic blocks of quartz which have broken away from the mountain, with large flutes flaked by percussion during the fall. If an earthquake were to shake this mountain, it surely would emit sparks and probably be luminous at night. A legend of a luminous mountain in the desert is preserved in Upper Volta, Africa, which probably refers to such an event.

The Stockbridge area has several north-south tending ridges which are appropriate for natural solar calendrical horizon markers. We explored one to the west of the Housatonic River. The summit was partly surrounded by an enclosure made of stone rows and earthworks, and a short row on the east slope directed the observer to a winter solstice sunrise in a prominent notch in the ridge to the southeast. In the valley between these ridges, we saw a pointed monolith, nine feet high with a cross-section three feet square, standing alone in a field (Figure 7–4); it could have been an observation point for an equinox sunset at a short stone horizon row on the hillside.

At one of Sergeant's first services at the mission, Konkapot and his family were baptized before a large assembly of Indians and whites, principally Dutchmen who lived in the Housatonic River valley. Unlike John Eliot's praying Indians, Konkapot took a vow, which said in part:

> I am convinced of the truth of the Christian religion and that it is the only way that leads to salvation and happiness. I therefore freely and heartily forsake heathenish darkness, and embrace the light of the Gospel and the way of holiness. . . .[18]

The vow continues in an eloquent style, obviously written by Sergeant. Since Konkapot did not speak or read English, the nagging question of whether or not he understood the vow remains unanswered. As we shall see later, other Indians of this time and place refused to accept Christianity when they did not understand English or the Mahican dialect.

John Sergeant wrote that Umpachene, who, unlike Konkapot, is not reported to have accepted Christianity, was an Indian priest or powwow and that in the early days of the mission the Indians gathered at his wigwam, which was about sixty feet long, and performed traditional ceremonies. Timothy Woodbridge was invited to attend on one occasion. The next day, he told the Indians that their ceremony was sinful, and they resolved never to do it again.

In 1736, the first year that Sergeant was able to pray with the Indians in their own tongue, the mission was consolidated at the Indians' request in their village of Wnahktukook:

> The Indians expressed a desire to dwell together and receive the Gospel, and requested that the interval land above the mountain might be granted to them, that they might settle thereon, on the west side of the Housatonic River.[19]

7–4 Standing stone, West Stockbridge, Mass.

On 25 March, the first day of their calendar year, the General Court granted the Indians a township six miles square, above Monument Mountain, which included the present towns of Stockbridge and West Stockbridge. Of this thirty-six square mile area, one-sixteenth was given to the first pastor, John Sergeant, and another sixteenth to Timothy Woodbridge, teacher, magistrate, judge of all courts, deacon of the church, and superintendent of Indian affairs on a salary from the General Court of Massachusetts.

This land, though outside the English purchase of 1724 and occupied by the Indians, was claimed by the English as the property of the crown because it was *legally* vacant. The terms of the 1736 grant required the Indians to give the Massachusetts General Court equivalent Indian land in exchange, and Konkapot agreed to give land east of the land sold in 1724. As he put it, "Yes, I am very willing the English should have what of the land they want as an equivalent, provided we have that land above the mountain, as you propose to us."[20] We cannot help but question the accuracy of such quotations which are obviously translations by the English or Dutch of the words of Indians who are reported to have been unable to speak English. But clearly Konkapot would not part with his village of Wnahktukook, and in fact directed that it be the location of the mission or praying village. A stream, known today as Konkapot Brook, flows into the Housatonic River at Wnahktukook, after passing through a swamp just east of Monument Mountain. The pile of stones at the south end of the mountain is only three quarters of a mile from the brook and is clearly visible as a horizon feature to the west. It could easily have been used as an equinox marker to record the first day of the year.

The Indians at Wnahktukook "were very fond" of the Dutch settlers, particularly Van Valkenburgh, and wanted them to stay, but the English missionaries found them troublesome and accused them of interfering with the religious work of the mission by selling and giving the Indians liquor. By 1739, the Dutch had been forced to leave. We cannot help but wish that we had the Dutch side of the story, in view of the fact that Konkapot was so fond of them yet professed such Puritan piety.

In the next phase of the story, Indians from various and distant parts of the country came to Stockbridge, as Wnahktukook came to be called, to live like the English and to be Christianized. By 1740, the Indian population was 120; in 1749 it was 218, later increasing to as much as 600. Four hundred was the average for the greater part of the life of the mission village.

In the fall of 1735, immediately after the ordination of John Sergeant as pastor of the Muh-he-ka-ne-ok, Indians arrived from far and wide, apparently having heard about the Christian revival taking place along the Housatonic. And a revival it surely was, because it coincided with the New Light revival among the Puritan settlers brought from England by George Whitefield and led in New England by Jonathan Edwards, then pastor at Springfield and later pastor of the Stockbridge Indians.

In November and December, 1735, Un-na-qua-nut, a Susquehannah Indian, visited and left two boys in the school for Christian training. In December, the Indians passed a resolution "to have no trading in rum," and later held a *Kentikaw* or dance in order to purge themselves of the effects of liquor taken at the Mohawk Great Council, which they attended occasionally. John Sergeant approved of this particular manifestation of the old Indian religion and attended the dance. Abstinence from liquor remained a keystone of the mission from then on.

After settlement of the mission at Stockbridge, the Indians raised questions of the white man's motives and expressed fears that the Indians were becoming enslaved. Umpachene, the powwow, asked why his people, neglected for so long, had suddenly been brought into favor. He wondered why they were asked many questions about the ownership of their lands and the origin of their titles to them. The reply from Colonel Stoddard, who had been influential in founding the mission and otherwise active in pushing back the frontiers of the Massachusetts Colony, was a recitation of part of the Royal Charter of the colony, as follows:

> To win and to incite the natives of the country to the knowledge and obedience of the only true God and Savior of mankind, and the christian faith, is in our Royal intention, and the adventurers free profession, the principal end of the plantation.[21]

If this was actually said and the Indians understood it, it is doubtful that they would have continued to support the mission.

By July 1736, many Indians from the Hudson River had joined the mission. In 1737, Chief Um-pau-mut, from an island in the Hudson, was baptized and a Shawnee Indian joined. Indians were admitted to membership in the church by a "halfway convenant," which meant that they had not yet experienced renewal but hoped to. This was done in order to encourage those who had not fully renounced alcohol, to do so, but it could have applied equally well to their old religion.

John Sergeant travelled to other places as part of his mission and brought many Indian families back with him to Stockbridge. In 1739, he travelled within a circle of about thirty miles radius of Stockbridge with much success. Stockbridge was incorporated that year, and six English families lived there. In 1741, he travelled to the Shawnees on the Susquehannah and to the Delawares east of them, a distance of 220 miles. A letter sent by the Stockbridge Indians to a Susquehannah Indian, probably written by Sergeant, reveals something of the Puritan attempt to put into words their perception of the role of Christianity in Indians' lives.

> In the end of the world you will see a good prepared if you embrace the Christian religion in truth; and if you believe it not, you will see a punishment provided. Formerly, our forefathers used to send messages one to another; but their speeches were nothing. They were wont in the conclusion of their speeches to say, "now I see the sun at noon, you shall always see clearly; you shall see nothing amiss!" But these things which they spake in darkness were nothing. The only true light which enlightens the eyes is the Christian religion.

The more candid reply from the Susquehannah was:

> It is true that we have one father above, and we are always in his presence. The Indians have one way of honoring and pleasing him, and the White people have another; both acceptable to him. I am glad to hear from my brother, and to cultivate friendship with him. He shall always find me here if he has any message to send; but Christianity need not be a bond of union between us. As for your teacher, I cannot understand him. If I could understand him, it might be well to hear him; but he speaks in an unknown tongue.

Electa Jones, who quotes these eloquent passages, does so to show that the Susquehannahs had been deeply prejudiced by the teachings of papists and that "their minds were not open to conviction." However, the two letters can be more reasonably interpreted as the arguments of rigid and fearful Puritans set against those of the Indians.

Sergeant had some success with the Delawares, who understood the language of the Muh-he-ka-ne-ok and sought Christian instruction. He made plans to obtain land and to set up a mission in New Jersey. At this point in the history, the Honorable Society in Scotland for the Propagation of Christian Knowledge appears as a sponsor of the Stockbridge mission. Their support continued, paying the pastor's salary, through the remainder of the century with a slight interruption during the American Revolution. The Society subsequently appointed David Brainard as missionary among the Delawares.

In 1740, the Moravian missionary C. H. Rauch established a mission among the Mohegan Indians at Shekomeko, near Kent, Connecticut, on the Housatonic River south of Stockbridge. The Indian missions of the Moravians or United Brethren were also supported financially from Great Britain, by the English Society for the Propogation of the Gospel in Foreign Parts. They were encouraged by George Whitefield, the New Light revivalist, John Wesley, founder of the Methodist Church, and David Brainard of the Stockbridge mission. The Brethren missionaries used methods rather different from other Protestant missionaries. They earned their livelihood by working for the Indians, lived and dressed like them, and were often taken for Indians. Thus their charges, the Christian Indians, as they were known, maintained their old ways of life, behaving quite differently from the Stockbridge Indians, who were encouraged to live like the English following the example of John Eliot. By 1745, the Brethren were forced to leave Shekomeko by death threats from the whites, whom the Brethren had prevented from selling liquor to the Indians. The Christian Indian community remained until 1763, under the direction of Indian assistants. The saga of the Brethren and their Christian Indians is one of frequent forced removals and persecution by whites and Iroquois Indians throughout the Northeast. As late as 1882, a group of ninety-six Christian Indians, men, women and children, were massacred one at a time with a cooper's mallet by renegade whites at Pittsburgh.[22]

At about the same time that Sergeant made his mission to the Delawares, a group of Nanticoke Indians joined the Stockbridge mission. The Nanticokes in their coastal Virginia homeland erected sacred, temple-like structures of earth and logs to house skeletal and funerary remains, stored on shelves until later ceremonial burial. Verrazzano had written of this region, "We saw no stone of any sort," and wood was the only reasonable load-bearing structural material available there. We mention these structures because they had an acknowledged ritual function and are very similar in design to New England stone chambers, many of which are to be seen in the Mahican domain, differing only in the material used, a natural regional choice.[23]

John Sergeant died in 1749. In early 1750, Ezra Stiles was invited to preach a few sermons at Stockbridge, which was in need of a pastor to succeed Sergeant. Only twelve English families lived there at this time, and it was clearly still an Indian town. Stiles knew he was being considered for the pastor's job, and he also found other attractions there. When he rode into town, he immediately became enraptured of John Sergeant's twenty-seven-year-old widow, Abigail.

As far as Stiles' papers tell, this was his first encounter with Indians. During his guest sermons and interviews, he professed Old Light views and tolerance similar to Sergeant's. He was concerned more with morals than with revelation and more with the message of the Scriptures than with their origins. He thought that his heretical views might not be found out until he had decided whether or not the ministry was for him and whether or not the Scriptures were divinely revealed. Even though he seemed headed toward marriage with Abigail, he did not tell her the full extent of his heretical views, but nevertheless, rumors of his association with New Haven Arminians and Deists reached Stockbridge. Timothy Woodbridge, who evidently included government spy among his many positions, learned from one of Stiles' pupils at Yale that he held Arminian views. As a result, Stiles was called to Boston for a religious examination. He consulted his father, Isaac, who, more astute to the ways of politics in religion, advised him that the commissioners would smoke him out and ruin his reputation forever. Therefore, Ezra declined the examination and the post and lost Abigail.

Jonathan Edwards, the noted New Light preacher, became the Stockbridge pastor in 1751 and served until 1758. During his tenure, the number of English families increased to eighteen while the number of Indian families was reduced to forty-two. Edwards was succeeded in 1758 by Stephen West, who held the post until 1818, during which period the number of European residents came to exceed the number of Indians. Dr. West had little use for Edwards' New Light ideas, but at one point he did go through a crisis in which he denied Christ as his personal savior. After a period of depression, he was reconverted and became a more fervent Christian than before. In 1775, John Sergeant, Jr., son of the first pastor, took on the task of teacher at Stockbridge.

From 1755 to 1783, the Muh-he-ka-ne-ok were caught in the middle of the white man's open warfare resulting from territorial ambitions. Most Indians resolved to "sit and smoke together, and see who will be the conquerors," but during the French and Indian Wars begun in 1755 the northern Iroquois, allies of the French, became hostile. Most of the River Indians planned to move west before the American Revolution, but waited until 1785 to actually do so. The places to which they travelled throughout the United States and the timing of the moves gave this migration its fascination from our perspective. They followed a more northerly route west than the Moravian Christian Indians who had preceded them by about twenty-five years, and encountered fewer and less severe obstacles.

For Native Americans, leaving their homeland was devastating. The Navajo people say, "In our traditional tongue there is no word for relocation. To move away means to disappear and never be seen again."[24] The first of many relocations for the Stockbridge Indians was to New Stockbridge, fourteen miles south of Utica, New York, where the Oneidas, grateful for their help against a powerful enemy in times past, had given them some land. Reverend Kirkland, the missionary to the Oneidas, estimated in 1784 that 1,000 Oneida Indians were expected to participate in the Christian mission, in addition to 80 Delaware Indians and 400 Stockbridge Indians. John Sergeant, Jr., son of the first Stockbridge pastor, was ordained in 1788 to the New Stockbridge ministry.

As the years went by, Indians from the Senecas, Onondagas and others joined in the mission. Chief Hendrick Aupaumut, of the Onondaga, who never professed Christianity, joined the New Stockbridge mission and argued for accepting the teaching of the whites in a speech at a Great Council. He attributed the Indian attraction to strong liquor and other sins to the temptation of the evil spirit and to their ignorance of their weakness. He asserted that they neglected to pray to the Great and Good Spirit for wisdom and strength, which must be done every day. This speech and others were delivered by Chief Hendrick but doubtless written by John Sergeant.

Chief Hendrick was well respected by the white settlers and was a firm friend of their institutions and ministers. He gave many speeches, during which his clear and authoritative manner doubtless was as influential as the spoken message, but in most cases he acted only as interpreter of material written by the white pastors. In his own right, he sought to gather the Stockbridge Indians or New York Indians, as they were later called, in a peaceful community where they would live in fellowship with the whites. While he was engaged in this endeavor, the famed Shawnees Tecumseh and his brother the Prophet were working for an Indian league which would halt white aggression. The Prophet sent forth "divine" instruction beginning in 1806 forbidding witchcraft, intemperance and other vices, including Christianity. The Shawnees, according to the Prophet, were created from the brains of the Lord of Life and shared his wisdom, but this wisdom was forfeited by vice and given to the white settlers. Not content, the whites were also taking the land by force, or purchasing it with goods made with borrowed skills. By reforming themselves, the Prophet held that the Indians would regain a right to all that the whites possessed. Chief Hendrick chose to support the Christian whites and sapped enough Indian support from Tecumseh and the Prophet to contribute to their downfall.

In 1819, a collection was taken up for the Jews, and Chief Hendrick read a letter from the Muh-he-ka-ne-ok to "their brethren who were camped about Jerusalem, the sachem and head men of the remnant of the children of Abraham, Isaac and Jacob, commonly called Jews." The letter tells of how the Indians were enraged to hear that Jesus had been killed by his own brethren, the Jews, and of how there are precious promises in store on the day of Israel's redemption. A great day was seen when Jews and gentiles would be received into heaven, called *Woh-un-koi-geu-wun-kun-nuk*, if all truly worship the Great and Good Spirit.

In 1818, the Indians at New Stockbridge, feeling the pressure of white settlement, left for the White River in Ohio, near the Indiana border, the land of the Miami Indians, whom Chief Hendrick mentions as the grandchildren of the Muh-he-ka-ne-ok. Before reaching this land, they learned that the Miamis had sold it, reserving the right to live on it for only three years. Failing in this location, they purchased 500,000 acres in 1821 on the Fox River in Wisconsin, twenty-two miles from where it flows into Green Bay. This move appears to have been partly engineered by the Ogden Land Company, which wanted to remove all Indians from New York State.

A year was spent in relocating to Wisconsin and many Indians who went there were not Muh-he-ka-ne-ok, or Christian. After considerable turmoil, all were forced by the government to remove again in 1833 because they were in the way of river improvements. They went to the east side of Lake Winnebago where the soil was richer and they lived peacefully until 1838. Then they were pushed to a tract west of the Missouri River reserved for New York Indians.

In 1839, seventy to eighty individuals of the Muh-he-ka-ne-ok, who, Jones comments, could well be spared, started for the Southwest. The government of the tribe was in transition from direction by chiefs to republicanism, and new rules were in effect which members of this group could not accept. Jones observes critically that they started out on the Sabbath, from which we can infer that they were backsliders from the Christian mission. They settled temporarily upon the lands of the Delaware Indians, five miles below Fort Leavenworth, Kansas, on the Missouri River, where disease reduced their numbers to less than thirty by 1851. Back in Stockbridge, the Muh-he-ka-ne-oks had been friendly with some Delawares who spoke their language and had joined the Christian mission, so it was natural that they would seek out the Delawares in the West. But Indians were not the only easterners at the junction of the Missouri and Kansas Rivers at this time. Joseph Smith, Jr., had led the Mormons there, to Independence, Missouri, where he designated the site of the first and greatest Mormon temple on a hilltop at a sacred Indian site marked by a mound of stones. Oliver Cowdrey, one of the Mormon leaders, told the Delawares in sermons that they "should be restored to all their rights and privileges, should cease to fight and kill one another; should become one people; cultivate the earth in peace, in common with the pale faces." Because of their religion and their support for the Indians, the Mormons were forced by the white residents to move north to a place they called Far West and ultimately to leave Missouri. All this happened the year that the Stockbridge Indians joined the Delawares in Missouri.[25]

Those that remained in Wisconsin finally moved in 1848 to land of their own selection, belonging to the Dakotas, in Minnesota at the mouth of the Vermillion River. A great treaty was made in 1851 between the United States and several tribes at Traverse de Sioux, setting aside Indian land, some of which went to the Muh-he-ka-ne-ok. The Plains Indians attending the treaty assembly were surprised at how the Stockbridge Indians associated with the whites on terms of equality, and resembled them in every way save color. White observers noted that the "squalid barbarism" of the Plains Indians contrasted greatly with the demeanor of the Stockbridge Indians.

While they had at first absorbed Christianity without giving up the old religion, over a period of 200 years the Indians of New England had changed and adopted many of the white man's ways. In the process, most gradually forgot much of the shamanistic ritual and the role of the natural land and sky, and the stone structures. In reviewing the history of this period, we can see this starting to happen in the seventeenth century, accelerating in the eighteenth and nineteenth centuries, until by the twentieth century, most Indian lore in New England comes not from strictly local heritage but from Indians throughout America, homogenized and Christianized.

8

Shakers and Shamanistic Christianity

The early history of New England is punctuated by many ventures in socioreligious separatism. Only vestiges are left of most, but several of these movements not only had considerable impact, but also were characteristic of the growth of America itself. The Shakers were such a movement. Over one hundred years after the founding of the New England praying villages, the Shakers established communal societies, some located on the sites of these villages.

We became interested in the New England Shakers because the location of their leading settlement in the formative years was on the site of the historical praying Indian village of Nashoba. We found that the landscape of this Shaker community at Harvard, Massachusetts, has the elements which we suggest signal an Indian sacred place. The Shaker area, directly west of the praying village in what is now the northeast corner of the town of Harvard, is a region of hills and wetlands with many earth and stone constructions of diverse age, size and complexity which exhibit special spatial relationships to natural landforms. Earth works can be seen in the bottom lands and adjacent to the swamps while the highlands feature many large perched boulders, balanced rocks and stone rows, some adjacent to earthen banks, as well as standing stones, prayer seats and stone mounds. The presence of these man-made structures on Shaker land suggests connections between them and the Shakers, and between the Shakers and Indians.

Though the American Shakers can claim antecedents in several European sects, including the English Quakers, their way of life, religious practices and theology after their arrival in America were in the main American in origin. Of the religious groups of New England which had originated in England, the Shakers probably came nearest to accepting the Indian way. Edward Andrews writes of the "curious affinity between the Shakers and the Indians."[1] This affinity, however, is quite natural if Shaker ritual and theology are compared with that of American Indian groups, although the Shakers may well have been unaware of the great similarity, which probably came about through subtle influences. From the contemporary record, we feel that Shaker practices may reflect Native American religious practices in New England in the eighteenth and nineteenth centuries, practices which we believe included the stone structures.

Shaker Origins

During 1742, some English Quakers near Manchester, led by Jane and James Wardley or Wardlaw, received into their group some individuals who had been associated with the Camisards, a radical sect of Calvinists from the Cévennes Mountains in France. Since the revocation of the Edict of Nantes in 1685 had made outlaws of all French Protestants, three and one-half million left France to escape conversion by torture and death by agents of Pope Clement XI. The Camisards were too poor to leave their homes and instead fought a war against the French government from 1702 to 1705 in which a force of 60,000 troops went against them. In defeat, the Camisard leaders were killed or dispersed, and the religious movement went underground until 1789 when the penal laws against Protestants were repealed. After 1705, scattered groups of Camisard refugees had held semisecret meetings in various parts of the British Isles. The courts in France considered the Camisards fanatics because their practices included fasting, trances, agitation of the body, prophecies concerning the end of the world and the second coming of Christ, calls for repentance, and the interpretation of celestial events and other natural phenomena as omens from God. Many of these practices were adopted by the Wardley's group, which broke off from the Society of Friends in 1747 and became known as "Shaking Quakers" or "Shakers."

In September 1758, Ann Lee or Lees of Manchester, born 29 February 1736, became acquainted with the Wardleys and joined them in their religious work.[2] From her childhood, Lee had had an abhorrence of the lusts of the flesh, often admonishing her mother against having sexual relations with her father, for which he attempted to whip her. Nevertheless, she was persuaded by her parents to marry Abraham Standerin, known as Stanley among Shakers, on 5 January 1762, and had four children in the next four years, all of whom died in infancy. She saw the deaths of her children as a divine judgment and began nine years of mortification and suffering, with intervals of release filled with visions and revelations.

Mortification of the flesh was so strongly ingrained into Ann Lee's perception that she stayed awake for days, wringing her hands so hard that they dripped with blood. Not only did she deprive herself of sleep, but she also denied herself every gratification of a carnal nature, eating and drinking only what was considered mean and poor. She became so weak and frail that she had to be supported and fed by others. During this period she experienced a complete conversion, feeling that she had been reborn into the spiritual kingdom. In 1770, the root and foundation of human depravity was revealed to her, namely, "living in the works of natural generation and wallowing in their lusts."

Ann was said to have spoken over twelve languages and in one story seventy-two different tongues. She considered herself married to Lord Jesus Christ and told her companions, "I am Ann the word." She held that cohabitation of the sexes was the cardinal sin and source of all evil, so she separated from her husband, who insisted on living in the flesh with her and having her bear children. Ann persuaded the Wardley group of Shaking Quakers that she had experienced Christ in his second coming, and they bestowed on her the title of Mother Ann or Mother of New Creation and let her assume leadership of the order.

Shaker theology held that God is bisexual, as manifested throughout nature by male and female elements, and in the Church by Jesus and Mother Ann, who were sometimes looked upon as brother and sister, but who, as mortals, were not worshipped. Accordingly, while Christianity was accepted, the Trinity was rejected, as was physical resurrection since Shakers believed that the day of judgment had occurred at the founding of their church. A sharp distinction was made between the spirit and the flesh, and by suppressing thoughts of the flesh and practicing celibacy, the Believers could live in a higher order surrounded by and in communication with the spirits of the dead.[3]

In 1774, after years of persecution, John Hocknell of Cheshire paid the bill for Ann Lee and eight other Shakers including himself to travel to the New World on board the ship *Mariah*. They chose to settle in the desolate wilderness country of New York, in a wooded, low swampland called Niskayuna (now Watervliet) by the Indians. For years there were no new converts to the faith. In 1779 Mother Ann, in the depths of discouragement, led her followers into the forest west of their dwelling, where she saw a vision of great numbers of converts coming soon. Early in 1780, the vision began to be fulfilled as many flocked to Niskayuna, as well as other religious centers, during the New Light revival.

At the same time, intense persecution of the Believers began, which continued until Mother Ann's death in 1784, heightened by the American Revolution. The Shakers were seen as traitors because of their pacifist doctrine, and their leaders were imprisoned for five months in Poughkeepsie. A group of antagonistic whites dressed as Indians attacked the house where Mother Ann was held. The Shakers were moreover accused of Papist tendencies because of their celibacy, obedience, confession of sins, and miracle-working by visions. They were also charged with inciting the Indians against the government, which may support our argument for an Indian-Shaker connection. However, many citizens thought these persecutions unjust and either supported or joined the Believers.

While the Shakers would not join armies or take oaths of allegiance, in this period they provoked violence in others by their uncompromising confrontation with unbelievers on the issue of lust. Also during this time the leaders practiced deliberate mortification of the flesh to such an extent that it led to the premature deaths of Mother Ann, her brother, Father William Lee, and Father James Whittaker.

Suffering Prophets and Shamans

Most religious leaders who have founded sects or who became recognized as prophets, messiahs, or saints, suffered greatly during their lives. If they experienced particularly great pain or recovered from near-death, their perceptions of the world took on a dimension unfamiliar to most people. In hunter-gatherer societies of the present and past, such people are described as healers, seers, and visionaries. They play the same role as the shaman in traditional Siberian culture, who undergoes a ritual rebirth and becomes an intermediary between the world of the flesh and the spirit world. The act of suffering has become ritualized and made part of the training of shamans in hunter-gatherer societies in all places and epochs. The different world view of such people is attributed by modern Westerners to either arctic hysteria or schizophrenia, but it is believed by the shaman-ritualist to be a true picture of the way things are. Westerners who have experienced near-death agree. Visionists in hunter-gatherer societies provide guidance and holistic council to relatively small numbers of people at a time and are very closely linked by ritual, tradition and genes to their believer-participants, whereas religious leaders of agricultural or industrialized societies inspire great numbers of people using the hierarchical and organizational methods of these societies.

Accurate observation of the surroundings enables the hunter-gatherer to live, so this faculty is valued greatly. In turn, it contributes to the profundity of the visionist-participant bond, making the participant a partner in prophecy with the visionist so that prophecies are self-fulfilled. The profound, personal links between the shaman in a hunter-gatherer society and the other participants are so very strong and the balance so carefully maintained that faultily sighted prophets are not tolerated. The balance is so precise that in many hunter-gatherer societies dishonesty is taken as a capital offense.

The quality of participation found in a hunter-gatherer society is also found occasionally in agricultural and industrialized societies in cases where the experiences of suffering of the religious leaders and their followers lead toward strong feelings of rebirth. Shamanism can exist alongside or be part of other religious practices.[4] We conclude that Ann Lee became a shaman, within a Christian religious framework.

Ann Lee's Mission

In 1781, Mother Ann set out from Niskayuna on a proselyting mission that lasted over two years and took her all over southern New England, but eventually focused on Harvard, Massachusetts. While in England, she had seen a vision of a place in America to which she was drawn but still had not seen prior to her journey, and she spoke of it often. She also said that her feelings drew her toward Upton, Massachusetts, the chamber site of Chapter 2.

Her route first took her south to Mount Washington, Massachusetts, then to Enfield, Connecticut, then to Grafton, Upton and Harvard, Massachusetts (Figure 8–1). Grafton and Harvard had been the sites of important Indian praying villages. When she reached Harvard, she said that she had found the place of her vision and made it her headquarters for the remainder of her life. At Harvard, persecution of the Believers reached its peak and continued for the three years that Mother Ann made it her base of operations. She said that she bore her sufferings in order to open the gospel to a lost world. In one instance she called on fishes, fowls, trees, grass, all living things, to pray to God for her, which further suggests a connection with Indian animism.

The Shaker mission at Harvard was first established at the home of Isaac Willard. Mother Ann later took up residence in the house of the deceased Shadrack Ireland, a well-known New Light Baptist preacher who had been a follower of Shaker-like doctrines of perfection, celibacy and the millennium. But Mother Ann said that the Baptists were opposed to the testimony of the Gospel and maliciously stirred up persecution of the Shakers, accusing them of being false professors who wished to be Christian without the cross.

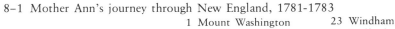

8–1 Mother Ann's journey through New England, 1781-1783

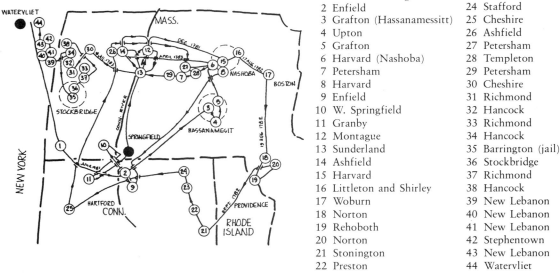

1	Mount Washington	23	Windham
2	Enfield	24	Stafford
3	Grafton (Hassanamessitt)	25	Cheshire
4	Upton	26	Ashfield
5	Grafton	27	Petersham
6	Harvard (Nashoba)	28	Templeton
7	Petersham	29	Petersham
8	Harvard	30	Cheshire
9	Enfield	31	Richmond
10	W. Springfield	32	Hancock
11	Granby	33	Richmond
12	Montague	34	Hancock
13	Sunderland	35	Barrington (jail)
14	Ashfield	36	Stockbridge
15	Harvard	37	Richmond
16	Littleton and Shirley	38	Hancock
17	Woburn	39	New Lebanon
18	Norton	40	New Lebanon
19	Rehoboth	41	New Lebanon
20	Norton	42	Stephentown
21	Stonington	43	New Lebanon
22	Preston	44	Watervliet

Nothing has been found describing meetings between the Shakers of the Harvard area and Indians, but very near the Shaker mission was the well-known praying village of Nashoba, and it is certain that Indians lived in Harvard and Littleton until the end of the nineteenth century. The experiences of Ann Lee and her followers indicate that the native people of New England felt an affinity with the Shakers. An Indian, upon meeting Mother Ann in the forest, described seeing a bright light around her and said that the Great Spirit had sent her to do much good. According to Shaker tradition, it was the Indians, and not other white Americans, who first noticed that the Shakers were unusual among religious groups in their concept of spirituality.[5]

During 1783, in spite of severe persecution and the suffering of the Believers, there was time for joy, as conversions increased. At New Lebanon, 400 people assembled in the orchard, and it seemed as if there were not enough food, but after the assembly there was more food left than before. The outdoor assemblies, necessary because no building would hold them, caused the grass to be trampled, but afterward the grass came back greener and lusher than before. A free offer of the gospel was given to all souls, whether in the present world or in the spirit world. This idea of the baptism of souls in the other world was taken up by the Mormon Church as a cornerstone of its theology. Some Indians came to an assembly and Father William Lee spoke to them in their own tongue, though he had no conscious knowledge of it. When Mother Ann returned to Niskayuna on 4 September 1783, after her mission, the Indians greeted her at the river crossing with, "The good woman is come. The good woman is come."[6]

But Mother Ann during this period had two sides. At times many were unable to tolerate her: "Her words were like flames of fire and her voice like peals of thunder." After these outbursts, she would be released from her sufferings and begin to sing with great joy and love and to gather people around her. She prophesied that after her death there would be peaceable times, which indeed came to pass.

William Lee, younger brother of Ann Lee, was born in 1740 and also led a tortured life. In England, when in tribulation he would reveal his trial to the Wardleys, who would encourage him and build him up. But when he went to his sister, she would tear him down and plunge him deeper into depression than before. He felt compelled to cry to God till he gained release through obedience to her counsel. Sometimes during these sufferings, he would vomit clear fresh blood. He spent his life in suffering and died like a bleeding martyr at age forty-four on 21 July 1784. He did not appear to die by natural infirmity, but rather to give up his life in suffering. Six weeks later, on 8 September, Mother Ann died, also with no visible appearance of bodily disease. Just before her death, she said, "I see Brother William coming in a golden chariot, to take me home."[7]

After the Lees' deaths, James Whittaker, a distant relative, was the only one left of those who came from England and also stood in the ministry. He felt called to be Mother Ann's successor, and was acknowledged as such after her death. Whittaker, who did not deny that he was the son of God, also suffered intensely, dying 20 July 1787 at the age of thirty-six. An unbeliever is quoted as saying, "Now James Whittaker is gone, the Shakers would return to their former ways again, and become good members of society, if it were not for Joseph and David Meacham; but they are so wilful, that they will keep up the delusion, and keep the people together."[8]

The first Shaker meeting house was built at Niskayuna in 1785 after the deaths of Mother Ann and Father William. The first communal societies were established after 1787 when Joseph Meacham led the movement and codified their theology, drew up laws of behavior and generally turned a wild orgiastic group into an orderly society, in which many found fulfillment and peace of mind. Life in the Shaker societies became authoritarian and highly ritualized with rigid taboos. Applicants for membership, who came for the most part from religious revivals, underwent a one-year period of instruction and trial.

The Nineteenth Century Expansion to the West

In the Kentucky revival of 1800 and 1801, missionaries from several Christian sects, including Methodist, Baptist and Presbyterian, conducted meetings at which worshippers experienced jerks, trances and other extraordinary behavior. Richard McNemar (1770–1839) was pastor at Turtle Creek of the largest Presbyterian congregation in southern Ohio, with some 500 members. In 1803 there was a major schism in the western Presbyterian Church and McNemar was among the leaders who broke away and formed a new sect called New Lights to escape from the authoritarian ministerial system. They founded the Presbytery of Springfield, Ohio, but this was soon abolished, in 1804, and in 1805 many of the New Light leaders, including McNemar, became Shakers, converted by Shaker missionaries sent out from New England to take advantage of the opportunities offered by the religious ferment of the Kentucky revival. McNemar wrote that in conversion he renounced no part of his former religious profession but his sins and those false doctrines intended to palliate and cover them.[9] This scholarly man became the single person most responsible for the success of the large and prosperous Shaker movement in the midwestern part of the United States.

Some of the New Light Presbyterian leaders who did not become Shakers eventually came to hate the Shakers, partly because they were drawing members from the New Light congregations. In 1810, Barton Stone, one of this group, led a mob of 500 armed men followed by 2,000 spectators to attack the Shaker Community at Turtle Creek. Stone wrote about the "lamentable departure of two of our preachers — into wild enthusiasm, or Shakerism. They have made a shipwreck of faith, and turned aside to an old woman's fables. . . . These wolves in sheep's clothing, have smelt us from afar, and have come to tear, rend and devour."[10]

The Kentucky revival had another dimension, a movement started by the Shawnee Indians to revive the religion of their ancestors. The whites who were caught up in the New Light revival saw this as an opportunity to missionize the Indians. In the fall of 1804, many Indians from different tribes assembled in southwestern Ohio and danced before the Great Spirit under the direction of the Shawnee Prophet.

The Shawnee Prophet, 1775–1836, was born a triplet and was the younger brother, by seven years, of Tecumseh. He was named Lalawethika in his youth, and Tenskwatawa, or The Open Door, after he became a visionary. He was an important, and for a time perhaps the most important, Indian leader in the struggle against the white man's depredations, and a key link in the Native American spiritual network that is crucial to our interpretation of history.[11]

Tecumseh and two other brothers of Tenskwatawa died in various battles against the frontiersmen in attempts at a political and military solution to the Indians' problems. The Prophet founded a religious movement that was an Indian response to the stresses placed upon the Native Americans by loss of lands, food shortages, white injustice and disease. From 1805 to 1811, this movement dominated Indian-white relationships at the frontiers, where the Indians were robbed and murdered at pleasure because the Christian whites were not held accountable for the abuse of non-Christians. The Indian response to stress was always first a spiritual one, but this was not understood by the whites, which explains why the history of America never suggests that the white man's religious beliefs might be at fault.

Lalawethika as a young man became an alcoholic. He was befriended by an elderly shaman, Penagashea (Changing Feathers), and, although he had not experienced a vision nor had he been trained as a shaman, he attempted to take the place of Penagashea after the latter's death in 1804. He was not successful, in part because of a plague brought by the white men to the Shawnee in 1805. During the plague, Lalawethika was found one day lying before his fire with eyes closed, apparently not breathing. While laid out for burial, he miraculously revived and told a story of his death, a visit to Heaven and Hell, and of his resurrection. He had not been allowed to enter Heaven but had looked on its wonders. In his vision he had also seen a place where souls of sinful tribesmen were subjected to fiery torture; drunkards were forced to swallow molten lead, but after atonement they were permitted to enter Heaven.

After his experience, Lalawethika changed his name to Tenskwatawa and created a religion which included a Christian-like Heaven and Hell as well as elements of Shawnee shamanism. His dogma aimed at reclaiming the Indians from bad habits brought on by the white man. He condemned alcohol and violence and urged returning to the traditional communal life and other past ways, while at the same time, he rejected traditional shamans. He explained this contradiction by the need to replace the old wasted medicine by a new medicine. His influence was increased by his prediction with great ceremony of a solar eclipse on 16 June 1806, from advance information he gleaned from astronomers preparing a station to observe the event.

In the Prophet's vision, the white people were portrayed as a great ugly crab that had crawled from the sea at Boston, created by an evil spirit. Later, whites were described as the spawn of the serpent, and contact between whites and Shawnees was discouraged. The Shawnees had traditionally been held by Algonquian-speaking Indians to be particularly prone to sorcery and the supernatural, and Tenskwatawa condemned Indian witches as agents sent by the evil spirit who had created the whites to instigate disorder among the Indians. These witches were thought to preserve in their medicine bags the flesh of the Great Serpent, also the servant of the evil spirit; they could become invisible or transform themselves into animals, and could cause illness and death by witchcraft. Many Indians who opposed the Prophet, primarily traditional shamans, were identified as witches and, if they did not recant, were killed by tomahawk and then burned, or else burned at the stake. It appears that Tenskwatawa defined witches as those shamans who opposed him. Particularly at risk were those Indians who had accepted the white man's religion. When criticized for witch hunting and executions, Tenskwatawa's followers replied that they had merely followed the white man's example.

Indians from many tribes in eastern and central North America came under the influence of the Prophet. Among them were Delawares, Chippewas, Ottawas, all of the Iroquois nations of New York, and Mohawks and Mohicans of New England. By 1810, the Prophet, having failed to halt the white man's incursions by religious revival, was sharing power with Tecumseh. The Battle of Tippecanoe in 1811 was more a personal defeat for the Prophet and his medicine than an American victory, and Tecumseh took over from his brother as leader of the Shawnee, ultimately aligning with the British in the War of 1812.

The Shaker mission to the Shawnee Indians was reported by Richard McNemar. On March 17, 1807, he, David Darrow and Benjamin Young, set out from Turtle Creek to meet the Indians at their village in Greenville, Ohio. There, they saw the Great House, 150 by 34 feet in size, where they were told that the Indians worshipped the Great Spirit. "Our prophet Lal-lu-e-tsee-ka converses with the Great Spirit and tells us how to be good. . . . He can dream to God." They asked to see Tecumseh and the Prophet. The Prophet at first refused to see them, pleading he had a "pain in the head," but he eventually relented upon hearing that they did not drink hard liquor. Through an interpreter, he said that he had been a doctor (shaman) and a very wicked man until about two years before, when he was struck with an awful sense of his sins and cried to the Great Spirit to show him an escape. He had then fallen into a vision in which he appeared to be travelling along a road which forked. The right was the way to happiness and the left to misery. The fork, he said, represented that stage in life when people were convicted of sin, and the punishment for drunkenness was particularly severe. The Great Spirit had warned him to tell his people to put away their sins in order to be good. Some of the chiefs who were wicked would not believe, so the Great Spirit told the Prophet to tell the people to separate from their wicked chiefs and come to the big ford where the peace had been concluded with the Americans.

McNemar and his brethren asked the Prophet if the Great Spirit had once made himself known to the world by a man that was called Christ. The Prophet answered yes. He also spoke against witchcraft, poisoning people, fighting, murdering, drinking whiskey, and beating wives because they would not have children. He went on to say that those who had been wicked confessed to the Prophet and four chiefs from the age of seven. McNemar asked how they learned to confess, and the Prophet answered that some Wyandots, who now believed in him, had once joined the Roman Catholics at Detroit. Roman Catholics, he said, confessed their sins but went and did bad again, whereas his people forsook their bad way when they confessed. When McNemar told the Prophet that Shakers did not drink whiskey, he rejoiced.

It was at dusk one evening, "and the full moon just rising above the horizon, when one of their [Indian] speakers stood up in an alley between the camps and spoke for about 15 minutes with great solemnity." McNemar retired for the night assured that, "Surely the Lord is in this place! And the world knew it not." The next morning, an Indian speaker mounted a log at the southeast corner of the village and in a loud voice began a service of thanksgiving to the Great Spirit, which continued for nearly an hour. McNemar and his colleagues were so impressed by the Indian gathering that they felt as if they were among the tribes of Israel on their march to Canaan. The Indians from many tribes were camped at Greenville in the cold of that winter, drawn together by a religious revival that was a direct result of disruption of their way of life by the white man. They had little to eat, and the Shakers gave the Indians what money they had and invited three or four of them to visit the Shaker community.

In mid-June, twenty Indians appeared at Turtle Creek and stayed four days. They held worship every day at their camp and on the Sabbath attended the Shaker meeting, behaving with order and decorum. The Shakers loaded twenty-seven horses with provisions and sent them with the Indians, an act of charity for which they were later persecuted by other whites.[12]

On 12 August 1807, Richard McNemar and Issachar Bates went to visit the Indian village at Greenville. They had little conversation with the Indians but attended their meeting from sundown until an hour after sunrise the next morning.

> The meeting was opened with a lengthy discourse, delivered by the prophet; after which they assembled in a close crowd, and continued their worship by singing and shouting, that might have been heard at least to the distance of two miles. Their various songs, and perfect harmony in singing, shouting, etc., rendered the meeting very solemn. But all this appeared far inferior to that solemn fear of God, hatred of sin, and that peace, love and harmony which they manifested among each other. [13]

On 29 August, fifty Indians arrived at Turtle Creek. As a result of their interactions with Indians, McNemar and Bates concluded that, although these poor Shawnees have had no particular instruction but what they received by the outpouring of the spirit, yet in point of real light and understanding, as well as behavior, they shame the Christian world. They [the Shakers at Turtle Creek] are willing that God should carry out his work among them without interruption, as He thinks proper.[14]

With these phrases, we see a Shaker community accepting the Indian way as equal in sanctity to their own and refraining from missionizing the Indians. It is clear from many Shaker writings that this position was consistent with the flexible Shaker theology which enabled the cult to absorb from others as well as to spread their doctrine through missionary efforts.[15]

The next event of importance to our story was that confused conflict known as the War of 1812, much of which was fought in the Midwest. The Americans attempted to acquire more territory by driving the British out of Canada, and many of the Indians who had been resisting American colonial expansion to the west joined with the British. The Ohio, Indiana and Kentucky Shakers were on the front lines of this war and were suspected of aiding the Indians who had become the enemy on two counts, first by being Indians and second by aiding the British. The Indiana Shaker community was destroyed and abandoned because of the war. After Perry's naval victory on Lake Erie, the British abandoned Detroit and withdrew to Canada with Tecumseh and 600 Indians. They made a stand at the Moraviantown, Ontario, Indian village, where United States troops led by General Harrison killed Tecumseh and burned the village occupied by the much-persecuted Moravian Christian Indians. Thousands of British and American troops fought in this battle, quickly decided by an American victory with little loss of white troops on either side. However, Harrison made a point of killing many Indians, including their leader, in order to destroy the British-Indian alliance,[16] a genocidal act that later contributed to his being elected President. At the negotiations which ended the war, the British urged formation of a large Indian reservation in the Northwest, but the Americans refused and the proposal was dropped. Ironically, during the war, Harrison had been kind to the Shakers who were friendly with the Indians and had protected them from mob violence.[17]

After the War of 1812, the Shaker communities of the West prospered and grew. There was little extraordinary in the church meetings for over thirty years. The Stockbridge Indians passed through in 1818 from New York on their way to Wisconsin under the auspices of the Presbytery of Ohio, the same group that had lost several leaders to the Shakers in 1806 and had organized mob violence in 1810 against them. The Shaker Society at Turtle Creek reached its peak membership of 600 in 1823, the largest of all Shaker communities, and was in decline thereafter.[18] By the 1830s, the Shaker journals had become distinctly secular, and several influential Shakers had resigned from the Society at Turtle Creek, by then called Union Village.

Mother Ann's Second Appearing

On 12 February 1837, a spiritual storm hit the Union Village meeting: "The church meeting today was the most extraordinary of the kind, that we ever witnessed in this place." This began an unexpected ten-year period of spiritual activity that spread to all the other Shaker communities, reaching Watervliet, the original Shaker community founded by Ann Lee, in November 1837, when a girl received revelations. The revival was seen as the supernatural work of God and was called Mother's Work. It was directed in the West from 1837 to 1843 by the credulous and intellectually weak Freegift Wells.[19]

The renewal had an unusual pattern, which was repeated in the different communities. Almost always it began with the younger members, who would be seized with involuntary jerks and other violent body motions or fall into trances. "John Ross, 10 years old, fell into a trance for 37 and 1/2 hours. Several other little boys are visionary." On 13 January 1839, there were "most powerful exercises in public meeting today. Common order and regulation out of the question. Many down on floor at a time. . . . These little visionists, 6–8, 10, 12 yr. old carried out of time. . . . Many times in company of departed friends."

In May 1839, at Union Village: "Family meeting visited by the spirits of departed Indians. They brought us presents. These Indians are often seen by those who are under inspiration. They have embraced Mother's gospel in the spiritual world." Visions of Indians became common through the 1840s. One sister began to speak in the Indian tongue and for some time afterwards could speak only in it. Foreigners were also seen in visions; curiously, Laplanders, whom we discuss in Chapter 9, were singled out for mention. Of course, Jesus Christ, in company with Mother Ann, was a frequent spiritual visitor.

Most of those who experienced trances, spinning, and violent shaking were young, some only five years of age. These sensitive people received "gifts" in the form of visions, songs, or revelations. The recipient would fall to the floor and become perfectly rigid. It appears that many of these were later considered unreliable and left the Shakers after they had grown up.

In 1839, the year of the most extravagant experiences, it is reported that Elder William Reynolds of Union Village, at the age of sixty-five, began turning over like a cart wheel from the residence to the church and back every Sunday, a practice he followed for three years. He would sometimes turn over fences. Clairvoyant episodes were common, including well-documented mental transmission of messages between the Societies at Union Village, Ohio, and New Lebanon, New York. Because of unfavorable publicity, Union Village decided not to admit spectators in 1839 and New Lebanon, the administrative headquarters for all Shaker activities throughout the country, issued an official ban on spectators at meetings and control on visitors to all societies in 1842.

In the spring of 1842, New Lebanon announced a revelation to an unspecified Shaker directing that twice a year, in May and September, for ten years, the members of all Shaker communities should worship on the highest point of land within each community. At the same time, each society received a spiritual name. Those which we have been able to track down are tabulated below, with the societies listed in order of their dates of organization.

Society	Spiritual Name	Place of Worship
Watervliet, N. Y.	Valley of Wisdom	(several, see below)
Mount Lebanon, N. Y.	Holy Mount	Holy Mount
Hancock, Mass.	City of Peace	Mount Sinai
Enfield, Conn.	City of Love	Mount of Olives
Canterbury, N. H.	Holy Ground	Pleasant Grove
Alfred, Me.	Holy Ground	
Enfield, N. H.	Chosen Vale	Mount Assurance
Harvard, Mass.	Lovely Vineyard	Holy Hill of Zion
Shirley, Mass.	Pleasant Garden	
Sabbathday Lake, Me.	Chosen Land	
Union Village, Ohio	Wisdom's Paradise	Jehovah's Chosen Square
Pleasant Hill, Ky.		Holy Sinai Plains
South Union, Ky.		Jasper (Gaspar's) Valley
North Union, Ohio	Valley of God's Pleasure	
Whitewater, Ohio		Lonely Plain of Tribulation

As can be seen from the list, not all sacred places are hills; some societies chose valleys or plains. At Niskayuna, in the town of Watervliet, later Colonie, New York, four families made up the Shaker Society with the spiritual name of Valley of Wisdom, shown in Figure 8–2. There were also four holy feast grounds and four fountains, one associated with each family.[20] In addition, three were located, respectively, at the Holy Mount, the Holy Vineyard, and the Holy Wisdom Fountain at the Spiritual River. We observed that the fountains of the North, G, and South Families, C, were horizon points at which the winter and summer solstice sunrise, respectively, could have been seen from the Holy Wisdom Fountain, H.

Other than the dictum from New Lebanon, the details of the origin of the special place of worship in each community are unrecorded, except for that at Union Village, called Jehovah's Chosen Square, a one-half-acre enclosure about two thirds of a mile northeast of the meetinghouse. Richard McNemar lived at Union Village until his death in 1839, after the start of the ten-year spiritual revival, and he was the only one left of the original group that had visited the Shawnee Indians in 1807. During the days leading up to the conversion of McNemar and his family on 24 April 1805, he had walked alone in the garden and grove behind his house, which was at the top of the highest hill. That very site later became the Shaker special place, Jehovah's Chosen Square. Here, it is said, a spiritual manifestation was revealed to McNemar which caused him to become a Shaker.[21]

The decade of increased spiritualism became known as "Mother Ann's Second

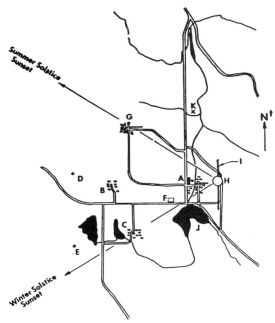

8-2 Astronomical alignments,
Spiritual City of Wisdom,
Watervliet, N.Y.
(after Filley, note 20)

Appearing." There was an intensification of religious zeal which reminds us of the early days when Mother Ann was alive. Visions were more frequent, more elaborate and more bizarre. Speaking in tongues increased. At the Holy Hill of Zion in Harvard, Massachusetts, 40,000 spirits were said to have gathered. This was a time of unusually vivid visions and violent shaking and whirling; sometimes members could speak only in an unknown tongue for days. Certain members, called instruments, had visions which were held to be direct communications from Mother Ann, and from Jesus. Some of the messages called for a revitalization of the communities which were held to have slipped from the personal influence of Mother Ann and succumbed to worldly temptations. Many Shaker publications about this period of spiritualism appeared at the time, some of them spiritual revelations in themselves. The headquarters at New Lebanon, New York, ordered that all spiritual revelations be recorded. However, except for that part dating after July 1845, the last part of the revival, this spiritual journal appears to have been purposely destroyed in 1904–5 because the Shakers came to be ashamed of the extravagances of the period.

It was during this period that Indian ways crept into Shaker ritual. Spiritual presents, imaginary gifts of all kinds, were given between individuals and, via an instrument, from departed saints. One spiritual present was a peace pipe. There was also talk of "grinding the evil, sensual principles in man with spiritual machines deposited in the center of the sanctuary by some of the aboriginal inhabitants of America." The Shakers believed in a duality of God, which they called Father and Mother, or Power and Wisdom. Mother Wisdom corresponds to the Indian's creator god, Kichtan, who was inaccessible, while Father Power is Hobomock, whom Indians sought in visions.

Shaker ritual expanded to include outdoor meetings at sacred places and bathing in spiritual waters, and to take in the spirits of Indians. A purification rite to purge the community of evil spirits, akin to the Indian sweating ritual, was constituted in 1842 and practiced for eight years. Each society, at its chosen sacred place, cleared about a half acre of land, sometimes called a feast ground, leveled and enclosed it, and laid out in its center a low-fenced hexagonal plot called "the fountain." At one end of the enclosure, a marble tablet called the Fountain Stone was placed. At Hancock, Massachusetts, which was typical of other Shaker societies in this regard, on the outer or back face was engraved,

Written and placed here
By the command of our Lord and Saviour Jesus Christ
The Lord's Stone
Erected upon the Mt. Sinai, May 4th 1843
Engraved at Hancock

On the inner face, a longer inscription stated that the stone marked the Lord's Holy Fountain and that no one polluted with sin might step within the enclosure, nor place hands upon the stone. It stated further that "I am God the Almighty in whose hands are judgment and mercy. And I will cause my judgments to fall upon the wilful violator of my commands. . . . For I have created all souls and unto me they are accountable."

The marble Fountain Stone on Holy Hill in Harvard, Massachusetts, conveyed a nearly identical message, but the Shirley, Massachusetts, Fountain Stone was more explicit about the curse on vandals. "Touch not my holy fountain, deface not anything on this Holy Hill for if this ye do, cursed shall ye be. . . . I have chosen this place and sanctified it unto myself."[22]

All except two of these Shaker stones are lost. In spite of the curse, between 1850 and 1880, the holy places were desanctified as the period of heightened spirituality came to a close. Henry A. Blinn, who lived in and mapped the Canterbury, New Hampshire, community, wrote of his role in the erection and desanctification of the feast ground. "At Canterbury, the place was designated 'Pleasant Grove.' A building forty feet long, fifteen feet wide, and one story high, was built for the protection of the people. . . . In 1847, a marble slab was purchased, six feet long, three feet wide and three inches thick. This was placed in the center of the enclosure." Blinn wrote that he engraved the lettering on the stone, erected it and, later on after meetings had been discontinued, removed the house, fence and the marble slab. Blinn's matter-of-fact account makes no comment on the fact that he both engraved the Lord's command on the stone and then violated it.[23]

Few Shaker maps show the feast grounds, but those at Canterbury, New Hampshire, and Alfred, Maine, indicate that the surrounding fence was oriented true north and east and parallel to the main streets and buildings of the communities. However, at Enfield, New Hampshire, a community associated with Canterbury, and at Harvard, Massachusetts, we observed that the fences and the fountain stones were oriented eighty-two degrees true, eight degrees different from the others. In the 1840s when the grounds were laid out, the magnetic variation was one-half of what it is today and eighty-two degrees true was within one degree east by the magnetic compass. It is tempting to assume that the Shakers merely oriented by the magnetic compass, but the practice of orientation to cardinal direction was not characteristic of Shaker architecture so we doubt it as the only reason for the orientation of the feast grounds and stones and have looked for other explanations. At Enfield, the feast ground overlooks the Shaker community on the shore of Mascoma Lake with Mount Cardigan dominating the eastern horizon. A small piece of the marble fountain remains because the stone was broken off during removal. It was carefully fixed in its foundation by iron shims (Figure 8–3) and is aimed at a horizon notch one degree to the south of the summit of Mount Cardigan, where the sun rises on 10 April and 3 September, dates of no particular modern significance (Figure 8–4). There

8–3 Enfield, N. H., fountain stone foundation with portion of marble slab remaining

8–4 Enfield fountain stone alignment to notch on Mt. Cardigan. A stone pile just outside the feast ground is on this line

was, however, a stellar event of note, the rising of three of the ten brightest stars in the sky, Betelgeuse, Procyon and Altair, within a three degree sector on the south slope of Mount Cardigan. The unusually large red giant Betelgeuse, the brightest star in Orion, the most brilliant constellation, rose in line with the fountain stone.

The Shakers who frequented this sacred place probably noticed the stellar horizon events at Mount Cardigan, as did the Indians before them, who would have recalled in their legends a more spectacular event that occurred in A.D. 1200 when all three stars rose at exactly the same place, in the notch, on Mount Cardigan.

The stellar explanation for the orientation of the fountain stone and feast ground fence may be a second instance of astronomical influence on Shaker sacred architecture, the first being the Watervliet solar alignments, both associated with the period of Mother Ann's Second Coming, a time when Indian spirits entered the meetings. The fountain stones may be in the tradition of Indian manitou stones which mark Indian sacred places and represent anthropomorphized spirits of nature, as we explain in Chapter 13.

At Hancock, outdoor ceremonies on Mount Sinai incorporating Indian ritual were held from 1838 to 1850. Mount Sinai is the Shaker name for a mountain 1845 feet in elevation, which overlooks the Shaker village from 700 feet above it on the north side. An area of about half an acre was cleared on the flat summit of the mountain, and then the fountain stone and its sacred enclosure were erected. A mile-long trail from the village was cut into the steep slopes, forming a spiral path to the summit. We followed this trail and found unmistakeable signs of stone and earthern works that were familiar to us from other New England sites with clear Indian, but without Shaker, connections. These structures include stone rows with large slabs, standing stones, rock stacks, and earthern ditches and banks, located as shown in Figure 8–5 and described here in the order they are encountered during the ascent. The first part of the trail climbs gradually beside Shaker Brook. A is a north-south length of stone row containing many Indian hammerstones, tailing tools, and perched boulders. B is a straight stone row without distinguishing features and is probably colonial. At its west end is a juncture with C, a length of stone row with groups of orthostats built in, ending in a sweeping curve to an opening, D, leading to a marsh on the west. The other side of the opening is formed by another stone row, E, which is curved near the opening but then straight. This opening and the two curved rows may have been designed to guide waterflow from a gulley on the adjacent hillside to the marsh. Next encountered is F, an overhanging rocky cliff about thirty feet high that could have provided shelter for aboriginal encampments. A low stone row runs along the top edge for about 100 feet. Stone row E ends and is continued by a row of intermittent boulders, G, spaced about five to ten feet apart, which continue until the land levels out in a plateau between hillsides through which the brook meanders. We have found frequent examples elsewhere of stone rows aimed to signal such hydraulic features. This plateau is likely to have been the place where the Shakers paused in their climb. On the

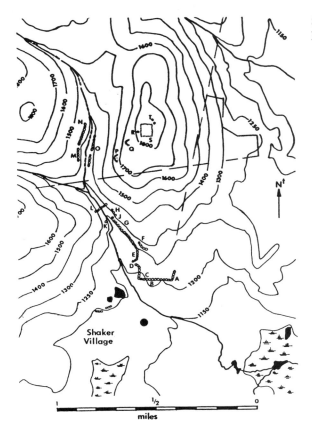

8-6 Balanced boulder on Mount Sinai

plateau at brookside are three small stone slabs, H, set in the ground in the manner of gravestones. Each has two chiseled holes through it, a design we have seen in Narragansett Indian gravestones. Nearby is an unroofed subterranean stone enclosure having two levels; the lower about seven feet deep is connected by a drystone, slab-roofed passage about fifteen feet long to the bank of the stream. We draw no conclusions about this structure, though we have seen others like it. Across the brook is a balanced boulder, K, shown in Figure 8–6. A stone dam, L, was built by the Shakers, with piping for water power. Although this engineering work clearly served the Shakers, the nearby balanced boulder marks the spot as one that was also of special importance to Indians. Farther along Shaker Brook, stone rows, M, N and O, are scattered on the hillsides, some with orthostats either singly or in groups. On the trail up the western slope of Mount Sinai is a semicircular earthern platform about thirty feet in diameter. Here the trail becomes overgrown, so we left it and climbed directly toward the summit. We next encountered a twenty-foot diameter circular earthern platform surrounded by a ditch and earthern bank, almost identical to structures at the Nashoba praying village site described in Chapter 11. We infer that these are related to the Indian vision quest. Immediately after climbing over the rocky edge of the summit plateau, we saw a small rock stack, R, like ones we have seen elsewhere as sightline markers for astronomical alignments, and also like the trail markers to Yurok places of vision quest, described in Chapter 9. A square of about one-half acre, S, has been cleared within the last ten years on the summit, presumably in preparation for developing the site as part of the Hancock Shaker Museum. On the other side of the square are two more rock stacks, T.

We view the remains on Mount Sinai as subtle indicators of an Indian presence and believe it was likely to have been an Indian sacred hill, as are many in the vicinity, before it was adapted to Shaker worship.

The ritual at Hancock on 18 September 1842 began the evening before in the village with fasting, confession, silent prayer and the distribution of spiritual "gifts," which included imaginary ornate clothing, white trousers spangled with stars, gowns of twelve beautiful colors and silver-colored shoes. Led by elders and instruments, the group of believers started at eight o'clock in the morning, marching two abreast, until they reached a spot halfway up Mt. Sinai at the walnut grove. There, they bowed and clapped and turned around, in love of departed brethren and sisters. Spiritual spectacles were distributed, the better to see visions. Then they continued up the hill singing a marching song. At the top, the instruments were anointed and urged to "act or move as the spirit directs." Imaginary incense was poured over them and mantles of strength draped over their shoulders (Figure 8–7).

Then, everyone present danced with energy, removing their coats and leaping, skipping, staggering and rolling on the ground. After more bestowal of spiritual gifts, an elder announced that a large white tub had been placed by the Saviour on each side of the fountain, one for the brethren and one for the sisters. Spiritual water vessels were produced, water dipped from the fountain, and all bathed. Brother washed brother and sister washed sister. All were spiritually scrubbed, sponged and rinsed. More spiritual gifts were distributed, including wine; all felt quite merry.

Then a stone altar was built upon the four foundation stones laid by the elders. From a pile of stones prepared for the purpose, each member brought a

8–7 Shaker mountain meeting
at Holy Hill of Zion,
Harvard, Mass.
(from Lamson, note 19)

living stone to the three brethren selected to erect the mound. When the "lead" had finished by placing four capstones on top, all made offerings of most choice things such as love, thankfulness, meekness and obedience. The fencing, marble slab, and stone altar were all material things, not spiritual. Stone piles seen today in the feast grounds may be the remains of these altars.

This was the first half of the ceremony. The second half commenced with clapping, bending, bowing, singing, and shouting, some in unknown tongues. A song was danced "in the quick manner while the Virgin Mary sprinkled love over the brethren and sisters and we gathered it as we danced." This was followed by gifts from famous men and women throughout the world. Then the spiritual seed was sown and watered. An instrument acting the role of a holy angel placed "small papers of seed" all around the fountain, followed by people sowing spiritually from baskets of seeds slung over their arms and afterward reaping the growth. Finally, the seed in papers was scattered over the holy ground and watered spiritually from pots the people carried on their shoulders. At this point, Indian spirits came into the meeting; their possible connections to the watered seed is left to the reader's imagination.

Shaker history from its founding through the nineteenth century records only a few instances of actual, as opposed to spiritual, contact between Indians and Shakers. Mother Ann herself was respected by the Indians about Watervliet, and William Lee preached to the Indians in New Lebanon. In 1807, the Shawnees participated in Shaker meetings and Shakers witnessed the Prophet's religious ceremonies in Ohio. All these communications occurred well before Mother Ann's Second Appearing in the 1840s, when Indians came to meetings only in visions or their spirits entered the bodies of the Shakers.

Immediately after the watering of the seed from papers, a brother announced that "there was a large company of natives that desired to come and unite with us." The Indians said that they had confessed all their sins and had the same Mother or creator that the Shakers had. The Indians entered the dance through Shaker instruments and there was a quick song,

> rather on the native order. . . . The brethren and sisters were very much pleased and united with their new visitors and asked them to sing another song more fully expressive of the native language. The natives sounded a brisk whoop and for some time they carried the day. The brethren and sisters and Indians shook hands, bowed, ran to and fro, caught one another, ran around one another giving and receiving love.

Finally, there was an elaborate spiritual feast, and at two-thirty in the afternoon, the worshippers returned to the City of Peace.

This was not the only instance of participation by Indian spirits in Shaker meetings. The Shakers provided spiritual instruction to the Indian spirits in all the various industries and trades followed by the brethren and sisters, and gifts flowed from the Indian spirits to the Shakers steadily until 1845. Directly after one of these exchanges, a display of lights was seen in the sky. The natives gave

their songs and dances, vision tunes, inspirational messages, spiritual presenta-
tions and various other gifts. While great exchanges took place between the
Indians and Shakers on a spiritual level, history lacks the complementary reports
of Shakers participating in and learning the Indian ways on a material level that
are necessary to prove the influence of Native Americans on Shaker concepts and
ritual. Nevertheless, this influence is supported by circumstantial evidence that
the Shakers were in many respects akin to the Indians. When people exchange
gifts by way of spiritual reciprocity as we believe the Indians and Shakers did,
the impact and quality of that exchange is great and lasting.

The Great Dances of the California Yurok, the Deerskin and Jumping Dances,
part of the world renewal ceremony and shamanic training ritual, are remarkably
similar to the Shaker ritual of 1837 to 1847. At each sacred sweat house of the
Yuroks on the Klamath River, a Jumping or Deerskin Dance is made in October
or April at the times of the great ceremonies of the year, world renewal and first
fruits. At one place, called Sa'a-Kepel, the ritual building of a fish weir replaced
the dance.

The dance ground is always the same and is the place that has preeminent
ceremonial sanctity among the Yurok. The dance begins with a formula recited
by an old man who is not a shaman. The formulas are full of the names of specific
places described very exactly, which are believed to have existed unchanged since
the time when there were no men in the world. There is nothing symbolic or
inherently religious in the appearance of the places evoked in the formula, nor
are the places prominent in myth. The formulas frequently call on rocks and
the spirits in the rocks. Kroeber lists forty rocks addressed by the formulas, including a "bold column" of rock at the mouth of a river, a large perched boulder
at the foot of a waterfall, other large rocks at the water's edge, and a stone altar
at river's edge.[24]

After the recitation of the formula, the dance begins and continues every afternoon, or sometimes morning and afternoon, for five, ten, or more days. The
numbers five and ten are important. The regalia for the dance is not sacred.
Only men can dance, but women can watch. During the dance, certain people,
both men and women, inhabit a house sanctified by tradition for this purpose,
fast and spend a number of nights in the associated sweat house.

Here is the sequence of events at a specific Jumping Dance at Weitspus which
lasts for two days. The formula reciter recites and an assistant prays and makes
offerings at eleven places identified by rocks or bushes along the path from the
village to the summit of the sacred mountain, named Kewet. There are three
such offering places in the village, five on the way up the mountain, one near the
summit, one at the summit, and the one under a sacred cedar tree, also on the
summit, where a fire is kindled and the dances are made. The people climb the
mountain starting in the early morning, following the formula reciter to the
top. There is line dancing by men and boys in small groups at the fourth to the
eighth stops and circle dancing by men at the ninth and tenth stops. At the sacred
tree, only men and boys dance, first in a circle, then separating into lines of three.

Under the tree, there is much wailing and lamentation in remembrance of the dead. At mealtime, there is relaxation and merriment; all camp for the night on the summit.

Both the Yurok shamanic dance and New England Shaker ritual start with an early morning procession up a sacred mountain, stopping at designated places where ritual is performed. At the top, the Yurok in the Jumping Dance kindle a fire and dance in a circle and in lines under the sacred tree. In the shamanic training, the novice spends a night in a stone prayer seat at the summit. Short aligned rock rows, rock circles and rock stacks are built along the track up the mountain. In New England, at the top of the holy hill, all the Shakers danced and a stone altar was built, a stone mound with four capstones on top. Also, at the summit a hexagonal fenced enclosure was built, at one end of which was placed a standing stone slab, called the fountain.

Indian Shakers

Learning of the Indian Shakers of the northwest coast of the United States gave us the first-hand historical evidence which verified our perceptions of exchange of religious ideas between Indians and European settlers and between Indian groups throughout America. It fit like a keystone into our assembled theories. A messianic cult, called Shakers, had intruded into the cultures of the Yurok, Hupa and Tolowa tribes of the Klamath River of northern California, among others.

As the contemporary reports by the Indians and Indian agents of the coastal regions of southern Puget Sound go, John Slocum, a Skokomish Indian about forty years of age, fell seriously ill sometime in the 1890s. The medicine men could not cure him, and he fell into a trance and was presumed to be dead. Some said that he had been "killed" by an Indian medicine man, who shot his *tamaneous* or guardian spirit into him. Slocum was laid out in state on a board, covered with a sheet and prepared for burial. After a time, reported to have been between six and forty-eight hours, he revived. He claimed to have been to the gate of heaven, where, looking back, he saw his body without a soul, as well as the wickedness of the evil medicine men, and of gambling and liquor. An angel told him to return to the earth, for he was not ready for heaven.

Slocum also claimed to have a message from God, and he commenced to set up a church and preach Christianity. He said that another message for healing would come later. About a year after his "death" and rebirth, he fell seriously ill again and was again expected to die. The medicine men could not help him this time either, but Slocum's wife, Mary, had a vision accompanied by an ecstatic shaking of her body. While Mary shook, John recovered. Mary's shaking was seen as the expected message from God for healing the sick, and it gave the church a needed renewal in which she had an important role. From this beginning, church ritual developed, which included special garments, hand-held bells, candles, and organized dancing incorporating shaking.[25]

Dancing to bring on a mystical state of mind is common throughout the history of man. In North America, traditional Indian dancing and much folk dancing of the later immigrants are organized forms of this phenomenon. Violent ecstatic shaking, however, is confined to a few religious cults of the eighteenth, nineteenth and twentieth centuries and to American folk dancing of the twentieth century.

Psychologist Julian Jaynes, speculating on the roots of this phenomenon, writes that in ancient times people were incapable of introspective thinking and acted in response to hallucinations coming from the right hemisphere of the brain. This reliance on gods led to the use of divination, dream omens and shamanism, which were the beginnings of astronomy. The most recent stage has been man's complete reliance on his reasoning powers, from the left hemisphere of the brain, to solve problems. Hypnosis, schizophrenia, religious frenzy, as well as poetry and music, are throwbacks to the ancient way of thinking.[26]

Jaynes sees the use of psychotropic drugs as the American Indian's way of contacting more profound realities in the face of a breakdown of his traditional way of thinking. This is analogous to the collapse of organized oracles in Europe which resulted in cults of induced possession. Jaynes' theory of the origin of religious frenzy such as shaking would explain the Indian Shakers. Mary Slocum's shaking can be seen as a reaction to the breakdown of the old ways brought about by the intrusion of white settlers and a foreign religion.

The church was incorporated in 1910 as the Indian Shaker Church, the name suggested by James Wickersham, their legal counsellor and public defender for many years. He was instrumental in giving the church a firm legal foundation able to resist attacks by both government and better established Christian churches aimed at eliminating shamanism from the Shaker ritual.

The Indian Shaker Church spread to the Indian reservations of the Olympic Peninsula and then to Oregon, British Columbia, northern California and to the Nez Percé of Idaho, although it did not flourish in Canada because of strong opposition by Roman Catholic Indians. In 1926, the cult was introduced to the Yurok Indians at the mouth of the Klamath River of California and over the next few years to the neighboring Hupas, Tolowas and Wiyots. These are the same Yuroks described earlier as being of Algonquin stock from eastern North America. They continued to use stone structures, identical to those found in New England, in the vision quest and training of shamans.

The Indian Shaker Church is a blend of Christian and Indian traditional forms. The shaking ritual for healing is shamanic, pure and simple, and the Christian overlay, which varies considerably from church to church, is also mostly shamanic. Shamanism is associated with arctic animistic religions because the name came from that source, but it is not a religion in itself. The concept of a shaman as a priest or healer of special training who is responsive to gods and spirits is a prominent ingredient of many religions, including the Christianity that the colonists brought to America. Probably contributing to the Yurok's ready acceptance of the new church was the fact that Yurok shamans were women and Mary Slocum led the native shamanistic part of the Indian Shaker Church.

Members of the dominant conservative wing of the church do not believe in the Bible. They hold that convictions based on private visions are the true sources of doctrine and that shaking is the most important feature of the church. Baptism, marriage and ordination are meaningless for most participants, who consider ethics a minor matter, but see Jesus Christ as the source of shamanic power. To them, a good Christian is a good shaman. The minor radical wing uses the Bible, but considers divine intervention in worldly affairs to be rare. It accepts Christ's teachings and relegates shaking to a secondary role, in this way, seeking common ground with other Christian churches.

In 1902, Lans Kalapa, leader of an early Indian Shaker group on the northern Olympic Peninsula, attempted to eliminate the cross from Shaker ritual. According to A. S. Reagen, school teacher among the Ouilente Indians of the region, Kalapa signed a document stating his views. If the document is authentic, which is likely, it reveals the situation not only in the Indian Shaker Church but also elsewhere where Indians have accepted Christianity. Kalapa held that the shamans were the leaders of the Indian Shaker organization and that they clothed their old performances with a very thin cloak of Christianity that would hide the shamanistic ceremonies and practices. This position is supported by an incident at the Hupa Shaker Church on the upper Klamath River in 1932, when some Indians had visions of "Indian devils" whom they claimed were "shooting" the Shakers with poison as they danced. Announcement of these visions precipitated wild chases to drive away the Indian devils. Among the Yurok, in particular, witch hunts and contests between shamans within the Shaker Church were common. Also among the Yurok, there was a faction which claimed to reject shamanism entirely, as well as all traditional Indian traits and beliefs, and would not take part in the religious dances. Today, the remaining Indian Shakers can cure one another with the shaking ritual, and some have clairvoyant power, including the ability to find lost articles.

The ritual elements of the Indian Shaker Church include the cross, candles, hand-held bells, a prayer table or altar, special garments worn during service, and church orientation. The long axis of the church is east-west with the altar on the east and entrance on the west, an orientation that is identical to pre-Reformation churches of Europe. The shaking, which began as an undisciplined frenzy, eventually became a well-organized dance beginning with all facing the prayer table, men in ranks on the left and women on the right. From these positions, the dancers form processions which may become counterclockwise circles, a men's circle alternating with a women's circle. They may weave between ranks across the hall and exchange a ritual handshake when passing another person in the procession. The rhythm is fast but forward progress is slow, as in many Indian dances. Heel stamping with either fixed or flexed knees produces three basic steps. Hand movements are also choreographed.

Anthropologist H. G. Barnett observed that the dance of the healing ceremony resembles the dances of the United Order of Believers in Christ's Second Coming, popularly known as the Shakers. He suggests that Wickersham may have passed along descriptions of ritual which he had seen among the Holy Rollers of Appalachia, but he writes that "the Indian Shaker religion has no connection with that sect [the New England Shakers]." Nevertheless, the similarities between the ritual of the New England Shakers and the Indian Shakers are indeed remarkable: 1) Both separate men and women in the dance. 2) Both refer to members as brothers and sisters. 3) Both use hand bells as signals in the service. 4) Both have the same symbolic colors, blue and white. 5) Both refer to the content of visions as "gifts." 6) Both refer to the dance as work or labor. 7) Many dance patterns are identical. 8) Footwork in the dance is very similar, in part identical. 9) Both are called Shakers. 10) Both speak in tongues during the service.

Reconstruction of Ritual Exchange

It is well established that the New England Shakers, while having a rigid code of personal behavior, were nevertheless receptive to theological ideas and ritual practices from other religions. The Indians were, in a similar manner, able to absorb Christianity into their traditional animistic religion. In addition to spiritual interaction, we have cited a few direct references to Indian participation in Shaker meetings and to the presence of Shaker leaders at Indian ceremonies. From this background, we think it possible to reconstruct the probable specific circumstances surrounding this cultural exchange between Shakers and Indians and suggest that the following scenario is how it may have happened.

Five hundred or more years ago there must have been a westward migration by eastern, Algonquian-speaking people to the Pacific coast. They naturally took their ritual with them and continued it there over the years. The next link was the passing down of this ritual and accompanying beliefs to succeeding generations, both those remaining in New England and those resettled in the American West. The tradition included the continued building of stone structures as ritual architecture.

The New England Shaker ritual performed within the meetinghouse was fully developed by 1795. Dancing was a mixture of local invention, Indian traditional ritual dance, and European country dancing. In 1807, a Shaker mission went from Turtle Creek, Ohio, to a tribe of Shawnees at Greenville, Ohio, where a revival had broken out among the natives. As a result of this meeting, Richard McNemar and his companions, after participating in Shawnee religious ritual, decided that the Indians did not require conversion to Christianity. From that moment on, these Shakers gradually incorporated Indian religious ideas and practices into the Society at Union Village, and these ideas eventually pervaded all the communities, reinforcing earlier Indian influences in New England. The Indian revival meeting in Shawnee territory included many different tribes, some probably from as far as California. McNemar probably picked up knowledge of the Indian ritual, including dance steps and possibly the Yurok ways of California. Similarly, knowledge of Shaker ways could have been conveyed to the Yurok as a result of this or similar meetings.

After 1807, both Christianized Indians and Indianized Shakers were active in the Midwest. Their knowledge of ritual and tradition surely found its way into the Ghost Dance and the Prophet Dance, to the Smohalla cult of the 1870s, and then to the Indian Shakers of Washington State. That the Shawnee Prophet and later John Slocum both experienced near death and revival, had visions of Heaven and Hell, and abhorred alcohol suggests possible direct communication between Indian peoples of the Midwest and Far West or a common stress and response. This transfer of religious beliefs and ritual was ignored by the white invaders as not relevant to Indian problems.

In 1818, the Christianized New Stockbridge Indians from Oneida, New York, mostly Iroquois, journeyed west, via southwestern Ohio where the Shakers were located, thus providing an additional religious link between East and West. They became famous in the Midwest because they sought to create a peaceful community where Indians lived in fellowship with the whites and because they had the manner and language of white men, contrasting sharply with the Plains Indians.[27]

Just when the idea of an outdoor sacred plot of land in each Shaker community became important is unknown, but it was probably some years before the official dictum from the Shaker headquarters at New Lebanon in 1842. In the 1780s, outdoor meetings in a New Lebanon orchard in which spiritual food was cooked and eaten anticipated to a small degree the mountain meetings of the 1840s. Also, the Union Village sacred plot dates back to 1805, and there is evidence that the western Shaker Societies acted independently of the leaders at New Lebanon. In 1867, the western Societies attempted to introduce democracy to Shaker administration but were overruled by the eastern Societies. It is not unlikely that the revelation announcing outdoor services twice a year on a sacred plot of land originated very early in the revival movement, based on ancient precedents, and was practiced in Ohio long before the official announcement from headquarters. It is also likely that the spirits of departed Indians that came to the meetings of 1839 included those individual Shawnees whom Richard McNemar and his companions knew in 1807.

The mountain ritual of the Shakers appeared on the scene in the 1840s. While the Indian ritual which parallels it may go back 500 or more years in New England, we cannot be sure. We only know that the Yurok practiced it in recent times. Therefore, we must consider a connection in the early 1800s between the Yurok of California and the New England Shakers. This could have been physical contact between peoples, or a psychic communication, a notion which cannot be dismissed out of hand, given the shamanic nature of the ritual. After all, the spiritual interactions during Shaker meetings also included Eskimos, Lapps, Chinese, Abyssinians, Hottentots and other people relatively unfamiliar to the Shakers.[28]

The cycle of religious transfer across space and through time is completed in the late nineteenth century when the Indian Shaker ritual was started on the West Coast, influenced as well by the old shamanic traditions. This scenario for the flow of ritual shows Christianity and Indian religion each being transferred across the country, the Indian possibly both ways. But always the two paths were intermingled. In the exchange, not only were the Indians Christianized, but also the white Christians seem to have sought a measure of Indian belief to temper the severity of their Calvinism. This trend continues to this day in evangelical churches of many persuasions.

Earlier, we asked about the Shakers' possible connection to the stone and earthen works at Harvard, Massachusetts. History has told us that the Shakers selected holy places on the landscape for their ritual, including hills and rivers, during the period 1837 to 1847. Also, the Shakers built stone altars at their holy places, and erected standing stones. Stone mounds remain today located just outside the fences which enclosed the feast grounds. It became the custom for each passerby to place a stone at the Harvard site where Father Whittaker was whipped, which resulted in a stone heap, following Indian tradition.[29] But this accounts for only a small part of the structures that we have seen on Shaker lands. We have shown that the Yurok Indians, whose ritual was like the one followed by the Shakers, built stone mounds, rows and enclosures for their ritual. In Chapter 4, we showed that perched boulders played a role among Indians universally. The perched boulders, balanced rocks, stone rows, stone mounds and earthworks of the Harvard, Massachusetts, Shaker village fit into this pattern of Indian ritual landscape.

In Chapter 11, we describe the stone and earthen structures that abound on the land of the Harvard Shaker Society, which is located at the site of the Nashoba Indian praying village. We infer from the circumstantial evidence, that here the ritual landscape architecture is the work of both Indians and Shakers, first by Indians, then by both working together, and finally by the Shakers. That the Shakers would ritualize the landscape is consistent with their practice of creating buildings, furniture and other utilitarian objects of sublime simplicity as a religious activity. The Midwestern Shaker sites are devoid of stone and earthen structures today because they were built on choice farmland and have been destroyed by cultivation. As an example, Jehovah's Chosen Square at Union Village, which was a grove of ash, oak and hickory trees with a spiritual fountain marked with a stone slab in the center, is now part of a large cornfield. It may not be a coincidence that the Union Village Shaker Society was situated between the Great and Little Miami Rivers only seven miles from Fort Ancient, built by the Mound Builders, one of the most impressive earth and stone ceremonial enclosures in the United States.

The stone and earthern structures of the Mound Builders will be examined in the next chapter, as well as similar structures throughout North America and Western Europe, in order to see what light they shed on the stone structures and ritualized landscape of New England.

9

Traditions of Stoneworks in North America, Europe and the Arctic

The Mound Builders

The Mound Builders of the American Midwest, identified with Adena (100 B.C. to A.D. 700) and Hopewellian (500 B.C. to A.D. 800) phases of Woodland Indian culture, are known best for extensive and elaborate earthworks. Less known is the important role in their culture of stone in mounds, linear works, effigies, platforms and other types of structure. In Chapter 1, we described stone burial vaults within Hopewellian earthen mounds in the Missouri River Valley, which date to about 2,000 years ago and have a striking similarity to some New England stone chambers. In fact, all of the types of stone structure that are found in New England are also found in Hopewellian constructions in the Midwest.

The stone rows, mounds and enclosures and earthen mounds and enclosures that are characteristic features of Adena and Hopewellian sites have aspects that are found also in New England. A stone heap near Chilicothe, Ohio, on a dividing ridge between streams, is described as remarkable by Squier and Davis. It is 106 feet long, 60 feet wide and 3 to 4 feet high, made from stones of all sizes, some of which came from the creek one-half mile below. There are many mounds of this description in New England. Prufer sees the Hopewellian phase of mound building as a cult superimposed on distinct cultures which had basically Algonquian traits and extensive trade networks. He also sees the architectural element of a mound blocking a gateway as characteristically Hopewellian. Intrusions of Adena and Hopewellian artifacts into New England are well established. Adena artifacts, including bird effigy stones, large plug-ended stone pipes, boat-shaped

9-1 Hopewellian bird effigy stone from Swanton, Vt., *l* (after Nadaillac, note 15). Adena bird effigy stone from Wenham, Mass., *r* (after Fetchko, note 1)

stones (Figure 9–1) and copper and slate gorgets, were reported in New England as early as 1868 by Perkins. Copper artifacts and axes from the Archaic Period of types which predate the Midwestern Mound Builders have also been found.[1]

Mississippian art (A.D. 800–1700), much of which may have been an outgrowth of Hopewellian, continued the building of groups of temple mounds which did not cover burials.[2] In Chapter 3, we showed that some New England mounds are contemporary with Mississippian (A.D. 1100) but generally of smaller size, without burials, and built primarily of rock rather than soil. We speculate that the stone and earthen constructs in New England may be the functional equivalent of the ceremonial earth and stone works of the Midwestern river valleys, perhaps indicating a connection with Adena, Hopewellian or Mississippian culture.

Groups of stone mounds are very common in the Appalachian Mountains, including effigies, large linear forms, platforms and cairns dated to the second and third centuries A.D. As usual, these sites of geometric earth and stone works yield few if any diagnostic artifacts or pottery. In Georgia in 1979, an effigy mound 300 feet long in the form of a serpent was discovered, surrounded by a group of fifty stone mounds.

Squier and Davis classify the Midwestern stone enclosures, usually located on high promontories overlooking the great rivers, as works of defense, while they classify the earthworks of various complex and curious geometries, usually located in the valleys, as sacred enclosures. The largest enclosure of the former class which they observed is Fort Ancient on the east bank of the Little Miami River thirty-three miles north of Cincinnati, Ohio. The Fort Ancient earthen and stone works were built by the prehistoric Hopewellian people between 300 B.C. and A.D. 600. These, like many similar structures usually called forts, form a huge walled enclosure a mile in length and three-and-one-half miles in circumference. They are built on a promontory jutting out into a gorge of the Little Miami, and outside the walls, the land drops off precipitously to the river 300 feet below, as shown in Figure 9–2. This dropoff would be the most striking feature of the site were it cleared of trees as it no doubt was when in use.

While Hopewellian implements, ornaments and pottery have been found in the walls and interior of the enclosure, the Hopewellian villages are found only outside of the enclosure. After the Hopewellians had disappeared, a later culture, inappropriately known as "Fort Ancient," built a village within the southern

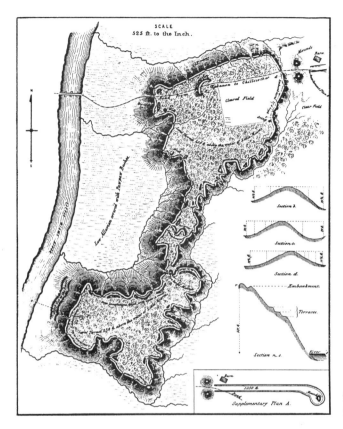

9-2 Fort Ancient, Ohio
(from Squier and Davis, note 1)

part of the enclosure and others elsewhere along the Little Miami. They lived there until the early seventeenth century. Recent thoughts lean toward the view that Fort Ancient was a place used for ceremonial rites, rather than a fort.[3]

In 1897, J. P. Hale described an irregular, elliptical enclosure of stone walls six or seven feet high and seven or eight miles in circuit on the upper reaches of Mount Carbon in West Virginia. Near the center of the enclosure were the supposed remains of two round towers twenty feet in height and diameter. After making the difficult ascent to 1,600 feet above the nearby Kanawha River and viewing the structures personally later in 1897, he published a revised account in which the "walls" became ridges of roughly piled stone twelve to fifteen feet wide and three to four feet high. Though there were in fact miles of these rows, they were intermittent and the eight mile circuit included long gaps. The "round towers" were piles of stone, one twenty feet in diameter and three feet high and the other a circular ridge of stones thirty-three feet in diameter. Hale wrote, "I feel quite positive that there never was a foot of built-up wall in all the series. I am sure that the ridges or windrows of stone remain today just as the builders left them ages ago." We believe that Hale's unusually perceptive obser-

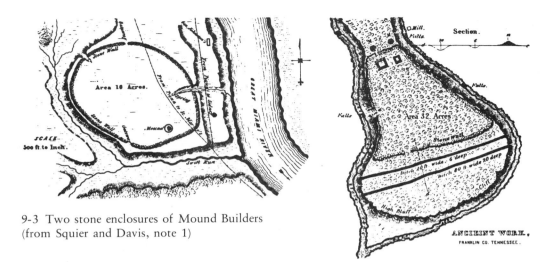

9-3 Two stone enclosures of Mound Builders
(from Squier and Davis, note 1)

vation was correct. Along the river at the base of the cliff is a large burial ground.
Nothing remains above ground to indicate burials, but each skeleton, facing
east, was covered by a pile of stones beneath the present-day surface of the ground.[4]

Elliptical stone enclosures on ridges are common among the structures described
and mapped by Squier and Davis in Ohio and Tennessee. Two of these are shown
in Figure 9–3, since established as Hopewellian. A twenty-acre hilltop enclosure,
shown in Figure 9–4, was used by the Seneca Indians of Ontario County, New
York, in historical times. Unfortunately it was destroyed by the Marquis de
Nonville, governor of Canada, in 1687, during a period of church tyranny
comparable to that in Puritan Massachusetts.[5] The location of this enclosure
bridges the geographical gap between the Midwest and New England, and its
destruction attests to its ceremonial and religious significance.

In New England, the stone enclosures known as Indian forts and other large
structures of earth and stone are similar in several respects to the works of the
Mound Builders. Characteristics such as orientation, relationship to rivers,

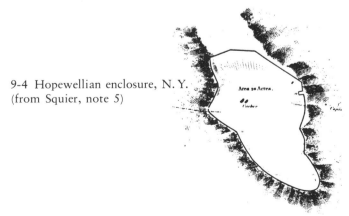

9-4 Hopewellian enclosure, N.Y.
(from Squier, note 5)

springs and lakes, avenues, acute-angle intersections, organization and design of mounds, effigy forms, all are similar. For the most part, the Midwestern structures are larger and make greater use of earth, differences that can be explained by the differences in topography and geology of the respective regions. For example, New England has none of the great flat-topped ridges which jut into the valleys of the Midwest and provide platforms for the great stone and earthen enclosures we have described. However, in northern Maine, we have mapped miles of stone structures retained by built walls which are five feet high and ten to twenty feet wide. These great causeway-like constructs wander across the hillsides connecting great stone mounds and natural landscape features, and bear no relationship to historical land boundaries. On one farm alone, we estimated that over 20,000 tons of rock had been dug, transported and built into these structures.

We infer that some of the New England works are contemporary with or older than the comparable works of the Midwestern Mound Builders. One consideration leads us to favor the New England stonework as earlier and perhaps prototypical. In places throughout the world where stone and earthen works are found near the coast, astronomy is vital to the landscape design and religion, whereas at inland sites, astronomy is less dominant and less sophisticated. We know that celestial navigation at sea, at many places and in many epochs, has been the inspiration for astronomy on land, and there is evidence that American Indians traveled on the deep ocean off the Pacific coast in historical times and off the Atlantic coast in prehistoric times.

Indian Ritual Stonework in Western North America

In addition to the Midwestern Mound Builders, there are native groups throughout the western part of North America who built stone structures as ritual architecture. These structures, found in a variety of natural environments, are also similar to those in New England. Although anthropologists are reluctant to impute cultural relationships between geographically distant peoples, particularly when the ethnographic and archaeological records of the practical aspects of daily life do not appear to support it, if this topic is examined from a broad perspective which includes environmental and religious considerations, a pattern of detailed similarities between distant groups emerges.

Far more is known about Indian ritual life in the western part of America than in New England, where it has been given short shrift in the anthropological literature. We suggest that much can be learned about New England Indian spiritual life by studying California Indians. Naturally there are differences between the religions of Native Americans in different geographical regions and in different epochs, but these differences are minor compared with the similarities. We see in New England in remarkable detail the same ritual para-

9-5 Cahuila Indian
sacred perched boulder,
Palm Springs, Calif.

phernalia and surroundings that are reported in the literature of the western parts of America.

Among the Chumash of southern California, close-grained, dense stones called charmstones, about six inches in length and carefully worked and polished, were collected from great distances, apparently for ritual use. At one Chumash sacred place, in an area enclosed by stones, two groups of charmstones were found. Each group was made up of ten oblong stones radiating outward from a central round stone that rested in a cup-like boulder. In addition, many charmstones were buried within the stone enclosure. A Chumash Indian from the Santa Ynez valley said that the medicine man would fast for a month and consume quantities of jimson weed broth before using the stones.[6] While walking about an Indian reservation in this region, Mavor noticed a large perched boulder on bedrock at the edge of a stream (Figure 9–5). There was a natural cavity in the boulder which upon inspection revealed a neat collection of charmstones, thereby identifying the boulder and its place as sacred.

The charmstones used in Chumash ritual were considered very powerful. The shaman arranged them in a circle of nine, ten, twelve or twenty, then shoved them violently together and sprinkled water over them. Various medicine materials were assembled about them, red ochre spread over the whole, and a dance performed around the stones. Among the adjacent Yokuts of the San Joaquin Valley, the stones are of a plumb-bob shape with a knob at one end and a point at the other. They were often hung on branches along streams to bring good fishing. Plummet-shaped stones are without doubt ceremonial objects, used as amulets or fetishes for luck in hunting and fishing and for rainmaking by shamans. A pervading creation myth among the Indians of southern and central California refers to a black, hard rock called *tosaut*, used to fasten the earth.

9-6 Plummets: charmstones, *left two* (after Chartkoff, note 9); Early Archaic, New England, *center one* (after Fowler, note 7); pendants, classified as fishing weights, *right two* (after Willoughby, note 7)

The word occurs among the Chumash as the name of the charmstones used by shamans. Many people of this region had similar sacred stones.[7] In spite of this clear documentation concerning the ritual use of charmstones, including the "plummet type," in California, archaeologists in the East insist that stones of identical design have only practical uses such as for fishing weights (Figure 9-6).

Also, in southern California, stones are used in fertility ritual. These stones are mostly natural boulders, in some cases worked by man, that resemble male and female genitalia. The sites where these rocks are found were used by the Kumeyaay Indians in their winter solstice ritual, and women of the tribe also went there to ensure fertility. Eastern Algonquin Indians made similar ritual use of similar rock formations in Ontario, Canada. According to McGowan, "It is possible that the Algonkian Indians believed that the fissure led to power hidden deep inside the rock, that it was the yoni, the entrance to the uterus of Mother Earth."[8]

Some sites in California are recognized as places created specifically for conducting ritual activities, based on rock structures, rock art and astronomical alignments. The Moki snake dance is held at a great rock stack located within the pueblo grounds (Figure 9–7). Often, there are no archaeological remains to mark such spots, and they are known only from historical records or current use.

9-7 Rock stack, Moki Snake Dance grounds, N. M. (from Starr, note 9)

Some such sites, particularly those with astronomical features, are usually found at some distance from settlements, where the horizon events could be seen more clearly and the ritual performance could be separated from everyday activities.[9] These facts probably explain why few if any subsistence artifacts are found at the places in New England we call ritual sites. This does not mean that subsistence activities were not sacred and without ritual, only that some rituals such as the vision quest are performed at remote locations.

The people of the Yurok nation live on the lower Klamath River near the Pacific Ocean in extreme northwestern California. While there are differences among the rituals of California Indian societies, the basic characteristic of shamanism as seen among the Yurok persists everywhere. This seems true even when the unique effects of secret societies and narcotics in some tribes and the pervading effect of the modern Ghost Dance phenomenon of 1872–1892, a reaction to the white man's destruction of Indian cultures, are taken into consideration. The Ghost Dance penetrated to the Indians of half of the United States, affecting those tribes that had experienced such cultural decay that a revivalistic influence could impress them, but it left most Californians untouched. This provides additional justification for seeking authentic American Indian ritual among the California Indians.

Recent California Ethnography

There are specific similarities between rock structures and their settings in New England and rock features of six types in a mountain range in the extreme northwest of coastal California. Following up on Kroeber's studies of the Yurok, Chartkoff reports that man-made rock cairns, alignments of rocks, hearth rings, stone stacks, stone rings and semicircular enclosures are used today by members of the Yurok Indians and their neighboring tribes for traditional religious activity including vision quests and ritual training.[10]

Before learning of this striking evidence from California, which associates the stone structures originally identified by Kroeber with Yurok shamanistic ritual, we had arrived at Native American ritual use of some of New England structures through the results of excavation of the stone mound at Freetown, Massachusetts, the prevalence of astronomical associations, and sparse New England ethnography. We had also seen many examples of the best known ritual tradition in New England, the Native American practice of leaving donation stones or branches in piles at important places.

The most complex California structures are U-shaped enclosures of laid up stonework called prayer seats by the Indians (Figure 9–8). They are typically six to twelve feet wide, three feet deep and one to two feet high. However, there are other types of construction, for example, a square twelve feet on a side in which one side is a large boulder. Few artifacts occur with prayer seats and they generally are found on high rock outcrops or mountain peaks. The opening

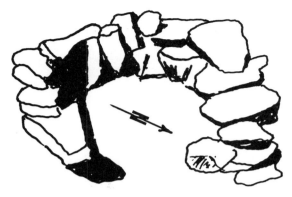

9-8 Yurok stone prayer seat
(after Chartkoff, note 9)

usually faces east or northeast, or toward other prayer seats or dominant mountain peaks or hills. Some prayer seats are placed below peaks and constructed as closed semicircular structures built against rock outcrops. Traditional physicians or shamans visit the prayer seats to gain and renew their healing powers, and at the seat they dance, fast, pray and meditate for up to ten days. Sometimes tool flaking is taught at the prayer seats.

Rock stacks of one to four rocks piled one on top of another on a larger rock or bedrock are found along the trails to the prayer seats. It appears that their construction is part of a ritual purification performed during the approach to the prayer seat. Hearth rings are built during the vision quest along the trail to the prayer seat when an overnight stay is made and also may be part of the ritual at the prayer seat. Curved and straight laid-up stone rows of six to twenty-five feet in length are found close to other rock features. Small rock circles which are not hearth rings are also found near prayer seats and may have a role in the ritual. Sometimes sweathouses are found at the ritual sites.

Cairns are rock piles with six to seventy rocks piled randomly and are distinct from rock stacks, which are orderly. Sometimes they approach pyramids in structure, however, and they may appear as pavements as well. Some cairns may be prayer seats that have been purposely destroyed after an individual has made his final quest, and some form astronomical alignments.

The Yurok, Wiyot, and Hupa mountain ritual is part of the world renewal ceremony, which also includes a brush dance. It contrasts with that of the lowland settlements of California, but Chartkoff sees both as part of a common cosmology. In the Yurok view, elevation conveys social importance, so that mountain prayer seats are closer to the source of power than lowland settlements. Chartkoff suggests that the lowland ceremonies celebrate acquired powers but that the power is acquired in the mountains.[11]

Ritualists pass along part of the ritual to one individual and part to another. In this way, the ritual changes over time because no individual knows the entire procedure used by his ancestors. This suggests that the act of performing the ritual was more important than the detailed materials or procedures. If this is true, one might expect considerable differences in ritual in widely separated

9-9 Circular stone enclosure, N. H.   9-10 V-shaped structure, Foxboro, Mass.

geographical areas even if transmission of the ritual is by direct contact. It is therefore remarkable that there would be such similarity, described throughout this book and summarized below, between the stones in New England and those at sites in northwestern California. These observations imply that the stonework is an unchanging part of tradition or that communication between peoples in these widely separated regions has been quite recent.

The structures in New England that appear analogous to the Yurok prayer seats include: 1) a rectangular low stone enclosure at Montville, Connecticut; 2) pits or enclosures on bedrock among stone mounds at Montville; 3) enclosures in Woods Hole, Massachusetts, surrounded by groups of stone mounds; 4) circular enclosures on a hilltop in New Hampshire (Figure 9–9); 5) V-shaped enclosures in New Hampshire, Foxboro, Massachusetts (Figure 9–10), and Foster, Rhode Island, built against large boulders (These have a remarkable resemblance to Hopi sun temples, Figure 9–11, which are often built as a partial ring structure of stones with a large rock forming the back.); 6) circular enclosures with openings in Foxboro, Massachusetts (Figure 9–12); 7) enclosures built into the Queen's Fort, Exeter, Rhode Island; 8) U-shaped enclosures in Boxborough and Lunenberg, Massachusetts, South Royalton, Vermont, and Foster, Rhode Island.

9-11 Hopi sun temple (after Fewkes, note 13)

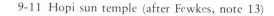

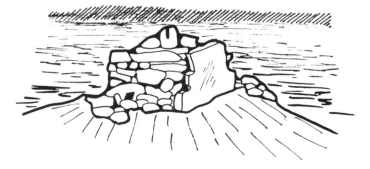

9-12 Circular stone enclosure, Foxboro, Mass.

We dwell on the Yurok of California not only because identical stone structures are found in association in similar settings in New England, but also because there is a connection between the people in both places on quite independent grounds. The Yurok and Wiyot people of California speak the Ritwan stock of the Algonquian languages of eastern and central North America. Based on linguistic analysis, their ancestors migrated into northwest California from the Saint Lawrence River area between A.D. 900 and 1100, toward the end of the Late Pacific Period. The archaeological record of northwest California shows that there was a hiatus in the cultural record between 500 B.C. and A.D. 1100 in the region ultimately occupied by the Yurok and Wiyot. They apparently migrated to a place where no one lived. In addition, the historic Yurok are known as skilled boatbuilders and navigators.[12] As we show later, Native Americans of the coast of Labrador had comparable skills thousands of years ago.

Stone Chambers and Kivas

An important question is whether or not the stone chambers of New England are in fact analogous to the Yurok prayer seats, or are the eastern counterpart of sweat houses or kivas, or all these things together, as Kroeber implies was the case in the West. Their design and construction is clearly more complex than the California structures, but they might be for winter use. They are frequently astronomically oriented and set on high places to give a panoramic view. The ceremonial kivas of the American Southwest survive from Archaic times and traditionally symbolize the womb of the earth from which the races of human-kind were born. Many of them, like the New England stone chambers, were built below ground and are associated with astronomical ritual. The idea that kivas are related to the ceremonial sweat house, used all over the world, has been frequently cited. For example, Kroeber writes, "A failure to connect the kivas and sweathouses would be more than short-sighted."[13]

The kivas of the Mesa Verde Cliff Palace were built of stone following an ancient traditional design with detailed features we have found at Calendar

One.[14] The corners of intersecting walls were rarely interlocked, and the floors are commonly hardened earth or the natural bedrock; it is not unusual to find the floor of the kiva quarried down a few feet. Small cup-like artificial depressions are sometimes found in the bedrock floors. At Mesa Verde, a smooth ovoidal stone with a flat base was found at the northwest corner of kiva H. It was supposed by the excavators, based on Hopi tradition, to be an idol, possibly an earth goddess. In addition, rock markings in the form of vertical parallel concave abraded grooves were found on the cliffs at Mesa Verde, similar to markings found on the walls of Hopi kivas. All these features of the Cliff Palace kivas are found at the Calendar One bowl stone chamber, and the similarities are unlikely to be coincidental.

Kivas at Mesa Verde typically have vertical ventilating shafts built into the walls of the structures. Kiva V, however, also has a horizontal subterranean passage, large enough for a person to crawl through, carved into the bedrock (Figure 9–13). This quarrying was done in addition to considerable lowering of the kiva floor into natural rock. The radial passage is intersected by a lateral passage from which a person can enter the kiva through a manhole in the floor. Similar arrangements of unknown function have been found at Anasazi Pueblo Bonito in Chaco Canyon and near Chama.

Another example of an inexplicably long entrance passage to a kiva is found on the Rio Mancos. Here, the cliff house is built in an indentation sixty feet wide and fifteen feet deep in the cliff forty feet above the river, as shown in Figure 9–14. The kiva is entered through an opening of twenty-two inches at the end of a straight passage thirty feet long.[15] These dimensions are almost the same as those of the Montville, Connecticut, long-passaged chamber described in Chapter 11, and a few other long passages to be found in New England.

9-13 Ceremonial kiva, Mesa Verde, Colo. (from Fewkes, note 14)

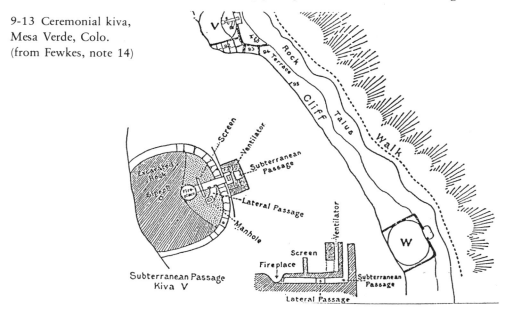

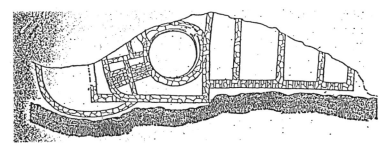

9-14 Kiva, Rio Mancos, N. M.
(from Nadaillac, note 15)

Europe and New England

There is no doubt that there are architectural similarities between the well-studied ancient stone structures of Europe and the stone structures of New England. Also, the design and crafting techniques of many organized stone markings and the signalling of alignments to celestial events on the horizon are much the same on the two continents.

The Native American's preoccupation with the spirituality of all things in nature was and continues to be shared by many people the world over, so that much of the ritual and its material remains are universal. For this reason, some immigrants to North America brought about very little change in this aspect of American culture. Also, we expect small effects from visitors whose ways contrasted sharply with the American cultures, until the Native Americans were physically displaced by Europeans whose culture was transplanted to America in the seventeenth century.

However, archaeological evidence suggests that an important cultural diffusion took place between about 10,000 and 2,000 B.C. through movement of people in the boreal and arctic regions of Europe, Asia and America. The ways of life and attitudes toward nature of the people in these two regions were probably similar except for the influences of differences in natural environment between the arctic and temperate zones.

Here, we describe our perception of how natural environment, independent invention, diffusion and transplantation brought about cultural change in prehistoric New England.

The Natural Environment

A tour of the sites of ancient standing stones and stone rings in Europe reveals to even the casual observer that these structures are located systematically upon the landscape. The spectacular sunrises and sunsets on the west coast of Scotland are marked by stones, sometimes aligning with notches in the island hills. When the air is clear, the brilliant red stripe on the sea between the observer and the sun demands our attention.

When following a valley down to the sea, there is usually a constricted place, perhaps where a glacier halted for a time. Here will be found a standing stone or perched boulder. When climbing across fields and hills, eventually the walker will reach a plateau where the distant sea comes into view accompanied by a broad panorama of hills, just as a stone circle thousands of years old appears. Follow a stream up from the sea coast and where there is a waterfall or a sharp bend in the stream, or a division of the stream into two branches, there will be a standing stone, previously invisible, suddenly projecting above the horizon.

The stones of New England were also placed to grace the natural scene, although the landscape is different, less maritime, and without a western seacoast. But rivers, hills and valleys still signal the places where the stones are found. Standing stones and cairns are generally in high places, while stone chambers are often low with a view across a pond to an elevated horizon. The locations appear to have been chosen partly to suit astronomical requirements and partly to grace the natural landscape in ways that ultimately became ritualized. In New England, there are probably more stone structures per square mile than in modern Europe, which is to be expected because the gradual destruction wrought by succeeding cultures has been at work for at least 2,000 years in Europe but, for only 400 years in New England. On the other hand, in Europe there is a continuing respect for ancient remains because of a general feeling of consanguinity. In New England no such bond exists, a fact reflected in callous disinterest in precolonial America, even though some people living today still practice the ways of their native ancestors.

Astronomy is the great cultural unifier, for many of the same events and objects in the sky are seen throughout the world by those who watch for them. We have chosen an astronomical site in Argyllshire, Scotland, on Loch Fyne, to show that even specific architectural similarities between Europe and America are probably mostly of independent origin with the possible addition of elements of an ancient diffusion through the arctic. The site, overlooking Brainport Bay, is probably one of the most revealing of the workings of such places in all of Great Britain. Unlike Stonehenge and other massive monuments, which are atypical of British astronomical sites, the constructions at Brainport are confined to small stones which blend into the natural landscape. In fact, before excavation there were hardly any man-made remains to draw attention to the site. It was defined by natural features of topography, particularly its fine view of the summer solstice sunrise over the hills at the head of Loch Fyne.

9-15 Brainport, site alignment to horizon

The Brainport site was discovered in 1976 by Col. P. F. F. Gladwin. In 1978, he published a description and, in 1980, theories about its astronomical use.[16] In 1982, Dr. Ewan Mackie of the Hunterian Museum, University of Glasgow, led an excavation that found archaeological evidence of features which had been predicted by the astronomical hypothesis, and established a Bronze Age date. Published in *Nature* in March 1985, it stands today as a premier proven astronomical site.[17] We have had similar predictive experiences in New England, both in Vermont and Massachusetts, where we suspected an astronomical site from strictly natural environmental clues and were able to verify our theory by discovering above-ground markers and underground features revealed by excavation.

The Brainport constructions lie on an uneven slope descending to the northeast. The main alignment to the summer solstice sunrise has three marker locations lined up over a distance of about 200 feet, in addition to distant foresights, a cairn and natural horizon features on the skyline twenty-seven miles away (Figure 9–15). The main rock outcrop was modified to form a notch with paving and two revetted terraces (Figure 9–16). It contains two sockets on the sight line for small standing stones, which were found fallen nearby. A few meters lower

9-16 Brainport, main platform stone revetments

9-17 Brainport, split boulder with quartz pavement

9-18 Brainport, gun sight through woods

and to the southwest is a group of two boulders, one of which is shown in Figure 9–17, with a space between them suitable for standing to observe the sunrise in line with the standing stones and notch at the first outcrop. A paving of small pieces of broken quartz surrounds these boulders. The group of features, all lined up to the summer solstice sunrise at distant peaks at the end of Loch Fyne, looks like the "sights of a huge rifle," in a cut through the woods (Figure 9–18).

Some 150 feet southwest of the boulders and about 22 feet higher is another rock outcrop which is paved, sprinkled with broken pieces of quartz, and revetted to form a flat platform. The sightline to the horizon from this platform is too high to use the "gunsight" except as a general directional guide but gives a grand and broad view of the sunset and all the other features of the site. This is perhaps a ceremonial station separate from the point for astronomical observations. Lack of habitation artifacts over the entire site shows the site to have been ceremonial and not a settlement, just as we have found in New England.

On a hilltop 700 feet northwest of the main alignment to the summer solstice sunrise and 130 feet higher lies a fallen standing stone 15 feet long, called the Oak Bank Stone, shown in Figure 9–19. We know that it lies where it fell because its socket is located at the southeast end. Nearby are two subtle rock carvings, each consisting of a groove 16 to 24 inches long with a cupmark at its center (Figure 9–20a). One points to the main outcrop of the main alignment (Figure 9–20b). After transferring the direction of the line from the second groove over to the base of the fallen stone, and cutting a swath through the forest, it was seen that this line pointed directly at a deep V-shaped notch one kilometer away, and to an equinox sunset alignment. This stone follows a pattern, in Scotland, of

9-19 Brainport,
Oak Bank Stone

single standing stones which mark the observation point for a solar alignment to
a distant natural horizon feature. The entire site is within a forestry plantation,
part of the recent extensive reforestation of the Scottish Highlands, so that, as
in New England today, trees must be cut in order to actually witness an astronomical event.

Gladwin also reports the results of naked-eye observation of the sun and
suggests that early observers may have used smoke haze to protect their eyes
from the blinding brightness of the sun. Apparently, distant skylines can be
seen surprisingly well through smoke of suitable density; they are seen best
through a thin, deep haze. To support this argument, Gladwin found a firepit at
the site, between the two standing stones on the summer solstice sunrise alignment, that may have been used to generate such a smoke haze to facilitate obser-

9-20 Brainport, grooved marks indicating
astronomical alignment at observation points

vation. At Upton, Massachusetts, we believe that the long, undulating chamber passage was also used as an optical aid to observation.

Many features of the Brainport site remind us of Calendar One, but the most reasonable explanation for this is that they are geographically universal. Gladwin first noted the astronomy using natural horizon features. Later, a string of stone structures along the solar sight line was found, and excavated artifacts showed use from 1800 B.C. extending into the Christian era, perhaps bridging the gap between the megalithic monuments and early Christianity. Sun worship was quite alive in the time of the Christian missionaries, as we show later. At first, Calendar One was similarly imagined as a calendar which used natural horizon features as foresights, in this case for the six major solar events from a common observation point.[18] Later, a principal alignment of a stone chamber, a C-shaped cairn and a notch on the horizon was discovered. Subsequent excavation hardened the evidence of astronomical use over a long period of time.

Standing stones and cairns have turned out to be suitable for both foresights and observation points on both sides of the Atlantic. A large fallen standing stone on the eastern ridge of Calendar One with an adjacent socket in bedrock is similar to the Oak Bank stone at Brainport. Terracing and pavement have been found at Calendar One, similar to that at Brainport, which appear to be part of the astronomical complex. The features of the sites, both at Brainport and Calendar One, flow naturally from the elemental needs of horizon astronomy for marking and ritualizing astronomical events and probably do not require conceptual or technological capabilities that would need cultural diffusion. The similarities are to be expected among people responding to the same environmental stimuli.

Early Christianity in Ireland and Great Britain

We have discussed the religions of both Native Americans and the historic European settlers in America because they help to explain the stone structures of New England and the circumstances under which these structures were remembered by some and forgotten by others in later generations. But there are serious gaps in the historical record which we believe can be resolved by turning to the more complete history of Europe. In Europe, a similar conflict between Christianity and the old natural religion occurred earlier and more gradually, especially in Great Britain and Ireland. The monks who brought Christianity to these islands from the continent were part of a religious invasion as were the English colonists who invaded America. We can, by examining parallel events, extrapolate to fill the gaps in American history and thereby add to the explanation of the origins and uses of the stone structures. This leads to new evidence that early Christian monks may have actually traveled to America and left subtle imprints on the design of stone structures.

The Celtic and Roman churches differed in organization, discipline and liturgy.[19] The religious community on Iona, which was the base for numerous Christian missions throughout Scotland and Northumbria, was unregimented and owed little if any allegiance to Rome. The monks lived in separate huts or cells grouped about an oratory. Saint Adamnan, ninth Abbott of Iona, who died in A.D. 704, described the first settlements as wattle and daub construction; the monks were a "secular clergy," presumably meaning that they were unordained and did not take a vow of celibacy, as required of all Roman Catholic monks from at least as early as A.D. 590. In the eighth century they came to be called Culdees, meaning worshippers of God, and had by then spread their influence widely.[20] They supplanted the Roman influence of Saint Ninian with a Celtic form of Christianity.

Recent astronomical research on Celtic structures suggests that the Culdee monks' dedication to Christianity was not exclusive and that the Druidic practices of their forbears played a continuing major role in their lives. Eleven stone structures used by Culdee monks in Scotland and Ireland have been found aligned to horizon observations of the sun or stars or both.[21] The willingness of Saint Patrick and the other early Celtic Christian monks to accept the pagan traditions and conform their teachings to them has been discussed by several recent writers.[22] The stone beehive structures and oratories of these early monks are better preserved in Ireland than in Scotland, so we must move temporarily to County Kerry in Ireland for the physical evidence of pagano-Christianity among the monks.

Here, where Saint Brendan and Saint Malkedar led religious communities in the sixth century A.D., there are several oratories in good repair, small rectangular buildings of elegant dry-wall construction. Though none has been archaeologically dated, they are presumed to have been built between A.D. 600 and 1200 (Figure 9–21). The oratories are usually oriented approximately east-west, with openings confined to a small elevated window in the east end and a low door in the west end (Figure 9–22). They are rather dark inside, even in broad daylight. Measurements at several oratories have shown that they were designed so that the rays of the equinox sunrise shine directly into the small window, illuminating the interior in a symmetrical pattern of light and shadow. Also, the sightline along the building axis toward the west is almost always directed at a distant

9-21 Gallerus Oratory, Dingle Peninsula, Ireland

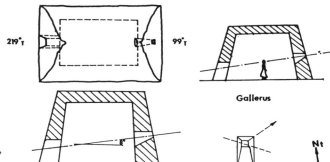

9-22 Equinox sunrise sightlines, Gallerus Oratory

natural horizon feature. In the cases of at least four oratories, the western horizon marker is a prominent hilltop which marked the setting of three of the eleven brightest stars in the sky between A.D. 600 and 1200, Betelgeuse, Procyon and Altair (Figure 9–23).[23] In A.D. 1200, the three stars set at precisely the same place, a rare and memorable event which may date the structures. In the nineteenth century, the stars had moved so that they set within a three-degree envelope, an event still notable enough to suggest its observation by the Shakers at Enfield, New Hampshire.

It is clear from this circumstantial evidence that the old nature religion which identified the sun and stars with the spiritual world was still an important or even dominant part of the lives of these Celtic monks, even though they also embraced Christianity.

The pre-Christian Celtic religion was somewhat similar to that of the American Indian, at least to the extent that it was a nature religion in which the sun played a prominent role and standing stones, cairns, springs, mountains, valleys, lochs, and rivers were integral parts, each with its spirit. Britain at this time was largely agricultural, whereas Native Americans were primarily hunter-gatherers when major European influence came in the seventeenth century. Shamanism originated among hunter-gatherers with the spiritual interaction of wild animals and plants

9-23 Western horizon from Gallerus Oratory, showing three bright stars setting at Sybil Head

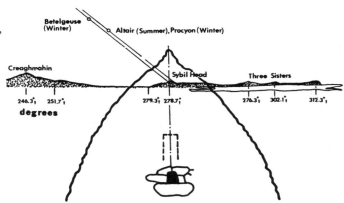

with humans. This spiritual richness became subdued with the introduction of agriculture and other technologies.

The Celtic Christian monks approached the native religion cautiously. The cross was at first quite naturally put on a standing stone located at a place sacred to the natives from time immemorial, which also served as an astronomical marker (Figure 9–24a). Noting the cup marks that occasionally decorate pre-Christian standing stones, the monks, according to a suggestion by Gladwin, incorporated inverted cupmarks or bosses on the design of their Celtic crosses (Figure 9–24d).[24] The addition of Christian symbolism to Native American

9-24 Celtic crosses
(clockwise from top 1)
a Cross carved on standing stone, Irish monastery
b Iona, seventh century
c Christianized standing stone, Point Aven, Brittany
d Standing Irish cross

9-25 Pictish symbol stone (from Cruden, note 19)

ritual objects was practiced by Jesuit and Puritan missionaries and probably by their possible predecessors.

Evidence of the attempts to mix Christianity and the pagan religion is clear at all stages of the process of Christianization. The Picts worshipped nature and depicted natural objects mingled with the sign of the Christian faith on their symbol stones. The stones, sometimes upright slabs and sometimes rude boulders, contain apparently abstract geometrical symbols in addition to realistic inscriptions of fish, animals and people (Figure 9–25). Those without the Celtic cross are artistically and symbolically pagan, while those with the cross may be the work of converts to Christianity.[25]

Unfortunately, we do not know what the Iron Age Druid priests, who were eventually displaced for the most part by the Christian monks, thought about these developments. But we do know that they had in their turn accepted the standing stones and stone rings of the Bronze Age people before them and incorporated them into their ritual. From the evidence of the inscribed crosses and Pictish symbol stones, it seems that the Druids need not have been deeply offended by the Christianization of their monuments. The sun worship remained as a circle on the Celtic cross and the pagan customs and deities were by and large simply retained by the new religion and given new names.

This process can be seen at Dunkeld, the ancient Scottish capital and seat of the Culdees. Dunkeld is located at a major bend in the River Tay on the verge of a great mountain barrier. Outside the present village is a sacred well known as Grews, formerly Sancta Crux. It has long been a place of pilgrimage and healing, where sacred rites were observed on May Day or Beltane, at least through the nineteenth century. The rites include certain stones of the place, which must be used.[26] Immediately above the well there is a cairn that must be traversed three times around and have a stone added.

9-26 Dunkeld Rocking Stone

The "Rocking Stone" on a hill 900 feet high overlooking Dunkeld Cathedral occupies a uniquely commanding position. It is oriented east-west and is traditionally an altar used by sun-worshippers. It weighs 20 tons and is supported by three small boulders (Figure 9–26), a type that is found worldwide and is often considered by geologists to have been perched naturally by a glacier in ages past. Some large Scottish perched boulders are true rocking stones, known traditionally as objects of veneration, such as two near Ben Nevis, shown in Figure 9–27. Christianity did not displace the old Celtic nature religion for over a thousand years after its introduction, and even to the present day the old ways persist in local regions, amalgamated with Christianity.

Stone Chambers

New England's stone chambers vary considerably in design. They may have short or long entrance passages, or no passages, and the plans may be circular, oval, or rectangular. The roofing is in some cases corbelled with central slabs, and in others uncorbelled. They are sometimes built into hillsides, sometimes built on the flat and mounded over with earth, sometimes dug deep into the

9-27 Ben Nevis rocking boulders

ground, or placed within quarried holes in bedrock. Often, bedrock makes up a side or the back of a chamber and sometimes large boulders are incorporated into the construction. The size and shape of the stones which make up the chambers vary with local materials. Their most consistent features are orientation toward a solar horizon event, roofing with stone slabs, dry-wall construction, and, frequently, roofed entrance passages.

As pointed out by James P. Whittall II in several publications, similar structures can be found in Scandinavia, Ireland, the British Isles, France, Spain and Portugal, built over a long period from 4000 B.C. to recent times.[27] Many of these were tombs, some were habitations, some were sweathouses and other religious structures, and some were of unknown use (Figure 9–28). There are compelling specific architectural similarities between stone chambers on both sides of the Atlantic, which have been the source of controversy about whether or not the New England chambers were built as a result of cultural diffusion by voyagers from Europe to New England.

Some European monks lived in small, stone circular beehive huts on isolated small islands off the coasts. These structures may have evolved as a logical habitation in these treeless places, but they could also have been part of the sacred architecture of the Iron Age inhabitants whom the monks wished to convert (Figure 9–29). The stone beehives of southern France, called bories, have Celtic origins before the Christian era, and the design has been continuously in use ever since in inland farming communities.[28] Arthur Mitchell provides rather startling evidence that it was common in the nineteenth century in the western isles of Scotland for families to inhabit beehive houses which were no different from similar structures in use for thousands of years.[29] He reports that a Captain Thomas saw fifty or sixty inhabited beehive huts on the islands of Lewis and Harris and certifies that one was built by a man living in 1858. The typical beehive is a circular dry-stone-walled structure of domed, corbelled construction with a central roof hole for ventilation. It is mounded over with earth, has about six feet headroom and is six feet in diameter. As far as habitability is concerned,

9-28 Sweathouse, Co. Caven, Ireland

9-29 Beehive house, Dingle Peninsula, Ireland

larger croft houses of rectangular construction with thatched and earthen roofs are quite similar and reported to be quite warm, if a bit smoky, in winter.

The origin of beehive huts on both sides of the Atlantic is obscure and may be different from the origins of standing stones, cairns and other ritual landscape architecture. In America, beehive huts are found throughout the United States as both tombs and ritual structures. In New England, where they have been noticed more than other works of stone, the widely held but unfounded view persists that they were built as root cellars by English settlers.

We see stone chambers as but one of many elements of a ritual architecture in New England that is part of a long, profound and continuing tradition including the natural landscape and many types of indigenous man-made structures. To consider stone chambers in isolation or solely as part of a nearby farmstead or other settlement is a distortion of the record. We see antecedents for most chambers in similar stone structures with established provenance among Native Americans in other parts of North America. One, nearby, is the stone building of arctic people of northeastern Canada which has origins in Archaic times. This tradition may go back to a time thousands of years ago when arctic people travelled around the northern world diffusing certain traditions down into the temperate latitudes. With a few exceptions, any specific architectural feature of New England chambers that has been mentioned in literature can be found elsewhere in North America, as well as throughout Europe.

One of these exceptions is the design of the Upton, Massachusetts, chamber. It has a long entrance passage roofed with slabs and a circular corbelled domed roof. As the passage approaches the chamber, each roof slab successively overlaps the previous one until a sufficient height is achieved for the passage roof slabs to fit smoothly into the roof corbelling of the chamber proper (Figure 2–4). Also, the passage widens out gradually as it approaches the chamber, a technique that not only provides visual continuity but also avoids the necessity of a huge lintel stone at the transition between passage and chamber in order to transfer the chamber roof load to the passage. Except for a few stone chambers in southern New England, this technique is known only in the great chamber tombs of Newgrange and Knowth in the Boyne valley of Ireland, and possibly in some ruined examples in Portugal (Figure 9–30 and 31). In other respects, the Irish

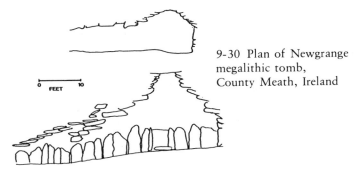

9-30 Plan of Newgrange megalithic tomb, County Meath, Ireland

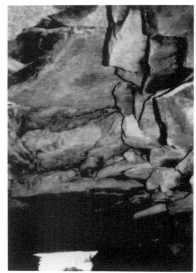

9-31 E. Thompson, Conn.,
stone chamber,
looking out entrance, *l;*
Newgrange megalithic tomb,
looking out roofbox, *r.* Note
similar structural transition
from passage to dome.

megalithic tombs are built quite differently, using, for example, vertical, megalithic slabs for walling rather than the New England horizontally laid-up walling.

In exploring a possible Irish connection, we have considered ways in which the design of Newgrange or Knowth could have been carried to America in the centuries before A.D. 710, when we believe, on astronomical grounds, that the Upton Chamber was used. The passage at Knowth has a number of souterrains burrowed under the surface like a rabbit warren, built of dry-walled masonry using small stones. These have been dated by occupational debris to an early Christian date, but they were found in 1967 and 1968 to intersect the earlier megalithic passages built of tall upright slabs, which lead to the main chambers of the mound. In fact, the burial chambers were discovered by following the souterrains.

The Boyne cemetery enjoyed considerable prestige among the Irish of the early Christian period, and the kings of Northern Brega appear to have lived near or at the mound of Knowth during this time. According to legend, during the 200 years previous to A.D. 700 there was considerable friction between the monarchs at Tara, only ten miles from Newgrange and Knowth, and the church-men. One of these, who came to Tara during this time and may have known about the tomb construction, was Saint Brendan the navigator, who may have carried this knowledge to America in the sixth century A.D..[30] Evidence of the navigational ability of the Irish monks is their settling of Iceland before the Norse. Icelandic records describe these monks as traditional shamans capable of feats of wizardry. The Old Icelandic calendar, which was regulated by solar horizon events on the natural landscape, appears to have been based upon navigational requirements in that its key points mark the navigation season. It is likely that this calendar was brought to Iceland by the seagoing monks from

9-32 Newgrange grand exterior as restored, showing astronomical roofbox above entrance

Ireland with both a tradition of shamanistic astronomy and seafaring.[31] In any case it is apparent that some of the Irish who lived at Knowth in the few centuries prior to A.D. 700, saw and knew the design of the interior of the megalithic tomb which was structurally similar to Upton.

Astronomy at Newgrange is rather different from that at Upton. Both have sophistication of different kinds. At Upton, an elaborate array of events is recorded by markers on the horizon, including the Pleiades and summer solstice sunset, which are important features of Native American cosmology in both North and South America. At Newgrange, there is a very special stone roofbox set in the passage which lets sunlight shine into the rear of the very long passage on the winter solstice sunrise (Figure 9–32). There appear to be no other events marked by this monument. But the Culdee monks need not have depended upon the astronomical design of the Irish megalithic tombs, which may have been unknown to them; they had their own practices which are revealed by the design of their oratories.

Similar architectural details, a circumstantial scenario of how they might have come from Europe, and evidence of astronomical alignments become relatively minor considerations in the total concept of Native American ritual architecture when the Upton chamber is considered as part of a complex consisting of a prominent hilltop, a valley, a pond and stream, and an elaborate array of stone rows and stone mounds interconnected by alignments to the setting sun and stars. Furthermore, there are specific similarities between the Upton complex and structures of the Hopewellian Mound Builders of the American Midwest, as well as those of the native astronomers of western North America and Peru, suggesting that if diffusion were a major influence on New England's native culture, its source may have been other areas of America, rather than Europe.

Some New England stone chambers could represent a joining of Native American and European skills and religious views, which were basically similar, differing only in detail. We do not exclude the possibility of occasional European visitors at any time over the past several thousand years. Those who managed to establish cordial relations with the natives would have participated with them in religious ritual and over time made their mark on it. The Culdee monks, who retained a large measure of Druidic tradition in their ways, and were not dominated by the organized religions of the Mediterranean area, were likely to have held beliefs not unlike those of the American natives and participated with them.[32]

Stone Rows

When the English colonists arrived in New England in the seventeenth century, they may have seen stone rows that were superficially like those they had known in England, made of laid-up boulders or split slabs of granite and slate. But many of the stone rows of New England are quite different from those we see in Europe today. Most European stone rows are straight, built without niches or embrasures or other special features. There are ancient examples, alignments of boulder rows and small slabs or standing stones that run for miles through the moorlands, and the great standing stone alignments of Brittany, structures not known in New England.

The pervasive stone rows of New England have many features that are not found in Europe. They connect both man-made features and parts of the natural landscape. The embrasures, curious methods of construction, wide rows, short rows, godstones in rows, slabs in rows which are typical attributes of ritual sites in New England are simply not known in Europe. Even at Upton, with its Irish-type structural detail, stone rows intimately connect the chamber to its place on the shore of a pond, and a pattern of stone rows connects the various foresights to astronomical events on Pratt Hill. Where special features are found in the stone rows of New England, they signal places of ritual architecture, an architecture which is in general similar to that of early people around the world, who were responding to the natural environment. But the special details of New England rows are the unique signature of their builders.

Marked Stones

We have observed and recorded many hundreds of stones with grooved markings on them, first in Vermont and then elsewhere in New England. We consider the concentration of these stones at Calendar One to be a characteristic of a ritual site. Most grooves that we have seen are straight, frequently arranged in parallel but also intersecting one another (Figure 9–33). In some places, they are arranged in specific patterns such as grids. Some were pecked with an impact instrument, and some were abraded into the rock. In central Vermont, most marks are in a weathered quartzite rock, with a thick rind of almost pure quartz from which the calcite bonding material has been leached out (Figure 9–34). The marks usually penetrate through but not beyond this friable layer. A few marks are found in the occasional granite boulders of the region, but no marks have been

9-33 Vermont marked stones: Blanchard stone, *l;* granite stone, *r*

found on the other common rock of central Vermont, mica schist, which is used for construction and tools. In Vermont, the marks are seen only at elevations between 800 and 1600 feet above sea level. They are found on stones of all sizes, in walls, in fields, on horizontal and vertical surfaces, on the ground surfaces and next to and into bedrock up to one meter below present ground level. Marked stones have been found in well-stratified excavations at a level associated with possible Archaic Indian pebble tools so that some of the marked stones of New England of simple grooved pattern may be a form of notation used by prehistoric Native Americans.

Similar marks are found in other types of rock, including granite, in other parts of New England. In some cases, where the marks have been created by abrasion, they have been recorded and called Indian sharpening stones. In cases where such marks appear to be organized we suspect that they are also a means of notation.

In the British Isles, we have identified stone markings similar to those in New England (Figure 9–35), and we have recognized them in definite prehistoric contexts including megalithic tombs of 3000 B.C. A random inspection of stone walls in Wales showed us that marks occur only near stone circles and standing stones of established ancient provenance. They are likely to have been partly the

9-34 Close-up of quartzite rind of Vermont stone   9-35 British prehistoric marked stone

result of independent development rather than diffusion because the marks could represent a basic type of numerical notation, perhaps with astronomical meaning, having a universal environmental inspiration. But there is also the possibility of cultural diffusion thousands of years ago by way of the arctic.

An additional possible explanation for the similarity between European and New England stone markings is that Jesuit priests, and perhaps earlier visitors, who were familiar with some types of European Ogam, may have noticed that the Native Americans made similar marks on stone for counting and taught them their use as a written language in order to record knowledge of their newly acquired European god. Barry Fell has concluded that some grooved markings on stone in New England, particularly Vermont, are similar to European Ogam script of early Christian times. He has even attempted translation of a limited number using European meanings.[33] While some marks may be related to Ogam, we are skeptical of translations because the perception of the marks on the rock, often worn or damaged, is subject to considerable variability from one observer to the next.

We have found that in transcribing stone markings to paper there is much room for interpretation and that it is difficult to classify the Vermont marks uniquely as Iberic Ogam without considerable imaginative license. We believe that proper interpretation of petroglyphs requires study both of the material, because natural cracks are almost always used in the message, and of the natural setting because this can be a key to the meaning and origins. Also, a large selection of examples in a region is necessary to establish patterns. We believe that few New England petroglyphs have been studied sufficiently to be translated. We do not claim, however, that epigraphic evidence of prehistoric Europeans in America does not exist, and we do support some of the proposals of Cyrus Gordon, Barry Fell and others that there are stone inscriptions in North and South America written in ancient European and North African languages.

The Arctic

The feeling of the arctic regions of our planet is difficult to convey in the words available for description or narrative in the languages of the temperate climates. It is a sensitive land where people are themselves very sensitive to subtle changes in their surroundings and are at peace with them. This enables its dwellers to sustain themselves without waste, and without gorging themselves on the environment's generosity.

The northern sky is very different from the temperate sky. In winter, it is always night, and the stars are seen continuously appearing in the east and setting in the west, determining the length of each day in the absence of the sun. In summer, the sun never sets, and in spring and fall the twilight is long because the sun approaches the horizon at a low angle. The change in length of each day is rapid,

9-36 Aurora Borealis (from Knox, note 34)

9-37 Lapp ritual, showing aurora, stone mound and fox (from Leem, note 34)

and the Aurora Borealis is a nightly display of color and electrical phenomena (Figure 9–36). In addition, the whole range of astronomical events observed and recorded in temperate and tropical regions is present. In the land of the Copper Eskimo, 69 degrees north, the horizon was important to the role of both the sun and moon as well as many bright stars. Eclipses were noted and parhelia (mock suns) were considered ominous. Arcturus signalled the start of the sealing season when it culminated at noon on December 12.[34] For at least the past 10,000 years, the people of the arctic have migrated east and west along the regions where the land and water or ice meet. They may see this not as a nomadic life of travel but one in which the earth moves under them, much as the sky moves above them.

The aurora surrounds the northern people. It is like a glowing blanket that warms everyone in a subtle and special way, that causes them to desire to maintain their place on earth. People of the north have incorporated the aurora into legends, in which it appears to be old women dancing in the more northern regions, and fire and violence in the mid-latitudes where the aurora is red. Both North American Indian and northern Europeans described the northern lights as merry dancers; in Sweden, the name polka comes from the Aurora. North American Eskimos, however, relate the northern lights to the realm of the dead. A drawing made in 1767 by K. Leem shows the northern lights as a fiery background for a Lapp performing a ritual before an altar of piled stones (Figure 9–37). It also shows a fox, thought in Lappland to be the origin of the Aurora, called Foxfire. In Canada, the Ottawa Indians believed that the lights were a message from their creator reminding them of his presence, and in Siberia, the Cuvash had such a belief. But in later medieval times, the trend was toward treating the aurora as an omen of war and destruction.[35]

We now know that the aurora is the visible manifestation of geomagnetic disturbances in the earth's upper atmosphere. It may be beautiful, awesome and fearful, but, in any case, it does have down-to-earth effects upon people. It provides light during the long arctic night and can act as a compass since north is at the highest point of the auroral arc. By the same token, it can disturb the earth's magnetism so that a magnetic compass is in error. Electrical disturbances on earth caused by the aurora are profound. Induced voltages great enough to power appliances or burn out fuses have not been uncommon. The physiological effects on man and animals caused by the aurora are similar to effects from microwave transmission and powerline fields.

Stone structures rather similar to the stone chambers of New England, Europe and Asia were used by the Thule people of northern Canada for winter dwellings up to about A.D. 1500, when they came to prefer the ice block house. The stone houses were circular or rectangular, set into a shallow excavation in the ground, built with stone slabs and wood or bone framing supporting a sod roof. They had long entrance passages roofed with stone slabs. Interior furniture of stone, bed, tables and floor paving reminds us of those at Skara Brae in the Orkney Islands, used in 2000 B.C. Extensive ritual paving of stone is known at Swedish prehistoric ritual sites, where long courses paved with cobbles extend for as much as 150 feet and are 15 feet wide.

In mediaeval Iceland, there is a rare reference to farmstead fencing for ritual purposes, after Christianity was adopted in A.D. 1000. Non-human folk, consisting of elves, trolls, giants and hidden people, and often referred to as the "people of the land," were attached to the landscape in ways that the old gods never were. Fencing was built to shut out these creatures from the farm. This practice reflected a cosmological view in which society was divided rigidly into those within the law and those without. People who broke the law were banished to the forest to live outside society and were considered in much the same category as elves and trolls. After A.D. 1000, this mode of thought appears to have been invoked in the conflict between heathens and Christians.[36]

The remains of the Komsa culture of coastal Lappland, of about 8,000 years ago, have remarkable resemblances to that of Archaic coastal North America. Artifacts are identical, including tools, implements, and structures. It is this similarity more than anything else that supports the idea of an ancient east-west Arctic migration of people during which cultural attributes filtered down to temperate latitudes both in Europe and America.[37]

There is a long tradition that the Lapps always lived in coastal northern Scandinavia. This view has been disputed by various foreign scholars who prefer a more recent southeastern origin of the present-day Lapps. But, geologists and botanists have proved that large areas of Lappland, including the coast, were free from ice during the latest Ice Age. During warming conditions, about 4000 B.C., the Lapps moved inland.

Lapp corraling systems for trapping reindeer include some features which appear to be ritual rather than serving directly as practical parts of the trap

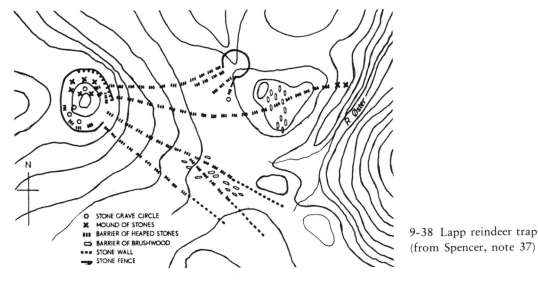

○ STONE GRAVE CIRCLE
✕ MOUND OF STONES
ⅲ BARRIER OF HEAPED STONES
▭ BARRIER OF BRUSHWOOD
••• STONE WALL
━ STONE FENCE

N

9-38 Lapp reindeer trap
(from Spencer, note 37)

(Figure 9–38). They include shallow depressions encircled by a low stone wall said to be the home of the giant, Stalo. Also, groups of stone mounds and "stone grave circles" in association are found at the sites. These do not seem part of the trapping system. They are rather like vision quest and mortuary sites.

In the old Lapp religion, like the Native American, all objects, animate or inanimate, possessed a spirit. The great forces of nature such as the sun, winds and fertility were major gods and direct personal contact with the spirits of nature was achieved by shamans in dreams or trances. The Lapps had sacred sites, called *seide*, which were in either public or private places, indoors or outdoors, and the locations usually kept secret. Sometimes the sanctuary was in a private home in which case there was a "sacred back door" for access to this place. More than 800 *seide* are recorded in Lappland. They are usually identified by a curious or awe-inspiring feature, a mountain peak or a gorge, unusual rock formations, curiously shaped trees, and waterfalls. At these places, a small idol of stone or wood was erected on a platform. This idol sometimes took the form of a human or animal shape (Figure 9–39), either as a naturally weathered stone or an artifi-

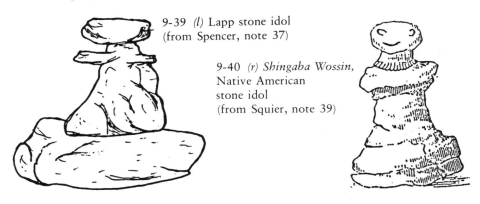

9-39 *(l)* Lapp stone idol
(from Spencer, note 37)

9-40 *(r) Shingaba Wossin*, Native American stone idol
(from Squier, note 39)

cially enhanced figure. It is recorded that in 1673, the Lapplanders worshipped an unhewn stone found upon the banks of lakes and rivers, which they called the stone god.[38]

Similar spirit stones are found in North America. Squier and Schoolcraft cite the finding of several "image stones" called *Shingaba Wossins* which are exactly like the Lapp idols. They were used in America in a similar ritual setting (Figure 9–40). In at least three cases reported by Squier, image stones were found in desert-like places where Indians might be supposed to have retreated to seek visions. At Pecos Pueblo in New Mexico in 1620, Father Ortega rounded up and smashed many idols of stone, and curiously painted stone slabs. Centuries later, archaeologists found these images, some repaired, hidden away. Pedro Fages, a Spanish soldier, wrote that Chumash idols of stick and stone figurines painted with colors and dressed with plumage were placed in the fields to protect, so they say, the crops. In addition, some 20 stone effigies of spirits, called godstones, were reported by Ezra Stiles to be used by New England Indians. It was said of these stones in Connecticut that the Indians placed their dead before them previous to burial and afterwards returned and danced around them.[39]

Shamanism is similar the world over. The novice shamans among the Algonquins, Yurok and Lapps all had to undergo strict training culminating in a successful journey to the spirit world. We have chosen to describe the details of the Yurok of California because their ritual probably approaches that of the ancient New England Indians more closely than any other that is known today.

Yurok shamans are women, and a candidate first cries and cries until she dreams of a dead person, usually a shaman, who puts a "pain" into her body, the possession of which makes her a shaman. She then fasts and dances in the sweat house for ten days under the direction of older shamans. She enters the sweathouse by the entrance in the middle of the long side which always faces a body of water and has a large area of stone paving in front of the house like a porch, quite similar to some New England stone chambers. The pain leaves her body and is reswallowed by her, a demonstration of control of the pain. She leaves the house through a small oval door, fourteen by ten inches, cut through the base of one of the planks that support the ridgepole and is closed by a snugly fitting plug of wood. The exit is some four feet below ground so a pit lined with cobbles is dug outside somewhat like a well.[40]

After this, in the seventh month after the winter solstice, she goes with a male relative to a prayer seat, or *tsektel*, on a sacred mountain top. Here she spends one night in chanting or dancing by a fire while her kinsman watches to see that she does herself no harm, because fasting, chanting and offering can be dangerous if not done correctly. In the morning her relative leads her back to the village, where she spends ten more days in the sweat house. After two years' training, again in the seventh month, which in Yurok tradition marks the heliacal rising of the Pleiades, she dances around a hot fire to "cook the pains," rendering them more amenable to the shaman's will.

9-41 Coffin Island, Labrador, standing stones (from Fitzhugh, note 41)

Ancient Migration

Some broad outlines of the prehistoric migrations of people across the Bering Strait from Asia to America have been established. More tentative are the circumpolar movements of people over land and sea, to which are attributed similar artifacts found in North America, Europe, and Asia. In coastal Labrador, Fitzhugh reports not only stone chambers, standing stones (Figures 9–41 and 42), and other structures similar to those of prehistoric Europe, but also refined tools of stone such as could only be used for sophisticated boatbuilding.[41] Toggle-

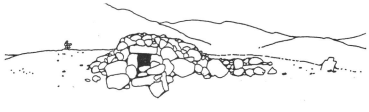

9-42a Stone chamber and burial mound, Nulliak Cove, Labrador. Note manitou stone at right.

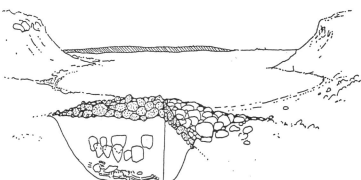

9-42b Maritime Archaic burial mound, over 4,000 years old, L'Anse Amour, Labrador

jointed harpoons from as early as 5,000 years ago have been found along the New England and Canadian coasts that were used in swordfishing, an art that requires a seaworthy and strong boat and offshore navigation. It took place when the rate of glacial melting was a maximum implying a warm period in the arctic. This evidence of an ancient maritime people in eastern North America opens the door to possible transatlantic adventures as early as 7,500 years ago in seaworthy boats by people accustomed to the deep sea.

The shamans of the Algonquin people were part of a world-wide tradition that probably goes back to these Archaic times. Their particular practices and traits are very similar to those of the Shamans of Siberia, from whom the name came. These connections between temperate and Arctic peoples imply that the similarities between the ancient Lapps and Algonquin Indians may result from major cultural diffusion which took place many thousands of years ago.

The idea of polar migration of Asiatic peoples 12,000 or more years ago is widely accepted. The Old Crow site in Alaska has been dated at 30,000 years ago, and earlier dates are claimed in isolated locations of California. These early dates demonstrate the possibility of intermittent migration over a very long time by people who eventually completed the circumpolar cycle. The northern arctic people have traditionally followed the north-south seasonal movement of the sun as part of living in tune with an ecological balance and have tended to migrate east toward the rising sun. The aurora borealis, which peaks in intensity at about 70 degrees north latitude, is a part of nature's balance and perhaps the more conservative peoples would have considered this an ideal latitude. Here, there is much sun at midsummer, and the aurora, the moon, and the stars illuminate the sky during the winter.

Circumstantial evidence favors the notion that there were probably many transatlantic crossings and even enduring settlements in New England by mariners between this ancient period and the fifteenth-century explorers and fishermen. The ways of the native people could well have been influenced by some of these foreigners, as history shows in later comparable situations. What we call the Indian way and the people we call Native Americans are probably a composite image, and their ways are described by what is to be seen on today's landscape, by the traditions and practices of the tribal remnants today throughout North America, and by the historical accounts of foreign observers.

10

Earthquakes and Vision Quests in the Land of the Mohegans

The cultural history of the Mohegan Indians since the sixteenth century sheds additional light on the Native American tradition of ritualizing the landscape and on what happened to this tradition when it was subjected to the territorial pressures brought about by the European colonies. When the white settlers first arrived in New England, the Mohegans, with the Pequots, occupied most of what is now southeast Connecticut. They were one of the tribes of the Mahican Confederacy and had probably migrated to this area from the ancient heartland of the Mahicans. As we have already seen, the traditional Mahican lands ran from the Green and Taconic Mountains west to the Hudson River, and included the sites of the Stockbridge mission experiment and many of the original Shaker communities. All of these lands contain a wealth of natural and man-made stone features gracing the countryside, features that we believe were an important part of the cosmology and ritual life of the Native American inhabitants.

In the days when the rivers were the primary travel arteries, the Hoosic was the major link between Massachusetts and the upper Hudson Valley. Draining the western slopes of the Green Mountains, a hard mass of quartzite and granite, it cuts through the softer limestone and schist of the Taconic range to the Hudson Valley. Here and there on the mountain ridges of both the Green and Taconic ranges are boulders of quartz which reflected sunlight makes appear as beacons of light to those in the valleys below. These boulders were called Manitou-aseniah or spirit stones by the Indians of the Hoosic Valley.

Near Lansingburgh Station, there is a vein of quartz-crystal, also called spirit-stone by the Indians and "Stone Arabia" by the Dutch. A town two miles from the Mohawk village of Tionnondogue on the Mohawk River, where the Jesuit mission of Saint Mary was founded in 1667, has the same Dutch name, presumably because of similar quartz formations.[1]

The powwows of the Hoosic Valley used this quartz-crystal to carve symbols of the Wakon-bird or spirit-dove in order to appease Hobomock during earthquakes, called Moodus upheavals. These stones have been found in the burial mounds of shamans, where a small opening was left for the flight of the Wakon-bird, which represented the soul of the departed. Mahican shamans carved Wakon-bird stones from slabs of quartzite or marble which were very similar to Christian tombstones. A bird carved on a godstone slab in Groton, Connecticut, shown in Figure 13–3 may be such a representation.

The pudding-stone cliffs accompanying the pre-Cambrian Green Mountain quartzite form structures which folklore has given names, such as the Weeping Rocks that overhang the highway at Hoosic pass in Pownal, Vermont. At Schaghticoke, a natural hollow obelisk of limestone nearly 70 feet high is known as the Devil's Chimney, named for an Indian ritual at this place to appease Hobomock. About 1812, sulphurous fumes were observed issuing from its aperture. It is located near Musical Falls, a wild, tumbling rapid through winding, cliff-sided gorges. Such places, where the water is broken up and natural sounds fill the air, were invariably seen as places of great manitou by the Indians.

On Rattlesnake Ledge of The Domelet in Pownal, a great heap of broken pieces of the Green Mountain quartzite bedrock is called Hobomock's Shrine. According to folklore, the Indians associated the quartzite with seismic noises and built stone piles at the places where the noises were heard. Where the Hoosic meets the Hudson, there is a stream called Dwaas Kill, which flows both ways depending upon the state of the waters about it. There is a similar reversing river in Tennessee where an island was the location of an important collection of Hopewellian ritual mounds and burials.[2]

There is a wall of boulders on Indian Point, a projection into Lake Onota on its western shore. Tradition holds that this wall, which appears to today's observer to be a work of art, was built by Indians. The lake, southeast of Pittsfield, was enlarged in 1864 from two smaller lakes separated by a causeway at Indian Point. Mount Honwee is a rounded summit located in the town of Hancock, Massachusetts, at the northwest corner of Pittsfield. While clearly in traditional Mahican lands, its name is Iroquois for "men," reflecting the intermingling of tribal lands during the seventeenth century.[3] Its status as an Indian mountain is probably similar to Mount Sinai of the Shakers.

There are perched boulders in the Mahican lands representing all of the types described in Chapter 4. Two are particularly prominent and accessible. One, after which a state park is named, is near the brow of a hill overlooking Pontoosuc Lake, just north of Pittsfield (Figure 10–1). It is a huge mass of white marble of roughly oval shape, nicely balanced on a single point. Before it settled, it could be rocked back and forth, causing vibration in the earth. Chief Hendrick

10-1 Balance Rock
(Atotarho's Duff),
Pittsfield, Mass.

Aupaumut of the Onondaga Iroquois, the same Chief Hendrick whose important role in the New Stockbridge mission in Oneida, New York, is discussed in Chapter 7, wrote that the balanced rock was known as Atotarho's Duff. Atotarho was the name of a dynasty of Iroquois kings who possessed supernatural powers. The first Atotarho had a complete table service made from the bones of his enemies and wore a cloak of venomous serpents to receive visitors. By contrast, the Atotarho involved in the origin of the balanced rock was a delicate and effeminate character. So the story goes, this young Atotarho was watching a group of youths playing "duff," a game which consists of placing one stone upon another, and then attempting to knock it off by throwing a third stone from a distance. The youths got to arguing, and, seeing the apparently weak youth nearby, laughingly challenged him to a test of strength and skill. He accepted and, to their terror, suddenly grew to giant size. Holding them fast by his glance, he seized the largest boulder to be found and balanced it where it now stands. According to tradition, the story of the Atotarho dynasty was passed down after that by a yearly rendition from atop the balanced rock.[4]

The interpretation of this oral tradition is unmistakable. The Atotarhos were members of a hereditary family who were both sachems and shamans. Some persons, such as Passaconnoway of the Pawtuckets, who combined both of these roles were considered to be extremely powerful.[5] The youth could have hypnotized the duff players or otherwise altered their perception so that he appeared as a giant and placed the boulder. Whether the actual origin of the balanced rock was glacial recession, weathering, or some unknown force controlled by the shaman is beyond our ability to judge.

In North Salem, New York, in the southern reaches of the Mahican territory, there is a monstrous pedestalled boulder of 90 tons, supported on the points of five standing stones set deep into the soil (Figure 4–21a). It is clearly similar to many structures, usually called dolmens, found all over the world, which are thought to have been places of ceremony and sometimes burial of ancient people. That this boulder could be solely the result of glacial forces is a notion with extremely low probability, and it does seem to possess spiritual power for those who perceive it. Its function and possibly its construction may follow a universal tradition transmitted via the Arctic many millennia past, as discussed in the previous chapter.

The Connecticut Mohegans and Pequots

Frank Speck, who studied the ethnology of the Mohegans in the first quarter of this century, had the use of a group of texts written in the Mohegan language found among the effects of Mrs. Fidelia A. H. Fielding, who died in 1908. She was the last Indian known to be able to speak this language. In addition, Dr. Speck lived among 122 remaining members of the tribe in 1920.

Mrs. Fielding wrote of the migration legend of her people, a story that is corroborated by several other oral traditions. A group of Mohegan Indians living near the Hudson River left their homeland shortly before A.D. 1600 and migrated east through southern Massachusetts, crossing to the Connecticut River before heading south to the seashore at Lyme, Connecticut. All the Indian traditions agree on this part of the story. This group, called Pequots, the destroyers, by the English, and Mohegans by the Dutch, settled in the region between the Connecticut and Pawkatuck Rivers on the lower Thames River, then known variously as the Little Fresh River, the Frisius River and the Pequot River. These lands, which are more than two miles from the coast, have a rugged and rocky terrain, with many streams, swamps and steep hills. It is a difficult place to farm and the land remains untended today. Their immigration displaced natives residing in the area, now known as the Narragansetts and Nehantics, who removed to Rhode Island and Niantic, Connecticut, respectively. Constant hostility existed between the Pequots and their neighbors from the time of their arrival.[6]

Another source is more specific about the migration from the Hudson Valley. Passaconnoway and Uncas, Great Sachems of the Mohegans and Hoosacs, ruled the homelands in the late 1500s until they were dethroned and succeeded by Uncas' nephew Aepjen-a-hican sometime before 1609. Passaconnoway went with his people to Pawtucket (Lowell, Mass.) and Uncas and the Mohegans moved to eastern Connecticut, where they adopted a new tribal name, Pequot, derived from the call of the wild turkey. Uncas returned periodically to attend councils on the Hudson River at Schodac.[7]

The Dutch were the first Europeans to settle coastal Connecticut. In 1613,

Adrian Block sailed the coast eastward to Cape Cod, kidnapping two Mohegan youths along the way and taking them home to the Netherlands. The Dutch established trade along the coast and obtained Indian land grants at Saybrook and Hartford. It was not until 1634 that the first English settlement in Connecticut was founded at Weathersfield. In 1635, four English plantations, settled from Massachusetts Bay, were set up on the Connecticut River. The Dutch observed that the Mystic River, also known as the River of the Sachems and Siccanernus, was the focus of the Pequot settlement, even though the name Pequot River was later given to the Thames.

By 1636, after apparently four successions of Pequot sachems, a dispute arose between Sassacus and another Uncas as to who should become sachem after the death of Wapigwooit, Sassacus' father. Most of the tribe remained faithful to the leadership of Sassacus, so Uncas was expelled from the country.

He first fled east with a few followers to the Narragansetts. Twice thereafter he was accused by the Pequots of treachery; each time he was pardoned by Sassacus and declined invitations to return. After English settlements became established on the Connecticut River, some "Connecticut River Indians" from Hartford joined Uncas and his band increasing it to a strength of seventy warriors. They returned to Pequot territory without permission, settled on the west bank of the Thames in the present town of Montville and part of Waterford, and assumed the tribal name of Mohegans. There was intermittent open hostility between Sassacus and Uncas.

Because the Pequots had become bold and hostile toward European settlers, an offensive war against them was commenced by the Massachusetts Colony in 1637, joined by the Narragansetts and by Uncas and his Mohegans. It appears, however, that this war may have been an accident based on a misunderstanding of a minor incident. John Winthrop ascribes the war to exasperation after a Massachusetts Bay Indian killed one Pequot, and, later two colonists were killed, probably accidentally by Pequots. There appears good reason to believe that the whole Pequot Nation, with their sachem, had been friendly to the English when they began their settlement in 1635. The war lasted less than two months and was marked by English atrocities, the beginning of an all-too-familiar pattern. Sassacus and a few survivors fled to the Mohawks on the Hudson for sanctuary, but they were killed, either because the Mohawks wanted to please the English or because they had been bribed by the Narragansetts.[8]

After the Pequot extermination, Uncas and the Mohegans claimed the land of the Pequots. In return for his aid in the war, Uncas remained under English protection for the rest of his life. On October 1, 1638, a tripartite treaty was signed among the English, Narragansetts and Mohegans, promising perpetual peace. Uncas yielded to the English the tract along the seacoast, retaining for his people the northern part of present-day New London County and parts of Windham and Tolland Counties. The number and strength of the Mohegans increased. A Mohegan fort was established on an eminence a short distance west of the present Mohegan Station, in full view of the surrounding hills of Norwich.[9]

In 1643, Uncas was authorized by the English clergy to carry out their sentence of death on Miantonomo, sachem of the Narragansetts. According to most sources, Miantonomo was slain on Sachem's Plain in Norwich, near the Shetucket River, a little south of its junction with the Quinebaug. Caulkins states that a monumental heap of stones was erected at this site, but "the heap of stones was doubtless in its origin a Mohegan pile," a marker erected where the tribe had been victorious. She also states that it was not a tomb and that Miantonomo was probably executed and buried somewhere in the woods of Windsor. She sees the rude tumulus on Sachem's Plain as at first three or four stones rolled together, which grew by donation to a memorable heap. The Narragansetts probably renewed their lamentation at the heap and cast stones on it. The heap was later removed by the landowner for a barn foundation, and today a granite pillar, erected July 4, 1841, commemorates the site.

Also in 1643, warriors of the Narragansetts invaded the territories of Uncas, and in 1645, a large force of Narragansett warriors under Pessicus poured into Mohegan country wreaking much destruction. This time, Uncas was forced to take refuge in one of his forts called Shantock Fort, where he was aided by the English with supplies and reinforcements. After this, there were repeated invasions by Narragansetts into Mohegan territory, until 1668, and many Mohegan "hiding places" in the woods for women and children were created during this period.

The remaining Pequots, who for some time were under the supervision of Uncas, eventually retreated to Mashantucket, their last reservation, 900 acres of craggy, forested hills and deep valleys in present-day Ledyard, Connecticut. In 1850, only ten remaining members of the tribe are recorded. The Mohegans were more successful than most New England Indians in preserving their tribal and cultural identity. In 1872, they were given individual titles to their lands and made citizens of Connecticut.

Speck writes that the Iroquois were more advanced in artistic and craft skills than the Algonquins. He also considers the Mohegans to have been influenced by the Iroquois, which is not surprising given their origins in the Hudson Valley. He notes that the Mohegan-Pequot culture was characteristic of a large area from Narragansett Bay to the Connecticut River and to the Massachusetts line, and identifies three tribal groups, original Pequot, western Nehantic and later Mohegan-Pequot. This is evidence of the composite character of eastern Indians which defies a breakdown into meaningful divisions that are entirely satisfactory.

According to Speck, the Mohegans believed in forest elves, fairies and river elves in former times, but only one kind is now remembered, the "little people," or dwarfs who lived in the woods. They made pictures and scratchings on the rock which stood on Fort Hill, since blasted out by road makers. Old glass bottles which are plowed out of the ground and brass kettles in graves were left by the little people. The last stories about the little people were told by Martha Uncas before 1900. She told about an Indian and his wife who lived here long ago, who saw dwarfs. One stormy night there was a rap on the door. When the woman opened it, there was a stranger who wanted her to come to care for a sick woman a long way off. She decided to go and packed her things and told her husband, who thought the stranger was a boy, although he was really a dwarf. He blindfolded her and led her far away in the storm until they reached an underground house. Inside, a dwarf woman lay ill on a bed of skins. The Indian woman then recognized them as dwarfs. When she was ready to return home the dwarf gave her presents, blindfolded her and led her back home. "People used to think that the stone mounds in this part of the Thames valley were made by the dwarfs."

In another story recounted to Speck, an Indian was aroused one night by a light that shone from a hill above her house. While she stood watching it, "she saw it ascend the hill to a small heap of rocks, where it blazed up and subsided. Then it moved to another rock and blazed high again, before subsiding as before. . . . The next morning she found no evidence of burning about the rocks. The incident was repeated a number of times and she thought she had been visited by spirits." People the world over have attributed spiritual properties to this class of luminous phenomena.

Speck describes a number of stone structures in the Mohegan lands. There is a Niantic legend about a cave called Devil's Den on the west bank of the Niantic River on a southerly spur of a ridge. The Niantics took refuge in the cave to escape the Mohawks who came after tribute; the narrow fissures in the rocks barred the ingress of any large body of men, provided there were a few to oppose them.

Cutchegun Rock, shown in Figure 10–2 with attached stone rows, is one of the largest detached boulders in New England and weighs 10,000 tons. It is located near Stoney Brook. Here in colonial times a Mohegan named Caleb Cutchegun lived in a cavity on the underside of the great rock. Mohegan tradi-

10-2 Cutchegan Rock, Montville, Conn. (from C. F. Wright, *Man and the Glacial Record*, New York, Appleton, 1898)

tion also mentions this as a resort of Uncas. It is said that Uncas held his council meetings on top of the rock, seated upon a flat rock for a bench, surrounded by seven other flat stones for his councilmen. These stones, however, have been rolled off the crown of the rock by vandals. Just north of the Pequot village in western Stonington, Connecticut, a bare rock not far from the summit of a hill shines like a light when seen from certain places at certain times. Because of this, the Indians named it Lantern Hill.

There are at least six known Indian villages that are called forts in the vicinity of the Thames River (Figure 10–3a):

1)	Black Point, Niantic Bay, summit ridge	Nahantics
2)	At head of Niantic River	Nahantics
3)	At head of Mystic River on Pequot Hill	Pequot
4)	Fort Hill on Mystic River near Sound	Pequot
5)	Fort Hill on Mohegan Hill, Montville (stone enclosure with earthworks)	Mohegan
6)	Fort Shantock on Crow Hill overlooking Thames rubble pyramid erected by the D. A. R.	Mohegan

Uncas's fort, located in Figures 10–3a and 10–3b and drawn in Figure 10–4, is described by Speck as an ancient stone enclosure on the top of Fort Hill. According

10-3a Mohegan lands between the Connecticut and Thames Rivers

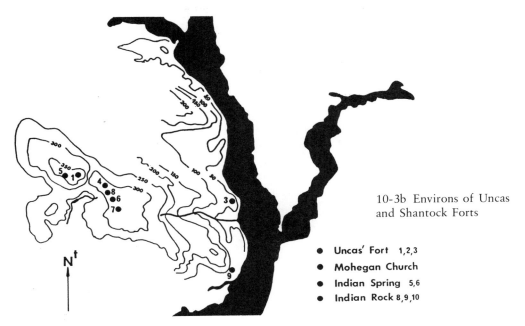

10-3b Environs of Uncas
and Shantock Forts

● **Uncas' Fort** 1,2,3
● **Mohegan Church**
● **Indian Spring** 5,6
● **Indian Rock** 8,9,10

to his description, which we have verified by observation, it has three sides made up of rocks and boulders. On the north, west, and south, the remains of a stone wall range from 6 to 8 feet across and 1 to 3 feet above ground, but there are no stones on the eastern side where the hill is the steepest. On the northeast corner of the main enclosure is a smaller one of large flat slabs laid upon a crown of bedrock. The Mohegans living in the area in 1920 remember this as having been the kitchen used when the fort was occupied. On the west, the wall is 180 feet long and on the north and south, 115 feet. The smaller enclosure is 30 feet square. Speck does not mention the prominent ditch and bank earthworks which we observed 100 yards to the west of the stone enclosures.

10-4 Uncas Fort

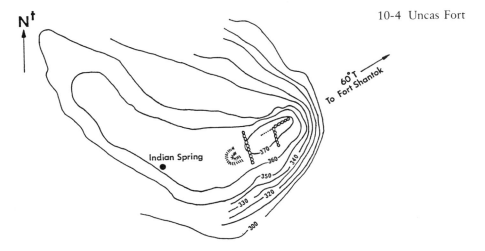

10-5 Devil's Footprint near Mohegan Church

10-6 Standing Stone at Mohegan Church

Near the Indian church, built in 1831 through the missionary zeal of Norwich English teacher Sarah Huntington, is a granite boulder (Figure 10–5), called the Devil's Footprint. There is a square crevice on its upper face about 8 inches deep and 6 inches on a side. Tradition has it that it always contains some water and it is bad luck to empty it. There is a legend that when the devil left the region, he stepped from the stone leaving the impression of his cloven hoof. He then went to Long Island where there is a similar impression near Montauk, also a place where Mohegans lived. A lone standing stone about 3 feet high, which Speck fails to mention, is set about 100 feet from the Devil's Footprint (Figure 10–6). There is a curious similarity between this folklore and the Breton legend of Mont Dol. There, a struggle took place between Saint Michael and the Devil in which the Devil was thrown down, making an impression in a rock and scratching it with his claw, but then escaped to nearby Mont St. Michel. Saint Michael then left the imprint of his foot on another rock in bounding from Mont Dol to Mont St. Michel in pursuit of his enemy.

There are several Indian springs, shown in Figure 10–3b, in the heart of the Mohegan settlement around Fort Hill. At these springs, water flows from a hillside through and over stone structures. Surrounding each spring are trees which were marked by fixing branches in unnatural bent positions when they were young, but Speck does not mention these. In some places nearby, pits are noticeable and appear as cavities in the fields. The present-day Mohegans call them "muggs" and store potatoes in them. According to Speck, certain individuals of the Mohegan are able to find water by means of a "crotched stick" of witch-hazel, wild apple or plum; witch hazel is also used as a divining rod for buried treasure. Also, men carry a long staff, which when let fall, divines the direction of game.

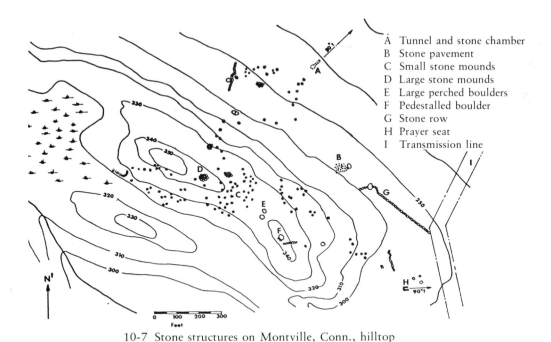

A Tunnel and stone chamber
B Stone pavement
C Small stone mounds
D Large stone mounds
E Large perched boulders
F Pedestalled boulder
G Stone row
H Prayer seat
I Transmission line

10-7 Stone structures on Montville, Conn., hilltop

A Hillside Prayer Seat

A vast collection of stone mounds, stone rows, enclosures, and perched boulders
is to be found in the rugged and rocky woodlands near the lower Thames River
within the present towns of Groton, Ledyard and Montville. This material is so
pervasive that one literally cannot drive along the country roads in the defoliated
seasons without seeing groups of stone mounds on hillsides and silhouetted
against the sky on hilltops. Yet, the material is known only locally and then
merely as something that has always been there.

We have selected one prominent place to represent this cultural material, a
hilltop in Montville of about 350 feet altitude. It overlooks a swamp of about
fifty acres. Unlike other local hills, it also has a small swamp very near the
summit. On and about the elongated summit we have counted about 150 stone
mounds and other curious man-made stone features (Figure 10–7).

The mounds are located in discrete groups. At the southeast end of the summit is an impressive boulder of about 100 tons perched upon three supporting
boulders. It stands majestically on its own rocky peak with no stone mounds
near it (Figure 4–21c). A concentration of stone mounds stands about 200 feet
to the northwest, and another 150 feet to the north and northeast. There are
none in sight in the other directions. The northwest summit is covered with

10-8 Stone mounds of hilltop group, Montville, Conn.

closely spaced mounds in a dense array with most less than 30 feet apart, many on bedrock and boulders (Figure 10–8). A few mounds, larger than the rest, cover large flat outcrops of bedrock near the summit of the hill. One end of the summit appears to be the domain of the great pedestalled boulder and the other that of the stone mounds.

We have seen large groups of stone mounds, 100 or more, throughout New England, often including a few much larger mounds among them. In some places these large mounds are retained by vertical dry stone walling several feet high as compared with apparently roughly piled stones. At Montville, the mounds are not walled, but some other groups in eastern Connecticut and Massachusetts are, as shown in the example of Figure 10–9.

10-9 Large walled stone mound, eastern Connecticut

On the northeast slope of the hill at Montville, below the stone mounds, there is a stone chamber, unique because of the great length of its passageway. James Whittall has published this chamber, and his drawing, Figure 10–10, shows a long narrow slab-roofed passage, which opens slightly at the interior end into a corbelled-roofed chamber. It meets the bedrock ledge, which has been quarried to serve as the back wall of the chamber. The alignment from the chamber to the horizon, which is elevated 2.2 degrees, in the direction of the chamber axis is 50 degrees true, and does not match any solar or lunar event, but could signal a star rise determinable only when we know the date. Whittall notes the similarity between this structure and souterrains of Ireland, Scotland and Cornwall, and draws attention to the very small entrance opening, 22 inches square, of the Montville chamber, which is similar to defensive restrictions or "creeps" in the European souterrains.[10] In our view, this chamber, and many others, could have as likely been built by Native Americans as by Europeans, in spite of specific architectural features which are found in Europe. It is quite possible that the chamber exhibits both Native American and European influence.

We do not know the identity of the builders of this particular chamber but less in doubt, in our view, is its function, which follows a pattern. Builders of many New England chambers devoted considerable effort to connecting the chambers structurally to bedrock, either by locating in suitable places or by quarrying the rock to suit the design. Most chambers are also aligned to observe celestial horizon events from within. We believe that the chambers are primarily sanctuaries built to connect the people with the earth manitou, as are kivas of the southwestern United States. Bedrock is relatively permanent and can be split or moved only by earthquake or other such great powers. By contrast, boulders can be moved by mere men and placed where they choose. The chambers also connect the earth with the celestial bodies, through the intermediary of the shaman, who knows when celestial events occur. Consistent with this theory, Cape Cod, which has no bedrock, has only two known stone chambers.

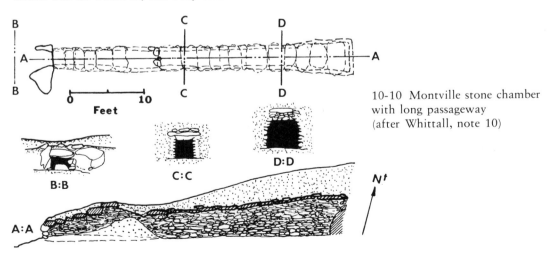

10-10 Montville stone chamber with long passageway (after Whittall, note 10)

At Montville, there are possible geographical relationships between the stone features on the hilltop and those on the eastern slopes. There are several short lengths of stone row; one, to the north, with an embrasure in it, points to the largest stone mound, which covers an expanse of exposed bedrock some 30 feet in diameter near the summit of the hill. The chamber axis also points to this mound. When observed from the short curved stone row to the west, the sun at the equinox rises precisely at the large mound. This row, which is perched upon a bedrock outcrop overlooking the upland swamp, is retained from collapsing by two iron tenons placed in holes drilled into the rock. Evidence of iron can imply either Indian or European construction. As we point out in Chapter 12, New England Indians used steel tools and ironwork from the seventeenth century and adapted their stone building to this change in technology. The short row near the perched summit boulder serves as a horizon marker for the equinox sunset when observed from an unmarked point on the hillside to the northeast of and in line with the stone row. The easterly short row below the summit, if extended to the northwest, intersects a short row attached to a large boulder and continues on to pass near the subterranean chamber.

During our exploration of the hilltop, we came to an area where there was a long outcropping of granite bedrock ending in a region that had been cleared of trees for the passage of a high voltage electrical transmission line, shown in Figure 10-7. At the eastern end of the outcrop and about 150 feet from the nearest of the four high tension lines, we experienced a crackling sound and felt distinctly uncomfortable. We wanted to leave the noxious place, but nevertheless we looked around and saw immediately a U-shaped stone structure of exactly the same shape as we had seen in pictures of prayer seats or tsektsels used in the Yurok vision quest of northern California. This one is a low, square stone enclosure, 8 feet on each side, open to the east (Figure 10-11). The sides are oriented precisely to true east, and an observer sitting or standing within the enclosure has a panoramic view to the east, where the sun rises over distant hills and valleys. He can also, by turning around, observe the setting summer solstice sun at the great perched boulder on the summit to the northwest.

10-11 Montville
prayer seat

This structure was an exciting discovery because we immediately and for the first time felt certain that it was an Algonquian prayer seat. We were reminded of the writings of Edward S. Curtis, known for his extraordinarily sensitive photographs of Indian life. Certain of his inferences from folk tales have been confirmed by recent anthropology. He wrote that many of the Flathead Indians of Montana were direct descendants of the Hurons, neighbors of the Algonquins in the East who had fled the slaughter of their people by Iroquois armed with the white man's guns in 1648. These Hurons went first to Green Bay, Wisconsin, where the Stockbridge Indians settled later when forced to move by the white man. From the West Coast came an elderly shaman of the Clayoquot people of Vancouver Island, who visited the Flatheads in 1700 and whose language was intelligible by the Flatheads. This story parallels the more recent finding that the Algonquian-speaking Yurok of the northern Pacific coast, who still use the stone mountaintop prayer seats, are descended from people who came from the Great Lakes centuries ago. We first heard of prayer seats because of the Yurok connection with the East.

Edward S. Curtis described in detail how the prayer seat was used in the Flathead three-day spring vision quest to relate the land and sky. Kukusim, son of the chief of the Flatheads, climbed the spirit mountain, probably on the vernal equinox, arriving at the summit at sunset, where he found a circle of stones. He sat on the west edge of the circle facing the dying sun and remained looking in that direction throughout the night, watching the stars, pausing only to build and tend a fire to ward off predatory animals. At sunrise, Kukusim moved to sit on the east edge of the ring where he watched the sun as it rose from the east to the south. At noon, when the sun was true south, he moved to the southern edge of the circle and watched the sun move from south to setting in the west. At sunset, he moved to the west to face the setting sun as he had done the evening before. With no food and little sleep, he continued this cycle three nights and two days, until on the third night spirits came and carried him over the clouds and mountain tops to where he heard the song of the spirits.[11] We felt sure that the stone prayer seat that we had found in Connecticut was used in just such a manner, augmented by the presence of the nearby high tension line.

We have seen many structures similar to the Montville prayer seat scattered widely over New England, always with a solar orientation, on or near a hilltop and surrounded by stone mounds and rows. We believe, based on ethnographic evidence from other parts of North America, that these structures are Algonquian "prayer seats" used in the vision quest ritual and that they may be the key to determining the origins and function of much stone structure.

The Montville structure had an unmistakably recent look about it. At the corners, where the stones are not interlocked, trees about 20 years old have grown, but the interior is free of trees even though it lies in a heavily wooded area. We read later that it is customary to plant four young cottonwood trees at the four corners of the enclosure at a place of vision quest in the Sioux tradition.[12] Next to the enclosure there was a pile of brush that appeared to be about twenty-five years old. Also, we know that the transmission lines and therefore the clearing were created about 1950. These circumstances all imply that the prayer seat was erected since 1950 in order to be located near the transmission line, as well as being part of the stone complex on the hilltop.

That high voltage, sixty-cycle power lines can affect human behavior through mental and physical changes is well known and a cause of health concern to those who live near them. In this instance, the effect was probably sought by someone in search of visions, because one of the effects of transmission lines is to cause hallucination and therefore better reception of visions. Studies suggest two mechanisms by which sixty-hertz power lines can affect human biology. The first effect is stimulation of neural receptors near the skin surface, commonly felt as tingling of the skin. The second is a more complicated transductive process at the cell membranes which seems to affect the transmission of neural impulses by altering the rate of calcium ion release from neural tissue. Measurements of electrical field strength about a grounded human body subject to an external field show that the field strength is increased about the head.[13]

The circumstances of a recent prayer seat at the easterly extremity of the site and the short stone row to the west retained by iron tenons imply historic construction and use of at least part of the site. Since the features are found in the traditional Mohegan hunting grounds, we infer that the users were and probably continue to be Mohegan Indians. It is curious that Frank Speck, who lived with the Connecticut Mohegans for two years, commented on but few stone structures in his folklore of the Mohegan lands. Either he did not know of the many others or purposely refrained from reporting on sacred places and objects.

"There Is a Bad Noise"

After we had studied the Montville region, we became aware of a hilltop site on the east bank of the Connecticut River, along the route taken by the Pequots during their migration. It is in East Haddam, overlooking the village of Moodus and the junction of the Salmon and Connecticut Rivers.

The site consists of a complex of most unusual stone rows, two stone chambers, many stone mounds, and mounds of earth and stone, as well as curious structures built into the rows. All features are related to the topography, geology and hydrology of the natural landscape in ways that we have recognized at so many other places in New England. Allan Martenson, who has been studying the site since 1978 and brought it to our attention, has postulated a number of astronomical alignments from stone features to astronomical events on the horizon.

Before describing the details of these structures, we want to point out the important connection between this location and Indian ritual, which has probably been preserved in historical records because the place has such a unique natural history. The hill on which Martenson surveyed is 430 feet above sea level and overlooks Cave Hill, one-half mile to the south, said to harbor an Indian cave. Further to the south about three-quarters of a mile, the site overlooks Mount Tom, a promontory where Salmon Cove divides into the Salmon and Moodus Rivers. Mount Tom is a very common name of hills in New England which are associated with flooding and ancient Indian ritual. The Indian name for this particular Mount Tom and the hills around it was Machemoodus, or "there is a bad noise," in the local Wangunk dialect.[14] The natives of this area during the seventeenth century were known as Machemoodus, from which the nearby village and river take their names. Cracking and rumbling noises and earth tremors have characterized Mount Tom and its surroundings from the seventeenth century to the present. The hills of the Moodus region are domes of gneiss and mica-schist and, as a contact area, like Calendar One, some mining has taken place.

The region about the village of Moodus is one of the three most seismically active places in New England, the others being northeastern Massachusetts and Ossipee, New Hampshire. Moodus seismicity is particularly shallow, and there is an anomalous earth structure with post-metamorphic faults which have been correlated with earthquakes.[15]

The local Indians were known for their religious activity and served as priests or shamans to other tribes. Pequot, Mohegan and even Narragansett Indians, with whom the other groups were constantly in conflict, went to Mount Tom and the Machemoodus powwows because they believed that the thunderings and quakings, called the Moodus noises, could only mean that this was the home of Hobomock, the spirit most sought after by the powwows of New England. The English colonists, as early as 1670, reported both the noises and extraordinary Indian ritual activity on the mountain. As they put it, "The Indians drove a prodigious trade at worshipping the devil."[16] The Devil's Hopyard, a wild and rocky region a few miles to the southeast, no doubt took its name from this activity.

The diaries of John Eliot and his colleague Danforth record a series of exceptional natural events. On February 1, 1660, there was a discernible earthquake, and on January 26, 1663, another earthquake. On November 4, 1667, there were strange noises in the air, like guns and drums, and on March 16, 1668, an earthquake shock was felt after there had been prodigies (extraordinary objects) in the heavens the night before.[17]

The 1663 earthquake was widespread in its effects. It was felt all over northeastern North America and described by the French in Montreal as a tremendous earthquake. Aftershocks continued intermittently for six months, accompanied by alarming phenomena. Ten days after the initial shock, a loud rumbling noise was heard throughout all of New France. Forest trees were set in violent motion, thrown from side to side. Ice on the lakes and rivers, some feet thick, broke and was thrown into the air with rocks and mud. Clouds of dust obscured the sky and water turned yellow and reddish, impregnated with sulphur. There were flashes of lightning and rocks cracked and rolled over each other.[18]

The Reverend Mr. Hosmer, the first minister at Haddam, wrote in 1729 that he experienced several hundred sounds over 20 years, sometimes almost every day, and many successively in minutes. He often heard the noises "coming down from the north imitating slow thunder, until the sound came near or right under, and then there seemed to be a breaking, like the noise of a cannon shot." Hosmer noted that the noises ceased after the great earthquake of 1727, centered at the mouth of the Merrimack River.[19] After the 1797 earthquake, centered near Moodus, stones of several tons weight were found removed from their places, and fissures were found in immovable rocks. In 1831, a person on top of Mount Tom felt as if a large stone had fallen down to the depths below from under the ground directly beneath his feet. The *Connecticut Gazette* of 20 August 1790 reported that a Dr. Steel from Britain dug up two pearls of great value near Salmon River which he called carbuncles. He prophesied a hiatus in the noises following his removal of the pearls, which did occur as predicted.[20]

The history of the Moodus area attests to participation of the native shamans with a geophysically active landscape that moved and produced light. This follows a pattern among cultures all over the world that have attributed religious significance to glowing forms that appear at areas of recurring earthquakes. History is also consistent with specific Algonquian legends and the concept of manitou.

Recent studies of light emission from rock fracture have suggested an explanation for many observed "mysterious lights" in nature and support our case for the importance of broken rock in Indian religious ritual. B. T. Brady and G. A. Rowell have proposed a mechanism, supported by convincing experimental results, in which the explosive process of rock fracture causes electrons, emitted from the fresh broken surface, to bombard the surrounding air and excite it to produce light. This theory explains satisfactorily how both large and small earthquakes which break the earth's surface can produce light.[21] Such phenomena as bright white lights the size of baseballs floating among treetops, luminous dust clouds moving along near the ground, sequential flashes from different points on a hillside, fireballs on the horizon, and glows at sea like a ship afire can now be explained by earthquakes.[22]

Quartz and other piezoelectric materials become incandescent when stressed by frictional sliding, and this has been suggested as a mechanism to support light generation because quartz is so commonly a part of cultural ritual. However, the experiments of Brady and Rowell have shown that this mechanism does not excite the air and therefore cannot produce the atmospheric lights that are characteristic of so much observed natural luminescence.

The stone structures on the hilltop at Moodus are shown in the map of Figure 10–12. The dominant feature is the 3,000 feet of oddly built stone rows. The rows are made with quarried slabs, from local quarries, set transverse to the row direction and leaning about 30 degrees from the vertical toward the west (Figure 10–13). In some places, the slabs are laid up in tiers. This curious construction may be related to the Moodus noises and quakes, either as a design that is resis-

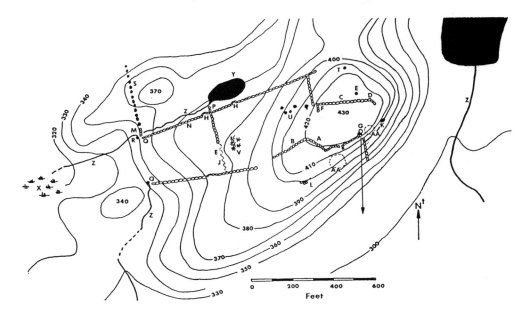

10-12 Map of stone structures and their natural surroundings at Moodus, Conn.

A, Saddle; B, Platform; C, Notched orthostats; D, Corner embrasure; E, Stone ring; F, High Row Corner; G, Larger stone chamber; H, Embrasures in row; J, Serpentine row; K, Lintel; L, Smaller stone chamber with platform; M, Short stone row of boulder construction; N, High section of slab row; P, Row meets pond outlet; Q, Row ends at spring; R, Stone-lined spring; S, Intermittent stone row; T, Rock outcrop due north of C; U, Stone mounds on bedrock; V, Earthen mounds; X, Swamp; Y, Pond (appears man-made); Z, Streams originating at stone rows; AA, Quarry

10-13 Stone row, Moodus, Conn.

tant to earthquake damage, or one in which the stones respond by rattling during an earthquake. The two major lengths of row, running generally in an east-west direction, both start in the west at springs, one of which is stone-lined. A little further to the west there is a swamp fed by one of these springs. The long rows proceed up a uniform slope to the summit of the hill, where the rows become more complex in geometry.

On the steep southeastern slope of the hill are two stone chambers built against and quarried into bedrock, and a complex of short stone rows on ledges which circumscribe and connect earthen platforms, all having a distant southerly view toward Mount Tom and Cave Hill. There are practically no boulders on this hill, and all structures are made from quarried granite or mica-schist. Throughout the site, placed in stone rows, are found worked stone slabs which we call either "spirit of the creator" or "godstone," from their appearance at ritual sites throughout New England and descriptions of such stones in historical records cited in previous chapters (Figure 10–14a and b). Specifically in Connecticut, such stones bearing a resemblance to the human head and shoulders have been found and called Indian gods by DeForest.[23] There are more of these shaped stones at the Moodus site than at any other known to us in New England.

The saddle, Figure 10–15 and feature A in Figure 10–12, consists of a large slab set in line with a stone row on exposed bedrock at the summit of the hill. There is a depression on its upper side which could be used as a sighting notch, most likely from some distant observation point. On each end of the slab, which is five feet wide, there is an additional large inclined slab leaning against it. A structure rather similar to the saddle is located about 15 feet to the northwest at about four feet lower elevation. Near the saddle, but around the corner of the

10-14 Godstones in stone rows, Moodus, Conn.

10-15 Great saddle
in stone row,
Moodus, Conn.

stone row, is a slab, B on the map, set in a horizontal plane so as to form a platform. It is bordered by large inclined slabs giving the appearance of a grand entranceway through the stone row (Figure 10–16).

In an east-west section of the northerly row system, there are two large rectangular slabs, C. One is built into the row and has an upper corner cut neatly from it. The other lies flat on the ground, with a similar corner cutout, and probably stood vertically at one time as a companion to the other stone. The two stones are separated by a six-foot space filled in by smaller stones. This structure, as do structures A and B, appears suitable for use as a distant astronomical foresight. All are also built sufficiently elegantly to imply ceremonial use.

There are three embrasures or U-shaped diversions in the stone rows, each occurring at an architecturally significant location. Embrasure D is at the end of a long stone row at the edge of the east slope of the hill. One embrasure H is next to the outlet of a small pond on the north which is marked also by a short length of stone row. The other embrasure H is opposite the center of the small pond, overlooking it as if it were intended for observing events at the pond.

10-16 Stone
platform in
stone row,
Moodus, Conn.

There are several stone rings, E, of about six feet diameter, barely visible above ground. Two of them are at the ends of or built into stone rows. Near the summit but on the north are two sections of stone row, F, which meet at a corner but are not interlocked. These row sections are five to six feet high and built with horizontally laid-up slabs and chunks of quarried rock. The rows appear similar to most rows called stone fences. They stand out here because of their height and the fact that they are built unlike any other rows on the hill. In our experience, they most closely resemble the Tunbridge, Vermont, Indian fort. Adjacent to this corner is found the major concentration of stone mounds on the hill.

Of the two stone chambers, the larger, G, is oval in shape, about 6 feet in diameter, with a corbelled roof (Figure 10–17). It has a passage about 5 feet long directed true south, and about one half of the chamber wall was quarried into the bedrock. Otherwise, it was built entirely of irregularly quarried stones, carefully and strategically placed in an elegant design. When discovered, there were but two feet of headroom in the passage and four feet in the chamber proper, but excavation by James Whittall reveals a full headroom of six feet in the passage and chamber and a bedrock floor.[24] Chamber L is smaller and less elaborate in design and construction (Figure 10–18). It is basically rectangular with one wall the bedrock and a parallel wall of large stones. Several slabs form a roof connecting the two walls, leaving headroom of about four feet. The sightline of an observer in this chamber or in front of it passes parallel to a long section of ledge, over a single lintel stone at a distance of some 400 feet, to a distant horizon notch. Martenson suggests that this sightline, whose astronomical declination is 30 degrees, was possibly a lunar extreme. The lintel stone, K, a slab about five

10-17 Large stone chamber, Moodus, Conn.

10-18 Small stone chamber, Moodus, Conn.

feet long and two feet wide, bridges the bedrock ledge and a split-off piece of rock. Both of these chambers are intimately connected to the bedrock and, in our belief, fit our theory of spiritual function. At this special place, where the mountain shakes, the role of seeking access to the spirit of the mountain has a special significance.

A barely perceptible serpentine row of stones, J, extends from one slab row to another. This row of perhaps 20 turns appears to be either a partially buried row of inclined slabs, whose tops barely break the surface, or an intentionally subtle feature. A row of intermittent stones, S, extends from the spring north down a slope for several hundred feet. The small pond, Y, appears artificial. It is dammed at the west end, possibly by an extension of the short row that meets it. Also, there are several earth and stone mounds, V, on the western slope of the hill.

In the Indian way, all of these stones which we have described, whether piles and placed boulders, split rock, or outcropping ledges, have spirits, as do the plants and animals and the forces of water, wind, and heat and cold which form the landscape. The Great Spirit is all of these taken together and is the land, sea and sky. The Native American tries to sense the world through the perception of the Great Spirit, and the shaman does it more completely than most. The stones help in this endeavor, and the luminous, glowing forms manifested by earthquake activity would have reinforced the native's concept of manitou. The historic Mohegan Indians moved from eastern New York and western Massachusetts to eastern Connecticut, to Canada, and to the Midwest. They kept their knowledge of spiritual things and built and used stone structures to communicate with the manitou wherever they happened to be, in the manner of their prehistoric ancestors. The continuation into recent times, among the Mohegans, of shamanistic ritual using stone structures and the natural landscape has led us to believe that they have been particularly zealous in preserving these traditions.

11

Nashoba

During the course of our work together, Byron moved to Boxborough in eastern Massachusetts, to be near his job. While walking the woods behind his house, he noticed stone mounds, perched boulders and curious stone rows, and, because of its easy accessibility, we began a study of the region. The deeper we probed the more exciting it became.

The Boxborough esker, a spectacularly large earth feature two and a half miles long, oriented northeast, lies between two extensive swamps in the midst of present-day Littleton and Boxborough. The esker is crowned by a narrow, sinuous, level ridge which has an average height of fifty-six feet above the adjacent wetlands. It is made of soil and igneous rock, mostly quartz, feldspar and biotite, whereas the underlying country rock is metamorphic. Stone rows, stone mounds and pits can be seen within the swamps and on the sides and top of the esker, and stone rows of granite boulders cross it in several places along its serpentine course.[1] This great earthen feature quickly became the focus of our research.

Muddy Pond, an elongated body of water, lies along the base of the east side of the esker, south of the swamp. Four stone rows emerge from its waters, two on the north end and two on the south end (Figures 11–1 and 11–2). The southwestern row climbs to the top of the esker, where it curves gently around a small platform from which there is a westerly view of Beaver Brook and the swamp below. The row then turns south, descends the west side of the esker, and curves

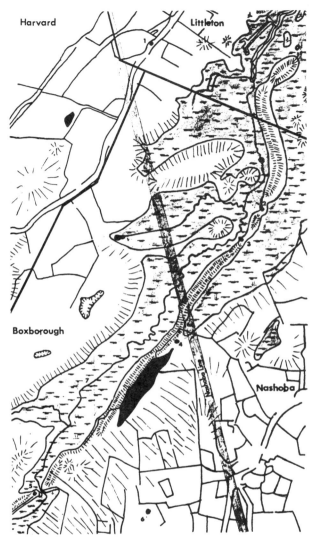

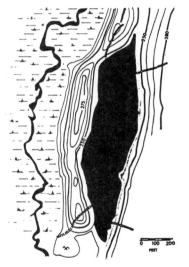

11-1 Boxborough esker and environs
1 Oak Hill northern chamber
2 Stone mound
3, 4 Earthern circles
5 Ditch and bank
6, 7 Large stone mounds

11-2 Boxborough esker at Muddy Pond

along a gentle slope to disappear into the swamp. Construction of this row may have occurred late in the seventeenth century, judging by marks of steel tools on several of the stones. There are balanced stones, embrasures and fire-burned rock along the row's course over the esker. Also, a viewer standing where the row enters the swamp can see the summer solstice sunrise over the row at the top of the esker.

The stone row that emerges from the water at the northwestern edge of Muddy Pond is directed north and climbs a curved path to the esker spine, which it follows for fifty yards before turning and ending at a man-made earthen platform just below and east of the spine (Figures 11–3 and 11–4). The platform was constructed by moving earth from the top of the esker over onto the eastern bank, resulting in a flat area below the crest, a practice we have seen at other locations.[2]

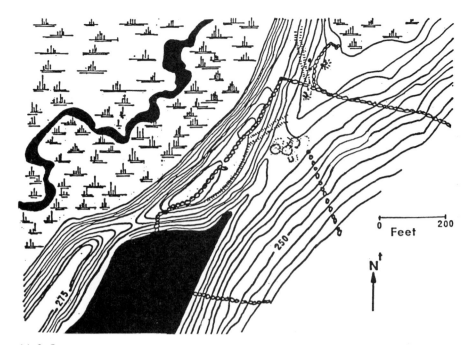

11-3 Stone structures at
north end of Muddy Pond

11-4 Stone row on esker
spine, looking south

Another stone row starts on the ridge line adjacent to the flat platform and can be considered an extension of the row just described, with an aperture of two yards width between them. The latter row continues north for sixty yards along the esker spine, then turns abruptly down the eastern bank, continues across a valley, then climbs uphill gently before stopping abruptly where it was cut off by construction of the dual lane highway, Route I–495. As the row reaches the valley, there is a three-foot-wide gap, just west of a junction with yet another stone row, this one curving gently from the edge of the swamp to the north. Two earthen pits are nestled in a level place on the eastern bank of the esker near this row intersection. The line of the stone row that crosses the valley undulates in this area, and it also undulates for several cycles at its lowest point in the valley, where we saw the rusted remains of a steel bucket. By now we had discovered that buckets and milk cans were documented as being ritual objects used in the Indian vision quest throughout America.[3]

As shown in Figures 11–3 and 11–5, the stone row that leads northward to the edge of the swamp ends with an embrasure and a small stone mound. Also, a U-shaped stone enclosure about two-and-a-half feet on a side and two feet high, nestled in an earthen mound and facing the esker, is located near the row at about its midpoint. Another similar structure, also facing the esker, is located just south of the row junction and aperture. Both of these U-shaped stone enclosures have the character and setting of prayer seats. Fire-burned rock, quartz, balanced rocks, manitou stones, and the remains of metal buckets are found throughout these rows.

A ramp, shown in Figure 11–5, has been constructed down the eastern bank of the esker northward from the man-made platform, and another ramp connects the row junction and aperture with another altered place on the esker spine to the north. This ramp directs a walker through the aperture in the stone row.

Three earthen circles, all about ten yards in diameter, and another U-shaped enclosure, three yards across, are located in the valley between these two ramps. Each of the circles appears to have been constructed by digging an annular ditch for three quarters of a circle and depositing the excavated material in the area

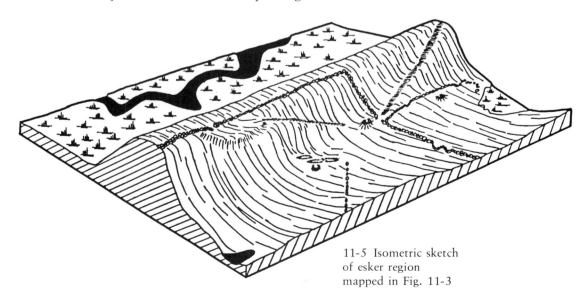

11-5 Isometric sketch
of esker region
mapped in Fig. 11-3

11-6 Summer solstice sunset
witnessed along stone row
to top of esker ridge

enclosed by the ditch. This created a circular area of slightly increased elevation almost enclosed by a ditch. Two of the circular earthworks have short elongated ditches, which face one another, in front of and near the undug quarter-circle, a Hopewellian design described in Chapter 9.

Solstice sunsets can be seen over horizon markers on the top of the esker from several marked positions in the valley. In 1987, a spectacular summer solstice sunset was witnessed from the row junction by looking along the stone row that climbs up the esker (Figure 11–6). A person sitting in the center of the circular earthwork nearest Muddy Pond can witness the summer solstice setting sun over an artificial horizon created by the platform and ramp on the ridge and the stone row that runs along the esker spine. Here, the row as seen from the earthwork emerges from behind the platform at the top of the ramp, and the gap in the row is a horizon marker for the solar event. From the center of the earthwork circle furthest from the pond, an observer can witness the summer solstice sunset at the highest elevation of the row along the esker spine, where there is a gap at the proper position.

Beaver Brook flows along the west side of the esker for most of its length and then winds through a gap near the southern end (Figure 11–1). Just south of the brook here is a fifty-foot-long earth and stone structure, consisting of a ditch and an adjacent bank, oriented north and south (A–A in Figure 11–7). The banked portion of the structure is a low stone row, with the ditch on the downhill side.

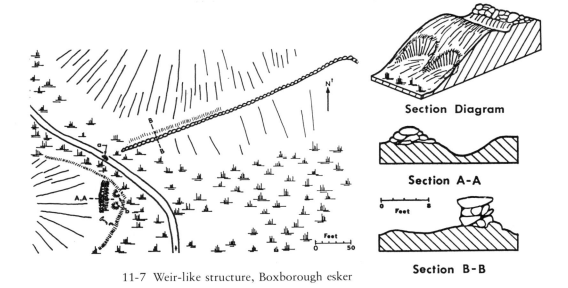

Section Diagram

Section A-A

Section B-B

11-7 Weir-like structure, Boxborough esker

Two pits, b, which face the swamp, have been excavated into the esker just beneath the ditch and bank. Nearby, on the north side of the brook and on the lower levels of the esker, a 525-foot-long stone row oriented west-southwest (B-B in Figure 11-7) terminates at the stream. A slight ditch and bank landform can be seen along the uphill side of this row. Were the stone and earthen features on both sides of Beaver Brook extended, they would intersect at the middle of the brook, a, where the water depth is usually less than three feet because of local rock structure in the stream. At times of high water level, the stonework on both sides of the brook would be submerged and would restrict flow, consequently diverting some of the water that would otherwise flow down the eastern side of the esker.

This stone structure on the banks and within a stream bears a resemblance to Native American fish weirs, yet another of the many types of native stone construction that participate with the whole environment and are part of ritual. Fish weirs are traditionally constructed of either wood or stone, and the skills required to build them of stone are the same as those required to construct stone rows.

In the town of Harvard, about one-half mile southwest of the Boxborough esker and Beaver Brook, a series of earth and stone structures have been placed along Elizabeth Brook, a stream that connects two swamps that are thirty-nine feet different in elevation (Figure 11–8). The stream, while flowing through the upper swampy area, undulates in response to flow modifiers consisting of large boulders (a), man-made stone mounds (b), and small embayments (h) along the watercourse. Immediately downstream of one of the stone mounds, this year-round stream is joined by a seasonal one, and thirty feet downstream of this confluence two parallel stone rows thirty-three feet apart cross the stream.

Downstream of the rows, the watercourse steepens sharply. Another stone

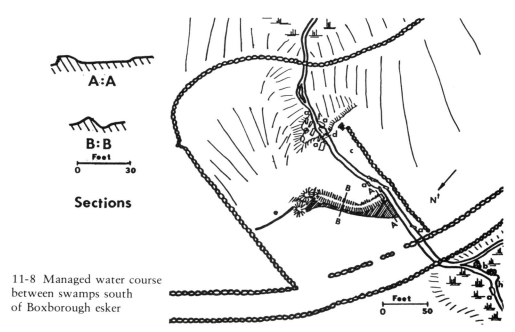

A:A

B:B

Feet
0   30

Sections

11-8 Managed water course
between swamps south
of Boxborough esker

row normal to the parallel rows follows along the south side of the stream and
down the hill, with a stone-paved area, c, between it and the stream. Also, a
manmade bank of earth and stone leads away from the stream on the north side
(AB). Immediately upstream of this bank is a ditch which is twenty-three feet
wide at the stream and narrows to seven feet at a distance of thirty-six feet from
the stream. The ditch continues down the hill and runs parallel to the bank for
another fifty-six feet, where both terminate at a shallow depression banked by
two small earth and stone mounds. A smaller ditch, e, runs out the other side of
the depression. This major ditch and bank construction could have been built to
divert water from the stream during periods of high water; the runoff water at
these times would have flowed along and down the ditch, between the two
mounds and on down the hill.

Meanwhile, the main stream bypasses the ditch and ninety-eight feet downstream plummets ten feet in a fall. Large quarried stone slabs, a, project into the
stream and were positioned along its course both above and below the fall. These
stones tend to retard and breakup the flow into white water, also directing it
toward the center of the stream. Several structured stone basins, f, are located
along the stream below the fall, and another stone row crosses the stream normal
to the flow seventy-nine feet downstream of the fall. The stream finally empties
into Boxborough Swamp fifty-six feet beyond the stone row.

At times of high water level, the flow of Elizabeth Brook between the two
swamps may be subject to changes in head and possibly to translating waves
because the placed stone obstructions contract the channel. Such surges of higher
water level caused by seasonal changes would have been of greater intensity in

the past on a burned-over landscape with fewer trees and less undergrowth to
absorb the water.

Boxborough Swamp has been drastically modified in recent years by building
and highway construction. Early local residents report that the area was, in large
part, wetland and included a pond, many stone walls, and a stream. These structures and those described above in the stream may have been used as a colonial
millrace, though no clearly colonial structures remain, but the subtle use of natural
materials and landforms, and the complexity make it unlike any known millraces.

Beaver Brook, Elizabeth Brook and the two swamps lie in a valley enclosed by
rocky ridges. On the summit of the ridge to the east of the falls were, until recently,
two boulders, one placed upon the other as a great rock stack. This structure,
shown in Figure 4–24b, which was just south of and in line with the Boxborough
esker, was destroyed in order to place a new corporate building adjacent to Route
I-495. On the ridge to the west, there is a single fifteen-ton boulder perched on
bedrock. Such prominent rocks, mentioned in Indian folklore throughout America,
are, in our opinion, clearly elements of the Indian ritualized landscape. In this
instance, they are, or were, related architecturally to the many stone works of the
esker region.

A short distance to the northwest of the hydraulic works just described and
west of the esker, there is another region, also near Beaver Brook, that reveals an
additional assortment of stonework. The structures located in Figure 11–9

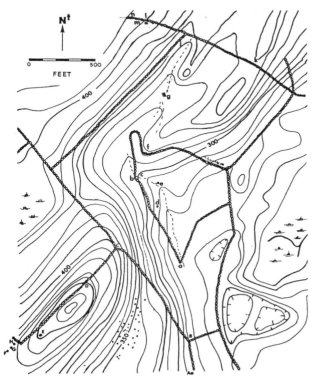

11-9 Stone features west
of Boxborough esker

include a complex array of stone rows, mounds, standing stones, etc., along both banks of a stream flowing south to join Beaver Brook.

In the central portion of the figure, a is an acute angled corner, where two stone rows meet at a stream (dotted line). At b, there is an embrasure in a stone row near c, a lintelled passage to permit flow of the stream beneath the row. A mound, d, about twenty-five yards in diameter and six feet high is located adjacent to the stream. It is circular and symmetrical except for an exposed ledge on its southern side, where numerous pebbles have been piled. This prominent mound lies at the center of the valley cut by the brook, surrounded by hills. The valley floor is surrounded by an irregular enclosure of stone rows. Feature e is a stone enclosure with a roof of stone slabs located at the edge of the stream and seasonally nearly full of water. It has an underground passage about five yards long extending from the water's edge uphill to an opening at the northeast end. The axis of the passage is aimed at the center of the large central mound.

In the northern region of Figure 11–9, g is a roughly built stone dam of quarried rock in a narrow natural cleft. North of this dam the land is nearly level, and the stream widens to a pool south of a stone row which runs uphill southeast and northwest of the stream. At the eastern summit is an embrasure, k, in the row, shown in Figure 11–10, such as we have seen frequently before. At the summit of the western branch of the row, there is a large rectangular orthostat, l, set in the row; beyond it is a triangular slab, m, and beyond that two more rectangular orthostats, n (Figure 11–10). This group of slabs, which signal the hill's summit, occurs over a twenty-yard length of the row. North of these orthostats about seventy-five yards, not shown, is a large boulder perched on an outcrop of ledge with a small stone wedged beneath it. It is clearly a horizon feature as seen from the valley to the southeast.

In the southwestern part of Figure 11–9, there is a prominent hill and an impressive standing stone at D, in a stone row. This monolith, shown in Figure 11–11, is about five feet high with a hooked point at its top. On the southwestern part of the summit is a large boulder, F, which partly covers a stone cist, three

11-10 Details of features,
northern part of Fig. 11-9

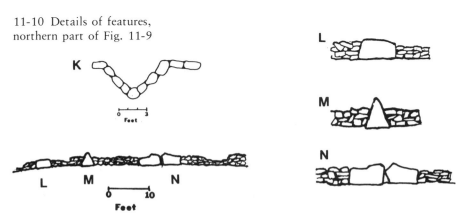

11-11 Details of features, southwestern part of Fig. 11-9

feet by one foot in plan and one foot deep made of slabs of stone (Figure 11–11). It would appear that it may have been a burial, formerly covered by the boulder which has since been moved aside. Near this cist, there is surface evidence of another subterranean stone enclosure, G, somewhat larger than the other. At H, at the same elevation and just below the summit, there is a circular depression, paved with small boulders, about five yards diameter, with a ten-foot diameter boulder lying in the center of the depression (Figure 11–11). This arrangement is quite unlike the natural terrain of ledges, quarry debris and soil and appears to have been built by humans as a ceremonial construction.

Shown at the bottom of Figure 11–9 as a group of dots is a field of stone mounds situated on a hillside plateau. There are about seventy-five small piles of broken stone, obviously quarried from the surrounding ledges. Some piles are made of elongated pieces of stone piled up parallel with one another (Figure 11–12). Most are piled on top of ledges or existing boulders as on Cape Cod.

11-12 Stone piles along Beaver Brook

11-13a Northern chamber,
Oak Hill

This site indicates landscape management and a sacred hilltop. It is typical of
sites found throughout the region and shows again the great extent and concentration of this type of stonework in New England.

Just west of the Boxborough esker lies a large ridge called Oak Hill, which
straddles the Harvard and Littleton town line. A stone chamber is located on
each end, the northern one aligned to the winter solstice and the southern to the
summer solstice. The northern chamber, located on the map in Figure 11–1 and
shown in Figure 11–13, is nested into a cavity carved into bedrock and has an
axis perpendicular to a stone row behind the structure. A small portion of the
bedrock was removed by quarrying with a hand-held steel stone mason's drill,
very probably of a flat cross section, leaving a hole having an irregular or multi-

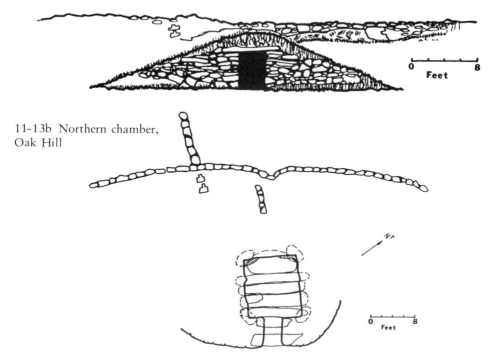

11-13b Northern chamber,
Oak Hill

lobed cross-section. This can imply either Indian or colonial workmanship over the past several hundred years. The chamber overlooks Beaver Brook and the Boxborough esker, and a person within looking out along its axis could have witnessed the winter solstice sunrise over Beaver Brook swamp at a horizon created by the esker. But the ancient horizon is no longer visible because part of the esker was mined away two decades ago and a barn obstructs the view. The efforts of George Krusen and Stanley Wirsig of Boxborough have led to the preservation of the remaining portion of the esker.

The chamber is sixty yards from the junction of the boundaries of the present towns of Littleton, Harvard and Boxborough. From an observation post at the back wall of the chamber where the axis of the passage, different from the axis of the chamber proper, meets it, an observer can see the winter solstice sunrise along the passage axis, a minor lunar standstill at the northern outer corner of the passage, and a major lunar standstill at the southern outer corner of the passage. The orientation of the Littleton-Boxborough town line is parallel to the minor lunar standstill alignment. This combination of solar and lunar alignments and a border connection suggests a native participation in the laying out of town boundaries. The structure was perhaps intentionally located at the end of a ridge system having an axis nearly normal to the sightlines to the winter solstice sunrise and the summer solstice sunset.

The southern stone chamber, shown in Figure 11–14, faces the direction of the summer solstice sunset. The chamber has a complex shape with a very long and narrow entrance. On entering, one encounters a short, tight passage, then turns a right angle to enter a longer passage that is only sixteen inches wide, which gradually widens as it approaches a small room on the right or southwest side, as shown in Figure 11–15. The chamber was built on the east side of a place which the first settlers called Bare Hill, near an area they called Wigwam Meadow and the Indian corn-planting area. The name Bare Hill reflects the native custom of

11-14 Harvard chamber

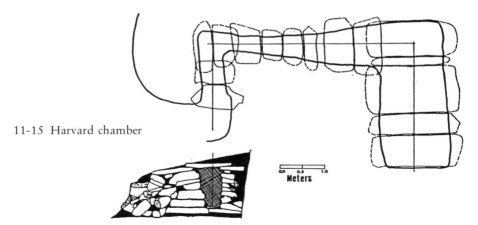

11-15 Harvard chamber

Meters

burning the trees and underbrush to create large open spaces, especially on hilltops. This way of cultivating a park-like landscape has been a native tradition for many thousands of years, a tradition that created an open landscape that was less subject to uncontrolled forest fires than is the case today. A clear landscape obviously gives a better view of the places where the land and sky meet, encouraging awareness of the earth's place in the celestial sphere and its annual passage in orbit. Bare Hill Pond, just west of Bare Hill, has two features that are probably related to this, a twenty-ton rocking stone on Sheep Island and a huge balanced boulder on the hilltop east of Sheep Island.[4]

The chamber is located adjacent to a small hill, 500 feet above sea level, and looks up to a horizon elevated three degrees above level. The alignment to the summer solstice sunset is identical in elevation, azimuth and distance to that at the Upton chamber in Chapter 2. Near the chamber is a swamp and an avenue defined by two stone rows that passes directly in front of the chamber. Two stone mounds are located nearby, one a circular mound on axis with the chamber main passageway, the other near the entrance. Manitou stones were found lying on top of the chamber (Figure 13–1b) and standing vertically in the nearby swamp. The entrance appears to have been modified by the later addition of the short passage extending at right angles from the original long passage, which is probably the reason that this complex floor plan is unique among New England chambers.[5] The mounds appear depleted of stones, suggesting that they may have supplied the stones used to add to the chamber's passage extension.

Oak Hill still retains its close connection with the cosmos today through Project SETI, Search for Extraterrestrial Intelligence, which operates a ninety-foot diameter radio telescope on the ridge. Also, the Harvard Center for Astrophysics maintains a battery of optical telescopes at the same location.

Among the earthen and stone works remaining in this region, some were acknowledged in the nineteenth century to have been the work of Indians. Two intersecting stone walls bounded the "Indian farm" and a "cellar hole" near

Fort Pond was thought to be the remains of an Indian dwelling. In addition, on the boundary with Westford, Mr. Francis Flagg, born in 1812, remembered a passageway roofed with large flat stone slabs running into a hillside near a barn. Opinions of the function of this stone chamber varied from a place of retreat during Indian raids to a structure for conveying water.[6]

The Place Called Nashoba

It wasn't until sometime after we had carefully studied and mapped the natural and man-made features of earth and stone along Beaver Brook and on Oak Hill that we seriously looked into the history of the region as written by the European colonists. We quickly discovered that the Boxborough esker was in or very near John Eliot's sixth Indian praying village, Nashoba. It was described by the English colonists as a plantation situated mostly in present-day Littleton but partly in adjacent Harvard, Boxborough, Acton, Westford, Groton and Ayer.[7]

Eliot's petition to the Massachusetts General Court for the establishment of Nashoba praying village was granted May 14, 1654, at the same time as Ockoo-cangansett (Marlborough) and Hassanamessit (Grafton), all in Nipmuck territory. The town was said to be roughly four miles square, which was typical of the size of most of the fourteen praying villages described by Eliot and Gookin. Nashoba in the Nipmuck language means "the place between" or "between the ponds," and the praying village was in an area that is rich in streams, swamps and ponds: Cobbs, Fort, Long, Mill and Nagog Ponds are all within the Nashoba praying village.[8]

The Nashua or Nashaway Indians, who were part of the group that Roger Williams called Nipmucks, occupied nearly all of this part of Massachusetts in the 1630s and 1640s. Because of family connections between sachems and other circumstances, the Nipmucks, Wampanoags and Narragansetts had close ties and in many ways acted as if they were of the same tribe. This example and others lead us to believe that the Indian tribal subdivisions and leadership hierarchies that were perceived by the Puritans and their successors were probably brought about in part by actions of the white settlers themselves due to their misconceptions and lack of appreciation of the Indian perspective.[9]

It becomes evident from town histories that each praying village of the first group of seven was interconnected with all the others of the group in ways that contributed more to maintaining Indian family networks and traditional ways than to Christianization. Family members were often spread through several praying villages. John Speen, for example, was the preacher at Natick while residing at Hassanamessitt and Nashoba. His name is found also on a Framingham quit claim deed made out in John Eliot's handwriting. Tahatawon, the sachem of Nashoba and his wife Kehonosquaw (Sara Doublet) participated in the

Musketaquid sale. Kehonosquaw, the daughter of sagamore John of Pawtucket, later married Oonamog, head of the Ockoocangansett praying village.[10] The identification of these individuals with important community events in widely separated regions may signify a lifestyle that was both communal and nomadic.

Most of the residents of the Nashoba praying village were from other places. Many of them came originally from Musketaquid (Concord), where they had been primarily hunter-gatherers who practiced limited farming, so that the communal life of the village was seasonal. Musketaquid, south of Nashoba, was, according to a contemporary description, a land of large open fields between rivers stretching from the great meadows on the north to the Boston Road on the south. Another historical account describes an earthwork, attributed to aboriginal origins, and mentions the finding of pipes and chisels, which frequently imply Indian ritual.

> Across the vale, south of Capt. Anthony Wrights, a long mound, or breastwork, is now visible, which might have been built to aid the hunter, though its object is unknown. Many hatchets, pipes, chisels, arrow-heads, and other rude specimens of their art, curiously wrought from stone, are still frequently discovered near these spots, an evidence of the existence and skill of the original inhabitants.[11]

But by far the most important artifacts left by the native inhabitants of the Nashoba region were the elements of ritual architecture on the landscape.

The historical record includes a description of a water management system engineered and constructed by Indians and later reused by colonists to power a saw mill. Also, the Nashoba villagers built two earthen dams and ditch systems that connected three brooks near what is now called Shaker Lane. "In the spring it made them a good supply." This type of system was common among native New Englanders, and there is a specific Algonquian word for it, Pemmoquitta-quomut, meaning "ponds joined by a ditch."[12]

The Indians who lived in the praying villages, taken collectively, had a great range of experience and learning, as well as religious backgrounds that were steeped in long tradition. They included artisans well versed in stone masonry, blacksmithing, and carpentry, and, almost certainly, shamans who not only understood the movements of the land and sky but also were specialists in medicine, healing, vision seeking, management and defense. No matter what the specialty, shamans were all trained within a structure of religious ritual. Because of this, it is highly probable that there were shamans in positions of influence at most of the praying villages. Their presence was probably reluctantly tolerated by the missionaries, John Eliot and others, because the cooperation of these leaders was necessary to the establishment of missions. The aged and much venerated Pawtucket sachem and shaman Passaconaway, child of the bear, lived near present-day Lowell, on the fringe of Nashoba Valley. He saw the praying villages as the signal presaging the end of the Indian ways. In a prophetic farewell speech to his children and people during 1660, he "warned them to take heed how they quarrelled with their English neighbors, for though they might do them some damage, yet it would prove the means of their own destruction.[13]

Passaconaway, if we can believe Gookin's estimate of his age as 120 years, or a descendant of the same name if we cannot, was formerly a great sachem of the Mohegans and Hoosacs. His nephew and successor, Wanalancet, became a sachem at Penacook, in New Hampshire, and as successor to Passaconaway was undoubtedly a shaman as well. He had much influence on the French, and probably was in touch with French praying villages along the St. Lawrence River, with Mississquoi, a Vermont praying village, and, as a result, with Calendar One.[14] These circumstances imply a pattern of interaction among Indian groups throughout New England, not only by trade or casual acquaintance, but also by lineage.

The venerated sachem and shaman of Sudbury, Massachusetts, Tantamous, also known as Jethro, was chosen by the Natick praying village elders to be the new preacher to the Indians of Nashua (Lancaster). Tantamous and his family of twelve were said to have lived on Nobscot Hill in Sudbury near a great stone mound, mentioned in records as early as 1654, and he was described as a soothsayer or powwow. The combination of powwow and Christian preacher is rare in historical records, but we believe that it was, in reality, a common occurrence. Another shaman, Wibbacowet had participated in Eliot's Christianizing effort from the beginning of the mission and questioned why it took the English twenty-seven years to get around to teaching the Indians to know their God.[15]

We believe that the shaman-preachers of Nashoba used the praying villages to maintain the Indian communication links, the sacred landscape and the stone and earthen structures in the midst of the encroaching white colonists. We believe that central to their world was the Boxborough esker (Figure 11–16). The esker

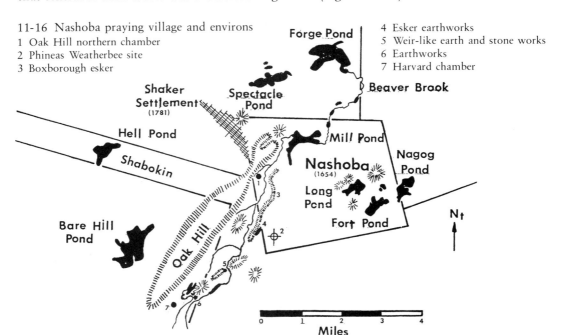

11-16 Nashoba praying village and environs
1 Oak Hill northern chamber
2 Phineas Weatherbee site
3 Boxborough esker
4 Esker earthworks
5 Weir-like earth and stone works
6 Earthworks
7 Harvard chamber

and other unusual natural landforms were probably considered sacred places in a manner similar to the Hopewellian serpent mounds of the American Midwest. Sophisticated water and land management, indicated by earth and stonework, could have played a practical as well as religious role.

The outcome of the Second Puritan War in 1676 caused Nashoba and the other praying villages to fall into decline as the lands were bought or taken by the encroaching English and increasing numbers of Indians melted into the colonial society and became invisible. But these villages were replaced by many new smaller villages because the only legal Indians in Massachusetts were those who had accepted Christianity.

Indians lived in Littleton up to the beginning of the nineteenth century. "Others now living or recently deceased, remembered Indians, or had seen their ovens and traces of huts near the pond [Fort Pond], on the island, as we call the flat edge where the mountain cranberry grows." From this report, Indians not only lived in a swamp in the heart of the Nashoba praying village, but on the edges of cranberry bogs, which we know today were frequently peat bogs and former white cedar wetlands.[16]

To date the region of Nashoba praying village has been less ravaged by developers than other areas, and, as we have observed, it still contains the ancient water control systems and ritual stone structures shared by all praying villages. These villages were located at sacred places chosen by the Native Americans within areas that they knew and which they and their ancestors had ritualized. Artifacts found in these areas indicate participation of the people with the land from many thousands of years ago to the present.

By tracing the history and physical environment of Nashoba and its surrounding settlements, including the lives of individuals who lived there, we came to visualize the natives' traditional sacred world view probably better than in any other community into which we have entered. All the influences about which we have written have acted on the place and the people of Nashoba, in ways that are unusually evident upon the natural landscape and in the written record. During the period from 1650 to 1850, the history of Nashoba tells about the impact of the native and English cultures upon each other.

The Shaker Land of Nashoba

The "curious affinity between the Shakers and the Indians" has already been discussed in Chapter 8, and Nashoba played a major role in Shaker as well as Indian spiritual life. Mother Ann Lee, founder of the Shakers, was drawn to the Nashoba praying village in a vision before coming to America, and she made it her base during her New England mission from 1781 to 1784. She may well have heard of Nashoba before the time of her vision of it, because early writings show that the missionary efforts of Eliot and others, and the locations of the praying villages, had long been widely known throughout England, due to the fund-raising efforts of the Corporation.[17]

An area adjacent to the western side of Nashoba, the northeast corner of the town of Harvard, was the place seen in Mother Ann's vision, a place occupied upon her arrival there in 1781 by people sympathetic to her and the Shakers. This land, in the highland region north of Oak Hill, is part of the Nashoba wetland system (Figure 11–16). Many large perched boulders, balanced rocks, unusual stone rows, standing stones, prayer seats, stone mounds, and artificial rock shelters are found in these highlands (Figure 11–17), and ditch and bank earthworks are located in the bottom lands and adjacent to the extensive swamps.

We have attempted throughout this book to show that balanced rocks, standing stones, and stone mounds were traditionally erected, modified and maintained by Native Americans. While the Shakers are known to have constructed stone tribute mounds, as well as a few standing stones at their outdoor places of ceremony (Figure 11–18), we have not seen records of Shaker traditions of respect for large balanced boulders or the other stone structures found at Harvard. But the presence of these structures and their relationships to natural landforms on Shaker land suggests connections. Were some structures built or used by the Shakers in cooperation with the Indians? Did the Shakers know of the memories in the landscape?

A large straight earthen bank of probable native origin is oriented from the Shaker village toward Zion Hill where the Shaker outdoor ceremonial area was carved from the ridgetop. Here, in 1842, the Shakers leveled an area of one-half acre by removing earth from the upper portion of the hill and moving it directly northerly down the slope (Figure 11–19).[18] The locations of the hilltop ceremonial areas were chosen by the most sensitive mystics among the Shakers, and

11-18 Standing stone in Shaker lands

11-17 Perched boulder in Shaker lands

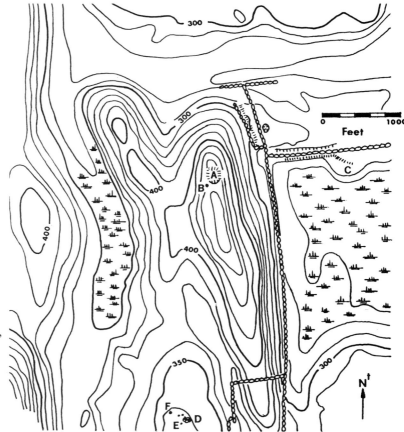

11-19 Shaker Hill of Zion,
Harvard, Mass.
A Cleared and levelled area
B Stone mound
C Earthern bank
D, E Stone rings and mounds
F Rocking stone

Indian and Shaker mystic communication was a part of Shaker ritual mentioned repeatedly in the journals. It is highly probable that the Indians still living in the Nashoba wetlands during the nineteenth century participated with the Shakers in combined religious ritual on both the physical and visionary levels of experience and that the Shaker ceremonial grounds on Zion Hill were former sacred places of Indian ritual (Figure 11–20).

The Shakers prohibited alcoholic beverages, but we have found whiskey bottles ranging from thirty to one hundred years old tucked away at several locations in the Shaker settlement. The most recent bottles were found carefully wedged up inside niches within stone row passages throughout an area of many rock outcroppings. Others were found carefully placed at a location one-half mile from this, where there had been rock quarrying, between a standing stone and a rocking stone which has a seat carved into its upper face. We suspect that the Brothers were not necessarily taking surreptitious swigs and hiding the evidence, but that Indians, and possibly Shakers too, were participating in an age-old ritual of respect for the landscape.

11-20 Stone features on Zion Hill
l, Stone rings
below l, Manitou stone in stone pile
below, Base of God's Standing Stone

Excavation at Nashoba Praying Village

In addition to our observations of the landscape and the history of Nashoba, we also consulted the record of archaeological excavations. In 1977, an excavation within the original bounds of the Nashoba praying village produced curious results, but these, and by implication many other excavation results, may not be what they have seemed. Phineas Weatherbee, described as a founder of the town of Boxborough, acquired land and at least one house from his father in 1742. The house stood until 1783, and was reported to have been on a 1744 town road that was two rods wide marked by two parallel stone walls of unknown date. The road was abandoned in 1788.[19]

A site suspected of being the location of the Weatherbee house was excavated (Figure 11–16). After brush clearing, four major features appeared: a cellar twelve by eighteen feet in plan lined with stone walls and filled with earth and rocks; a stone-lined well; a ten-foot diameter pile of stones between the well and the cellar; and an adjacent earth and stone mound about four feet high and twenty-three feet in diameter. In addition, there were scattered rocks presumed to be the remains of a house foundation.

An assortment of colonial artifacts was recovered from throughout the site, most dated between 1740 and 1780. These included broken ceramics, iron and brass hardware, bottle fragments, and cutlery. Most of the artifacts were of European origin but the total assemblage was similar to that found in recent excavations of Wampanoag Indian burials of the seventeenth century which suggest that items of European manufacture played an important role in Indian ritual of this period.[20] One type of artifact particularly suggests an Indian ceremonial presence. Thin, aqua-colored window glass, dated to the seventeenth century by an intact triangular pane and pieces of lead, was found broken into "extremely small sherds" distributed uniformly about the perimeter of the site, as if donated to a special place.

It seems to us that there are subtle signs of an Indian ritual presence which may have been superimposed on a genuine colonial farmhouse site or may have been the purpose of the original construction. Even the stone walls which line the roadway could be Indian ritual features, because they do not necessarily postdate the road. After all, the road was abandoned in 1788 because it was difficult for vehicular travel, implying that it may have been an Indian trail. The distributing of broken colored glass and the collecting of colonial household implements and ceramics for ritual use are common Indian practices. The doubtful house foundation and uncertain historical attribution make this location a candidate for a praying Indian site where the old ways were kept secretly under the watchful eyes of John Eliot.

Seismic Activity at Nashoba

Eskers, narrow ridges of gravelly and sandy drift, have traditionally been explained by stream deposition beneath a receding glacier. But recent research implies that the glacial theories for some landforms, including possibly eskers, may be incorrect. New information about seismic activity in New England and along the Atlantic coast during the past few thousand years, challenges the glacial theory of the formation of fissures in the soil, formerly called ice wedges by glacial geologists. These fissures were thought to be cracks caused by thermal contraction and expansion of the land about 12,000 years ago. However, fissures in the Hain quarry of western Massachusetts, which are twelve feet deep and one hundred thirty feet long, are now claimed by some geologists to be due to eruptions of soil that had been liquified by seismic shaking, and much more recent than the Wisconsin IV glacier. One fissure was dated by radiocarbon 14 to about 1,050 years ago. Even today the rumbling of trucks past the quarry causes eruptions of mud. A similar phenomenon has been observed in Charleston, South Carolina, where sand geysers spewed sand out of the ground forming pyramids tens of feet high after a large prehistoric earthquake. At Cape Ann, Massachusetts, it is claimed that two earthquakes in the 1700s liquified the soil as well.[21]

This new information permits us to suggest that the Boxborough esker could have been formed or at least modified by seismic activity in the past few thousand years. It is only four miles west of the Fort Hill-Nagog pond area that has an earthquake tradition. We can also suggest that some swamps, particularly shaking bogs which are common in Indian lore, may have been formed by seismic activity and continue to respond to it. The Boxborough esker and the surrounding Beaver Brook wetland area of Nashoba are rich in sand and gravel formations and would be expected to manifest the various seismic phenomena which accompany earthquakes.

Evidence from archaeological finds in soils of supposed glacial age must also be considered in this new light. The recent discoveries about sand geysers and soil liquifaction in seismically active locations suggest that artifacts found far below the surface may have been churned and buried by relatively recent soil dynamics, and may be much more recent than the 10,000-year-old glacial debris, that overlies them would imply.

We have already described how earthquakes at Moodus, Connecticut, were considered a manifestation of the spirit Hobomock and how shamans came there from all over New England to seek him. This evidence that shamans participated with the earth's pulse as seen, heard and felt at areas of recurring seismic activity led us to explore the history of earthquakes at Nashoba and their possible role in the spiritual life of the people. Nashoba is a seismically active area. It lies in northeast Massachusetts where a major postmetamorphic fault system has been intruded by igneous rock; a local fault zone coincides with Harvard and other ridges in the neighborhood, and with Beaver Brook. There was seismic activity during the praying village era, from 1654 to 1725. In addition to local earthquakes along this fault, earthquakes having their centers as far away as New York and Canada were frequently felt here because New England earthquakes attenuate very little with distance from the epicenter.[22] The knowledge of these events spread widely. It was recorded in 1846 that,

> Near unto this town is a pond wherein at some seasons there is a strange rumbling noise as the Indians affirm; the reason whereof is not yet known. . . . Some have conceived the hill is hollow, wherein the wind being pent, is the cause of this rumbling, as in earthquakes. . . . The pond where the rumbling noise occurred is, of course, Nagog. Traditions are plenty of rumbling noises, sometimes said to be like the discharge of cannon in the vicinity of Nashoba Hill, which is near Nagog Pond, but I have not heard of any occurring of late years. They were probably earthquakes.[23]

It is not surprising that such awesome natural events would be remembered as part of the spiritual life of the praying village, because Nagog Pond lies in the eastern part of its original bounds.

A very energetic earthquake was felt in 1755 in Nashaway Valley. Many of Harvard's people suffered severe dysentery the following year and the resulting forty-three deaths were attributed to the earthquake. Another earthquake, occurring in 1884 and felt at Nashoba, was centered about the mouth of the Hudson River and was felt from Maryland to New Hampshire.

Linear magnetic anomalies, with greater than average magnetism, generally occur at places of stress concentration and faults in the earth's crust; i.e., areas of seismic activity. A 1977 aeromagnetic map of New England shows anomalies southwest of Cape Ann and on a linear fault zone that extends from Lowell, Massachusetts, southwest to East Thompson, Connecticut, passing through Nashoba. We have superimposed a map of the locations of the first seven Indian praying villages on the map of magnetic anomalies. As shown on Figure 11–21, villages 3, 4, 5 and 6 all lie on the linear fault and villages 1 and 2 were adjacent to other local anomalies. This impressive correlation of seismic activity with the locations of praying villages supports our theory that these places were selected in part because of their seismic activity, which indicated that they were abodes of the spirit Hobomock.[24]

While wondering about the effect of earthquakes upon rock structures, we learned that the hills of Cape Ann, Massachusetts, New England's region of greatest seismic activity, contain an unusually large number of balanced and pedestalled boulders. A person can excite the ground and other stones by rocking a boulder, but earthquakes provide a periodic excitation from the earth itself, which may have rocked some of these boulders. Experience with the behavior of buildings during earthquakes shows that most earthquake energy causes response at periods less than about three quarters of a second; codes specify natural oscillating periods of buildings greater than this to avoid amplified forces caused by synchronism. Disappointingly, all except the smallest rocking stones have natural rocking periods of one to three seconds and would, therefore, be out of synchronism. To date we have not been able to experience the behavior of a rocking stone during an earthquake, because it cannot be scheduled, but such an event can be imagined as a mysterious gentle jiggling of small amplitude, perhaps a more desirable manifestation of Hobomock than the rare event when a large rocking stone would be thrown from its perch.

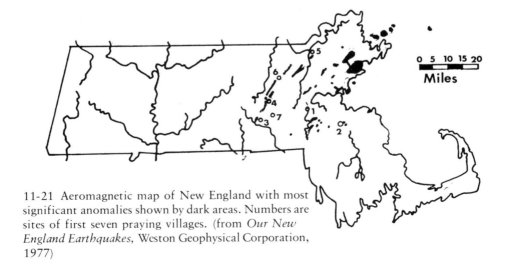

11-21 Aeromagnetic map of New England with most significant anomalies shown by dark areas. Numbers are sites of first seven praying villages. (from *Our New England Earthquakes*, Weston Geophysical Corporation, 1977)

However, other rock structures such as piles of boulders, stone rows, and the rows of inclined slabs at Moodus, Connecticut, have shorter periods and could have been designed to synchronize with the earthquake period-response spectra. They may have been carefully shaped and arranged to respond to earth movements, and an ordered network of tuned rocks could all oscillate when stimulated by seismic activity at the more active places on the landscape. This suggests that the tuning of rocks to seismic periods could have been part of the act of seeking Hobomock and that the excitation of the earth was seen as a manifestation of this spirit.

Some rock structures may have been designed to be sensitive seismic instruments which enabled shamans to monitor activity and to sense the slightest tremor which might presage greater, more widely felt quakes. The shaman, with this warning, would be in a position to gather people at seismically active areas to witness earthquakes and earth glows. This in turn would increase both the political power of the shaman and his knowledge of natural phenomena.

The strongest recent earthquakes felt in the towns of Boxborough and Harvard occurred during the spring and fall of 1985. On October 15, an earthquake registered 3.1 on the Richter scale, and on October 19 and 25, yellow-orange, brightly glowing pockets of air were witnessed and reported by several people on Woodchuck Hill, Oak Ridge, in Harvard near the Boxborough border.[25] New evidence, described in Chapter 10, indicates that such observations of light anomalies were caused by the recent seismic activity.

The mythologies of many cultures include personal experiences with luminous phenomena at high places and in wetlands. According to Basque legends, a glowing light, called *Arguiduna*, seen in the marshes and forests signalled calamity and was a manifestation of spirits of the dead.[26] Tibetan monks considered mountaintop glowing events to be manifestations of a bodhisattva. The Algonquian peoples spoke of the will-o'-the-wisps, the fairies of the swamps that carried glowing balls of light. The most complete observations of mysterious lights come from the Yakima Indian reservation in Washington State, where baseball-sized bright lights floating among the tree tops are apparently the result of tectonic strain and accompany increasing earthquake rates. The same phenomenon is often observed in wetlands or swampy areas, known as regions of methane production and reduction. Seismic activity of the land, when it fractures rock, probably contributes to methane reduction by the release of electrons that excite the local atmosphere to a glowing condition.

A narrow corridor of land extending from Nashoba praying village was drastically altered by seismic activity in a way that provided food for legends. Shabokin or Shabikin, also called Stow Leg, was a strip of land about seven miles long and one mile wide that extended into the central western side of Nashoba, as shown in Figure 11–16. The Oak Hill northern chamber is sixty yards from the Nashoba praying village boundary surveyed by Danforth in 1686 and at a corner of Shabokin. Shabokin was excluded from the adjacent towns of Lancaster and Groton at their incorporation in 1663 and 1655 and remained native territory until it became part of the town of Harvard on its incorporation in 1732. According to historical records, this strip of land was used by the Nashoba Indians as a way to hunting and trapping lands to the west,[27] but we think there is more to the story than that.

A local tradition describes an event at Hell Pond, now called Mirror Pond, within Shabokin and adjacent to Shabokin Hill. The pond is 100 feet deep and the hill 100 feet higher than the pond. As told by a native of the area,

> An Indian, a true son of the soil, is made to tell as a legend of his tribe, that a century or two ago before the pale-faced strangers came from beyond the seas, a lofty hill rose where the clear waters mirror the sky in the Shabakin woodlands; one night the earth trembled and in the morning the hill was not, and in its place slept this little lake overshadowed by the gloomy pine forest, its depth equaling the height of the vanished hill.[28]

This catastrophic event, which so altered the landscape, may have been a case of sand liquefaction caused by seismicity. The shaking of an earthquake can, within minutes, turn firm sandy soil that is saturated with water into a fluid that can no longer support the weight above it, and a hill becomes a pond.[29]

The true significance of this strip of land may be revealed by its name. Shabokin means the "place of the departed souls," a meaning that provides a spiritual as well as a physical connection between Shabokin and Nashoba praying village. Algonquins describe a bluish light that they see leaving the body soon after death; the Mohegans call this the Wakon-bird or spirit-dove, which represents the departing soul. We have shown that rocks fractured by earthquakes can produce lights in the atmosphere and that there is a record of seismic activity at Shabokin. This suggests that luminous glows created by earthquake were perceived as departed souls.[30]

We discovered in Chapter 2 a similar case of a strip of land retained by the Indians because of its spiritual and practical importance, at the Hassanamessitt (Grafton) praying village. This pattern of corridor landforms, strips of remaining native areas between lands taken by the English colonists, suggests that the resultant land boundaries were dictates of the natives and had great spiritual significance.

Earthquakes and seismically generated lights were important in the beliefs and everyday life of the historic Indians of Nashoba, as well as the Mohegans of Connecticut and the Hudson Valley. The seventeenth and eighteenth centuries seem to have been an era of considerably more seismic activity than today, and we suspect that stone structures were built to withstand these earthquakes and respond to them in a controlled manner, in ways that are no longer appreciated in New England. The link between natural events and human society was supplied by shamans.[31]

Who Built the Stone Structures?

Although the origins of the Nashoba earth and stone works cannot be known for certain, we observed here, as at many other sites in New England, striking similarities to structures elsewhere in North America recognized as being of Native American construction, particularly to those built by the various cultures making up the Mound Builders of the American Midwest.

For example, there is a heretofore unrecognized hydraulic stone work east of the Nashoba praying village, where an elongated, angled bank, a stone row, and a bank and ditch surround a swamp in Acton (Figure 11–22). A stream passes through the point where the stone row and the angled bank meet. At the other end of this bank, a smaller curved bank, a, meets a straight ditch and bank, b. Squier and Davis recorded an ancient Indian enclosure, probably Hopewellian, on the bank of the Great Miami River near Dayton, Ohio, that had a similar arrangement of earthworks on a larger scale (Figure 11–23).[32]

In 1984, Byron, while perusing the contours of a topographic map of part of Nashoba, noticed lines indicating many closely spaced, parallel curved banks covering an area of about fifty acres, at a river oxbow, bearing a remarkable resemblance to an elaborate Archaic earthwork at Poverty Point, Louisiana, built about 3,000 years ago.[33] The larger features of the plans of the two sites are compared in Figure 11–24. Three years later, when Byron returned to this Nashoba site, he found a vast array of earthen banks varying in height from eight to twenty feet, having steep sides with narrow ridges on top and spaced at intervals of fifty to one hundred feet. This is the largest complex of such structures that we know of in the Northeast.

We commenced mapping the site, searching historical records and local knowledge, consulting geologists and mining engineers, and, most important, observing the works and their surroundings in the light of our experience. We

11-23 Earthwork, Great Miami River, Ohio (from Squier and Davis, note 32)

11-22 Ditch and bank, Acton, Mass.

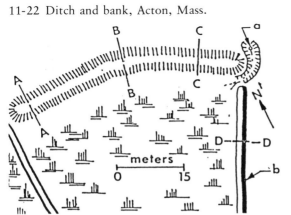

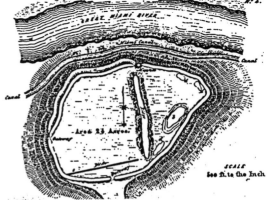

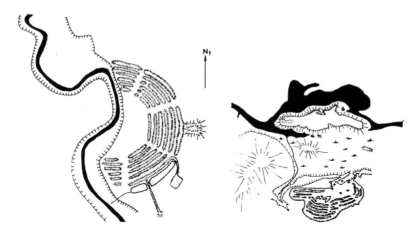

11-24 Nashoba earthern banks compared with Poverty Point, La., same scale

speculated that these puzzling structures could be, at one extreme, a major example of the ancient Mound Builders' art and, at the other, the tortured landscape left by modern sand and gravel workings, or perhaps even a mixture of the two, as unlikely as that may seem. It is not unknown for earthworks to be built using modern machinery by descendants of older cultures following the ancient traditions. On more than one occasion we have pursued the study of earth- and stoneworks which appear even on close inspection and by historical record to be the spoil of recent quarrying, strip-mining, sand and gravel operations, field clearing and the like, motivated by little more than a hunch or subtle clue. This approach was rewarded here by our discovery of the familiar signs of a recent Native American ceremonial presence and an elaborate but subtle array of banks of both earth and stone, individual and in networks, which are integrated into the geometry of the larger banks, accompanied by evidence of horizon astronomy. These features are to us as compelling as the obvious and uncanny similarity of Nashoba to Poverty Point in general plan, size, and elements, including avenues, causeways and conical central mounds.

In Figure 11–25 we show a plan of a ten-acre portion of the site, illustrating some of its subtler central features. The three large curved banks to the west are connected by lower banks to form a single three-fingered form. The large banks were probably built, as indicated by the positions of the cliff scallops, beginning with the one furthest from the cliff by successively cutting back the cliff and moving the earth to the banks. To the south, the end of a large bank resembles the mouth of a serpent swallowing or disgorging a low curved form. Nearby, a small bank partially blocks the opening between the groups of large banks. In the center of the map, low three-to-six-foot-high banks enclose irregularly shaped spaces.

The large central conical mound A (Figures 11–25 and 11–26) fits neatly into the curves of the three-fingered group of large banks and a true east-west line passes through it and the region of greatest curvature of each of these banks. Just north of mound B, a low earthen enclosure contains a pile of pebbles about three feet in diameter, some showing evidence of use as hammer stones, and a group of cut tree branches was found bundled and laid upon the southern bank of the enclosure. An observer sitting in the pit C on the equinox could see the one-foot-diameter disk of the sun set at the elevated horizon formed by the summit of mound A. All of the features just described are typical features of Hopewellian works in the Midwest.

A complex array of serpentine stone, as contrasted with earth, mounds and banks, are shown in the northeast part of Figure 11–25 associated with a spring and the pond it feeds. Near these banks, a heavy wire mesh has been shaped into an inverted U to enclose a space suitable for a person to sit within, a type of structure familiar from other sites. There is a tree about fifteen years old at each corner of the rectangular area on which the mesh was placed, that has grown up through the mesh. Several similar structures are located near the stone banks and mounds.

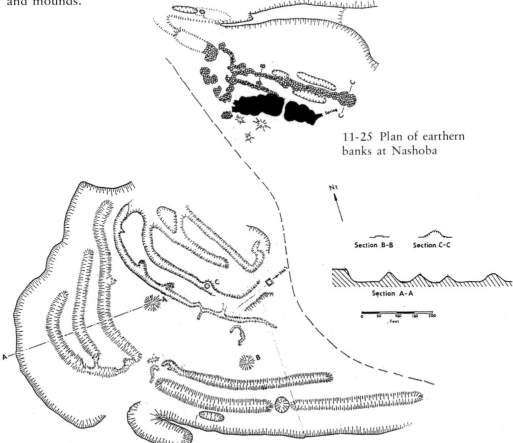

11-25 Plan of earthern banks at Nashoba

11-26 Conical earthern mound
among Nashoba earthern banks

At several places, usually within pits, we saw collections of rusted pots and pans, buckets, and whiskey and patent medicine bottles. These collections of stones, brush and other materials which have patterns of size and shape, are usually dismissed by New Englanders as refuse pits, but in the West and Midwest they are known to be donations associated with the vision quest. From these and other clues, we sense current ceremonial use of this site and have refrained from divulging its location out of respect for the place and the people who may still consider it sacred. Where we see clues to recent ritual practice, as shown by this example, we remain open to the possibilities that the sites may be both recent and ancient, practical and ceremonial, European and Indian.

Donation piles and caches of items the white man today considers junk or trash, such as rusted pots and pans, bed springs, automobile parts and the like, abound at Indian sacred places. Shamans often collected such material and even included it in their medicine. A stone mound in Nashoba was found to contain three alarm clocks which probably served in this capacity. The custom of assembling no-longer-used material objects is known mainly as the result of modern industrial planned obsolescence, but it has been part of society for a long time, though with a different rationale. A Middle Eastern tell made up of broken pottery and bones may have been a refuse pile but it was also a home and a sacred place. A pile of the white man's junk placed by an Indian may be a collection of objects each having a spirit, placed at a sacred place to acknowledge the spirituality of these and all things.

Empty whiskey and patent medicine bottles are frequently seen cached in niches between stones or in pits at places where we sense Indian ritual from other structures and the natural environment. We have observed pits in the earth and depressions in rock piles filled with empty or broken whiskey bottles, often located at the intersections of stone rows (Figure 11–27). We have also observed bottles, of ages ranging from one hundred forty years ago to the present, carefully placed within niches in stone rows, at places where stone had been quarried,

11-27 Whiskey bottle donation caches

buried underneath stone chamber flagstone floors, and within stone mounds at the edges of wetlands. We have come to believe that the donation at sacred places of liquor and its bottles was and continues to be a widespread ritual practice among Native Americans.

The increased stresses of Indian life induced by the white man's ways may have been a major factor in the Indian's difficulty in controlling the use of alcoholic beverages, leading to John Eliot's description of Nashoba as a place of great affliction. But there is evidence that consumption of alcohol in moderation and as a part of ritual tradition was part of the Indian way before the coming of the white man. When the first English settlers arrived at Nashoba, the Indians were growing apples, which they pressed. The fermented liquor, hard cider, was used for their own consumption, so the English and the Dutch were not the only sources of strong drink, though they did apparently introduce distilled liquors. Speck describes traditional practices still active in the 1920s in which New England Indians had places set aside which they called taverns. There, alcoholic drink was consumed while they participated in rituals which prepared them for the vision quest. The participants donated a portion of the drink to the earth and consumed the rest. The empty bottles were respectfully placed within a pit.[34]

The first European colonists of New England built their farms on land that had been ritually cleared by the Indians. As these colonists took over land previously managed by natives, the natives in turn absorbed elements of the European culture. The colonists intended to hook the Indians on imported technology as a means of subduing them, but the Indians took only what was useful to them and rejected the rest. Few people today take into account that European metal stoneworking tools were widespread among the native population of New England in the seventeenth century and were used for the native traditional stone construction. Among the goods traded with the Indians for pelts and the like were stoneworking tools such as steel chisels, drills and hammers. In early Norwalk, Connecticut, Daniel Patrick exchanged metal tools and drills for land. The natives of Maine preferred the European metal tools to jewelry for trade goods.[35]

The supply of steel tools increased in the praying village period, when they were ordered from England by Eliot and Gookin so that the natives could construct their villages. These practical gifts encouraged the natives to join with the English settlers in cooperative projects. It is said that Eliot encouraged the praying village peoples to build stone walls and to construct ditches about their villages and lands. This may explain why the number of Native American stone masons and builders in present-day New England far exceeds their proportion of the general population.

The steel tools inspired the natives, who had long traditions of stone construction, to create methods of quarrying stone different from their traditional ways. We suspect that adaptation to this technology occurred rapidly among people who previously had made large works with stone tools. The marks of iron and steel tools have been observed on stones at many sites throughout New England where stone features include embrasures, standing stones, orthostats, recent grave stones, astronomically aligned stone rows, stone mounds and pavements. They range in location from the highlands to the lowlands and wetlands, and were executed by Native Americans to be decorative and symbolic, as well as to manage the landscape for more practical ends.

Why Think the Structures Are of European Origin?

We are taught, in our written history, to believe that the strictures placed upon the Indians, while they were accepting John Eliot and the Christianity of the English, severely destructured their family, social, and religious lives. However, this was not necessarily so, because acceptance of and agreement with their new, imposed life styles were two very different positions in the minds of the Indians. The praying villages of New England in the seventeenth and eighteenth centuries were places where Indian traditional beliefs and practices were kept alive, not destroyed as was the intention of the missionaries. The Native Americans were desperately attempting to cope with the white man's invasion and sought creative ways to get around the English pressures. In some cases, the colonists used the praying villages as a means for enlisting Indian skills and manpower in the military adventures of European powers, but, for the most part, the natives were able to benefit by using the new lines of communication set up by the Christian missions throughout New England, eastern Canada, New York State and the American Midwest to replace the traditional ones that had been disrupted.

Historical evidence shows that Indians of seventeenth-century Nashoba were practicing the ancient rituals under the direction of their leaders, who included shamans committed to the traditional beliefs and practices. The shamans were sometimes also the teachers or preachers of the new religion, but, in any event, all Indians appointed as Christian preachers had a world view very different from that of the English missionaries. They went out from Natick, the training center, to help their people both adapt to and resist the English influence. By the time the second group of praying villages were set up, this Indian objective had been well established.

The atrocious English treatment of the praying Indians during the Second Puritan War caused most of the known native population of New England to seek sanctuary within the rules of behavior of the white man. First encouraged by John Eliot, this behavior required that the natives dress and appear like the English, actions that caused them to become invisible to future generations of European settlers. After the war, Natick was the only one of Eliot's praying villages to maintain its native character, which it did for over one hundred years. The Indians who returned to Nashoba lived, to all appearances, like the white people, probably realizing that this offered their only hope of a future. English settlers quickly moved into the area because it provided them with ready-made cleared land, apple orchards, and flood control systems along Beaver Brook. While only natives who had accepted Christianity were counted in the official population of the praying villages, there were others present who also changed their appearance and blended into the English background which gradually dominated the region, so there were always more Indians around than were acknowledged. The people of Nashoba and their descendants, the Nipmuck people, have lived in a state of social invisibility in central Massachusetts for over two centuries.

Historical reports of Indians in the nineteenth and twentieth centuries show that the invisible Indian persists within the recent American culture. There is evidence of the persistence of ancient religious traditions among Iroquois Indians at the Six Nations Reserve near Brantford, Ontario, at the beginning of this century. Years after a period of intense Christian missionary activity, a belief system was still intact that stressed social mobility through participation in longhouse activities, through knowledge of traditional rituals, and through rejection of white traits. Salvation was not acquired through civilization, but was attained only in the afterlife. Dreams, healing societies, and witchcraft thrived among a people who lived in white clapboard houses and adopted white agricultural methods. Their calendar was still based on the ancient tradition. The mid-winter festival, dominant as in earlier times, functioned as a thanksgiving to all spirit forces. An orderly social system was continued by means of a code based on ancient tradition and subject to change only by traditional practices.[36]

Even shamans have acquired the ability to go unnoticed in modern society, and the native respect for them continues. Other surviving Indians have learned the disappearing skill which has enabled them to affect the character of New England towns by participating in their development. Some Rhode Island towns were built largely by Narragansett stone masons and carpenters. The white man's written history records that these people acquired their skills from the English, whereas in reality they only acquired their steel tools. The Indians until recently have not seen fit to call attention to this rearrangement of history and probably view it as just another example of the white man's exploitation.

However, Indian society will become more visible to the mainstream society as the remains of the ancient native tradition of landscape management become recognized. Hydraulic water management systems across the country, constructed by Indians, ascribe to native cultures the same achievements as to the so-called advanced societies. This leads to the possibility that hunter-gatherers have, with more understanding, directed their environment just as much as have the advanced societies that prefer the method of conquest over participation. While Europeans talked about the weather, the rituals that related the Indians to their environment enabled them to alter the weather in their favor, through such techniques as burning over the land.

Most historical records of stone fence and wall building by the English colonists place the start of the bulk of this activity at about 1700, when the number of visible Indians in New England had decreased by more than ninety percent from 1620 due to disease and war. This implies that most Indian stonework was built before 1700, after which ritual stonework was confined to subtler works deep in the woodlands. When Indians were employed by the white people to build stone structures, their use of European tools such as steel rock drills, hammers, and steel reinforcing rod gave the mistaken impression that the structures were built by Europeans. However, their native origin is indicated by traditional features such as astronomical orientation, embrasures, gaps between boulders, and inclusion of manitou stones. And Indian stone rows are frequently of sizes and shapes that fit the landscape as ritual architecture but serve no European practical purpose.

The ancient tradition of large-scale stone construction among Algonquian-speakers, the historic accounts of this native stone construction, the nature and quantity of stonework on the New England landscape, and the deliberately low social visibility of Indians since the time of the Second Puritan War lend support to the hypothesis that Native Americans constructed the majority of New England's stone rows and other stone structures. This was done both in the prehistoric and historic periods; in many cases, a single structure was built, used, modified and reused during a long time that spanned both periods.

We have often wondered why New England history and folklore repeatedly attribute stonework to European colonists when its origins are either unknown or probably Indian. Here, in two folkloric accounts of events at the Natick praying village southeast of Nashoba during the Second Puritan War, we show how the authors were compelled to insert this view into their work. The point is equally applicable to Nashoba. About three miles southeast of the meetinghouse at the Natick praying village, Noanett Brook flows north into a sharp bend of the Charles River. This brook was dammed at three points, creating a chain of ponds at successively higher elevations. The dams were built of unmortared stone with stone-lined sluiceways. Near the uppermost pond and what is today called Noanett's Peak are the remains of an iron ore reduction plant which includes a stone smelting furnace, a water-driven mill for crushing the ore, and residual iron ore and slag.

The valley of Noanett Brook, which is still remote from buildings and roads, was the domain of Noanett, a sachem who appears in the Dedham town records of 1661, 1663 and 1664. He, along with John Eliot, Waban, and John Speen, was a defendant in a 1661 suit by the town of Dedham aimed at retracting the praying village grant of 1651 and thereby forcing the Indians out of Dedham to the west. These records imply that Noanett was a leader of the praying village, but Natick legends portray him as a bold and haughty sachem, who had been exiled from his tribe to the place of the ironworks, and who would have no traffic with the white man.

We have come across two stories that tell of Noanett and this locale. A poem, written in the style of Longfellow's *Hiawatha*, tells of the love between Noanett's son, Harry Bird, who had become one of John Eliot's praying Indians, and the daughter of Daniel Takawambpait, the Indian preacher who succeeded John Eliot as pastor of the Natick Church in 1690.[37]

A similar story, told in a novel written in 1894, with some of the same historical characters and events, describes the ponds, stone dams, and ironworks accurately and in some detail and attributes them to the sachems Noanett and Pomham and their people. Pomham was the great sachem of Shaomet, Rhode Island (Warwick), and, during the Second Puritan War, second only to Metacom in influence. He was killed at Medfield, just south of Natick, on July 25, 1676, just eighteen days before the execution of Metacom at Bristol, Rhode Island, and appears in both folkloric accounts thereof.[38]

Superimposed on both of these stories is a theme which betrays the compulsion of folklore to invoke European origins of all stone structures. In this case, the tendency is particularly potent because Indian involvement in this stonework is acknowledged. In manufacturing a European connection, the author of *King Noanett* reveals Noanett as actually a disguised royalist Englishman hiding from the Puritans, who had, incidentally, executed General Whalley, one of the regicides. The other author, in his love story of Noanett's son and Takawambpait's daughter claims that their Indian nation had sprung from Viking adventurers who rowed up the Charles River to Natick and started families with the Indians, who for generations thereafter spoke Norse. Hundreds of years after the Norse had left, the white man came again and brought destruction to the nation. We are not concerned about whether or not these stories could be true, only point out that the authors were compelled by a long New England tradition to invoke European origins to explain stone structures.

12

Back to Calendar One

Our research method, in which we focus on the interrelationship between the land and the sky to learn about ancient people, was conceived and produced its first results at Calendar One. We first visualized Calendar One only as the natural bowl whose east and west ridges marked a grand natural calendar, a place where humans must have participated in the daily, monthly and yearly cycles marked by the movement on the horizon of the celestial bodies and the seasonal changes in the land. However, as we explored more of the surrounding countryside, we found many more stone structures and evidence that the landscape had been subtly altered by humans in what seemed to us to be a ritualized manner. By letting our sights and thoughts expand to more distant horizons, as we sensed the ancient ritualists would have done, we gradually discovered what seems to be an interconnected network of sites scattered throughout the hills and valleys on both sides of the First Branch of the White River in parts of the towns of South Royalton, Sharon and Tunbridge. But our focus remained at the bowl.

It was at Calendar One that we first saw all of the features that we have since seen patterned throughout New England. It was also here that we first realized that the builders of the stone structures were probably Native Americans, an impression based on subtle clues such as chopper stones, red ochre deposits, marked boulders, magic stones, astronomically significant horizons marked by standing stones or stone mounds, and our intuitive feeling of sacred space. Since the first discoveries at Calendar One, we have experienced other ritual places with different attributes and have in turn used the new feelings and knowledge gained from them to understand Calendar One better. Each year we have returned to Calendar One in what has become a renewal ritual of our own.

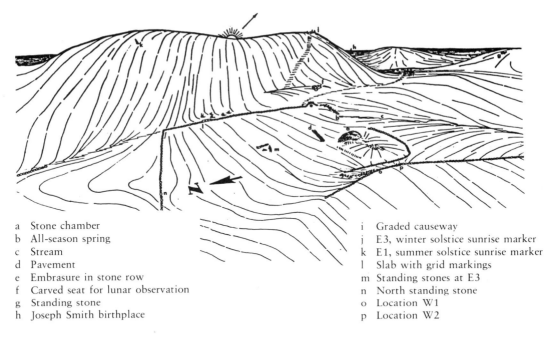

a	Stone chamber	i	Graded causeway
b	All-season spring	j	E3, winter solstice sunrise marker
c	Stream	k	E1, summer solstice sunrise marker
d	Pavement	l	Slab with grid markings
e	Embrasure in stone row	m	Standing stones at E3
f	Carved seat for lunar observation	n	North standing stone
g	Standing stone	o	Location W1
h	Joseph Smith birthplace	p	Location W2

12-1 Calendar One from the west, showing bowl and east and west ridges

The topographic sketch map of Figure 12-1, made from a three-dimensional scaled model, shows the major features of the Calendar One bowl. It provides a general orientation and feeling for the landscape and identifies specific places mentioned in this chapter as well as in Chapter 1.

Joseph Smith, Jr., and Calendar One

One of our usual camping spots at Calendar One is in a camping ground at the official birthplace of the Mormon prophet, Joseph Smith, Jr. This site is one mile from the bowl where we have focused our studies on the stone features, but some people place his birth in the bowl itself. Smith was born on December 23, 1805, within a few decades of the first recorded white settlement in the area. While he lived in the vicinity for only the first six years of his life, he was, at an impressionable age, exposed to the stone chambers, standing stones, stone mounds and marked stones which abounded in the neighborhood. Because of these circumstances and his later expressions of interests in Indians, we speculated from the beginning that we might eventually find connections between Smith, the history and revelations of the Mormon Church, and the ritualized landscape of Calendar One.

Joseph was the fourth child of Joseph and Lucy Smith, whose homestead was on the boundary between the towns of Sharon and South Royalton. Joseph, Sr., taught school in the winters and worked the farm he had rented from his father-in-law, Solomon Mack of Sharon. Mack and his family were considered religious dissenters because they subscribed more to the strength of individual religious experience than to traditional organized followings, opinions which led Mack to write an autobiography about the manner in which he was converted to the Christian faith. He was somewhat of a mystic in his old age, when he described lights and voices haunting his sick bed. His daughter Lucy embraced Antinomianism, the belief that faith alone, not obedience to moral laws, is necessary for salvation. For her, freedom and integrity of religious experience had at all costs to be preserved. Her husband approved of the separation of church and state and was dissatisfied with any sect that claimed to know the true answers. Lucy and Joseph, Sr., did not join a religious denomination for the twenty years they resided in New England.[1]

The first years of Joseph Smith, Jr.'s life were spent in the vicinity of the Calendar One stone structures. All of these features have marked stones either built into them or nearby, some of which we believe to be a class of petroglyph. Such lithic monuments and their uses are described in several places in Genesis, with which young Joseph became familiar.

In 1813, after the Smith family had moved eastward to Lebanon, New Hampshire, the second son, Hyrum, brought a fever home from school, from which eight-year-old Joseph incurred a severe infection. This nearly led to his leg being amputated, prevented only by having a portion of the bone below his knee chiseled away, without medication or anesthesia. He was sent to convalesce in Salem, Massachusetts, where he recovered rapidly but was left with a limp for the rest of his life. Lucy's religious philosophy probably caused her to interpret her son's ability to endure this ordeal as a sign that great things were to be expected from the boy. The experience may have set the stage for Joseph's later role as a reborn visionary, teacher and prophet — in short, a shaman.

The sickness collapsed Joseph, Sr.'s hopes for prosperity, and the family returned to Norwich, Vermont, in time to suffer the year without a summer, 1816. Severe cold, induced by the great volcanic eruption of Mount Tamboro in the East Indies, shrouded the countryside, bringing snow in June and July, freezing trees, and causing failure in food crops and large losses of livestock.

A great migration of people took place from hilly and rocky New England to the more inviting flatlands of the West, and the Smiths were among these migrants. The effect of all of these changes to people's lives brought about a flurry of religious activity, with new forms of religious expression sweeping the country. Many religious groups had found sanctuary and room for growth in New York State. The Shakers built community halls in Eodin Bay in 1826. Jemima Wilkinson, who thought herself to be Christ and was known as the Universal Friend, set up her sect in Jerusalem. At the heart of all this activity was Palmyra, two-thirds of the distance from Albany to Niagara Falls and a booming community in 1817. A bill had just passed the New York Assembly that called for one of the greatest engineering feats of the generation, the construction of the Erie Canal to connect the Great Lakes with the port of New York, and Palmyra was on the planned route. Palmyra at this time had a population of about 4,000 and was close to larger communities. It was in this dynamic environment of inflation, religious freedom and opportunity that the young Joseph Smith grew into manhood.

The land around the town of Palmyra once supported untold numbers of Native Americans. Many ancient Native American earth and stone mounds accompanied by ditch and bank earthworks have been found in Ontario County where Palmyra is located, and in the adjacent counties of Genesee and Seneca.[2] They are frequently found at high places, at the confluence of rivers, at or near bends in rivers or streams, and near cedar swamps and springs. Indian mounds filled with stone and copper artifacts dotted the landscape. There were eight prominent mounds within twelve miles of Smith's home, and new mounds were being discovered frequently. The ancient ruins were reported in the 1818 Palmyra *Register* to have been built by the Mound Builders, who had made great advances in the arts of civilized life. Another article in the 19 September 1821 Palmyra newspaper, *The Western Farmer*, reported that skeletons, fragments of pottery and several brass plates had been found during excavations on the Erie Canal. The mystery of the Mound Builders attracted young Joseph's attention and, according to his mother, he gave amusing recitals of his theories about the Mound Builders before he was twenty years old.

Smith in Palmyra was surrounded by cults that were rejecting the orthodox Calvinism of the seventeenth and eighteenth centuries. Like others, his religious beliefs blended the supernatural and the rational in a way that reflected the common thread of religious change in pioneer America. He accepted part of the Indian natural religion, at least in its ritual, and was also familiar with the popular view of his time that the Indians were descended from Hebrews, and were one of the ten tribes of Israel. As we noted in Chapter 6, this theory had been popular in America since early colonial days and had been espoused by Edmund Winslow, Roger Williams, Cotton Mather and Jonathan Edwards, among others. It is likely, however, that Smith learned about it from Ethan Smith's book, *View of the Hebrews, or the ten Tribes of Israel in America*, published in 1823, the year that Mormon history records for Smith's first vision concerning the golden inscribed plates.

Whether or not Smith heard of the brass plates found at the Erie Canal, he quite likely could have read James Adair's *History of the American Indians* published in 1775, where the Creek Indian plates and their origin from the Great Spirit were described by Old Brackett, an aged Creek Indian from the town of Tuccabatchey interviewed by William Bolsover in 1759. He described two brass plates about eighteen inches in diameter and five copper plates, the largest of which was eighteen inches long and seven inches wide. They were shaped like axeheads or breastplates and one circular plate was stamped AE. Old Brackett said that there were many more, some larger, some with writing, and that they had been given to his people generations ago by "the man we call God."

This was the earliest recorded description of these and similar plates of copper and brass that appear in folklore of the Shawnee and Creek Indians. In summary, the traditions hold that the plates were gifts from the Great Spirit, were sacred objects upon which the health and prosperity of the people depended, could only be touched by shamans, and were to be carried with each clan wherever it went. They were used in the green corn ceremony and sometimes buried with chiefs. In addition, there is a tradition that a person "without beginning" came from the "Source of Life" and told the Creeks that after a while a great many white people would come from the east and drive the Creeks away, but that they were always to carry these vessels; also, the Shawnees would unite with them.

From the physical nature of the Creek plates, which have been examined by some writers, they appear to have been of European origin, probably seventeenth-century Spanish, and were venerated by the Indians upon their first appearance because of their unfamiliarity and exotic origins. This veneration, known among other Indian groups in North America, has continued for many generations,[3] a tradition that can explain the continued appearance of European tools, implements and other possessions in Indian graves and at Indian sacred places in America. The pots and pans, whiskey bottles, and bed springs that were donated at places of vision quest were probably direct functional descendants of the brass and copper plates of Spanish invaders.

When the golden plates were revealed to Joseph Smith, Jr., in 1827, he brought into play both the European tradition attributing exotic origins to the Indian people and the Indian tradition attaching spiritual attributes to inscribed metal plates. The *Book of Mormon*, which Mormons believe to be the translation of the golden plates and a companion volume to the Bible, was first published in 1830. It concerns itself primarily with the history of two tribes from Jerusalem, Nephites and Lamanites, from 600 B.C. to A.D. 421. According to the *Book of Mormon*, the family from which both tribes were descended built a ship in 590 B.C. and sailed across the great waters to the promised land. Between 590 and 588 B.C., the Lamanites were cursed because they would not "hearken unto the word of the Lord." They were turned black, became idle, and were loathsome to the Nephites. After many centuries of conflict between the two tribes during which both alternately became virtuous and wicked, the Lamanites destroyed all except twenty-four of the Nephites at a great battle at the Hill Cumorah in A.D. 385. At this time the golden plates and two stones fastened to a breastplate were deposited in the hill to be delivered to Joseph Smith, Jr., in A.D. 1827, when he responded to directions from the angel Moroni. Some of these golden plates were reported to contain extracts from the brass plates of Laban, the first metal plates mentioned in the *Book of Mormon*, which were taken from Laban by Nephi and which contained the Hebrew scriptures and genealogy.

Mormons believe that the promised land was America and that the Lamanites became the Native Americans, who were bereft of Christianity until later Christian missions from Europe took up the call. There are details in the *Book of Mormon* which imply a resemblance between the Lamanites and Native Americans, as well as shamanistic practice. The period covered by the book coincides with the bulk of Adena and Hopewellian moundbuilding, a connection that was unknown in Smith's time. Although the *Book* does, by implication, recognize Native Americans and their religion, it advocates Biblical religion and presents the Lamanites as candidates for conversion.

The clearest evidence of the importance of Indian sacred places in the Mormon religion comes from the presence of Indian stone and earthen mounds at the most sacred Mormon sites and associated with the most sacred Mormon events. Seeking places for the Mormons to settle in the American Midwest, Joseph Smith, Jr., located the site for the first and greatest Mormon temple on a hilltop in Independence, Missouri, in 1831. He stood upon the summit, where to the west was only prairie all the way to the Rocky Mountains, and imagined both white men and Indians flowing to a great temple. At the site was a pile of small stones which designated the spot as sacred to the Indians. Smith located the northeast corner of the temple lot at this stone pile, which has since been destroyed for a nearby road foundation. The temple was never built because the Mormons were expelled from Missouri, in part, because of their friendship with the Indians.

The stone mound is said to have received donations of stones by natives from both the Atlantic and Pacific coasts of North America. It was probably the key to planning the first temple, located midway between the oceans and on a native shrine. We visited the hilltop site in 1982, now surrounded by city buildings, and saw the stone markers and the great tree, only a sapling in 1830, and visualized the place as an Indian sacred site. It is preserved today by the Church of Christ, which owns the property and continues as a small remnant of the original Mormon Church of 1830, whose priesthood traces back to Joseph Smith, Jr., and the angel Moroni. The beliefs and practices of this church differ markedly from the Church of Jesus Christ of Latter Day Saints, named in 1838, whose headquarters are in Salt Lake City, Utah, and from the Reorganized Church of Jesus Christ of Latter Day Saints in Independence, Missouri. The Reorganized Church was founded as a separatist movement by Joseph Smith, III, eldest son of Joseph Smith, Jr. The Church of Christ rejects most of the later innovations such as baptism of the dead, celestial marriage, polygamy, first presidency and high priests, and temples other than those in Independence and Jerusalem.[4]

Joseph Smith went on to designate the sites of three other temples before he died in 1844, and temples were actually built on two of these places. At Nauvoo, Illinois, the temple, now a ruin, was built atop a bluff overlooking a bend in the Mississippi River, surrounded by ancient remains of the Mound Builders. Smith excavated a skeleton from an Indian mound nearby on the Illinois River. At Kirtland, Ohio, a similar site was chosen in 1833. In 1838, the Mormons moved

from Independence to Far West. Here in upper Missouri, on a high bluff overlooking the Grand River, an Indian ruin which looked to Joseph Smith, Jr., like
an altar was discovered. Brigham Young and several other followers of Smith
laid the cornerstones for a temple at this site on 26 August 1839, and Smith
announced a new city to be called Adam-ondi-ahna, the land where Adam dwelt
after expulsion from Eden.[5]

We found evidence of Indian influence on Joseph Smith's religion at the most
sacred Mormon sites at Palmyra, New York. When we visited that great drumlin
called the Hill Cumorah, we found a group of stone mounds precisely where
Smith wrote that he had found the golden plates, "on the west side of this hill,
not far from the top."[6] And in the sacred grove where Smith had four visions of
the angel Moroni and the golden plates, there was a group of the now-familiar
stone mounds, frequently part of the Indian vision quest, with a manitou stone
on top of one (Figure 12-2). There was also a large boulder nearby, perched on a
stone row.

Quite apart from the controversies surrounding Joseph Smith's life, the origin
of the *Book of Mormon*, and any other aspects of the Mormon Church, Smith
stands as one of the few influential American religious leaders of the seventeenth
through the nineteenth centuries who actually incorporated some understanding
of Indian ways and the Indians as a people in his spiritual work. We suspect that
his youthful impressions, formed first at Calendar One and later at Palmyra,
probably through contact with Native Americans, influenced him in building
the Mormon religion in this way.

12-2 Stone mound at Joseph Smith, Jr.'s sacred grove, Palmyra, N. Y. Note rock stack
and manitou stone held by Byron Dix.

Evidence of Ritual Activity at Calendar One

Since 1979 we have been tramping the hills and valleys of Calendar One and over the years have discovered similar and seemingly connected sites scattered over an area of many square miles. We have found evidence of many human activities, some that we believe were ritual activities outside or on the fringe of previous New England archaeological experience. These include the working of bedrock, the selection, marking and placing of large and small stones, the use of white quartz, quarrying, fire, and special tools and implements, and the special recognition and observation of land and sky.

In 1984, after an interval of five years, we renewed the excavation of the Dairy Hill monolith. We had discovered in the first excavation that the monolith, a large flat pointed slab, was balanced on bedrock which had been carefully worked and altered to support it. Now, after experience at other sites throughout New England, we felt we were in a better position to reevaluate our previous findings and to make new discoveries about the site. Accordingly, we uncovered to bedrock an area of eight square yards adjacent to the monolith on the uphill northwest side. Just underneath the present soil we discovered a pile of broken white quartz two square yards in extent, placed on bedrock (Figure 12–3). Within the pile we found a deposit of red ochre, and adjacent to it were two large boulders of quartzite with grooved markings, shown in Figure 12–4. We also discovered a set of grooved markings on the base of the monolith at its southern end (Figure 12–5), where there is a cavity in the bedrock. The chopping tool found in our first excavation among the supporting quartz boulders at the base of the monolith (Figure 1–7) could have been used to make these grooved markings and then ritually donated to the boulder pile.

The summit of Dairy Hill is dotted with several large trees that appear to have been altered and shaped during early periods in their lives. In some cases, the trunks and branches are twisted or bent in curious ways that suggest that they may be part of the tradition of tree marking which is practiced today at Indian

12-3 1984 excavation, Dairy Hill monolith

12-4 Markings on boulders beside Dairy Hill monolith

12-5 Markings on base of Dairy Hill monolith

12-6 U-shaped enclosure
near Dairy Hill monolith

sacred places. One of these marked trees stands near the monolith on its south side and another on its north side, so that the flat face of the standing stone is bracketed between them. Also near the monolith is a U-shaped low stone enclosure, with an opening facing south, toward the noon sun (Figure 12–6). The shape, size, construction and location near a hilltop and near a standing stone and stone mounds invite comparison with the prayer seats used in vision quests by Algonquian-speaking Indians of California.

A ditch and bank partially surrounds the summit of Dairy Hill near the monolith and the marked trees. A large stone mound built upon a sizable white quartz outcropping of bedrock lies near the southern end of the earthen bank. At the northern end there is a very ancient-looking standing stone of rotting quartzite, ready to crumble away if it were struck. A cross section of the ditch and bank was excavated and in it were found charcoal and an assortment of stone hammers, scrapers and other basic tools on an ancient soil contour.

In all of our many excavations at Calendar One, we removed soil down to the mica-schist and quartzite bedrock, which usually lies less than three feet below ground level.[7] Invariably where we have excavated, the bedrock has been modified by humans to form grooved markings, niches to support standing stones, or unaccountable geometrical designs. There are rectangular or rounded holes, organized quarried slabs and piles of quarried quartz found on and within the bedrock. This has led us to believe that either large expanses of bedrock were naturally exposed during ancient times when it was worked by people, or a great amount of excavation was accomplished to gain access to bedrock. We believe that bedrock was seen as the connection between people and mother earth and that it was also believed to be the source of rumblings and earthquakes.[8]

In addition to the pile of quartz beside the Dairy Hill monolith, we have frequently found pieces of quartz throughout New England in stone rows or otherwise as part of stone structures. Indian lore refers to the ability of quartz rocks to reflect sunlight at a great distance, and this, along with other properties, is probably the reason quartz is very much a part of the Calendar One design. It

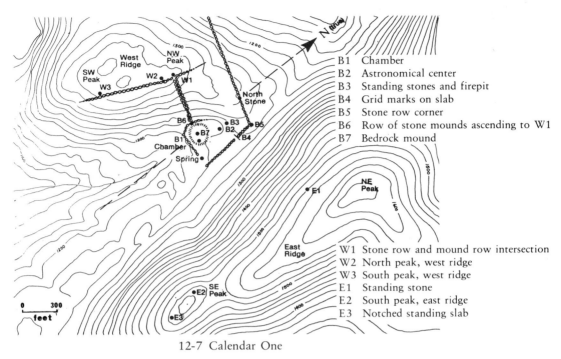

B1 Chamber
B2 Astronomical center
B3 Standing stones and firepit
B4 Grid marks on slab
B5 Stone row corner
B6 Row of stone mounds ascending to W1
B7 Bedrock mound

W1 Stone row and mound row intersection
W2 North peak, west ridge
W3 South peak, west ridge
E1 Standing stone
E2 South peak, east ridge
E3 Notched standing slab

12-7 Calendar One

is known to emit light both as a result of rock fracture and from piezoelectric stressing, as pointed out in Chapter 10. Two outcrops of major quartz veins are incorporated into the plan of the Calendar One bowl (Figure 12–7). A quartz outcrop lies on the west side of the east ridge among the standing stones at E3. This can be seen from the bowl and from the west ridge and reflects the afternoon sun. Another prominent outcrop of a vein that runs across the bowl is located centrally on the saddle to the north connecting the ridges, above and to the west of site B3. This beacon faces south and would therefore reflect the sun through-out the day at all seasons and the moon at night.

Two large rectangular quarried blocks of white quartz are set into the stone row on the west ridge south of the summit, shown in Figure 12–8. They contrast

12-8 Quartz blocks
in west ridge row

strikingly with their background and surely were placed to be seen from the bowl and the east slope. Since these are integral with the stone row, the date of their use is given by the date of construction of the stone row. We therefore excavated adjacent to the stone row and found that it was built on bedrock two feet below the soil surface, a design that is rather too elaborate for a sheep fence, a function that some would casually attach to this and many other stone rows. The date, however, remains unknown.

Soon after we had finished excavating, the day turned into evening, and we noticed an unmistakable glow about the many broken rocks as we backfilled the excavation. We also observed that when we struck one piece of quartz against another, sparks were emitted. We imagined that Indians sitting at night on this and other hilltops where many stone flakes from the knapping of stone are found could have produced an appreciable amount of light by this activity, perhaps having spiritual significance. Could it be that rock fracturing in many cases might have been primarily for the religious experience rather than for practical toolmaking?

Frequently, we have found tool-shaped stones within our excavations at Calendar One which are made of the soft schisty quartzite common in the region and therefore seem inappropriate for serviceable tools. We found a great many of these in the bowl chamber and at first speculated that they might have been throw-away tools for quarrying the bedrock. William Fowler, a perceptive New England archaeologist, has provided evidence for an attractive alternative possibility. He found indications of similarities in cremation practices between a Rhode Island Archaic Indian site and one of modern Aborigines of Tasmania. He attributed the similarity to common underlying concepts of a spirit-controlled universe, as we have done in similar comparisons elsewhere in this book. He observed that at the Flat River site in Rhode Island, crudely chipped tools of soft schisty quartzite, the same as we find in Vermont, were made expressly for the cremation ceremony. As flames developed, the tools were thrown into the fire, where they cracked readily because of their low-grade material, thereby releasing the spirits. In Tasmania, 3,000 years more recently, supposed sharp-edged knives were made of a soft stone, unsuitable for working tools, and burned with the body. In burning, the stones gave off an iridescent greenish-blue flame which represented ascent of the tools' spirits to the same spirit world as that of the deceased.[9] The stones that we have found may have a somewhat similar origin but perhaps not as part of a cremation ritual. Many of them are shaped like manitou or god stones but on a smaller scale and are found associated with tool-like stones. Perhaps all should be classed as "spirit stones."

The site which we call Genesis, another stone slab on Dairy Hill introduced in Chapter 1, was first dug in September, 1979, exposing a stone mound on bedrock beside the slab. We returned in August, 1986, and reopened the excavation, left untouched for seven years. This time, we went at the task with confidence and established a well-stratified soil profile which included the green hard layer two feet below ground. Part of the stone mound was within this layer. There were few stones present other than those making up the mound, so that a broken

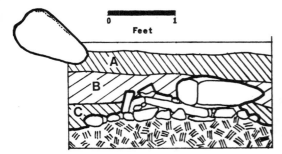

12-9 Genesis excavation before
removal of stone mound
A Humus; B Sandy soil; C Green

12-10 Genesis marked boulder

green pebble of hard metamorphic rock, set in the green layer between the mound and the marked standing stone caught our attention readily. The green stone fits nicely into the hand, with an exposed surface clearly battered from much use as a hammer or, more likely, a hand anvil. The layout of the features excavated is shown in Figure 12–9.

We removed the stones of the mound and saw before us a continuous expanse of bedrock into which, beneath the center of the mound, had been carved a rounded depression. Beside it and also under the mound's former position, was an elongated carved depression shaped like a projectile point directed toward 48 degrees true. This site, which today is identified at the surface only by the marked standing stone (Figure 12–10), appears to be quite ancient and is located on a small horizontal rock platform, on the west slope of a major hill within the Calendar One complex. At least three stone chambers can be seen from this platform.

At site B2 in the bowl located in Figure 12–7, the astronomical center selected by Betty Sincerbeaux and Byron during their early exploration of Calendar One, an excavation was made to determine if there was an underground marker. A considerable cavity was found in the bedrock, which is of unknown significance, and the three soil layers were seen clearly stratified, with small tools in all three layers. A small quartz projectile point was found in the middle layer.

Site B3, located near the astronomical center in the bowl, consisted, before excavation, of two little standing slabs barely a foot high, forming an ell-shaped pocket between them. Byron thought that they might have been used to position the feet of an observer for correct observation of the horizon markers. A person standing with his feet placed in the niche formed by the two standing stones

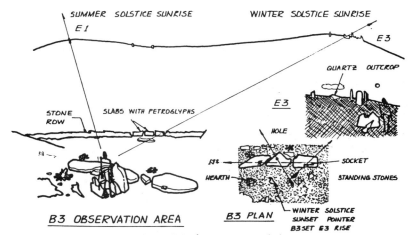

12-11 B3 observation sightlines

could observe the summer solstice sunrise at standing stone E1 on the east ridge and the winter solstice sunrise over the notched slab E3 (Figure 12–11).

Upon excavation, we found that it was much more. We cleared and dug a sixteen foot square area down to bedrock. The two little stones turned out to be standing stones nearly four feet high, made from the weathered mica-schist with decorative quartz intrusions. They were wedged into a deep recess in the bedrock, shown in Figure 12–12. Nearby, there were three large flat slabs lying in contact with the bedrock arranged in a north-south row with holes and recesses carved into them (Figure 12–13). Wooden staffs placed in the holes could have served as nearby approximate markers for the solar sightline to the ridgetop. In the north-

12-12 Excavation at B3

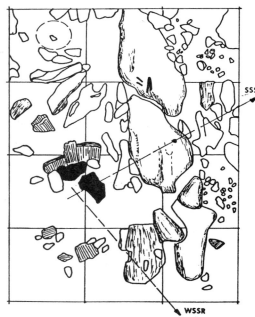

12-13 B3 excavation plan, one meter squares

12-14 E3 fallen standing stone

east corner of the excavation, we found a stone-lined fire pit filled with charcoal sealed from the atmosphere by over a foot of soil. A carbon 14 analysis showed the charcoal to have been created between A.D. 1240 and 1500.[10]

At the southern end of the east ridge, we excavated the collection of stone slabs near E3, most of which are now lying down. If erect, they would have appeared as shown in Figure 12–11 on the horizon as viewed from location B3. We know this because we located some of the bedrock recesses in which these slabs had been placed before they fell over. The largest stone, over six feet long, lies in the position in which it fell, with a foundation niche in the bedrock at one end which precisely fits the stone (Figure 12–14). We simulated the fall of this stone by pushing over a model stone, set in its recess. It fell into exactly the same position that the real stone occupies on the hilltop with respect to its socket. In Chapter 9, we cited a similar situation in Scotland with a recumbent standing stone lying beside its socket. On Burnt Hill in Heath, Massachusetts, due south of Calendar One and just west of the Connecticut River, there are fourteen standing stones wedged into sockets in the bedrock, which we believe form a ritual site similar to the one at Calendar One. In particular, at the Heath summit a group of five stones, shown in Figure 12–15, gives an aspect similar to our reconstructed view

12-15 Heath standing stones

12-16 Heath standing stones wedged into bedrock, *above.* Same stones showing alignment to summer solstice sunset, 1987, *r.*

of E3 at Calendar One. At Heath on 21 June 1987, Byron witnessed the summer solstice along an alignment to the distant horizon marked by two of these stones, as shown in Figure 12–16.

In the Calendar One bowl, a large embrasure was built into the north-south stone row south of the stones with the grid markings that Byron saw on his first visit. The axis of symmetry of the embrasure coincides with the sightline from the bowl chamber to the equinox horizon sight-line. We excavated this elaborately shaped structure, which, as we by now had come to expect, extended down to bedrock, as shown in Figure 12–17. The only artifacts found were suspected ancient stone quarrying tools of unknown date. In expanding the area

12-17 Excavation of embrasure east of bowl chamber

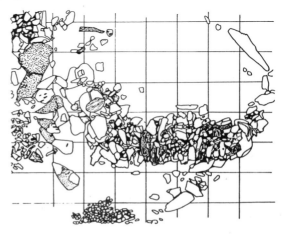

12-18 Excavated pavement between chamber and spring, Calendar One bowl

of excavation from the embrasure westerly down a slope about 100 feet to the all-weather spring between the chamber and the embrasure (Figure 12–1), we uncovered an area about 30 feet wide and found that it was completely paved over with rocks, most about six inches across, laid on the bedrock which was near the surface. At the spring, a built stone enclosure formed a pool about three feet in diameter which does not freeze even in Vermont's cold winters. This extensive pavement may well cover a much larger area and is similar in depth and construction to the pavement nearer the chamber which was excavated by James Whittall in 1984 and dated by charcoal analysis to A.D. 1300 to 1600. This latter pavement is a large shallow assemblage of broken rock located just northeast of the chamber on a gradual slope (Figure 12–18). It is sixty feet long and ten feet wide, with many pieces of quartz and burned quartzite, lying just beneath the present soil surface. It also contains brick fragments which may have been souvenirs or trophies taken from colonial structures during burning raids in the historic period.

The Age of Calendar One

The evidence of geological and astronomical events, as well as that of archeological excavations implies that human ritual activity took place at Calendar One over a great span of years from the ancient past continuing up to the present.

The most recent glacier which covered New England had receded from most of Vermont by about 12,000 years ago, leaving a land of rounded hills and valleys and deposited sand, gravel and boulders. As it receded, it formed Lake Hitchcock, a great body of water filling the Connecticut River Valley from Connecticut to Canada. The lake was dammed by glacial debris at present-day Middletown, Connecticut, for at least 2,000 years, and until about 10,000 years ago maintained a water level about 650 feet above sea level. Then, just about the time that the last remnants of the ice sheet had retreated as far north as Calendar One, the dam failed and the lake level fell about ninety feet. The valleys of the White River and its branches were fingers of the new, lower Lake Upham.[11]

One clue to a date for Calendar One is the fact that no stone chambers or marked stones are found below 700 feet above sea level along the valleys of the Connecticut River and its tributaries in Vermont. This is about 150 feet above the level usually estimated for ancient Lake Upham, which existed up to about 8,000 years ago, and could imply that the lithic traditions started before this date and continued only in the places of previous structures.

In Chapter 1 we suggested a date, based on soil stratigraphy, as early as 10,000 years ago and an astronomical date of 3,500 to 2,700 years ago. Continuing the astronomical approach, a datable astronomical event which took place in prehistoric times may have been observed by people who came to the Calendar One sacred site to witness it. At this stage of our work, we can assert with some confidence that celestial events visible to the naked eye were indeed such an important part of the ritual life of ancient people that they certainly would have observed and recorded all major events. The observation in question used only three stone markers, shown in Figure 12–7, the notched slab on the east ridge, E3, the west ridge peak, W2, and the intersection of two low stone rows on the west ridge, W1. We calculate that about 3150 B.C. observers could have witnessed a very special astronomical event, the acronical rising just after sunset of Sirius in the direction of the winter solstice sunrise and within one or two days of the winter solstice. The acronical rising of a celestial body is its last rising, after having been visible every night for several months, before it disappears below the horizon for a certain period.

We suggest the following scenario for this unusual event. The date of the winter solstice would have been known from previous measurements of sun position. For several mornings before the solstice, observers standing at position W1 on the west ridge could have witnessed the sun rising in the notched stone E3 placed near the southern peak of the east ridge. Each evening before sunset, they could have climbed from the bowl using an easy path to W2, the west ridge peak marked by the crest of a stone row. Within one or two days of the solstice, just after the sun had set in the southwest and the sky had darkened, they would have seen Sirius rise over the same stone marker, E3, where the sun had risen that morning as seen from W1 (Figure 12–19). The event would have had a special ritual importance to the people at Calendar One because of the coincidence of the date of acronical rising of the brightest star in the sky with the winter solstice. As has already been mentioned, the winter solstice was the most important day of the year to the Algonquins, the time of the feast of dreams, when communi-

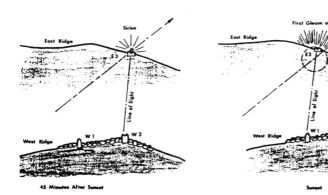

12-19 Acronical rise of Sirius

cation with all spirits is sought, including those of the stars. At each place where this event could have been witnessed, which depends upon the local topography, it would have occurred annually during only one ten-year period in the past 6,000 years, at a date which can be calculated.

The stone marker, E3, on the east ridge provides the distant observer with a horizon marker notch one-twentieth of a degree wide, or one-tenth of the sun's diameter. Our experiments showed that the unaided eye can detect a notch as narrow as one-sixtieth of a degree, so that detecting the event is feasible. The notched stone itself, lying on its side as shown in Figure 12–20, may, before 3150 B.C., have been erected vertically with its pointed left hand end at the top. In this attitude, it would have projected over three feet above the ground and would have been quite similar to several other standing stones in the vicinity, which we have identified as astronomical markers. It may, at a later date, have been laid on its side and altered to provide the notch that was preferable to a point for sighting.

Examining astronomical events of this complexity is important because it tells us about the probable abilities and inclinations of these prehistoric people, as well as suggesting dates. In order to watch this rare event, considerable planning

12-20 E3 notched marker stone

after the first year it was noticed would have been required. The event would have been repeated once a year on the winter solstice for as long as the star set in the notch. Each year, the star would have moved 0.005 degrees because of precession of the equinoxes. If people did observe these events, then they had the ability and motivation to set up repeated trials to determine how to design the arrangement of observation points and horizon foresights. They also probably had previously recorded acronical events of other stars and had a tradition of recognizing them. These speculations become highly probable when we recall from Chapter 2 that people in Europe, Asia, and South America built structures in ancient times to record just such an acronical stellar event as we have described.

After 3150 B.C., as the centuries passed, oral tradition would have told of how Sirius had moved away from the notched stone. In 2424 B.C., another very bright star, Rigel in the constellation Orion, would have appeared in the notch as Sirius had before, using the same observation point. The date of the acronical rising of Rigel was disappointingly about seventeen days before the winter solstice, but the heliacal rising was on the summer solstice.[12] During that event, Rigel rose just before sunrise in the northeast. Rigel, which classical authors have referred to as an ancient calendrical sign, would have risen within the notch for only ten years, as had Sirius many centuries before.

While geology and astronomy indicate dates thousands of years ago for the use of Calendar One, the radiocarbon 14 dates from charcoal in excavations have provided later, protohistoric dates. We have already mentioned that charcoal analysis from excavations in the bowl of site B3 and the pavement near the chamber yielded dates from A.D. 1240 to 1600. These dates were further supported by the excavation of another standing stone in the southern part of the bowl, this one also made by James Whittall in 1984. This three-foot-high slab was half-buried in soil and set on bedrock in a niche apparently prepared for it, as at all other such sites excavated. A firepit and a red ochre deposit adjacent to the stone dated to A.D. 1370 to 1660.[13]

Some structures at Calendar One appear to have been built since A.D. 1600. The two rectangular stone enclosures with parallel axes at the top of the natural rock mound into which the chamber is built, shown in Figure 12–21, are probably in this category. The elongated enclosure is subdivided into three or four small cubicles. The unworked stones of these structures project a few inches above the soil and give the appearance of the foundations of small buildings, but none of the enclosures is built on bedrock, which lies only twelve inches below the surface. Instead they are placed on soil and, from the presence of bricks and European artifacts integral with the structure, are presumed to have been historic.

It is tempting to jump to the ethnocentric conclusion that these are the remains of nineteenth-century farm buildings built by white settlers, but there is no specific basis for this. No known historical record mentions these structures or many others throughout Vermont of a similar character. Also, there are other stone structures that look superficially like building foundations, sometimes

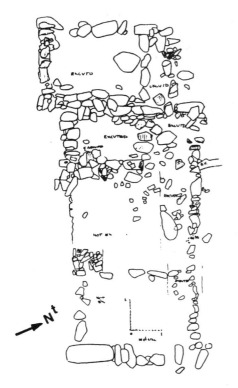

12-21 Rectangular enclosures on chamber mound, Calendar One bowl

made of rock quarried with steel tools, and that have been used as such in many cases. Some have a curious mixture of architectural patterns, including tightly laid masonry, loose boulder rows, non-vertical walls and acute angled corners. It is likely that many of these structures were built by Vermont Indians, who, through contact with the French, Dutch and English for 150 years, possessed the white man's steel stone-working tools and long experience in their use before Vermont's late English settlement about 1750.

The white settlers who built in Vermont in the late eighteenth century used the well-developed technology and mature architecture of New England at that time. The situation was very different from the settlement of the Plymouth colony in 1620. Yet all across Vermont we see stonework that, while it has some construction characteristics similar to those of the white man, is of a different, we think ritualized, architectural style, containing very ancient parts. We suggest that it was a common practice in Vermont for stone structures built by Indians prior to 1750 to be adapted by white settlers to building foundations, cellars, and other parts of farm buildings.

The various dates from 10,000 years ago to the present that have been determined by various circumstantial methods are useful only as general suggestions. However, taken as a whole they indicate a great span of years for ritual activity at Calendar One, which included celestial observation, erection of stone structures and the use of firepits. By comparison with other sites, we have come to believe that Calendar One may have been the oldest ritual site that we have seen in New England and that it is possibly still in use.

More important, in our view, than establishing any specific ages or cultural groups is recognizing and trying to understand the concept of the spiritual quality inherent in all things, manitou, represented by the ritual architecture of Calendar One. This transcends all other characteristics of humans' relationship to land and sky and forms the building blocks of spiritual appreciation. As our understanding of our natural world changes, so does our view of the spiritual world so that the sun, stars, earthquakes, lights, sound, rock fracture, and other natural phenomena are honored and responded to by the stone and earthen structures.

Calendar One and the Indian Road

There are features of Calendar One that make it appear to have been a major meeting place where people gathered for ritual observances, coming from distant places over a long period of time. In addition to the astronomical significance of the different sites in the complex, it seems that, in the absence of trees, there would be notable visual sightlines between many of these features. The sightlines interconnect them to such an extent that a visual communication system could spread a message very rapidly throughout the whole complex.

Calendar One was probably used by shamans from many different parts of the Northeast, not only because of its astronomical observatories, but also because it is a geologic contact area where metamorphic and igneous rock come together and metals are formed, including copper, lead, gold and silver. Quartz is also formed. Seismic activity in such places tends to have dramatic light and sound effects, regardless of the magnitude of the activity.

The stone structures that grace the landscape would have been designed to follow the earth movements during such activity, a concept that gives insight into the meaning of balanced rocks and serpentine stone rows, which would respond with oscillations but not be destroyed. The world view of people living in tune with nature would consider the design of such structures to be an appropriate response to natural events. They would interact with the elements of nature both on a small scale, such as the personal act of participating in a sunset at a specific place, and on a larger scale, such as visualizing a vast network of astronomical alignments across the countryside. The stone structures discussed throughout this book were intended to participate with the environment not only during the clear skies on the solstices but also during the flooding periods following the snows, during the windy seasons and the burning periods. In other words, the architecture of native people participated with nature in all of its cycles. The well-engineered bridge of Natick described in Chapter 6 may well

12-22 Rivers of Vermont
and ritual site locations

represent a sound understanding of the river water's behavior throughout the seasons, rather than merely skill in the art of bridge construction. Similarly, when the natives of Martha's Vineyard left spaces between the stones of their rows to let the wind blow through, it represented a profound sense of nature. In the same vein, earthworks found in lowlands soften the harshness of flowing water during seasonal flooding.

Rather than being a unique sanctuary in a remote wilderness, known by only a few shamans, we believe that Calendar One was one of many such sacred places near well-traveled routes and known throughout the Northeast. The major waterways of Vermont are shown in Figure 12–22. Also shown are four places in Vermont which we have come to call ritual sites and which all lie very close to a true north-south line west of the Connecticut River at west longitude 72 degrees 30 minutes. The most northerly site is in Washington, where the most elevated stone chamber known is built into a hillside at 2,000 feet. The sightline from the entrance along its axis leads across a natural bowl, somewhat like Calendar One, to the center and peak of a short, arched stone row of white quartz on the horizon. Next, to the south, is Calendar One. South of it in South Woodstock,

Calendar Two has as its focus a stone chamber at 1,600 feet altitude, with a winter solstice sunrise orientation. Continuing south, a hilltop location in Putney contains a complex of chambers and standing stones. None of the four sites departs from a true north-south line by more than two and one-half miles, and none is far from a waterway.

A traveler from Massachusetts or southern New Hampshire headed for Lake Champlain, and perhaps Montreal as well, would find a nearly continuous water route across Vermont by going up the Connecticut to White River Junction. There, he could go up the White River and its First or Second Branch to a one-mile portage across to one of the branches of the Winooski River. From there, the route, covering most of the distance across Vermont, is all downhill, down the Winooski to Lake Champlain. This route was called "The Indian Road" and was known to Native Americans throughout the Northeast. It was the path taken by the Indians who burned Royalton in 1780.[14] If the First Branch of the White River is chosen, the route passes through Calendar One and the high Washington site.

We suggest that sacred places like Calendar One were selected and used both because of their local environment and because they were on major arteries of communication for millennia past. In the seventeenth century, Calendar One was on the main route between the Indian villages of New England and Canada, and the travellers included Indians from the praying villages of both Puritan New England and Catholic New France. As colonial settlers moved into Vermont in the eighteenth century, the natives made the sacred places more clandestine in order that they and the activities that went on at them would be invisible to the white man and his missionaries. After the American Revolution, many Vermont Indians retreated northward, and most of the Abenakis who remained went underground. Their strategy was perhaps best described by John Moody, who writes, "The Abenaki survived into the twentieth century by adapting to western society as if it were another part of the natural world."[15]

13

Manitou

Shamanism, Geomancy and Manitou

The Siberian origins of shamanism may be the most promising source for learning the meaning of manitou. The concept of a primary creator may be at least one million years old, and more recently the two oldest racial stocks in North America continued this idea. They are the Algonquin of the Northeast, among whom the supreme deity is known as *Kichtan* or *Kitschi*, and the Wiyot of northern California, who call it *Gudatrigakwitl*.[1] The Wiyot join with the adjacent and culturally similar Yurok to constitute the "Algonquins of California," and their languages are united in the Ritwan stock of the Algonquian language family.[2] We have observed that stone structures used by the Yurok of California for shamanistic ritual are similar to the structures of New England, as would be expected because cultural similarities often follow language similarities. These ancient Native Americans descended from the Paleo peoples of northern Siberia, and their shamanistic practices would be expected to resemble those of the parent stock.

Among these ancient Siberian peoples are the Gilyaks. They believe in a supreme god named *Kur*, which is never portrayed. They do, however, make effigies of the second level of deity, called *nibach*, the lords of the beasts, forest, sea and mountains, which are said to resemble men in every respect. In the course of time, a multiplicity of spirits appeared which inhabit every space and every object in nature. The Gilyaks have no idols which are worshipped as gods but do have anthropomorphic effigies made of stone or wood which serve as the abodes of spirits. The effigies are called *lekan* and the inhabiting spirits *chaitan*. The lekan are given an honored place in the home and are sacrificed to, but they are also chastised and thrown away or burned. They have no connection with the supreme god.

These three levels of spiritual ideas may be historically successive. If so, first there was the supreme god, then the lords of nature were added and finally the chaitan. It would follow that the Algonquin manitou, which is descended from this root, would be comparable to the Gilyak chaitan. Hobomock would correspond to the lords of nature, and Kichtan would be the supreme deity, or Great Spirit.[3]

Another source for understanding the meaning of manitou is Chinese geomancy or *feng-shui*. Manitou appears to be inseparable from geomancy, the concept of the world as a place where all activities and objects, both in the natural and supernatural domains, are connected in some subtle manner.[4] Geomancers believe that the natural order can be sensed and tuned into by traditional practices, much as shamans do. While usually confined to eastern Asia and intimately involved with traditional Chinese Taoist philosophy, feng-shui, literally wind-water but, more generally, living with the rhythms of the land and seasons, would be expected to have or have had counterparts in other parts of the world, including America.

The elaborate practices of feng-shui used in selecting propitious natural sites for towns, homes and tombs and in modifying the landscape to improve them are based largely on common sense and knowledge of natural science. To this art are owed the disciplines involving the systematic use of magnetism, navigation and geography. The crux of feng-shui is the life force of the earth, *ch'i*, which flows through the earth like an underground stream in veins called dragon lines. The most favorable places are those with the greatest amount of ch'i flowing. This, in turn, is related to its rate of accumulation and dispersal. The practitioner learns to recognize natural and man-made influences which are favorable or detrimental to the flow of ch'i. He does this through observations of landforms, waterflows, horizon profiles, directions, the locations of constellations, and through intuition.[5]

In general, straight watercourses and land contours, flat plains, cold winds, isolated boulders and other land discontinuities are not propitious to the flow of ch'i, whereas curves, blended landscapes and rich soil are. With respect to these considerations, the straight ley lines visualized in England by Alfred Watkins and the straight geodesic lines sensed by many others in more recent years represent the antithesis of dragon lines.[6] On the other hand, the descriptions of curved lines of force sensed by Guy Underwood in England are not unlike descriptions of dragon lines. What Underwood called blind springs at the locations of ancient megalithic standing stones could be analogous to places having a great flow of ch'i.[7]

The architectural techniques practiced in feng-shui to bring forth a flow of ch'i and to suppress the appearance of *cha*, noxious vapors, include altering the courses of streams and rivers to include bends, planting trees to hide discontinuities in the landscape, curving the paths of roads and railways to prevent rapid dispersal of ch'i, and changing the shapes of hilltops. Hilltops are symbolized by various elements, such as fire, metal, earth, etc., which should be compatible when viewed from the selected site.

The ideal spot for a feng-shui practitioner, that is, one having the greatest flow of ch'i, is called a dragon's lair, where the dragon, who is male, and the tiger, who is female, are united in sexual intercourse. Its general features are that it is protected from high winds, screened on the north by hills or trees, close by a slowly meandering stream, nestled in the embrace of hills like an armchair, and has a distant view to the south. A dwelling place at a dragon's lair should have its entrance on the south side, while a tomb should have its entrance on the north.

The Calendar One bowl fits perfectly the description of a dragon's lair selected by feng-shui, an exciting development because it confirms our intuitive attraction to the site, but not a remarkable one. It does not mean that Chinese geomancers were walking the hills of ancient Vermont practicing their art. We think that feng-shui contains universal ideas propitious to the harmonies of the natural world and that those who selected Calendar One as a sacred place were in tune with these ideas.

Some recent theories attempt to analyze and understand geomancy. Morpho-genetic fields, which are postulated as fields of influence that cause characteristic forms in living organisms that are genetically maintained, may represent a factor in life that is not recognized by the physical sciences and may help to explain geomancy.[8] Also, that obscure and diffuse phenomenon known as earth energy, described broadly as patterns of energy or force fields on earth, may link critical points on earth with the health of all life. This theory holds that ancient people sensed these points, which became their sacred places.[9] According to the theory the places of ritual, which we have described throughout this book, related to natural phenomena such as seismicity, could also be critical parts of earth energy fields. In addition, the local patterns of man-made structures may signal the people's sensitivity to these fields. Another theory, building upon this, holds that the presence of dedicated people at the sacred places over millennia produced energy fields. Perhaps the data we have presented in this book will contribute to the testing of these theories.

Throughout previous chapters we have described man-made stone structures and natural rock formations which we believe were and continue to be part of Native American religious ritual in a shamanic tradition. We believe that the stones were considered to be both inherently spiritual and symbolic of spirituality, and that they were elements of a spiritual form o andscape architecture. They marked sacred places, signalled astronomical events and both recognized and participated in various natural processes such as seismic activity, hydrology, piezoelectric effects, and esker and swamp formation. Next, we want to single out a class of stones which appear to have been specially selected for their spiritual qualities and worked to enhance them. We call them *manitou stones*.

Manitou Stones

These stones usually have a shape resembling the upper human torso and head.
Often, they appear to have been made from rectangular slabs by breaking off the
upper corners symmetrically about a vertical axis. Others have a similar irregular
hexagonal shape but are more subtly worked. Many are portable and vary in size
from that of hand tools to three-foot-long slabs placed loosely in stone rows or
in the ground; some are larger and set permanently. These anthropomorphized
stones are found throughout North America as part of Indian ritual. Called
godstones by the European colonists, they include Hopi spirit-of-the-creator
and earth goddess effigies found in kivas, wood and stone divinities found among
Algonquin Indians of Canada, stone idols used among Indians of New Mexico
during the time of the Spanish missions, godstones used by eighteenth-century
Mohegans, image stones found at places of vision quest, Indian charmstones
such as plummets used in shamanic ritual in California, *Shingaba Wassins* or
spirit stones found among many American Indian peoples, symbols of the Wakun
or sacred bird used to appease Hobomock in New England, Atabeyra figures
used by the Arawak Indians of Puerto Rico, slabs found in Maritime Archaic
settlements in Labrador, and stones found near prehistoric Hopewellian burial
mounds in Ohio.[10]

In New England, we have usually seen manitou stones in or near stone structures
such as stone rows, mounds and chambers, but some are set in the ground in
cemeteries, giving the appearance of gravestones. In Chapter 3, we described a
propped slab of hexagonal shape dated to at least 900 years ago, found in the
excavation of a stone mound. In the eighteenth century, Ezra Stiles found an
Indian godstone at a place in Connecticut of Indian "worship in ages past."[11]
The shape of these stones is very like ritual slabs known throughout the world,
such as anthropomorphic god images of the Lapps and the Greek stone pillars
surmounted by the head of the god Hermes. He is said to have originated as the
spirit of stone piles placed along roadsides and also appeared as an ancient Celtic

13-1 Manitou stone from Harvard, Mass.,
compared with ritual shouldered stone
from Taiwan (from Pearson, note 12)

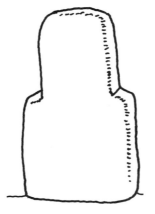
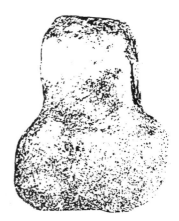

deity, meaning diviner. In the Near East, the same shape was called Tanit and represented the mother goddess or earth mother. Ritual "shouldered stones" identical to some New England manitou stones were found in eastern Taiwan and dated to A.D. 0 to 1250. They represent the cultures from which colonists (A.D. 1250–1600) of the nearby Ryukyu Islands came, people who built stone walls, stone enclosures and single standing stones (Figure 13–1). This archetypal

13-2 Manitou stones from southern New England having clear head and shoulders aspect:
l, Acton, Mass.
below, Heath, Mass.
bottom l and r, Groton, Conn.
See also Figures 3-7 and 10-14.

anthromorphized form, found world-wide and often associated with a creative force and male and female principles, may have originated before the last ice age.[12]

We present a gallery of manitou stones found in southern New England in Figure 13–2, stone slabs having clearly the characteristic crude head and shoulders shape. In Figure 13–3, also New England manitou stones, the shape is less clearly anthropomorphic but still recognizable. A stone found at Calendar One, shown in Figure 13–4, is exactly like Archaic quarrying tailing tools found in soapstone

13-3 Manitou stones from southern New England of less defined shape:

clockwise from top l
a Freetown, Mass.,
   in stone mound
b Freetown, Mass.,
   under stone mound
c Royalton, Vt.
d Groton, Conn.,
   with inscribed
   Wakun bird
e Falmouth, Mass.,
   in stone row

13-4 Quarrying tool from Calendar One, Vt., of friable material, which may be a hand-held manitou stone

quarries of southern New England. The Vermont stone is a friable mica-schist that will not last as a tool and was probably a ritual stone, a hand-held manitou stone. Figure 13–5 shows a variety of image stones from various sites in North America outside of New England, except for one from Lappland for comparison,

13-5a Image stones at Marietta, Ohio, mound (from Squier and Davis, note 10)

13-5, cont. Image stones from North America outside New England

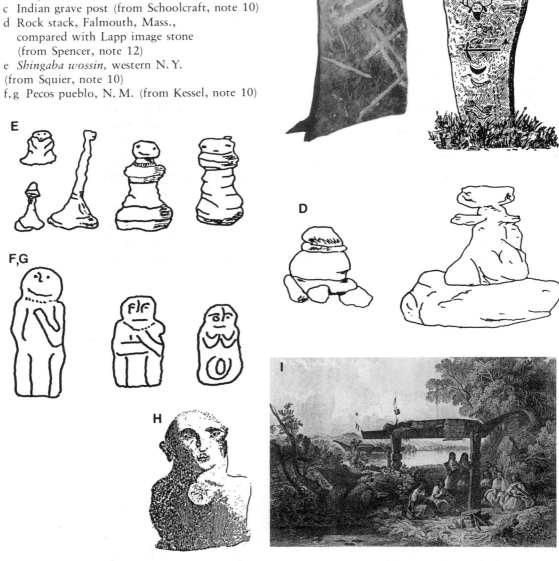

b Susquehannah, Penn.
c Indian grave post (from Schoolcraft, note 10)
d Rock stack, Falmouth, Mass.,
    compared with Lapp image stone
    (from Spencer, note 12)
e *Shingaba wossin*, western N.Y.
(from Squier, note 10)
f,g Pecos pueblo, N.M. (from Kessel, note 10)

h Stylized drawing of manitou stone from Mound Builders' ritual site, Natchez, Miss.,
    with inscription on center front
i Chinook burial structure with manitou stone and ritual hanging bucket (from
    Schoolcraft, note 10)

13-6 Row of manitou stones, Groton, Conn.

to establish the universality of this ritual object. Occasionally a row of manitou stones, such as the one in Figure 13–6 from Groton, Connecticut, is seen.

Many stones have the size and shape of traditional colonial gravestones, and we have observed the corner-notched form in cemeteries, but uninscribed (Figure 13–7). In addition, in Connecticut, Indians placed the dead before "godstones" previous to burial and danced about them. Historical observers noted that the Wakun bird effigy was similar to Christian tombstones and that the shape appeared to be a human head and shoulders.[13]

This similarity of manitou stones to gravestones of colonial New England leads to a theory that could explain a curious incident described by Ezra Stiles.

13-7 1725 colonial gravestone in Brewster, Mass., compared with manitou stone in Vt. cemetery

In 1741, Indians of Connecticut, who had previously concealed their godstones from the white settlers, gave up to the English a number of stone and wooden "idols."[14] The Indians, who had never used gravestones before the white man came, observed the colonists' introduction of this ritual to the New England landscape, which began in the late seventeenth century. In imitation of the white man, they may have modified their manitou stones and started using them as part of their burial ritual, laying the dead before the stone as the record shows.

When the English saw the Indian manitou stones and were told their meaning, they were probably reminded of pagan and animistic elements in their own heritage which they now associated with Satan; the god of the old society was transformed into the devil of the new. Expecting to be praised by the English for their efforts to adapt to white attitudes in their concept of manitou, the Indians would have been sorely saddened by their consignment to the Puritans' fiery hell for idolatry and may have reacted by turning in their manitou stones to the white men as a symbol of their rejection of the Puritan religion. But in Canada some Europeans held a different view. Father Joseph Lafitau, who lived at Caughnawaga, was more tolerant and saw the Indian manitou stones as a universal form that represented the spiritual and creative forces of peoples from all over the globe.

During the seventeenth and eighteenth centuries, the English settlers lavished their artistic creativity upon their gravestones. The ornamentation included solar images that suggest a relationship between the sun and the soul; in this and other cases these stones serve as records of colonial philosophy, and H. M. Forbes considers them the equivalent of Alaskan Indian totem poles, which were the Northwestern equivalent of the New England manitou stones.[15] During this period, the Indians would have believed that the white men perceived their gravestones as spiritual, which indeed they did before the stones became architecturally stereotyped.

Corner-notching a sacred Indian stone may have been analogous to Christianizing a standing stone by attaching or incising a cross, as was done widely in the

13-8 Standing stone modified into manitou stone, Lyme, Conn.

British Isles, Ireland and Brittany in medieval times (Figure 9–24). Many slabs in New England appear to have been corner-notched after they had been placed ritually to mark an Indian sacred place. For example, in Lyme, Connecticut, there is a large standing slab near chambers and curious stone rows which appears to have been modified in this way. It has been notched unsymmetrically following the grain of the stone, as if worked after emplacement (Figure 13–8).

We might expect that manitou stones that were modified to look like English gravestones would date from the historical period and be confined to places where the colonists attempted to Christianize the Indians. And, indeed, many manitou stones are found at the Indian praying villages, but they are also found at places of Indian ritual that have no known connection with Christianity, such as the hilltop at Moodus, Connecticut, where shamans came to seek Hobomock. Thus, the corner-notched feature of many stones in rows may be a traditional feature, or a later modification added to include the white man's power and thereby increase the manitou of the place, or as a condescension to the white man's ways.

A carved stone (Figure 13–9) which Byron Dix discovered in 1976 in Glover, Vermont, carries the idea of Christianized spiritual stones a step further. This stone, found in a stone pile on top of a large boulder in a highland swamp near the Barton River which flows into Lake Memphramagog, appears to represent a complete robed human figure. It may have been made by French praying Indians under the tutelage of or inspired by the Jesuit priests of Canada in the seventeenth or eighteenth century as an image of the Virgin Mary, or it may represent an ancient native goddess. There is a very similar stone figure in the museum at Niebla, in southern Spain, shown in Figure 13–9b, which is claimed to be a votive

13-9 Earth mother figurines: a, Glover, Vt.; b, Niebla, Spain (from Whishaw, note 16)

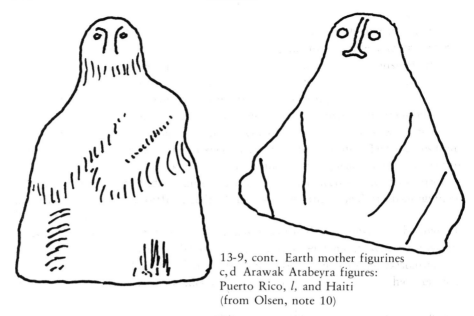

13-9, cont. Earth mother figurines
c,d Arawak Atabeyra figures:
Puerto Rico, *l*, and Haiti
(from Olsen, note 10)

Iberian sun and moon priestess found near a fourteenth or fifteenth-century convent named El Convento de la Luz (Convent of Light), perhaps because of ancient pre-Christian associations.[16] The mixing of ancient sun worship and Christianity at work here was a documented part of the Roman Catholic Church's approach to the American Indian missions. To the Jesuit missionaries in Canada, the supernatural world was ever present, and they gave prospective converts a votive image of the Virgin Mary with the hope that a vision of her would appear.[17] Perhaps the Glover image stone served this purpose.

Two other similar stone figures, shown in Figures 13–9c and d, are images of Atabeyra, the Arawak goddess of the moon, the sea and fertility, probably dating between A.D. 1000 and 1500.[18] All of these very similar votive images represent the spirit of the earth mother, a concept familiar to New England Indians as well, but which they symbolized quite differently. The mainland American Indians had a more ecological view of mother earth than that which the image of a Virgin Mary inspired. In one manifestation, the power of the universe was seen in the sacred pipe, and, when it was no longer efficacious, it was returned to mother earth from whence it came.

Manitou and other spirit stones changed in shape with time and with geographical location, as shown in Figure 13–10, and they probably also changed in meaning. Some historical records of eastern North American Indians report stone images and grope for their meaning, but several eighteenth-century writers denied the existence of idols or images. In 1823, Tennessee Indians claimed that they and their forefathers never made, used, or worshipped stone idols.[19]

Yet, many stone human effigies have survived and been found, although those of wood, such as the human-headed posts portrayed in John White's 1584 paint-

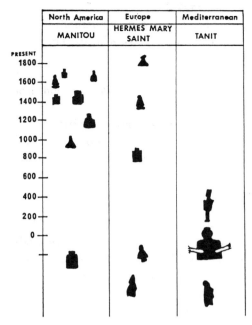

North America	Europe	Mediterranean
MANITOU	HERMES MARY SAINT	TANIT

13-10 Variation in shape of manitou stones and other spirit stones with epoch and location

ings of the Secotan settlement, have perished (Figure 13–11). Many human effigies have been found near the great Midwestern mounds. Two "Indian busts," heads and shoulders of near natural size, chiseled from stone, were excavated along the bank of the Cumberland River and given to Thomas Jefferson. Small stone idols of heads and shoulders, twelve to sixteen inches high, have been found in all of the southeastern states.[20] Squier published an apt description of manitou stones in 1849: "A stone which from some natural cause assumed the shape of a man or an animal was held in special esteem. . . . Artificial means were sometimes

13-11 Wooden image posts at Secotan, N. C., painted by John White in 1584

adopted to heighten the fancied resemblance. . . . Such objects were regarded as fit dwelling places for some manitou or spiritual influence."[21]

In 1873, Charles Jones found objects of this description in mounds and refuse piles "which doubtless answered some superstitious purpose in the hands of a conjurer, priest or medicine man." He concluded that the stone idols were "a sort of religious machinery," like the charms of medicine men, and occupied a position far inferior to the sun or Great Spirit.[22]

If we interpret the meaning of manitou stones in this light, it appears that they probably represent the abodes of spirits which Algonquins would call manitou. However, they also can include some aspects of Hobomock, the leading day-to-day operative spirit, especially in locations such as the summit of Mount Moodus in Connecticut, where the depths of the mountain are considered the home of Hobomock, who makes the bad noises. The anthropomorphism of manitou stones may reflect the tradition of nibach or lords of nature, which may predate the concept of manitou.

Manitou and Irish Monks

Limited numbers of Irish Culdee monks may have visited coastal New England between A.D. 500 and 1000 and participated in some stone construction and shamanistic ritual with the Indians. When the Indians revealed their manitou stones, the visiting monks probably saw themselves within these anthropomorphized stones and at the same time recognized their shamanic character. Early Icelandic records describe the monks who maintained the early monastic centers on the coasts of Ireland and Scotland and on the western islands as shamans who mixed Christianity with their traditional Druidic world view. According to these early accounts, the Irish monks were wizards with second sight who could change into animals and induce earthquakes and eclipses.[23]

These Irish adventurers would have found much in common with the native shamans, even to the wearing of animal skins, masks and body paint during their ritual. They would have exchanged spiritual, poetic and musical gifts, including sacred rhythms, prayers, religious notation and symbols, much like the later exchange between Native Americans and the Shakers during the middle of the nineteenth century.[24] Though the Native Americans probably learned the arts of stone construction at the chamber level from their contacts with people from the arctic and from the south and west of New England, special features such as those found in the Upton chamber could have been contributed by the Irish monks.

Inscriptions in languages of the shores of the Mediterranean, found at various places throughout North America, have been attributed to early European visitors.[25] The Irish monks who may have visited the Americas during the fifth to the tenth centuries were probably at home in Greek and Hebrew as well as Old Icelandic, and could therefore have been responsible for some inscriptions. An alphabet known to have been used by the Irish monks during this period, and by Druids before them, was Ogam, which was expressed by grooved markings on stone, nicks in wood or bone, hand and leg signals, and the like.[26] If the monks had travelled to New England, we might see evidence in North America of this alphabetical notation system. While stones with grooved markings are widespread, most appear to be calendrical or numerical rather than alphabetical.

Manitou

There is a tremendous amount of stone construction on the New England landscape which has gone unnoticed by the white man and forgotten by most of the remaining people of Indian descent. Its bulk probably dwarfs all other records of the Indian past, and its implications may eclipse in cultural significance all past results of New England archaeology and ethnology. It implies a great amount of communication and commonality of perception among people throughout America over the past several millenia, a fact which the white man has been slow to recognize.

Native Americans today in the eastern part of North America, while having limited understanding of traditional stonework through their direct ancestral lines, have learned of it through the pan-Indian movement from Native Americans in other parts of America where the destruction of the Indian way by the white man was more recent or less complete.

We perceive manitou as the spiritual quality possessed by every part or aspect of nature, animate or inanimate. Things relate to each other by means of this quality, which may be good or evil, temporary or permanent, fixed or changing. Manitou includes aspects of the natural world that are sensed but not understood.

The stone structures in general form a religious architecture that participates with the land and sky and reflects the quality or manitou of all things in nature. They are a reminder of the religious heritage of Native Americans in the midst of a modern world dominated by different spiritual perceptions. Stones were seen as habitat for much manitou and were at the same time symbolic of the quality itself.

Manitou stones mark places as the abodes of spirits and are symbolic of particular kinds of manitou. They are part of world-wide practices using anthropomorphic and other figures to protect crops, to heal, to aid visions and to aid spirits after death. Many stone artifacts found in excavations are manitou stones, and therefore spiritual symbols as well as functioning tools; some are specially made for spiritual qualities and have no practical function, such as the many ones of material unsuitable for tools which we found at Calendar One.

Some phenomena considered entirely spiritual by people of the past are perceived today mainly through their material elements. For example, the various manifestations of seismic activity in the earth and electromagnetic activity in the earth and sky have played major roles in the spiritual life of Native Americans.

By attempting a broad view of archaeology, we have found that New England offers a unique insight through its varied landscape and carefully placed stone constructions which have left a record of man's relationship to the natural order. The stars, the sun, the moon, the planets, the mountains and valleys, the rivers and streams, the lakes, the meadows and the seacoast are all a part of the stone structures. Native Americans of New England were experienced in stone construction at the level of roofed enclosures, both in building to last and in design for the proper relationship of man's works to his natural environment. The prevailing view that Native Americans in the east confined their use of stone to hand-held tools, weapons and implements of subsistence is quite false. Stone played a cosmological role of vital importance. The record suggests that astronomical events were recorded as both cosmological and calendrical guidelines over several millennia, practices which included short and long range astronomical and visual alignments linking centers of activity.

The native acceptance of European steel stoneworking tools obtained through trade for services, goods and lands encouraged both ritual and secular native stone construction. During the sixteenth and seventeenth centuries, the Dutch, English and French all participated in this trade with the Indians. As a result, at least one-half of all New England stone rows were probably constructed during this period by native stone masons following traditions that may be at least 10,000 years old. The new stone cutting and splitting technology using steel tools only served to blur the white man's history of Native American reverence for and work with stone.

We conclude that many European colonists in New England got on well with the Native Americans and that religious beliefs and ways of the two groups differed less than written records and archaeological research has led us to believe. In particular, we believe that certain English colonists acquired the skills and practiced some of the ways of native shamans, either to further their colonial objectives or because of sincere religious belief. European visitors as early as A.D. 500 could have brought religious practices and ways of subsistence that were so incorporated into those of the Native Americans that today's archaeological research would have a difficult time discerning the difference between artifacts of the superimposed cultures.

Many pure-blooded Indians are reported, even in early historical times, to be indistinguishable by color or facial features from the English colonists. Therefore, genealogical research has focused on English names given to Indians by the colonists. In most praying villages, the Indians dressed in the same manner as the English, even in the seventeenth century. For these reasons, it became very difficult to trace Indian ancestry, particularly if it was purposely kept hidden.

We believe that this phenomenon, which we call "invisible Indians," has misled investigators in their interpretations of stone rows and other stone structures. When the historical record reports stone structures built by people with English names and to all appearances of English ancestry, they may have been built by people of Indian ancestry following age-old traditions of their people. And the pervading spirit of those traditions, *manitou*, still lives and has much to teach our modern world.

Notes

Prologue

1. W. B. Goodwin, *The Ruins of Great Ireland in New England* (Boston: Meador, 1946), 401.
2. E. Kenyon, ed., *The Indians of North America* (New York: Harcourt Brace, 1927), I, 261. Selected from *The Jesuit Relation and Allied Documents; Travels and Explorations of the Jesuit Missionaries in New France, 1610–1791*, ed. R. Goldthwaites.
3. Roger Williams, *A Key Unto the Language of America*, (London: 1643), 20.

1. First Discovery in Vermont

1. William Tomkins, *Indian Sign Language* (New York: Dover, 1969).
2. William B. Goodwin, *The Ruins of Great Ireland in New England* (Boston: Meador, 1946), 401. New England stone chambers are built of dry-stone walling with slab roofs. They vary considerably in size and shape, the largest being about ten by twenty feet in inside dimensions. Some are freestanding and mounded over with earth. Others are built into natural hillsides. Some have entrance passages; some do not. Corbelling of the roof and passage is common.
3. Byron E. Dix, "A Possible Plinth Monument in Central Vermont," *Epigraphic Society* 3 (no. 60, 1976). Byron E. Dix, "An Early Calendar Site in Central Vermont," *Epigraphic Society* 3 (no. 51, 1975).
4. James W. Mavor, Jr., *Voyage to Atlantis* (New York: Putnam, 1969). James W. Mavor, Jr., "The Riddle of Mzorah," *Almogaren* (Graz, Austria, 1976).
5. William A. Haviland and Marjory W. Powers, *The Original Vermonters* (Hanover, N. H.: University Press of New England, 1981).
6. L. C. Aldrich and F. R. Holmes, eds., *History of Windsor County, Vermont* (Syracuse: Mason, 1891), 761.
7. June W. Potts (now Miller), "Dairy Hill" (Master's Thesis, Goddard College, Plainfield, Vt., 1981).
8. H. Nash, *Royalton* (Royalton, Vt.: Royalton Historical Society, 1975), 134. Potts, "Dairy Hill," 12.
9. E. M. Lovejoy, *History of Royalton, Vermont with Family Genealogies 1769–1911* (Royalton: Town of Royalton and Royalton Women's Club, 1911). Francis Jennings, *The Ambiguous Iroquois* (New York: Norton, 1984), 176. Z. Steele, "Steele's Narrative," in Aldrich, *Windsor County*.
10. I. Dunklee, *Burning of Royalton, Vermont, by Indians* (Boston: G. H. Ellis, 1906), 85–86.
11. Potts, "Dairy Hill," 19, 26.
12. The mineralogical constituents of a sample of the grey-green C soil from Calendar One was analyzed by Paul Bowker and Ray Hall of the U. S. Geological Survey. The results as percentages by weight were as follows: Quartz, 39%; Feldspar (K), 1%; Feldspar (Na + Ca), 13%; Vermiculite-Mica, 17%; Illite-Mica, 19%; Chlorite, 9%. Separation to clay minerals shows most of larger silicates, "phylo" one in silt fraction; i.e., most clay minerals are not clay size.

13. Dix and Mavor, "Heliolithic Ritual Sites in New England," *New England Antiquities Research Association Journal* XVI (no. 3, 1982), p. 78. William S. Fowler, "Magic Stones and Shamans," *Bulletin Massachusetts Archaeological Society* 36 (no. 3 and 4, 1975).

14. T. T. Waterman, "The Religious Practices of the Diegueno Indians," *American Archaeology and Ethnology* 8 (no. 6, 1910). Horatio N. Rust, "A Puberty Ceremony of the Mission Indians," *American Anthropologist* 8 (no. 1, 1906): 28–31.

15. William S. Fowler, "The Horne Hill Soapstone Quarry," *Bulletin Massachusetts Archaeological Society* 27 (no. 2, 1966). Dix and Mavor, "Heliolithic," 77, 78.

16. Potts, "Dairy Hill."

17. Elizabeth L. Coombs, "Symbolism at the Burying Ground" (Section 3 of The Memorial to Cyrus Standing Bull, unpublished note in public domain, 1979). The Yantacaw of the New Jersey Lenape, planted trees, then trimmed and tied them to symbolize history and to throw a shaped shadow during ritual at the equinox sunrise.

18. Byron E. Dix and James W. Mavor, Jr., "Progress Report on New England Archaeo-astronomy," *Bulletin Early Sites Research Society* 10 (no. 2, 1983): 13–24.

19. Byron E. Dix and James W. Mavor, Jr., "Two Possible Calendar Sites in Vermont," in *Archaeoastronomy in the Americas*, ed. Ray Williamson (Los Altos, CA: Balena Press, 1981).

20. W.R. Wedel, "Archaeological Investigations in Platte and Clay Counties, Missouri," *Smithsonian Institution Bulletin* 183 (1943). G. Fowke, "Antiquities of Central and Southeastern Missouri," *Smithsonian Institution Bulletin* 37 (1910). William W. Fitzhugh, "Maritime Cultures of the Central and Northern Labrador Coast," *Arctic Anthropology* XV (2, 1978).

21. Byron E. Dix, James W. Mavor, Jr., and June W. Potts, "Progress Report on the Calendar I Area in Central Vermont," *Archaeoastronomy* III (no. 1, 1980).

22. Potts, "Dairy Hill."

23. T. Largy, "An Unusual Notched Pendant," *Bulletin of Massachusetts Archaeological Society* 46 (no. 2, 1985): 52.

24. Alexander Thom and Archibald S. Thom, *Megalithic Sites in Britain and Brittany* (Oxford: Clarendon Press, 1978), 170.

25. Vincent Scully, *The Earth, The Temple, and the Gods* (New Haven: Yale, 1962).

2. A Pleiades and Sun Sanctuary at the Source of Waters

1. William B. Goodwin, *The Ruins of Great Ireland in New England* (Boston: Meador, 1946).

2. Byron E. Dix and James W. Mavor, Jr., "Possible astronomical alignments, date and origins of the Pearson stone chamber," *Early Sites Research Society Bulletin* 8 (no. 1, 1980). Also Byron E. Dix and James W. Mavor, Jr., "Heliolithic Ritual Sites in New England," *New England Antiquities Research Association Journal* XVI (no. 3, 1982).

3. D. H. Kelley and J. Glass, "Report to Early Sites Foundation" (unpublished manuscript, 1955). James P. Whittall II, "A Report on the Pearson Stone Chamber," *Early Sites Research Society Bulletin* 7 (no. 1, 1979).

4. W. Brigham, *An Address delivered before the inhabitants of Grafton on the first centennial anniversary of that town* (Boston, April 29, 1835).

5. R. C. Winthrop, *Life and Letters of John Winthrop* (Boston: Ticknor and Fields).

6. D. B. Johnson, *Upton's Heritage* (Canaan, New Hampshire: Phoenix, 1984), 43, 44.

7. H. S. Wood, "Lake Whitehall," *Hopkinton Historical Society* (Hopkinton, Mass., 1952).

8. *Worcester Spy* (Hopkinton Springs, Worcester, Mass., before 1850).

9. C. P. Bowditch, *An Account of the Trust Administered by the Trustees of the Charity of Edward Hopkins* (Hopkinton, Mass.: 1889).

10. D. A. Connole, "Land Occupied by the Nipmuck Indians of Central New England 1600–1700." *Massachusetts Archaeological Society Bulletin* 38 (no. 1 and 2, 1976).

11. James P. Whittall II, "Amerindian Stonework Tradition," *Early Sites Research Society Bulletin* 9 (no. 1, 1981).

12. James W. Mavor, Jr., and Byron E. Dix, "New England Cedar Wetlands in Native American Ritual," in *Atlantic White Cedar Wetlands*, ed. Aimlee D. Laderman (Boulder, Colo.: Westview, 1987). H. F. Walleing, *Map of the town of Upton* (Philadelphia, Pennsylvania: Kollner, 1851).

13. The observation point is two feet below and twenty-three feet east of the bottom of the chamber entrance lintel stone. We assumed the observer's eye level to be five feet above the floor and used an area four inches wide to allow for the separation distance between the eyes. From this observation point the horizon has an elevation above level which varies from 3.25 to 3.46 degrees, and the steepest possible observation line from the observer's eye position passes through the underside of the entrance lintel stone at an elevation of 4.5 degrees. Thus the horizon is below the lintel stone and can be seen with a minimum of one degree or 100 feet of sky above it.

14. Gerald Hawkins, *Beyond Stonehenge* (New York: Harper and Row, 1973), 207.

15. All of the stars except for the sun move slowly across the sky, as seen from earth, apparently on the surface of the celestial sphere, about one-half degree per century, because of the periodic, top-like wobble of the earth's axis, known as precession.

16. A. F. Emerson, *Early History of Naushon Island* (Boston: Howland, 1981), 354, 361.

17. J. H. Carmody, "Paper on the Nipmuck Indians," *Worcester Historical Society Bulletin* III (no. VII, 1964).

18. W. T. Olcott, *Star Lore of All Ages* (New York: Putnam, 1931). Heliacal and acronical events refer to the rising and setting of stars when the sun is just below the horizon. Each star makes one such event on each of four days annually, the dates changing at the rate of one day in 100 years because of precession. All dates are given in the Gregorian calendar for convenient reference to solar events. The English settlers of New England used the Julian calendar until 1752.

    Heliacal rise date: the first day on which a star is visible, having been invisible for a time because of its proximity to the sun, near the eastern horizon before sunrise.

    Heliacal set date: the last day on which a star is visible near the western horizon after sunset.

    Acronical rise date: the last day on which a star is visible near the eastern horizon after sunset.

    Acronical set date: the first day on which a star is visible near the western horizon before sunrise.

19. Observations and calculations of heliacal dates differ by as much as several days depending upon light conditions, and elevation, so we cannot be more precise here. We have been guided in part by careful field observations by Anthony Aveni and his associates. Anthony F. Aveni, *Skywatchers of Ancient Mexico* (Austin: University of Texas, 1980), 116.

20. R. T. Zuidema, "Catachillay," in *Ethnoastronomy and Archaeoastronomy in the American Tropics*, ed. Anthony F. Aveni and Gary Urton, *Annals of the New York Academy of Sciences* 385 (1982).

21. J. Broda, "Astronomy, Cosmovision and Ideology in pre-Hispanic Mesoamerica," in _Ethnoastronomy and Archaeoastronomy in the American Tropics_, ed. Anthony F. Aveni and Gary Urton, _Annals of the New York Academy of Sciences_ 385 (1982).

22. S. Tarrow, "Translation of the Cellere Codex," in L. C. Wroth, _The Voyages of Giovanni de Verrazzano_ (New Haven: Yale, 1970).

23. Roger Williams, _A Key to the Language of America_ (London: 1643).

24. R. J. Burnham, _Burnham's Celestial Handbook, Vol III_ (New York: Dover, 1978).

25. A. L. Kroeber, _Handbook of the Indians of California_ (New York: Dover, 1976), 75.

26. R. J. Ford, "Gardening and Farming before A.D. 1000: Patterns of Prehistoric Cultivation North of Mexico," _Journal of Ethnology_ 1 (no. 1, 1981): 6–27.

3. Stone Mounds in Massasoit's Domain

1. Eric Sloane, _The Seasons of America's Past_ (New York: Wilfred Funk, 1958).

2. _Atlas of Boundary Lines of Bristol County_ (Taunton: Bristol County Commissioners).

3. James W. Mavor, Jr., and Byron E. Dix, "Ritual Stones of Cape Cod," _Cape Naturalist_ 2 (no. 1, 1982): 2–12. Also, James W. Mavor, Jr., and William M. Dunkle, Jr., _Falmouth Historical Commission Archaeological Resource Report_ (Falmouth: 27 February 1981).

4. Letter from Mass. Historical Commission to William M. Dunkle, Jr. (1979).

5. F. Freeman, _The History of Cape Cod, Vol. 2_ (Boston: 1860). James W. Mavor, Jr., and William M. Dunkle, Jr., "Rediscovered Indian Rock Was a Colonial Landmark," _Falmouth Enterprise_ (15 February 1980); 1, 6.

6. Cecilia D. Fuglister, "Fragment of a poem found in the papers of Albert S. Bowerman, given to Arnold B. Gifford, April 1968," (Unpublished note, 1968). Also, Indian Shanks is referred to in C. W. Jenkins, _Three Lectures on the History of the Town of Falmouth_ (Falmouth: 1843).

7. James W. Mavor, Jr., "Stone Mounds and Stone Rows," in Mary L. Smith, ed., _The Book of Falmouth_ (Falmouth: Falmouth Historical Commission, 1986).

8. Milton Travers, _The Wampanoag Indian Federation_ (Boston: Christopher), 29.

9. Fred Rhines, "Indian Burial Site Found," _The Herald-News_ (Fall River, 17 June 1983): 1.

10. E. Almeida, "Director says Indian 'burial site' not authentic," _The Providence Journal_ (22 June 1983): Sec. B, p. 1.

11. Gretchen Fehrenbacher, "State spurns Indian theory, won't study Freetown rocks," _The Standard Times_ (New Bedford, 25 June 1983): 5.

12. Gretchen Fehrenbacher, "Freetown won't step into dispute over stone mounds," _The Standard Times_ (New Bedford, 26 July 1983).

13. F. Huntington, et al, _Preliminary Report on the Excavation of Flagg Swamp Rock Shelter_ (Cambridge: Institute for Conservation Archaeology, Harvard University, 1982).

14. Carbon 14 samples are identified as Geochron Company Numbers GX–9783 and GX–9784.

15. C. K. Wilbur, _The New England Indians_ (Chester, Connecticut: Globe-Pequot, 1978), 24, 77. William S. Fowler, "Spirit Worship," _Narragansett Archaeological Society of Rhode Island_ (June, 1982): 9. Numerous excavation reports such as: W. A. Ritchie, _The Archaeology of Martha's Vineyard_ (Garden City, New York: Natural History, 1969). Maurice M. Robbins, "Wapanucket," _Massachusetts Archaeological Society_ (1980). James P. Whittall II, "Excavation — Monolith A Site, South Royalton, Vermont," _Early Sites Research Society Bulletin_ 11 (no. 1, 1984): 35.

16. Byron E. Dix and James W. Mavor, Jr., "Heliolithic Ritual Sites in New England," _New England Antiquities Research Association Journal_ 16 (no. 3, 1982): 75.

17. Frank Waters, _Book of the Hopi_ (Ballantine, 1963), 39.

18. The soil down to 2½ feet is clearly stratified into a top layer, 4 inches of loam, a middle layer, 2 feet of yellow-orange sand, and a lower layer, a light-grey sand and gravel. The pH was an acidic 5.25 throughout the soil profile and phosphorus and nitrogen contents were very low.

19. Robbins, "Wapanucket," 1980.

20. J. Josselyn, *An Account of Two Voyages to New England Made During the Years 1638, 1663* (Boston: Veazie, 1865), 157.

21. O. Fowler, *An Historical Sketch of Fall River, with notices of Freetown and Tiverton* (Fall River: B. Earl, 1841), 59.

22. A. S. Philips, *The Philips History of Fall River, Fascicle 1* (New York: Dover, 1941), 127–135.

23. Fowler, *Fall River* (1841): 12, 13.

24. Benjamin Church, *The History of King Philip's War*, ed. H. M. Dexter (Boston, 1865).

25. Fowler, *Fall River*, 1841, 60,61. Philips, *Fall River*, 1941. H. M. Fenner, *History of Fall River* (New York: Smiley, 1906), 14.

26. *Plymouth Colony General Court Records* 6 (no. 44, March, 1681). "Plan titled Pocasset Purchase," *Freetown Historical Society* (Freetown, 1747). "Layout of the Great Lots in Tiverton with a highway, etc., 1715," Document No. 172 of the Rev. Pardon Gray Seabury Collection, New Bedford Free Public Library (New Bedford, Mass.).

27. Original 1715 deed of Great Lots of Pocasset Outlet, Tiverton, in archives of the New Bedford Free Public Library, part of the Gray Collection of manuscripts.

28. H. A. Dubuque, *Fall River Indian Reservation* (Fall River: 1907), 39.

29. Dubuque, *Fall River*, 1907, 4, 30. Philips, *Fall River*, 1941.

30. Dubuque, *Fall River*, 1907, 39.

31. Fowler, *Fall River*, 1841, 37–41.

4. Native American Traditions of Stone and Earthworks

1. Thomas Morton, "New English Canaan or New Canaan," in Charles F. Adams, *The New English Canaan of Thomas Morton* (Boston: The Prince Society, 1883), 173.

2. J. R. Stilgoe, *Common Landscapes in America, 1580–1845* (New Haven: Yale University, 1982).

3. Amelia F. Emerson, *Early History of Naushon Island* (Boston: Howland, 1981), 354, 361.

4. Benjamin F. Wilbour, *Notes on Little Compton* (Little Compton, Rhode Island: Little Compton Historical Society, 1970), 28. Ida S. Proper, *Monhegan, The Cradle of New England* (Portland, Maine: Southworth, 1930), 224.

5. A. Edwards, *Cape Cod, New and Old* (1918), 226.

6. F. W. Huntington, et al, *Preliminary Report on the Excavation of Flagg Swamp Rock Shelter* (Cambridge: Institute for Conservation Archaeology, Harvard University, 1982).

7. Joan H. Carmody, "Paper on the Nipmuck Indians," *Worcester Historical Society Bulletin* 3 (no.7, 1964): 37–45. James W. Mavor, Jr., and William. M. Dunkle, Jr., "The Stone Piles of Falmouth, Massachusetts," *Second Report to the Falmouth Planning Board* (February 20, 1981). James W. Mavor, Jr., and William M. Dunkle, Jr., *Falmouth Historical Commission Archaeological Resource Report*, (Falmouth, Massachusetts: Feb. 27, 1981). James W. Mavor, Jr., and Byron E. Dix, "Ritual Stones of Cape Cod," *The Cape Naturalist* 2 (no. 1, 1982): 6–12. James W. Mavor, Jr., and Byron E. Dix, "New England Stone Mounds as Ritual Architecture," *Early Sites Research Society Bulletin* 10 (no. 2, 1983): 2–12.

8. Francis Jennings, *The Invasion of America* (New York: Norton, 1976).

9. Frank G. Speck, "The Memorial Brush Heaps in Delaware and Elsewhere," *Bulletin Archaeological Society of Delaware* 4 (no. 2, 1945): 19.

10. Byron E. Dix and James W. Mavor, Jr., "Stone Chambers, Indians and Astronomy," *Vermont History* 50 (no. 3, 1982): 181–191.

11. Speck, "Brush Heaps," 1945. E. G. Squier, "Aboriginal Monuments of the State of New York," *Smithsonian Contributions to Knowledge* 2 (Washington, D. C.: Smithsonian Institution, 1849): 67–74. J. W. DeForest, *History of the Indians of Connecticut.* (Hartford: Connecticut Historical Society, 1851). Frank Speck, "Native Tribes and Dialects of Connecticut — A Mohegan-Pequot Diary," *American Bureau of Ethnology* 43 (1924): 262, 263. J. C. Huden, *Indian Place Names in New England* (New York: Museum of the American Indian, 1962).

12. B. D. Keene, *History of Bourne* 184, (Yarmouthport, Mass.: 1937). C. E. Banks, *The History of Martha's Vineyard, Volume I* (Edgartown: Dukes County Historical Society, 1966), 229. B. O. K. Reeves, "Six Millenniums of Buffalo Kills," *Scientific American* 249 (no. 4, 1983): 120. B. Brown, "The Buffalo Drive," *Natural History* 32 (no. 1, 1932): 76.

13. Edward J. Lenik, "The Riddle of the Prehistoric Walls of Ramapo, New York," *New England Antiquities Research Association Journal* 10 (no. 3, 1974): 47–51. Salvatore M. Trento, "A Stone Cairn Excavation, Mastens Lake, New York," *Early Sites Research Society Bulletin* 9 (no. 1, 1981): 16, 17. Frank Glynn, "Excavation of the Pilot's Point Stone Heaps," *Bulletin of the Archaeological Society of Connecticut* (no. 38, August 1973): 77–89.

14. William C. Noble, "Vision Pits, Cairns and Petroglyphs at Rock Lake, Algonquin Provincial Park, Ontario," *Ontario Archaeology* 11 (1968): 58. J. R. Swanton, "Social Organization and Social Usage of the Indians of the Creek Confederacy," *Forty-Second Annual Report of the Bureau of American Ethnology* (1924–25): 391. D. I. Bushnell, "Archaeology of the Ozark Region of Missouri," *American Anthropologist* 6 (1904): 297. John Eddy, "Astronomical Alignment of the Big Horn Medicine Wheel," *Science* 184 (no. 4141, 1974): 1035–1043. A. B. Kehoe and T. F. Kehoe, "Solstice-Aligned Boulder Configurations in Saskatchewan," *Canadian Ethnology Service, National Museum of Man, Ottawa* Paper Number 48 (1979): 32–39. J. W. Fewkes, "Hopi Shrines Near The East Mesa, Arizona." *American Anthropology* 8 (1906): 346–375. J. L. Chartkoff, "A Rock Feature Complex from Northwestern California," *American Antiquity* 46 (no. 4, 1983): 745–760.

15. William B. Goodwin, *The Ruins of Great Ireland in New England* (Boston: Meador, 1946), 35, 36.

16. Giovanna Neudorfer, *Vermont's Stone Chambers, An Inquiry Into Their Past* (Montpelier: Vermont Historical Society, 1980). Revised from 1979 version, *Vermont's Stone Chambers: Their Myth and their History.*

17. L. H. Morgan, in "Houses and Home-Life of the American Aborigines," *Bureau of American Ethnology* 4 (1881), doubted that any North American Indians could quarry stone for building purposes and claimed that they were unable to erect permanent structures in stone.

18. Byron E. Dix and James W. Mavor, Jr., "Stone Chambers, Indians and Astronomy," *Vermont History* 50 (no. 3, 1982).

19. Neudorfer, *Stone Chambers*, 6.

20. Jennings, *Invasion of America*.

21. H. S. Nourse, *The History of Harvard, Mass. 1732–1893* (Clinton, Massachusetts: Printed for W. Hapgood by W. O. Coulder, 1894).

22. Douglas E. Leach, *Flintlock and Tomahawk* (New York: Norton, 1958), 127.

G. M. Bodge, *The Narragansett Fort Fight, Dec. 19, 1675* (Boston: 1886). C. R. Woodward, *Plantation Yankeeland* (Rhode Island: Cocumscussoc Association, 1971), 39. N. S., *A Continuation of the State of New England* (Boston: 1676), 96.

23. C. G. Calloway, "Rhode Island Renegade: The Enigma of Joshua Tefft," *Rhode Island History* 43 (no. 4, November, 1984): 141.

24. *Rhode Island Historical Society Collections* SSV (no. 2, 1932): 35.

25. *Narragansett Historical Register* 1 (1882): 9.

26. H. B. Hammond, "Plan of Queen's Fort, 1865," *Rhode Island Historical Society Collections* 16 (no. 4, October 1923). S. S. Rider, *The Lands of Rhode Island as they were known to Canounicus and Miantunnomu* (Providence: author, 1904). "Ruins of the Wall of Queen's Fort," *Rhode Island Historical Collections* 24 (no. 4, October 1931). W. Kent, "Sketch of Queen's Fort," *Rhode Island Historical Collections* 16 (no. 2, April 1932).

27. E. G. Squier, "Aboriginal Monuments of the State of New York," *Smithsonian Contributions to Knowledge* (No. 2, 1849): 87.

28. Byron E. Dix and James W. Mavor, Jr., "Progress Report on New England Archaeo-astronomy," *Early Sites Research Society Bulletin* 10, (no. 2, 1983): 16. Figures 4–11, 4–12 and 4–13 are from E. G. Squier and E. H. Davis, "Ancient Monuments of the Mississippi Valley," *Smithsonian Contributions to Knowledge* (No. 1, 1848).

29. B. D. Keene, *History of Bourne from 1622–1937* (Yarmouthport: Swift, 1937), 63.

30. Samuel de Champlain, *(1603–1632) The Works of Samuel de Champlain, 6 volumes*, ed. H. P. Biggar (Toronto: The Champlain Society). John W. DeForest, *History of the Indians of Connecticut* (Hartford: Hamersley, 1853). Warren K. Moorehead, "Certain Peculiar Earthworks Near Andover, Massachusetts," *Bulletin of Philips Academy, Andover, Department of Archaeology* 5 (1912): 51–55. Charles C. Willoughby, "Certain Earthworks of Eastern Massachusetts," *American Anthropologist* N.S. 13. (1911): 566–576. Charles C. Willoughby, *Antiquities of the New England Indians* (Cambridge: Peabody Museum, 1935).

31. Ripley P. Bullen, "Forts, Boundaries, or Ha-Has?" *Massachusetts Archaeological Society Bulletin* 4 (no. 1, 1942).

32. Keene, *Bourne*, 180–183, 198.

33. O. Fowler, *An Historical Sketch of Fall River.* (Fall River: B. Earl, 1841). Also F. M. Peck and H. H. Earl, *Fall River and its Industries* (New York: Atlantic, 1877). Also, H. M. Fenner, *History of Fall River* (New York: Smiley, 1906), 54.

34. The ideal situation used for calculation was an elastic, circular cylinder on a flat support, such as is used for the design of roller bearings. See R. J. Roark, *Formulas for Stress and Strain* (New York: McGraw-Hill, 1938), 242–244. Typical properties of granite are: compressive strength, 19,000 psi; shear strength, 4,000 psi; Youngs Modulus of elasticity, 7,000,000 psi.

35. D. Guynes, "The British Antiquary and The Rocking Stone," *New England Antiquities Research Association Journal* 20 (no. 1 and 2, 1985): 1–17.

36. D. Kirkpatrick, *The City and The River* (Fitchburg: Fitchburg Historical Society, 1971), 49, 50.

37. *Lunenburg, The Heritage of Turkey Hills, 1718–1978* (Lunenburg: Lunenburg Historical Society, 1978).

5. The Land and the Sky

1. Declination is the angular distance of a celestial body north or south of the celestial equator, the projection of the earth's equator on the celestial sphere. Declination in

the sky corresponds to latitude on earth, and the declination of the celestial equator is zero, as is the latitude of the earth's equator. The sun follows the celestial equator on the days of the equinox.

2. Euan W. Mackie, *Science and Society in Prehistoric Britain* (New York: St. Martin's Press, 1977).

3. T. T. Waterman, "Yurok Geographical Concepts," in *California Indians*, ed. R. J. Heizer and M. R. Whipple (Berkeley: University of California Press, 1971), 472–474.

4. Thomas Morton, "The New English Canaan, 1637" in *The New English Canaan of Thomas Morton*, ed. Charles F. Adams, Jr. (Boston: The Prince Society, 1883), 172–173. Morton describes burning of the uplands twice a year, in spring and in fall, in order to provide easier passage through the forests. Only the wetlands retained their growth of large trees. Morton observed that trees in New England grew as they did in English parks.

5. G. M. Day, "The Indian as an Ecological Factor in the Northeastern Forest," *Ecology* 34 (no. 2, 1953): 334. C. Gamble, "The Artificial Wilderness," *New Scientist* (10 April, 1986): 50.

6. Francis Jennings, *The Invasion of America* (New York: Norton, 1976).

7. A. P. Kershaw, "Climatic change and aboriginal burning in north-east Australia during the last two glacial/interglacial cycles," *Nature* 322 (3 July 1986): 47–49.

8. R. Lewin, "Fragile Forests Implied by Pleistocene Pollen," *Science* 226 (5 October 1984): 36–37.

9. Kershaw, "Climatic change," 47–49.

10. Gamble, "Artificial Wilderness," 52.

11. LaVan Martineau, *The Rocks Begin To Speak*, (Las Vegas: K. C. Press, 1973), 13.

12. ibid., 38, 44.

13. ibid., 42, 43.

14. William A. Neilson, editor-in-chief, *Webster's New International Dictionary, Second Edition, Unabridged* (Springfield: Merriam, 1947), 49, 1268.

15. J. W. Deforest, *History of the Indians of Connecticut* (Hartford: Hammersley, 1853).

16. Douglas E. Leach, *Flintlock and Tomahawk* (New York: Norton, 1958). Good bibliography of King Philip's War.

17. Benjamin F. Wilbour, *Notes on Little Compton*, ed. Carlton C. Brownell (Little Compton: Little Compton Historical Society, 1970), 13.

18. Benjamin Church, *The History of King Philip's War, Part I*, ed. H. M. Dexter, (Boston: Wiggin, 1865), 50–52.

19. James W. Mavor, Jr., and Byron E. Dix, "New England Cedar Wetlands in Native American Ritual," in *Atlantic White Cedar Wetlands*, ed. Aimlee D. Laderman (Boulder: Westview, 1987).

20. W. K. Moorehead, "Certain Peculiar Earthworks near Andover, Massachusetts," *Bulletin V, Philips Academy* (Andover, 1912). Charles C. Willoughby, *Antiquities of the New England Indians* (Cambridge: Peabody Museum, 1935), 277–279.

21. Neal Salisbury, *Manitou and Providence* (New York: Oxford, 1982), 137.

22. J. L. Chartkoff, "A Rock Feature Complex from Northwestern California," *American Antiquity* 46 (no. 4, 1983). Also, William C. Noble, "Vision Pits, Cairns and Petroglyphs at Rock Lake, Algonquin Provincial Park, Ontario," *Ontario Archaeology* 11 (1968): 58. L. Bonfanti, *New England Indians* (Wakefield: Pride, 1970).

23. Ripley, P. Bullen, "Forts, Boundaries or Ha-Has?," *Massachusetts Archaeological Society Bulletin* 4 (no. 1, 1942). J. G. Gosselink and R. E. Turner, "Hydrology in Freshwater Wetland Ecosystems," in *Freshwater Wetlands*, ed. R. E. Good, D. F. Whigham and R. L. Simpson (New York: Academic Press, 1978), 63. Also M. W. Weller, "Management of Marshes for Wildlife," in *Freshwater Wetlands*, 275–278.

24. Frank Speck, "Native Tribes and Dialects of Connecticut," *American Bureau of Ethnology* 43 (1924): 262, 263. J. Josselyn, "An Account of Two Voyages to New England." *Collections of Massachusetts Historical Society, 3rd. Serial* 3 (1833): 211–354. (First published London 1675.)

25. J. C. Huden, *Indian Place Names in New England* (New York: Museum of the American Indian, 1962).

26. M. L. Norton, "The Story of Fall Mountain" and "Indians of Bristol and Vicinity," in *Bristol, Connecticut*, no author, (Hartford: 1907), 15, 125.

27. R. L. Myers and P. A. Peroni "Approaches to determining aboriginal fire use and its impact on vegetation," *Bulletin of the Ecological Society of America* 64 (no. 3): 217. Weller, "Management" and Gosselink and Turner, "Hydrology," in *Freshwater Wetlands*, 28. B. L. Turner, and P. D. Harrison, ed. *Maya Raised-Field Agriculture and Settlement at Pulltrouser Swamp* (Austin: University of Texas, 1984).

29. E. G. Squier, "Aboriginal Monuments of the State of New York," *Smithsonian Contributions to Knowledge* (no. 2, 1849): 67–74.

6. Indians Meet Jesuits, Pilgrims, Puritans and Quakers

1. C. L. Evans, "Early Breton Voyages to Canada," in *Proceedings of the First International Brendan Conference, 8–14 September, 1985, Trinity College, Dublin* (Dublin: in press). I. S. Proper, *Monhegan, The Cradle of New England* (Portland, Maine: 1930), 46, 56.

2. Proper, *Monhegan*, 43, 45, 49, 59, 75, 90, 111, 114, 130. Richard Hakluyt, *Hakluyt's Voyages* (New York: Viking, 1965), 293.

3. Francois DuCreux, *History of Canada or New France, Vol I* (Toronto: Champlain Society, 1951, Reprint of Paris: Cramoisy, 1664), xvi, 111–115. This book is the official summary of the Jesuit Relations covering the period 1625–1644. The most complete modern publication of the Jesuit Relations is Reuben G. Thwaites, ed., *The Jesuit Relations and Allied Documents: Travels and Explorations of the Jesuit Missionaries in New France, 1610–1791* (Cleveland: 1896–1901). This seventy-three volume work contains the original French, Latin and Italian texts with English translations and notes.

4. Joseph F. Lafitau, *Customs of the American Indians Compared with the Customs of Primitive Times, Volume I,* Translated into English by W. N. Fenton and E. C. Moore, (Toronto: Champlain Society, 1974), xlviii, 114, 129. Original Paris, 1724.

5. Armand Louis de Lahontan, *New Voyages to North America . . . Written in French . . . Done in English, Volume Two* (London: Bonwicke, Goodwin, Wotton, Tooke and Manship, 1703), 20.

6. Lafitau, *Customs, Volume I,* 171, citing Father DuTertre, *Historie Naturale des Antilles* (Traite 7, Part 3, Volume 2), 371.

7. Father Le Jeune, *Relation, Volume VI* (Paris: 1634), 191.

8. DuCreux, *History, Volume I,* 85, 90, 165–167, 197.

9. Christian LeClerq, *New Relations of Gasperia, with Customs and Religion of the Gaspesian Indians*, trans. W. F. Ganong (Toronto: Champlain Society, 1910), 215. Original, Paris, 1692.

10. Lafitau, *Customs, Volume I,* 154, 241, 243.

11. LeClerq, *Gasperia*, 137, 146, 190, 193.

12. Lafitau, *Customs, Volume I,* 217, 236.

13. Lafitau, *Customs, Volume I,* 219.

14. Lafitau, *Customs, Volume I,* 233, 234.

15. J. Norman Emerson, "The Puckasaw Pits and the Religious Alternative," *Ontario*

History 52 (no. 1, 1960): 71–72. William C. Noble, "Vision Pits, Cairns and Petro-glyphs at Rock Lake, Algonquin Provincial Park, Ontario," *Ontario Archaeology* 11 (1968): 63.

16. Thomas Morton, "New English Canaan or New Canaan," in Charles F. Adams, Jr., *The New English Canaan of Thomas Morton* (Boston: The Prince Society, 1883). Original edition, 1637. Also William Bradford, *History of Plymouth Plantation, 1620–1647* (New York: Knopf, 1963), 204–210. Original edition, 1648. Both Bradford and Morton wrote from observation about the activities at Ma-re Mount. Their perspectives were quite different; Bradford failed to mention that there was an old English pagan May Day festival. Our interpretations of Ma-re Mount and Morton are drawn from these two original sources.

17. Neal Salisbury, *Manitou and Providence* (New York: Oxford, 1982), 158.

18. Brian Branston, *The Lost Gods of England* (London: Thames and Hudson, 1974), 175, 189, 200.

19. Bradford, *Plymouth*, 26.

20. William Bradford and Edward Winslow, *Mourt's Relation or Journal of the Plantation at Plymouth*, ed. H. M. Dexter (Boston: H. M. Wiggin, 1865), 41. Original edition 1622, London.

21. Ibid., 1–59. Bradford, *Plymouth*, 1963, 64–72.

22. H. M. Dexter, in his introduction to the 1865 edition of *Mourt's Relation*, concluded that the events during the latter part of 1620, that is from September through March, for the year began on March 25 among the English until 1752, were chronicled by William Bradford (1590–1656), and those from March 25 through December, 1621, by Edward Winslow (1595–1654). Dexter concluded on page xviii that these journals were not intended to be printed, and furthermore were published without the authors' knowledge or consent. Most of the events were described also, with less detail and some conflicts, by Bradford between 1630 and 1646 in his *History of Plymouth Plantation* and in Nathaniel Morton's *New England's Memoriall*.

The dates of solar events with which we are concerned are given below in the Julian calendar of the time, ten days earlier than our present Gregorian calendar, and considering that the year started on March 25:

Winter solstice	December 11, 1620
Spring equinox	March 10, 1620
Summer solstice	June 11, 1621
Fall equinox	Sept. 13, 1621

All of the principal episodes involving contact with Indians, as selected by Bradford and Winslow, are given below:

Monday, Dec 11, 1620	Shallop's first landing at Plymouth.
Friday, Mar 16, 1620	Samoset arrives at Plymouth.
Thursday, Mar 22, 1620	Massasoit and party of sixty including Squanto arrive at Plymouth.
Monday, Jun 11, 1621	Winslow, Hopkins and Squanto meet with Massasoit at Sowams.
	Journey to seek lost boy among Nausets.
Tuesday, Aug 14, 1621	Journey to Nemaschet in defense of Massasoit against Narragansetts and to avenge supposed death of Squanto.
Thursday, Sep 13, 1621	Nine sachems affirm allegiance to King James. All sent messengers to this end at once.

Tuesday, Sep 18, 1621   Voyage to Massachusetts in shallop.
Tuesday, Dec 11, 1621   Winslow wrote annual report letter to England.

Bradford, who reportedly wrote that Hopkins, Winslow and Squanto set out for Massasoit's home on June 10, wrote also between ten and twenty-five years later that it occurred on July 2. Dexter, *Mourt's* editor, prefers the later date because June 10 was a Sunday and the Pilgrims would not have started out on the Sabbath. The narrative of the journey, which lasted five days round trip, identifies the third and fourth days as Thursday and Friday, days which fit neither a June 10 or a July 2 start. We do know that the party was anxious to reach Massasoit on the second day, which, *Mourt* claims was June 11, and pushed on late on the first day on Squanto's advice in order to accomplish this.

In a conflict between Winslow's portion of the *Relation* and Bradford's writings decades later, Winslow lists Squanto as guide and himself as a participant in the search for a lost boy among the Nausets, which they began on June 11. Bradford does not specify who went on this journey and dates the event to late July. Morton's *New England's Memorial* (1667) lists Hobomock and Tuckamahanon without Squanto and gives no date.

Mourt's Relation stands as the earliest and most authoritative source, and the coincidence of episodic and solar dates stands regardless of how the inconsistencies between accounts are resolved.

23. Nathaniel Morton, *New England's Memoriall* (Boston: Crocker and Brewster, 1826), 55, 62, 63. Fifth ed., originally published 1667 at Cambridge, Massachusetts. Also Bradford, *Plymouth*, 84.
24. E. Altham, "Letter to Sir Edward Altham September, 1623," in S. V. James, Jr., *Three Visitors to Early Plymouth* (Plymouth: Plimoth Plantation, 1963).
25. W. T. Davis, *Ancient Landmarks of Plymouth* (Boston: William, 1883), 154.
26. The stonework along Beaver Dam Brook was discovered by the late Stanley Deane and by Martin Abramo of Whitehorse Beach, Massachusetts.
27. Frank Speck, "Native Tribes and Dialects of Connecticut," *American Bureau of Ethnology* 43 (1924): 262, 263.
28. E. H. Byington, *The Puritans in England and New England* (Boston: 1897), 43.
29. The source for the material on John Eliot, unless otherwise noted, is D. E. Winslow, *John Eliot, Apostle to the Indians* (Boston: Houghton-Mifflin, 1968).
30. W. E. Thwing, *History of the First Church in Roxbury, Massachusetts 1630–1904* (Boston: Butterfield, 1908), 31.
31. Michael J. Crawford, *History of Natick, Massachusetts, 1650–1976* (Natick: Natick Historical Commission, 1976), 10. Also, *Natick Milestones* (Natick: Natick Public Schools, 1963), 21.
32. A. C. Bouquet, *Comparative Religion* (London: Pelican, 1953).
33. E. Hall, *The Ancient Historical Records of Norwalk, Connecticut* (Norwalk: Mallory, 1847), 52.
34. Daniel Gookin, "Historical Collections of the Indians in New England," *Collections of the Massachusetts Historical Society, First Serial* (1792): 141–227.
35. Clara E. Sears, *The Great Powwow: The Story of the Nashaway Valley in King Philip's War* (Boston: Houghton-Mifflin, 1934), 174, 190.
36. George M. Bodge, *Soldiers in King Philip's War* (Leominster: Author, 1896), 393, 396.
37. F. S. Drake, *The Town of Roxbury* (Roxbury: Privately printed, 1878), 181.
38. An antiquarian, *Blue Laws of New Haven Colony; Quaker Laws of Plymouth and Massachusetts; Blue Laws of New York, Maryland, Virginia, and South Carolina* (Hartford: 1838).

39. Unless otherwise noted the sources for material on Martha's Vineyard are Charles E. Banks, *Martha's Vineyard, Vol. 1* (Edgartown: Dukes County Historical Society, 1966), 12, 117, 214–216, 219, 221, 237, 238, 496–498; and Banks, *Martha's Vineyard, Vol. 2, Town Annals*; Edgartown, 19, 67–69, 83, 149, 170, 171; West Tisbury, 117; Chilmark, 17, 24, 35, 73; Tisbury, 31, 38, 131; Oak Bluffs, 24. The quotations from Thomas Mayhew, Jr., are taken from H. Whitfield, "The Light Appearing more and more toward the perfect day," in *Massachusetts Historical Collections, Third Serial* 4 (1651): 109, 110.

40. William S. Simmons, "Conversion from Indian to Puritan," *The New England Quarterly* 52 (no. 2, 1979): 209.

41. Daniel Gookin, *Massachusetts Historical Collections* 1 (1674): 141–227. C. E. Swift, "Cape Cod, the Right Arm of Massachusetts," in *Register, Yarmouth, Massachusetts* (1897): 93.

42. Francis Jennings, *The Ambiguous Iroquois* (New York: Norton, 1984), 367, 368.

43. Ibid., 126–134.

44. J. F. A. Smith, *The History of Pittsfield, Massachusetts from the year 1734 to 1800* (Boston: Lee and Shepard, 1869). D. K. Richter, "Rediscovered Links in the Covenent Chain: Previously Unpublished Transcripts of New York Indian Treaty Minutes, 1677-1691," *Proceedings of the American Antiquarian Society* 92 (Part 1. April, 1982): 60, 61. Jennings, *Iroquois*, 148, 194.

7. The Eighteenth Century

1. Edmund S. Morgan, *The Gentle Puritan* (New York: Norton, 1983).

2. R. Terry, "Ezra Stiles," in *Early Religious Leaders of Newport, Eight Addresses of 1917* (Newport: Newport Historical Society, 1918), 149.

3. Ezra Stiles, "A Birthday Memoir," (1767).

4. A. Holmes, *Life of Ezra Stiles* (Boston: 1798).

5. W. Walker, *A History of the Christian Church,* (New York: Scribners, 1918), 487. J. S. Judah, *The History and Philosophy of the Metaphysical Movements in America* (1967), 23.

6. M. E. Marty, *Pilgrims in Their Own Land* (Boston: Little Brown, 1984), 110.

7. Ezra Stiles, *The Literary Diary of Ezra Stiles, Volume 1, 1777–1781* (New York: Scribners, 1901), 76. J. M. Davidson, *Muh-he-ka-ne-ok, A History of the Stockbridge Nation* (Milwaukee: Chapman, 1893), xvii.

8. Stiles *Literary Diary*, Volume 1, p. 385.

9. Morgan, *Puritan*, p. 167.

10. Ezra Stiles, *The Literary Diary of Ezra Stiles, Volume 2,* (New York: Scribners, 1901), 424. Stiles, *Literary Diary, Volume 3*. E. G. Squier, "Aboriginal Monuments of the State of New York," *Smithsonian Contributions to Knowledge* 2 (1849): 162, 163.

11. Ezra Stiles, *Itineraries* (New Haven: Yale University, 1916) 385.

12. A. C. Bouquet, *Comparative Religion* (London: Pelican, 1953), 252.

13. The primary sources for material in this section are:

Electa F. Jones, *Stockbridge, Past and Present: or Records of an Old Mission Station* (Springfield: 1854), 47, 52, 67, 68, 86, 90, 101, 131. Jones reports events over a 120 year period, up to 1851. We infer that she supports the idea of Christianizing Indians so that they may live in fellowship with the white settlers. She is critical of the white man's treatment of the Indians in forcing them further and further west, but she attributes this to whites who do not meet her New Light Puritan standards. Jones also believed, as did many of her contemporaries, that the Stockbridge Indians were descendants of a lost tribe of Israel. She also held that both the

Indians and the English settlers were descendants of ancient Scythians. As a result of these views, there is a large and obvious gap in Jones' book, the pre-Christian life and beliefs of the Indians. While, on the one hand, there is a wealth of detail about the Indians which is rare in a New England town history, it is confined entirely to the views of Christian missionaries.

   C. J. Taylor, *History of Great Barrington, Massachusetts* (Great Barrington: Bryan, 1882), 55, 56, 61, 73, 75.

   J. M. Davidson, *Muh-he-ka-ne-ok, A History of the Stockbridge Nation* (Milwaukee: Chapman, 1893), ix, 2, 13, 16. This book draws on the oral history of the remnant of Stockbridge Indians who settled in Wisconsin and is authoritative for the westward migration of this unique group.

   D. D. Field, *An Historical Sketch, Congregational, of the Church in Stockbridge, Massachusetts* (New York: John Gray, 1853), 7, 10.

14. J. W. Barber, *Historical Collections of Massachusetts* (Worcester: Dorr, Howland, 1839).
15. Jones, *Stockbridge*, 62.
16. G. C. Niles, *The Hoosac Valley* (New York: Putnam, 1912), 8.
17. E. W. C. Campbell, "An Archaeological Survey of the Twenty-Nine Palms Region," *Southwest Museum, Los Angeles, Paper* (no. 7, 1931): 24–39.
18. Jones, *Stockbridge*, 42.
19. Taylor, *Great Barrington*, 63.
20. Ibid., 64. Also Francis Jennings, *The Invasion of America* (New York: Norton, 1976), 135, 136.
21. Jones, *Stockbridge*, 56.
22. R. M. Willett, *Scenes in the Wilderness: Labours and Sufferings of the Moravian Missionaries among the North American Indians* (New York: Sandford, 1842), 10–187.
23. C. A. Weslager, quoted in William H. Wroten, Jr., *Assateaque* (Centreville: Tidewater, 1972), 9, 10. S. Tarrow, in L. C. Wroth, "Translation of the Cellere Codex," in C. Wroth, *The Voyage of Giovanni Verrazzano* (New Haven: Yale University, 1970).
24. P. Whitesinger, *Navajo Poster* (1986).
25. Fawn M. Brodie, *Noone Knows My History* (New York: Knopf, 1945).

8. Shakers and Shamanistic Christianity

1. Edward D. Andrews, *The People Called Shakers* (New York: Dover, 1963), 169.
2. Unless otherwise noted, the material on Mother Ann Lee is from (No author) *Testimonies of the Life, Character, Revelations and Doctrines of Mother Ann Lee, and the elders with her* (Albany, New York: Weed and Parsons, 1888), 3, 4, 5, 8, 10, 55–57, 65, 101, 135–141, 161, 262–266.
3. Mark Holloway, *Heavens On Earth* (New York: Dover, 1966), 64. J. G. Davies, P. van Zyl and F. M. Young, *A Shaker Dance Service Reconstructed* (Birmingham, Alabama: Institute for the Study of Worship and Religious Architecture, University of Birmingham, 1984).
4. Nicholas Tolstoy, *The Quest for Merlin* (London: Hamilton, 1985), 141.
5. Andrews, *Shakers*, 300.
6. Andrews, *Shakers*, 301.
7. Andrews, *Shakers*, 49.
8. Edward R. Horgan, *The Shaker Holy Land* (Harvard, Massachusetts: Harvard Common, 1987), 38.

9. Andrews, *Shakers*, 78. R. E. Whitson, *Shaker Theological Studies* (Bethlehem, Connecticut: The United Institute, 1969), 7.

10. J. P. Maclean, "Shakers of Ohio," in *Fugitive Papers Concerning the Shakers of Ohio With Unpublished Manuscripts*, (Columbus, Ohio: Heer Printing, 1907), 366.

11. Material on the Shawnee Prophet is from R. D. Edmund, *The Shawnee Prophet* (Lincoln, Nebraska: University of Nebraska, 1983), 22, 24–29, 33, 36–40, 42–54, 93–116, 189. Edmund cites letters between General Harrison and the Secretary of War and disagrees with some popular histories and encyclopedias.

12. McNemar's visit to Greenville and the Indians' visit to Turtle Creek are from Maclean, "Shakers of Ohio," 353–358. Maclean quotes an unpublished report by McNemar, who based his narrative on his own journal and those of David Darrow and Benjamin Youngs.

13. *Shaker Journal of Union Village, 1805–1890*. A microfilm copy of hand-written records from various sources in archive of Warren County Historical Society Museum Library, Lebanon, Ohio, Aug. 12 and 29, 1807.

14. Maclean, "Shakers of Ohio," 360.

15. R. E. Whitson, *Shaker Theological Studies* (Bethlehem, Conn.: The United Institute, 1969), i–v.

16. S. C. Goodrich, *A Pictorial History of America* (Hartford: E. Strong, 1844), 710, 711.

17. A. White, and L. S. Taylor, *Shakerism: Its Meaning and Message* (Columbus, Ohio: Heer Press, 1910), 118.

18. Andrews, *Shakers*, 292.

19. Unless otherwise noted the sources for the Shaker revival are: Andrews, *Shakers*, 43, 157, 158, 161, 162, 165, 166, 168–170; Maclean, "Shakers of Ohio," 389, 392, 394, 396–400, 402; Horgan, *Holy Land*, 71–80; and *Shaker Journal*, 12 February 1837, 13 September 1838, 7 and 13 January, 1839, May, 1839, 1 September 1842. Andrews is the source for the Hancock ritual and Horgan for that at Harvard. Figure 8–7 is from David Lamson, *Two Years Experience Among the Shakers* (West Boylston, Mass.: by author, 1848).

20. D. M. Filley, *Recapturing Wisdom's Valley* (Albany, New York: Albany Institute of History and Art, Publishing Center for Cultural Resources, 1975).

21. H. S. Philips, *The Shakers* (Lebanon, Ohio: Warren County Historical Society, 1959), 9.

22. Transcribed by J. W. Mavor, Jr., from the photograph published in Horgan, *Holy Land*, 87.

23. Robert P. Emlen, *Shaker Village Views* (Hanover: University Press of New England, 1987), 107, 108.

24. A. L. Kroeber, *Handbook of the Indians of California* (New York: Dover, 1976), 53–57, 69, 70.

25. The source for the material on the Slocums and Indian Shakers is H. G. Barnett, *Indian Shakers* (Carbondale, Illinois: Southern Illinois University, 1957), 14, 26, 58, 64, 139, 142, 204, 260, 334, 440.

26. Julian Jaynes, *The Origin of Consciousness in the Breakdown of the Bicameral Mind* (Boston: Houghton Mifflin, 1976), 4, 440.

27. Electa F. Jones, *Stockbridge, Past and Present* Springfield: Massachusetts, 1854).

28. Andrews, *Shakers*, 169.

29. Horgan, *Holy Land*, 41.

9. Stoneworks in North America, Europe and the Arctic

1. E. G. Squier, and E. H. Davis, "Ancient Monuments of the Mississippi Valley," *Smithsonian Contributions to Knowledge* (no. 1, 1848). O. H. Prufer, "The Hopewell Cult," *Scientific American* (December, 1964). G. H. Perkins, "On an Ancient Burial Ground in Swanton, Vermont," *Proceedings of the American Association for the Advancement of Science* 22 (1873): 76–100. P. Fetchko, J. Grimes and W. Phippen, *Stone Age in New England* (Salem, Mass.: Peabody Museum, 1976), 21.

2. Peter Farb, *Man's Rise to Civilization as Shown by the Indians of North America from Primeval Times to the Coming of the Industrial State* (New York: Dutton, 1968), 222, 223.

3. R. G. Morgan, *Fort Ancient* (Columbus: Ohio Historical Society, 1965), 13, 15.

4. J. P. Hale, *History and Mystery of the Kanawha Valley* (Charleston, West Virginia: West Virginia Historical and Antiquarian Society, 1897), 10–12. J. P. Hale, *Some Local Archaeology* (Charleston, West Virginia: West Virginia Historical and Antiquarian Society, 1898), 7–14. H. C. Shetrone, *The Mound Builders* (New York: Appleton, 1930), 240, 241.

5. E. G. Squier, "Aboriginal Monuments of the State of New York," *Smithsonian Contributions to Knowledge* (no. 2, 1849): 67–74. Francis Parkman, *The Old Regime in Canada, Part IV* (Boston: Little Brown, 1922), 410, 414, 445.

6. D. B. Rogers, *Prehistoric Man of the Santa Barbara Coast* (Santa Barbara: Santa Barbara Museum of Natural History, 1929). L. G. Yates, "Charmstones or Plummets from California," *Annual Report of the Smithsonian Institution* (Washington, D. C., 1889): 296–305.

7. A. L. Kroeber, *Handbook of the Indians of California* (New York: Dover, 1976), 638, 936. W. S. Fowler, "Significant Plummet Discoveries," *Massachusetts Archaeological Society Bulletin* 36 (1975): 31. Charles C. Willoughby, *Antiquities of the New England Indians* (Cambridge: Peabody Museum, 1935).

8. Charlotte McGowan, "Ceremonial Fertility Sites in Southern California," *San Diego Museum Paper* (no. 14, 1982): 17.

9. Joseph L. Chartkoff, and Kerry K. Chartkoff, *The Archaeology of California* (Stanford: Stanford University, 1984), 209, 211. F. Starr, *American Indians* (Boston: Heath, 1899), 174.

10. Joseph L. Chartkoff, "A Rock Feature Complex from Northwestern California," *American Antiquity* 46 (no. 4, 1983): 746–753.

11. Chartkoff and Chartkoff, *Archaeology*, 1984, 211.

12. Kroeber, *Handbook*, 1976, 109–120. Chartkoff, "Rock Feature," 1983, 757.

13. Kroeber, *Handbook*, 1976, 794. J. Walter Fewkes, "Hopi Shrines Near the East Mesa, Arizona," *American Anthropology* 8 (1906): 350, 358.

14. J. Walter Fewkes, "Antiquities of the Mesa Verde National Park," *Smithsonian Institution Bureau of American Ethnology Bulletin* 51 (1911).

15. Marquis de Nadaillac, *Pre-Historic America* (New York: Putnam, 1884), 209.

16. P. F. F. Gladwin, "Discoveries at Brainport Bay, Minard, Argyll," *The KIST*, Natural History and Antiquarian Society of Mid-Argyll (no. 16, Autumn 1978); "Thoughts on the Use of the Brainport Bay Structures," *The KIST*, (no. 19, Spring 1980).

17. Euan W. Mackie, P. F. F. Gladwin and A. E. Roy, "A Prehistoric Site in Argyll?" *Nature* 314 (no. 14, March 1985): 158–161.

18. Byron E. Dix, and James W. Mavor, Jr., "Two Possible Calendar Sites in Vermont," in *Archaeoastronomy in the Americas*, ed. R. Williamson (Los Altos, California: Ballena Press Anthropological Papers No. 22., 1981).

19. S. Cruden, *The Early Christian and Pictish Monuments of Scotland* (Edinburgh: Her Majesty's Stationery Office, 1964).

20. E. Stewart, *Dunkeld, An Ancient City* (Dunkeld: Burns, 1926), 15.

21. James W. Mavor, Jr., "Astronomy and Shamanism Among the Culdee Monks," *Bulletin Early Sites Research Society* 12 (no. 1, 1985): 2–17.

22. Christopher Bamford, "The Heritage of Celtic Christianity," *Lindisfarne Letter 13* (West Stockbridge: Lindisfarne, 1982): 10, 11.

23. Mavor, "Culdee Monks," 1985.

24. Gladwin, "Thoughts," *KIST*, 1980.

25. Cruden, *Pictish Monuments*, 1964.

26. Stewart, *Dunkeld*, 1926.

27. A sampling of reports can be found in the following issues of the *Bulletin of the Early Sites Research Society*: 5, (no. 1, Feb. 1977), 6 (no. 1, May 1978), 8 (no. 1, June 1980), 10 (no. 1, Dec. 1982), 10 (no. 2, Dec. 1983), 11 (no. 1, Dec. 1984). Also, *Sean Seomrai Cloiche De an nua-shasana* (Rowley: Early Sites Research Society, 1977).

28. P. Coste, *Pierre Seche en Provence* (Forcalquier: Les Alpes de Lumiere, 1986).

29. Arthur Mitchell, *The Past in the Present* (New York: Harper, 1881).

30. J. J. O'Meara, *The Voyage of Saint Brendan*, translated from Latin (Ireland: Dolmen, 1985). Also, Tim Severin, *The Brendan Voyage* (New York: McGraw-Hill, 1978).

31. James W. Mavor, Jr., and Byron E. Dix, "An Icelandic Horizon Calendar, Key to Vinland," *Proceedings of Brendan Conference*, (Dublin, Ireland, 1989).

32. Mavor, "Culdee Monks," 1985.

33. Barry Fell, *America B. C.* (New York: Quadrangle, 1976).

34. P. Jenness, "The Life of the Copper Eskimo," *Report of the Canadian Arctic Expedition 1913–1918, Vol XII* (Ottawa: 1922), 179. T. W. Knox, *The Voyage of the Vivian* (1884). K. Leem, *Beskrivelse over Finnmarkens Lapper* (1767).

35. A. Brekke, and A. Egeland, *The Northern Night* (Berlin: Springer Verlag, 1983). S. I. Akasofu, *Aurora Borealis* (Alaska Geographic Society, 1979).

36. A. Rothery, *Iceland, Bastion of the North* (London: Melrose, 1948).

37. A. Spencer, *The Lapps* (New York: Crane-Russack).

38. ibid.

39. E. G. Squier, "Aboriginal Monuments of the State of New York," *Smithsonian Contributions to Knowledge*, Vol 2 (1849). Henry R. Schoolcraft, *Historical and statistical information, respecting the history, condition, and prospects of the Indian tribes of the United States, Vol I–VI* (Philadelphia, 1851–57). J. L. Kessel, *Kiva, Cross and Crown* (Washington: National Park Service, 1979). H. J. Priestly, ed. *A Historical, Political and Natural Description of California by Pedro Fages, Soldier of Spain* (Berkeley: University of California Press, 1937). E. G. Squier, *Transactions AAAS* (III): 192.

40. A. L. Kroeber, *Handbook*, 1976, 64–66, 80.

41. William Fitzhugh, "Maritime Archaic Cultures of the Central and Northern Labrador Coast," *Arctic Anthropology* XV (no. 2, 1978): 61–95.

10. Earthquakes and Vision Quests in Mohegan Lands

1. G. C. Niles, *The Hoosac Valley* (New York: Putnam, 1912), 6, 7. N. Greene, "Fort Plain-Nelliston History," *Fort Plain-Nelliston Historical Society* (Publication No. 5, Fort Plain, N. Y., 1947): 19.

2. Niles, *Hoosac*, 8–14, 30, 41, 106. Thomas N. Lewis and Madeline Kneberg, *Hiwassee Island*, (Knoxville: University of Tennessee, 1946), 1.

3. J. F. A. Smith, *The History of Pittsfield, Massachusetts, from the Year 1734 to 1800* (Boston: Lee and Shepard, 1869), 25, 28, 45.

4. G. Greylock, *Taghonic; The Romance and Beauty of the Hills* (Boston: Lee and Shepard, 1879), 78–83.

5. William S. Simmons, *Spirit of the New England Tribes* (Hanover, New Hampshire: University Press of New England, 1986), 42.

6. Frank G. Speck, "Native Tribes and Dialects of Connecticut — A Mohegan-Pequot Diary," *American Bureau of Ethnology* 43 (1924): 205–280.

7. Niles, *Hoosac*, 23–25.

8. See Francis Jennings, *The Invasion of America* (New York: Norton, 1976); also Richard Drinnon, *Facing West: The Metaphysics of Indian Hating and Empire Building* (Minneapolis: University of Minnesota Press, 1980); also Frances M. Caulkins, *History of New London, Connecticut, from first survey of the coast in 1612 to 1852* (New London: 1852).

   The contrast between European and Native American concepts of warfare at this time is striking, as evidenced by an incident related by Caulkins. On the 16th of May, 1637, John Mason's troops destroyed the Pequot stronghold at the head of the Mystic River. During the march south to Pequot Harbor, the troops were continually harassed by Pequots but no one was killed. During the march, Mason's Mohegan allies encountered Pequots who shot their arrows high into the air and waited until they came to earth before firing another. Mason wrote, "They might fight seven years and not kill seven men."

   Another incident which illustrates the nature of Indian "warfare" before the coming of the white man and firearms took place on the shores of Lake Champlain between Algonquian and Iroquois groups and showed that skirmishes were highly ritualized and seldom was anyone hurt. There was much exchange of threats and insults and out-of-range shooting of arrows; results were seldom decisive. This ceremonial venting of anger was replaced by guerilla warfare brought by the English and French. (C. G. Calloway, "Green Mountain Diaspora: Indian Population Movements in Vermont, c. 1600–1800," *Vermont History* 54 [no. 4, 1986]: 165.)

   It is worth noting that Caulkins, reflecting a view of the Pequot War that was common as late as 1852, also wrote that the Pequots were swept away by the colonists without misgivings or conscience, and that "an overuling power was indeed making use of their instrumentality, to accomplish his wise designs. . . . God is now acknowledged and honored in a region that for ages had been devoted to the worship of evil spirits."

9. Except where otherwise noted, historical information on the history of Connecticut is drawn from the following sources.

   H. A. Baker, *History of Montville, Conn., formerly the North Parish of New London, from 1640 to 1896* (Hartford: 1896).

   Frances M. Caulkins, *History of New London, Connecticut, from the first survey of the coast in 1612 to 1852* (New London: 1852).

   F. M. Caulkins, *History of Norwich, Connecticut* (1874).

   John W. DeForest, *History of the Indians of Connecticut: From the Earliest Known Period to 1850* (Hartford: Hamersley, 1853).

   Frank G. Speck, "Native Tribes and Dialects of Connecticut — A Mohegan–Pequot Diary," *American Bureau of Ethnology* 43, (1924).

   J. Hammond Trumbull, *The Public Records of the Colony of Connecticut* (Hartford: Brown and Parson, 1850–1890). (Reprinted, New York: AMS and Johnson Reprint Corporation, 1968).

   "John Winthrop's Journal, Volume One," *New York Historical Collections* 1 (New Series): 295.

   R. C. Winthrop, "Letter from John Winthrop to William Bradford, July 28, 1637," in *Life and Letters of John Winthrop* (Boston: 1867), 194–200.

10. James P. Whittall II, "Hunt's Hill Site–Souterrain, Montville, Connecticut," *Bulletin of Early Sites Research Society* 11 (no. 1, 1984): 7–12.

11. Edward S. Curtis, *Indian Days of the Long Ago* (Yonkers: World Book, 1915) 52–54, 208–221.

12. T. E. Mails, *Sundancing at Rosebud and Pine Ridge* (Sioux Falls: Center for Western Studies, 1978), 64.

13. M. G. Morgan, H. K. Flory, I. Nair and D. Lincoln, "Power Line Fields and Human Health," *IEEE Spectrum* (February, 1985): 62-68.

14. J. C. Huden, *Indian Place Names of New England* (New York: Museum of the American Indian, Heye Foundation, 1962).

15. J. R. Rand, and R. J. Holt, "Tectonics and Earthquakes of Massachusetts from a Regional Context," in O. C. Farquhar, ed. *Geotechnology in Massachusetts* (Amherst: University of Massachusetts, 1982), 463, 464.

16. C. B. Todd, *In Olde Connecticut* (New York: Grafton, 1907), 146.

17. F. S. Drake, *The Town of Roxbury* (Roxbury: Privately printed, 1878), 15, 16.

18. S. G. Goodrich, *A Pictorial History of America* (Hartford: E. Strong, 1844), 270.

19. J. E. Tebel, "Earthquakes in New England," *Cape Naturalist*, 13, (no. 1, 1985): 63.

20. Todd, *Connecticut*, 147, 149.

21. B. T. Brady, and G. A. Rowell, "Laboratory investigation of the electrodynamics of rock fracture," *Nature* 321 (29 May, 1986): 488–492. Also, general theories of light emission during fractures of crystalline compounds, called triboluminescence, may apply to rocks. See L. M. Sweeting and A. L. Rheingold, *Journal of American Chemical Society* (April 29, 1987).

22. J. S. Derr, "Luminous phenomena and their relationship to rock fracture," *Nature* 321 (May 29, 1986): 471.

23. DeForest, *Indians of Connecticut*.

24. J. P. Whittall, II, "Moodus Chamber," *Early Sites Research Society Bulletin* (1985).

11. Nashoba

1. N. A. Allen, *Master Plan for the Nature Conservancy's Beaver Brook Valley Preserve, Part I, Section 1* (Boxborough: Town of Boxborough, Massachusetts, 1981), 9.

2. E. D. Andrews, *The People Called Shakers* (New York: Dover, 1963), 161.

3. T. E. Mails, *Sundancing at Rosebud and Pineridge* (Sioux Falls: Augustana College, 1978), 63–66.

4. H. S. Nourse, *History of the Town of Harvard, Massachusetts* (Harvard, 1894), 64, 67.

5. Byron E. Dix, and J. W. Mavor, Jr. "Heliolithic Ritual Sites in New England." *New England Antiquities Research Association Journal* 16 (no. 3, 1982): 69, 70.

6. F. Priest, *Proceedings of the Littleton Historical Society, 1894-5* (no. 1, 1896): 12, 21.

7. H. J. Harwood, "An Historical Sketch of the Town of Littleton," in *History of Middlesex County, Massachusetts* (1890), 2, 5, 6.

8. Daniel Gookin, "Historical Collections of the Indians in New England," *Collection of the Massachusetts Historical Society for the year 1792* (Boston, 1792), 77. T. T. Sykes, *History of Littleton, Massachusetts* (Littleton, 1952), 11. J. C. Huden, *Indian Place Names of New England* (New York: Museum of the American Indian, 1962), 137. Mark Holloway, *Heavens on Earth: Utopian Communities in America 1680-1880* (New York: Dover, 1966).

9. M. A. MacLeod, "The Great Sachem of the Nashaways," *Archaeological Quarterly, Massachusetts Archaeological Society* 7 (no. 2, Fall, 1985): 5–7. F. C. Pierce, History of Grafton, Worcester County, Massachusetts (Worcester: Author published, 1879), 17–23. John W. Barber, *Historical Collections of Massachusetts* (Worcester: Howland, 1839).

10. Gookin, "Historical Collections," 71.

11. Lemuel Shattuck, *A History of the Town of Concord* (Boston: 1835), 3.

12. C. Stearns, "Letter to H. J. Harwood, August 1894," *Proceedings of the Littleton Historical Society* (no. 1, 1894–95). Huden, *Indian Place Names*, 179.

13. H. A. Hazen, *History of Billerica, Massachusetts* (Boston: Williams, 1883), 104.

14. G. G. Niles, *The Hoosac Valley, Its Legends and Its History* (New York: Putnam, 1912), 24.

15. Alfred S. Hudson, *History of Sudbury, Massachusetts* (Sudbury, 1889), 6–12. Alfred S. Hudson, *The Annals of Sudbury, Wayland and Maynard, Massachusetts* (By author, 1891), 32. Shattuck, *Concord*, 2, 6, 25.

16. W. Waters, *History of Chelmsford, Massachusetts* (Lowell: Courier Citizen 1917), 100, 101. J. W. Mavor, Jr., and B. E. Dix, "New England Cedar Wetlands in Native American Ritual," in A. D. Laderman, ed., *Atlantic White Cedar Wetlands* (Boulder: Westview, 1987).

17. Andrews, *Shakers*, 169.

18. Ibid., 161.

19. W. T. Brandon, "Middlesex Farm: An Archaeological Perspective from Rural Massachusetts," *Dublin Seminar for New England Folklife Annual Proceedings* (1977): 65–67, 69–73.

20. William W. Fitzhugh, ed., *Cultures in Contact*, (Washington: Smithsonian Institution, 1985), 69–73.

21. S. Weisbord, "New Traces of Ancient Eastern Quakes," *Science News* 130. (1986): 6. Also, "When the Earth Quakes the Sand Blows," *Science News* 127 (1986): 78.

22. J. R. Rand and R. J. Holt, "Tectonics and Earthquakes of Massachusetts from a Regional Context," in O. C. Farquhar, ed., *Geotechnology in Massachusetts* (Amherst: University of Massachusetts, 1982), 461, 464. F. S. Drake, *The Town of Roxbury* (Roxbury: Privately printed, 1878), 15, 16.

23. Harwood, "Littleton," 2, 5, 6.

24. Rand, "Tectonics," 464. G. LeBlanc, R. J. Holt, G. Klimkierig, and J. C. Johnston, "Earthquakes and Mafic Plutons, Some Instrumental Data," in O. C. Farquhar, ed., *Geotechnology in Massachusetts* (Amherst: University of Massachusetts, 1982). Figure 11–21 is from *Our New England Earthquakes* (Weston Geophysical Corporation, 1977).

25. T. McQuiston, "Second UFO Sighting in Boxborough," *The Beacon* (Boxborough, Oct. 31, 1985), 1, 5.

26. M. Monteiro, *Legends and Popular Tales of the Basque Peoples* (New York: Stokes, 1891).

27. Nourse, *Harvard*.

28. Ibid., 66.

29. I. Peterson, "Liquid Sand," *Science News* 128 (October 12, 1985): 234, 235.

30. Huden, *Indian Place Names*, 228. William S. Simmons, *Cautantowit's House: An Indian Burial Ground on the Island of Conanicut in Narragansett Bay* (Providence: Brown University, 1970). Niles, *Hoosac*, 41.

31. In Iceland, for example, whose continuous history goes back 1,000 years, it is known that the ancient, carefully built cairns with vertical-walled exteriors have withstood the severe tectonic activity of that island. Many cairns and other ancient stone

structures in New England appear capable of similar integrity. Recent research into the mechanical and electrical processes in earthquakes may show that these seismic phenomena played an even greater role than we have imagined.

32. E. G. Squier and E. H. Davis, "Ancient Monuments of the Mississippi Valley," *Smithsonian Contributions to Knowledge* (no. 1, 1848): Plate VIII, op. p. 21. Byron E. Dix, and J. W. Mavor, Jr., "Progress Report on New England Archaeoastronomy," *Bulletin of Early Sites Research Society* 10 (no. 2, 1983): 16, 17.

33. Philip Kopper, *The Smithsonian Book of North American Indians* (Washington: Smithsonian, 1986), 150–154. Francis F. Marcus, "Solar Riddle of an Ancient Earthwork," *New York Times* (November 22, 1981), E11.

34. D. E. Winslow, *John Eliot, Apostle to the Indians* (Boston: Houghton-Mifflin, 1968). J. Greenberg, "Natural Highs in Natural Habitats," *Science News* 124 (November 5, 1983): 300, 301. Frank G. Speck, "Native Tribes and Dialects of Connecticut, A Mohegan-Pequot Diary," *American Bureau of Ethnology, Smithsonian Institution* (no. 43, 1924). Frank G. Speck, "The Memorial Brush Heaps in Delaware and Elsewhere," *Bulletin Archaeological Society of Delaware* 4, (no. 17, 1945).

35. E. Hall, *The Ancient Historical Records of Norwalk, Connecticut* (New York: Mallory, 1847), 31.

36. D. P. Foley, "The Rural Six Nations Traditional Belief System: 1870–1914," *Man in the Northeast* (no. 14, Fall 1977): 19–33.

37. C. E. Eliot, J. A. Stanton, W. Elliott and E. Eliot, *Proceedings at the Reunion of the Descendants of John Eliot* (Natick, Massachusetts: 1901), 65–73.

38. F. J. Stimson, *King Noanett* (Boston: Lamson Wolffe, 1896), ix, x, 204-207, 260-264, 296-309.

12. Back to Calendar One

1. Except where otherwise noted, biographical material on Joseph Smith, Jr, is taken from Fawn M. Brodie, *Noone Knows My History* (New York: Knopf, 1945).

2. E.G. Squier, "Aboriginal Monuments of the State of New York," *Smithsonian Contributions to Knowledge* 2 (1849). Henry R. Schoolcraft, *History, Condition and Prospects of the Indian Tribes of the United States, Vol 1* (Rochester, New York: 1851).

3. John R. Swanton, "Religious Beliefs and Medicinal Practices of the Creek Indians," in *42nd Annual Report of Bureau of Ethnology, 1924–25* (Washington, 1928), 503-510.

4. A. M. Smith, *Temple Lot Deed,* (Independence, Missouri: Church of Christ, 1973). A. M. Smith, *A Brief History of The Church of Christ* (Independence: Church of Christ, 1981). J. M. Case, *The Stones* (Independence: Church of Christ).

5. P. Nibley, *Brigham Young The Man and His Work* (Independence: Zion, 1936), 26. M. E. Peterson, "Why We Build Temples," in *Temples of the Church of Jesus Christ of Latter Day Saints* (Salt Lake City: Church of Jesus Christ of Latter Day Saints, 1981). L. B. Andrew, *The Early Temples of the Mormons* (Albany: State University of New York, 1978).

6. Joseph Smith, Jr., *The Pearl of Great Price* (Salt Lake City: Church of Jesus Christ of Latter Day Saints, 1968).

7. The bedrock constituents of Calendar One are referred to as the Waits River and Gile Mountain formations. They are metamorphic rocks containing mostly quartz which appears in two general forms, foliated mica-schist and a homogeneous quartzite, fifty percent quartz, forty percent calcite, with some magnetite, which weathers to

a crumbling brown rind. Large structural members are usually made from quartzite and hard tools from mica-schist.

8. Byron E. Dix and James W. Mavor, Jr. "Heliolithic Ritual Sites in New England," *Journal of New England Antiquities Research Association* 16 (no. 3, 1982): 78.

9. William S. Fowler, "Spirit Worship," *Report of the Narragansett Archaeological Society of Rhode Island* (1982): 8.

10. Geochron Laboratories Carbon 14 Sample GX-8629, 580 130 B. P.

11. J. P. Shafer and J. H. Hartshorn, "The Quaternary of New England," in *The Quaternary of the United States,* ed. H. E. Wright, Jr., and D. G. Frey (Princeton: Princeton University Press, 1965), 121, 122.

12. See note 2, Chapter 2.

13. James P. Whittall, II, "Excavation — Monolith 'A' Site," *Early Sites Research Society Bulletin* 11 (No. 1, 1984).

14. C. G. Calloway, "The Conquest of Vermont: Vermont's Indian Troubles in Context," *Vermont History* 52 (no. 3, 1984), 163, 174.

15. John Moody, quoted in J. K. Fadden and J. Bruchac, *The Wind Eagle* (Greenfield, Massachusetts: 1985).

13. Manitou

1. I. Lissner, *Man, God and Magic*, trans. J. M. Brownjohn, (New York: Putnam, 1961), 88.

2. A.L. Kroeber, *Handbook of the Indians of California* (New York: Dover. 1976), 112.

3. Lissner, *Man, God and Magic*, 231.

4. Nigel Pennick, *The Ancient Science of Geomancy* (London: Thames and Hudson, 1979).

5. Stephen Skinner, *The Living Earth Manual of Feng-Shui* (London: Routledge and Kegan Paul, 1982).

6. Alfred Watkins, *The Old Straight Track* (London: Abacus, 1974).

7. Guy Underwood, *The Patterns of the Past* (London: Abacus, 1972).

8. Rupert Sheldrake, *A New Science of Life* (Los Angeles: J. P. Tarcher, 1981).

9. Sigfrid Lonegren, *Spiritual Dowsing* (Glastonbury: Gothic Image, 1986), 35, 36.

10. Frank Waters, *Book of the Hopi* (New York: Ballantine, 1963), 39. J. Lafitau, *Customs of the American Indians Compared with the Customs of Primitive Times, Vol I* (Toronto: Champlain Society, 1974), 103–114. J. L. Kessell, *Kiva, Cross and Crown* (Washington: National Park Service, 1979), 110, 111, 168. Ezra Stiles, *The Literary Diary of Ezra Stiles, Vol 2* (New York: Scribners, 1901), 424. J. W. DeForest, *History of the Indians of Connecticut* (Hartford: Hammersley, 1853), 25. J. L. Chartkoff and K. K. Chartkoff, *The Archaeology of California* (Stanford: Stanford, 1984), 112. E. G. Squier, "Aboriginal Monuments of the State of New York," *Smithsonian Contributions to Knowledge* (No. 2, 1849): 162, 163. G. C. Niles, *The Hoosac Valley* (New York: Putnam, 1912), 8, 30, 41. Fred Olsen, *On The Trail of the Arawaks* (Norman: University of Oklahoma, 1874), 332. Ted Timreck, and Will Goetzman, *Polar Culture of the Red Ochre People*, a film featuring interviews with W. Fitzhugh, R. Tuck, and others; previewed at American Museum of Natural History, New York. E. G. Squier, and E. H. Davis, "Ancient Monuments of the Mississippi Valley," *Smithsonian Contributions To Knowledge. Vol. 1,* (1848): Plate 45, op. p. 138. Henry R. Schoolcraft, *Historical and statistical information respecting the history, condition and prospects of the Indian tribes of the United States,* Vol. I–VI (Philadelphia, 1851–57). Josiah Priest, *American Antiquities and Discoveries in the West* (Albany: Hoffman and White, 1838), 224.

11. Ezra Stiles, *A History of Three Judges of King Charles I* (Hartford: 1794), 75–84. Also, Stiles, *Literary Diary,* 538–539.
12. A. Spencer, *The Lapps* (New York: Crane-Russack). P. Grimal, ed., *Larousse World Mythology* (New York: Putnam, 1963), 128. Richard J. Pearson, *Archaeology of the Ryukyu Islands* (Honolulu: University of Hawaii, 1969), 125–128.
13. Squier, "Aboriginal Monuments of New York." Niles, *Hoosac Valley,* 8, 30, 41.
14. Stiles, *Literary Diary,* 508.
15. H. M. Forbes, *Gravestones of Early New England* (New York: DaCapo, 1967), 2.
16. E. M. Whishaw, *Atlantis in Andalucia* (London: Rider, 1929), 89, op. p. 92.
17. Francis Parkman, *France and England in North America, Part 2* (Boston: Little, Brown, 1867), 108.
18. Olsen, *Arawaks,* 332.
19. C. C. Jones, Jr., *Antiquities of the Southern Indians* (New York: Appleton, 1873), 430. J. Hayward, *Natural and Aboriginal History of Tennessee* (Nashville: 1823), 226.
20. Jones, *Southern Indians,* 436, 439.
21. Squier, "Aboriginal Monuments of New York," 171, 172.
22. Jones, *Southern Indians,* 430, 439.
23. James W. Mavor, Jr., "Astronomy and Shamanism Among the Culdee Monks," *Bulletin Early Sites Research Society* 12 (no. 1, December 1985): 2, 3. W. A. Craigie, "Gaels of Iceland," *Proceedings of the Society of Antiquaries of Scotland* VII (Third Series).
24. E. D. Andrews, *The People Called Shakers* (New York: Dover, 1963), 166, 167.
25. Cyrus Gordon, *Before Columbus* (New York: Crown, 1971), 175–187.
26. Robert Graves, *The White Goddess* (New York: Farrar, Straus and Giroux, 1948), 113–115.

Index